DATE DUE

FARM BUILDER'S HANDBOOK

Under construction in New Hampton,
Iowa—240 feet controlled environment poultry
house, capacity of 10,000 birds. *Republic Steel
and Iowa Lumber Dealer*

FARM BUILDER'S HANDBOOK

With Added Material for Pole Type Industrial Buildings

second edition

by **R. J. LYTLE**

with chapters by

MERLE L. ESMAY, Ph.D.
Michigan State University

ARTHUR J. MUEHLING
University of Illinois

LARRY D. VAN FOSSEN
Iowa State University

GEORGE E. BRUNNER, Jr.
Metal Building Review Magazine

engineering consultants

ROBERT J. MANSFIELD, P.E.

JOHN PEDERSEN
Manager, Midwest Plan Service

STRUCTURES PUBLISHING COMPANY
Farmington, Michigan   1973

Manufactured in the United States of America.

Book designed by Richard Kinney.

Current Printing (last digit)

10 9 8 7 6 5 4 3 2 1

International Standard Book Number: 0-912336-05-6
Library of Congress Catalog Card Number: 72-90111

Structures Publishing Company
Box 423, Farmington, Michigan 48024

CONTENTS

What is a farm builder? He is a firm or an individual doing building contracting work for the modern "Agricultural businessman." This "Agricultural businessman," unlike his father, no longer has the time, desire, or the knowledge to build his own buildings.

Farm building as it is today hardly existed fifteen years ago. Experienced farm builders like yourselves came from many parts of the construction industry. In a very short time, largely on your own, you have developed construction techniques uniquely suited for modern industrialized farming. Reflecting economy and a high rate of obsolescence, the buildings you build are an increasingly important factor in making America pre-eminent in agricultural production.

Because of the location of your construction sites, you have not been saddled with rigid, slow-to-change building codes. Neither have you had to bear stifling trade union restrictions or jurisdictional disputes. Your future is bright. Rapid developments in agricultural engineering continue to accelerate the trend to confinement housing. Increased cost and lack of availability of farm labor steadily increase the demand for your product.

Within the farm building industry, many of you specialize in certain areas such as pole buildings, poultry, swine or dairy housing, silos, greenhouses, steel buildings, etc. Some of you furnish and install the equipment and design complete production facilities. Others furnish only the building on a foundation by others.

Many dedicated agricultural engineers in agricultural colleges throughout the country have played no small part in the development of this industry. Their testing, studies and design services have been and will continue to be of great assistance to the farm builder.

Because of the considerable economy of the post and pole buildings which you have developed in a few short years, a good part of the average pole builder's business today is industrial or commercial buildings. It is for this reason that we include span tables at a code-approved 50 lbs. per square foot. This provides the additional safety factor for human occupancy.

My study of the industry leads me to believe that many of you will become full service "Agri Builders," offering industrialized agriculture a complete service from planning, engineering, construction, financing, sale and installation of equipment to remodeling as the technology changes. This "General Farm Builder" will subcontract parts of the work to specialists while retaining total control of the project. This is an exciting prospect in a truly growth industry.

Statistically, Farm Building News reports this picture of you and your industry. *(The industry's rapid growth has outdated figures like these rapidly in the past.)*

The total industry builds between five and six billion dollars in farm buildings annually. This is a sizable percentage of total building construction. Individually, you average between $300,-000.00 and $400,000.00 annually *(but a few do over five million).* Seventy per cent of your work is farm building.

In 1971 you averaged 70 buildings which you sold for an average of $7,000.00 each. However, some in specialized fields averaged $50,000.00 per building.

Making up the averages, some of you are small growing builders; others are farm building departments in lumber yards.

You work within about 150 miles of your base but some go 1,000 miles.

Why This Book?

Prior to the first edition, the engineering department in my Panel-Clip Company increasingly received calls from customers for engineering assistance on parts of the structure not in our sphere (roof trusses). These requests for help came not only from a few new inexperienced builders, but from old hands as well. Traveling around the country, I talk to many farm builders. They have a divergence of opinion about many aspects of the structures they build. Then, too, there are always a few unprincipled builders (as there are in all facets of construction) who compete on price alone by offering shoddy construction.

One builder uses a 2 × 10 for a job that another uses only a 2 × 6. Discussion of this project with a number of farm builders revealed that not only would this book help them to build better, but would tend to upgrade the quality of the work of some of their price-only competition. This is not a detailed guide for the Do-it-yourself farm-builder, nor will it help the uninitiated to become farm builders. To properly use this book, you must already have a broad construction knowledge.

In almost all other types of construction the builder is "quality controlled" by architects, building code inspectors, FHA inspectors, etc. Since this is not true of farm building, in some respects this book will provide a "minimum standard" to protect the buyer. Of course, there is no substitute for the competence and integrity of the farm builder.

How the Handbook Was Written

Prior to the first edition, over a period of many months I accumulated all that I could find on farm building from manufacturers, Agricultural

Engineering Departments and farm builders. A wealth of material was received and catalogued.

For this second edition, we sent out several hundred questionnaires to purchasers of the first book. The responses to these largely dictated the changes and additions in this book. Dr. Esmay and Professor Muehling updated their earlier excellent work on Special Buildings, Controlled Environment, and Waste Management. We were able to enlist the help of Larry Van Fossen of Iowa State University to do the chapter on Grain and Silage Storage. George Brunner, Editor and Publisher of the Metal Building Review magazine, provided us with the chapter on Metal Buildings. John Pedersen, manager of Midwest Plan Service, assisted me in updating the first six chapters on structural subjects. It was necessary to update many of the tables in Appendix A, Structural Design Data, because of the recent change in lumber standards.

Our approach has been, as with the first edition, to make this a genuine handbook, including information which will be truly useful to you and in a form you will find readily accessible. The answers to "How long can I make it?", "Out of what material?", "How far apart," and "How to fasten it?" are given plainly and simply.

Wherever possible, I tried to make the structural parts of the book the result of engineering calculations. Some parts are based on what I could find among you as "Good Practice." So don't be surprised if you disagree with some of the recommendations.

Change

If you will take your copy of the first edition of this book and compare it with this second edition, you will be amazed at the changes that have taken place in only four years. In addition to the technical changes, your editor and authors have become more skilled at presenting the material.

In the years ahead, this rapid rate of change will continue and we plan subsequent editions and/or supplements to insure the utility of this book.

How to Use The Handbook

First, scan the book from cover to cover. This will give you the best idea of what is available to you for future use.

Decide from the map in Appendix "A" which load zone or zones you operate in. For your convenience, you will find all of the tables for each zone grouped together. If the tables specify a certain species—grade lumber group, for example, this is exactly what is meant. Make no substitutions unless you are sure the strength is equal. The tables have been modified to reflect the new lumber standards, where those affect the engineering.

Suggested Farm Builder's Library

This handbook is intended to provide the farm builder with basic reference data. There are a number of publications available to you through material manufacturers and agricultural engineering departments that should be of considerable help to the farm builder. Keep your library up to date and keep it organized for ready reference.

A number of publications of particular value to farm builders are prepared by the Midwest Plan Service, Iowa State University, Ames, Iowa, 50010. They are available from them or from the Agricultural Engineering Department of State Universities in the Midwest. Write for their free catalogue and order what you need.

Chapter 1

PLANNING, SITE SELECTION & PREPARATION

100 Objective: To assure that construction planned will be:
a. An efficient use of the capital investment.
b. structurally sound.
c. located to not interfere with other farm operations or cause a public nuisance.
d. located with access to other buildings, water supply, utilities, and waste disposal.
e. oriented to minimize adverse weather effects.
f. spaced to minimize or confine fire losses.

101   Planning

The farm builder, along with the farm owner or manager, should write down the objectives of a proposed construction program. Include a layout of the area to be used, such as the contour sketch, Det. 101. Recommended scale 1″ = 20′.

101-1   Select the system or building to be constructed.

101-2   In view of the rate of technological change, it may be desirable at this point to consult with an Extension Agricultural Engineer or County Agent to insure that the program incorporates all of the latest developments.

101-3   Develop an "as built" plan of both the plot and buildings. Indicate items not included in the farm builder's contract on Plans by "NIC" (Not In Contract) or "By Others" or "By Owner" to avoid misunderstanding.

101-3.1   Plot Plans should incorporate—
a. Grading Plan
b. Water Supply & Lines
c. Waste disposal, including effluent lines, lagoons, etc.
d. Windbreaks
e. Feed lots
f. Access Roads
g. Fences
h. Existing buildings
i. Direction of prevailing winds
j. Power lines, new and existing

101-3.2   Building Plans should incorporate—
a. Floor plan showing equipment to be installed or stored, location of windows, doors, fans, dimensions of manure pits, lighting layout, etc. Recommended scales: 1/4″ = 1′-0″ is common for houses and small buildings; use 1/8″ = 1′-0″ for larger ones.
b. Section through the building should show general construction details and as much of the equipment installation as relates to the design of the building. Recommended scale 3/8″ = 1′.
c. Detail drawings should show details of the structure or installation of equipment which are critical or non-standard. Recommended scales 1/2″ or 1″ = 1′-0″.

102   Site Selection—In selecting a site for a farm building program, consider the following factors:

102-1   Water Supply. Calculate water requirements to determine the adequacy of existing or proposed water supplies. Should there by any doubt about the adequacy of new wells, they should be drilled before construction begins.

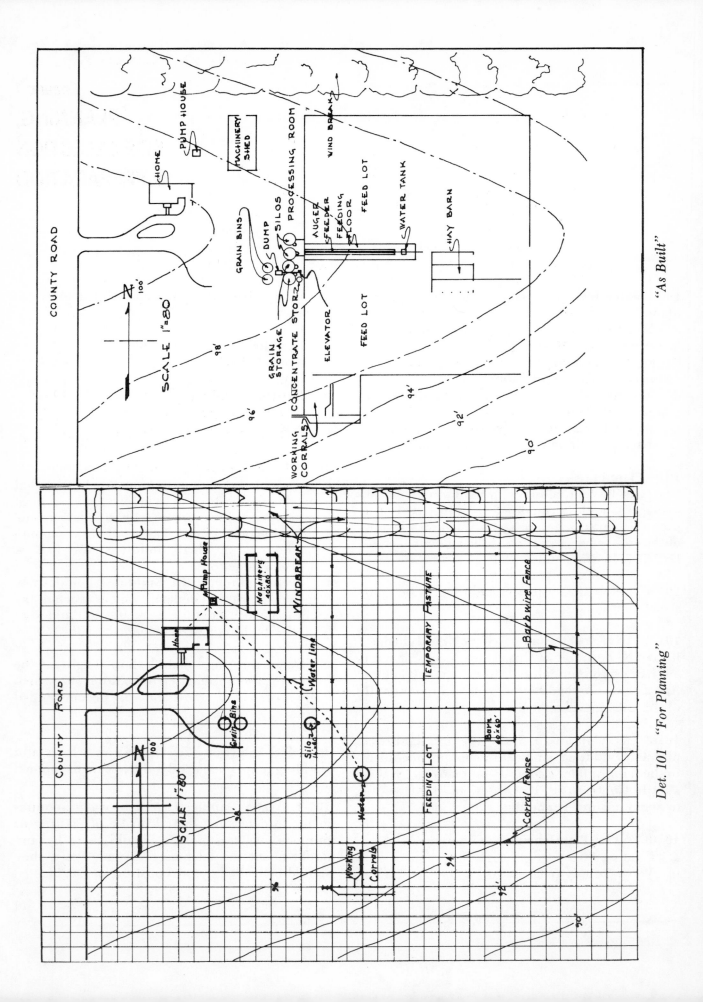

Det. 101 "For Planning"

"As Built"

LAYOUTS THAT PLACE BUILDINGS IN PROPER RELATION TO HOUSE, PREVAILING WINDS, AND ACCESS ROAD

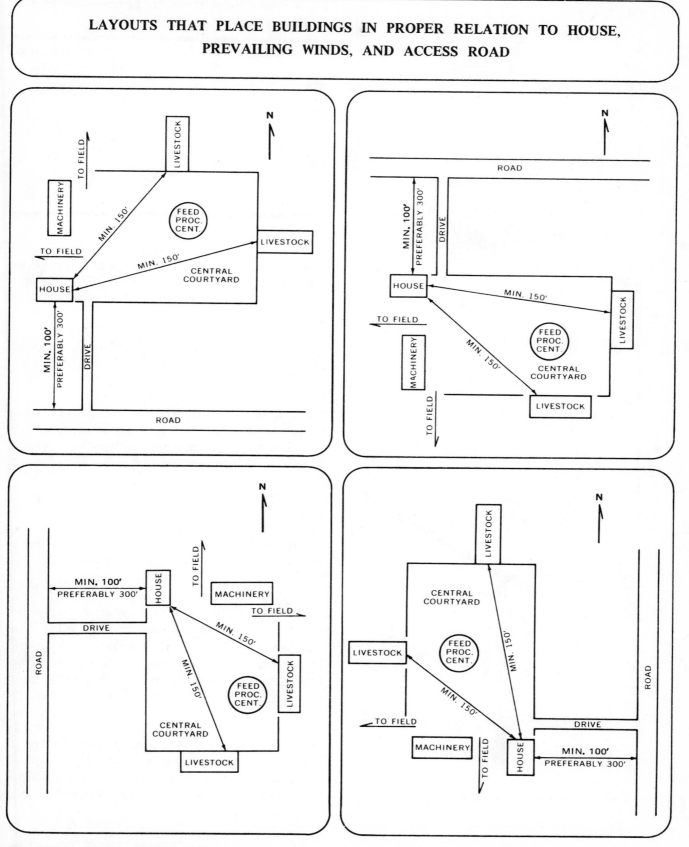

Det. 102-5   Granite City Steel Co.

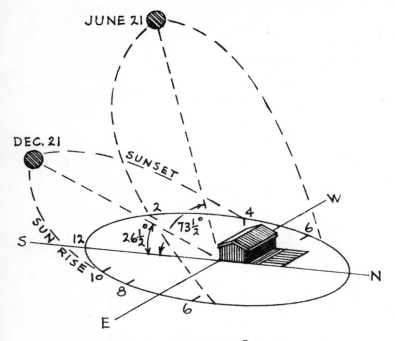

Position of Sun at Noon (40° Lat.)

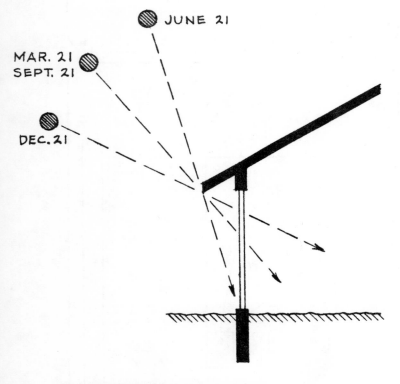

Sun at Noon (South side of bldg.)

Daily Water Requirements (Temperature of 50°F)

Water for:	Daily Water Requirements (Gallons)
Milk Cows	30
Beef or Dry Cow	12
Horse	12
Hog	4
Sheep	2
100 Chickens	6
100 Turkeys	10
Flushing Stables and Washing Dairy Equipment	20

102-2 Drainage. Natural drainage should be good or capable of modification at minimum cost. Plan grading and eliminate low spots before building.

102-3 Soil. Firm for footings. No rock out croppings or high water table. Avoid unstable soils or use floating slab foundation.

102-4 Prevailing Winds. Get information from nearest weather bureau. Face the long, open side of buildings away from prevailing winter winds. Keep livestock downwind of the house in summer.

102-5 Accessibility to road and manure disposal area.

102-6 Distance from residences or public areas to avoid a public nuisance from odor. See Det 102-5

102-7 Power Supply—New installations, particularly confinement housing, require substantial new power capacity. Calculation of needs should be made in accordance with equipment manufacturer's specifications. Appendix B. may be used as a guide. Contact local utility for capacity statement.

102-7.1 Power Supply—Emergency. (See 700-3) Livestock in total confinement are dependent on power-operated fans, feeders, etc. Power failure for any extended period may result in substantial losses. Plan an emergency power supply, or at least a warning system.

102-7.2 Install wiring in accordance with the National Electrical Code.

103 Orientation of Buildings

103-1 The coolest buildings are generally long buildings oriented with the long dimension east and west, with small areas facing east and west. To minimize summer heat gain, use a white roof.

103-2 Shadows—Locate structures to avoid continuous shadows in feed lots and livestock areas. Snow and frozen manure accumulate on the north side of buildings, bunks, silos, etc.

103-3 Microclimate. Data from your local weather station is applicable to a wide area. Examine the proposed building location for any unusual climate factors, such as wind, snow accumulation, cold "pockets," heavy rainfall, etc.

103-5 Sun—Det. 103-1 shows the importance of locating the building and overhangs to take advantage of, or minimize, the effect of the sun heat and light. In most areas, open buildings to the south or southeast to be protected from winter winds.

103-6 Windbreak Planning—See Det. 103-6

104 Site Preparation

104-1 Remove all stumps.

104-2 Concrete floor—remove all topsoil and organic material grade or fill to 12 inches below top of finish floor.

104-3 Fill—Use sand or gravel, minimum 8″ thick. Pit run gravel is satisfactory, but remove all stones over 6″.

104-4 Earth or Gravel Floors—remove all topsoil and organic material.

105 Grading and Drainage (For Grading & Drainage of Livestock areas. See Par. 703-6.1)

105-1 Protective slope around buildings. Slope downward from building foundation and water wells to lower areas or drainage swales. Minimum length—10′; minimum fall—6″.

105-2 Minimum Gradients
a. Concrete or other impervious surfaces—1/16 in./ft (1/2%). A minimum of 1/8 in./ft is usually needed to avoid ponding.
b. Pervious surfaces
  1. In extremely dry area—1/8 in./ft (1%).
  2. Other areas—1/4 in./ft (2%).
  3. In areas of heavy rainfall such as Florida, Gulf Coast, Hawaii and Puerto Rico special drainage design may be required.
c. Avoid conditions leading to prolonged standing of water at any season.

105-2.1 Maximum Gradient
a. Avoid slopes over 1 in./ft (5%) in animal or machine traffic areas.
b. Other areas—2′ horizontal to 1′ vertical.
c. If slope is held by satisfactory existing vegetation or rock outcropping, no limit when present and future stabilization is assured.

105-3 Storm Water Disposal

105-3.1 Control runoff from feed lot and loose housing areas. Connect gutters and downspouts to drainage lines to direct roof run off to natural drainage areas. Protect downspouts from animal or equipment damage.

105-3.2 Where downspouts are not connected to drainlines, install splash blocks of concrete or other durable material. Minimum size 12″ × 30″.

105-4 Trough and Downspout Sizes

Roof Area (sq. ft.)	Trough Diameter	Downspout Diameter
100 to 800	4″	3″
800 to 1000	5″	3″
1000 to 1400	5″	4″
1400 to 2000	6″	4″

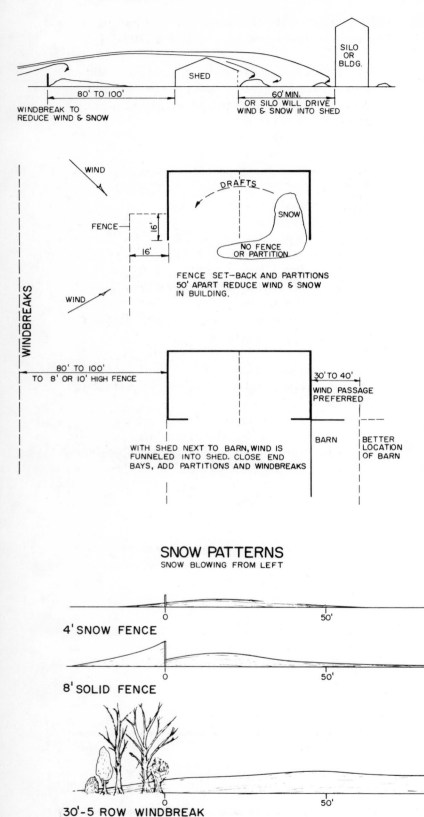

WINDBREAK TO
REDUCE WIND & SNOW

80' TO 100'

SHED

SILO
OR
BLDG.

60' MIN.
OR SILO WILL DRIVE
WIND & SNOW INTO SHED

WINDBREAKS

WIND

DRAFTS

FENCE

16'

16'

SNOW

NO FENCE
OR PARTITION

FENCE SET-BACK AND PARTITIONS
50' APART REDUCE WIND & SNOW
IN BUILDING.

WIND

80' TO 100'
TO 8' OR 10' HIGH FENCE

30' TO 40'

WIND PASSAGE
PREFERRED

BARN

BETTER
LOCATION
OF BARN

WITH SHED NEXT TO BARN, WIND IS
FUNNELED INTO SHED. CLOSE END
BAYS, ADD PARTITIONS AND WINDBREAKS

SNOW PATTERNS
SNOW BLOWING FROM LEFT

0   50'   100'

4' SNOW FENCE

0   50'   100'   150'   175'

8' SOLID FENCE

0   50'   100'   150'   200'   300'

30'-5 ROW WINDBREAK

103-6 Windbreak Planning
For Buildings & Lots

Orientation

Buildings, lots, and other areas to be protected should be located within the area of wind protection but beyond the expected snow catch. Local experience is the best indicator on the distance facilities should be placed from shelter belts.

Generally, shelterbelts should be 100 to 300 feet away from protected areas. The shorter distance is suitable where snow accumulation is less severe.

Snow Catch

The sketches indicate the approximate shape of the snow catch to be expected behind the different types of windbreaks.

The total amount of snow caught, and therefore the extent of the leeward drift, is a factor of how much snow is caught by other breaks or natural basins, and total seasonal accumulation.

Note that the total amount of snow will be much larger (perhaps 50 times) behind the trees.

106 Fire Safety

106-1 General—The considerable and increasing investment in farm buildings, machinery, equipment, livestock, and feed, and the cost of business interruption, make it important to include fire safety in a farm building program. Consult your insurance agent for guide lines to minimize rates. The following are general rules.

106-2 Separate liquid or gaseous fuel storage from other buildings by at least 60'.

106-3 Separate other buildings with metal siding and asphalt or metal roofs by at least 40'.

106-4 Consider sub-dividing buildings into compartments with masonry firewalls and self-closing fire doors as follows:—no more than 5000 sq. ft. total floor area in each compartment in:
a. Hay and bedding storage, tobacco curing and stripping, mechanical crop drying *(excluding small grains),* livestock feed grinding and preparation, furnace and boiler rooms.
b. Animal and poultry brooding *(where supplementary heating equipment creates an additional fire hazard)*—no more than 10,000 sq. ft. total floor area in each compartment of any other building.

106-5 Provide lightning protection for all buildings. (See Det. 106-4). On buildings to about 158' long, put grounds at each of two diagonally opposite corners. On longer buildings, put grounds at intervals of 100' around the outside. Bolt or rivet conductor cables and grounds at least 6' from telephone and electric wires. Drive ground pipe down until you reach permanent moisture (usually 6' to 10'). Complete path from eaves with 1/2" galvanized pipe, 3/8" steel cable or No. 2 copper cable. At least 18" of cable should be in contact with roof. Connect all metallic parts of building, such as pipe or ventilators, to grounding system. Protect nonmetallic roofs and projections, such as cupolas, with lightning rods.

106-6 Water for fire protection.

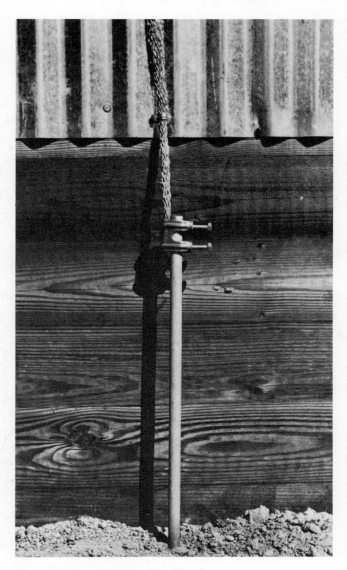

Det. 106-4 Granite City Steel

106-6.1 Construct ponds for water for fire protection accessible to, and within 500' of, major buildings.

106-6.2 A pump for firefighting should have a minimum capacity of 300 gallons per hr at 30 psi. If electrically operated, supply the pump by a power line independent of all buildings.

106-7 Factory-Made Chimneys. Should bear an Underwriter's Laboratories label and be installed to the manufacturer's specifications.

107 Knock-Out Panels. In long livestock or poultry buildings, having doors at the ends only, consider easily-removed panels in strategic locations along the walls of the building. Red painted panels removable from either side can:

a.   Provide emergency escape from the building.

b.   Provide access for firemen.

c.   Provide additional openings for removal or replacement of livestock or poultry.

d.   Open for additional ventilation during power failures. (Not a substitute for emergency power generation facilities).

Chapter 2

EXCAVATION, FOUNDATIONS AND CONCRETE WORK

200 Excavation, Foundations and Concrete Work

201-1 Extend excavation for footings or foundation walls at least 6″ into undisturbed soil that will provide adequate bearing, except when bearing is on a stable rock foundation.

201-2 When the bearing capacity or stability of the soils is questionable, soil analysis, bearing tests or special foundation design are recommended.

201-3 Holes drilled for poles shall be of sufficient diameter to permit the installation of a pad as required by Appendix A, unless the bottom of the hole is flared to the proper diameter.

202 Frost Line

202 Frost Line—Except as otherwise recommended, extend exterior wall footings, foundation walls and pole pads below frost line. Determine frost depth from custom and experience in the area, the average and extreme depth of frost penetration and the susceptibility of the soil and site to frost action. Great variations occur in a small area.

203 Concrete

203-1 Strength—Ready-Mixed Concrete shall have a compressive strength, at 28 days, of at least that specified by the engineer. Where not otherwise specified, use a minimum of 2000 psi for non-structural concrete.

203-2 Air-entraining cement is recommended for all concrete exposed to freezing and thawing, livestock wastes, milk equipment cleaning compounds, etc.

203-3 Table 203-3 is a guide for ordering Ready-Mixed Concrete for farm buildings.

203-4 For small jobs where batching and mixing operations are done on the job, concrete mixed according to Table 203-4 will provide plain concrete meeting minimum standards. Increasing the amount of water per sack of cement greatly decreases strength.

203-5 For job mixed air entrained concrete, use cement to which an air entraining agent has been added by the cement manufacturer.

203-6 Place concrete continuously where possible, or provide construction joints with dowels for stress transfer. Vibrate, or spade and rod, concrete thoroughly between forms and reinforcing.

Allow time for strength of concrete to develop before subjecting to loads. Strip forms around slabs after 3 days, walks after 7 days, and self-supporting floors after 10 days.

203-7 Concrete shall be properly cured. Allow sufficient time for strength to develop before subjecting to load.

203-8 Cold weather concreting.

In freezing weather, protect walls until thoroughly set, but not less than two days. Take

Table 203-3 A Guide for Ordering Ready-Mixed Concrete

Specifications for medium-consistency concrete (3 in. slump)	Flatwork *(with 1-1/2″ maximum size aggregate)*			Formed work *(with 3/4″ maximum size aggregate)*		
	Severe exposure *(garbage feeding floor, floors in dairy plant)*	Normal exposure *(paved barnyards, floors for farm buildings, sidewalks)*	Mild exposure *(Bldg. Footings concrete improvements in mild climates)*	Severe exposure *(mangers for silage feeding, manure pits)*	Normal exposure *(reinforced concrete walls, beam tanks, foundations)*	Mild exposure *(concrete improvements in mild climates)*
Cement Content Minimum number of bags per cubic yard of concrete	7	6	5	7 3/4	6 1/2	5 1/2
Water Content Maximum number of gallons per bag of cement	5	6	7	5	6	7

Order air-entrained concrete for all concrete exposed to freezing and salt action. For 1 1/2-in. maximum size aggregate, specify 4 to 6 percent air content. For 3/4 and 1 in. maximum size, specify 5 to 7 percent air content. *(Portland Cement Association)*

Table 203-4 Concrete Proportions (Field Mixing)

Maximum size of coarse aggregate	Approximate Cement sacks per cubic yard	Maximum Water Gals. per sack	Approximate proportions[1] (by volume) per sack of Cement		
			Cement	Fine agg.	Coarse agg.
3/4″	6.0	5	1	2-1/2	2-3/4
1″	5.8	5	1	2-1/2	3
1-1/2″	5.4	5	1	2-1/2	3-1/2
2″ [2]	5.2	5	1	2-1/2	4

1 For concrete not subject to freezing and thawing, the above proportions may be varied to use up to 5% less cement and 10% more fine aggregate.

2 Not recommended for slabs or other thin sections.

special precautions if placing concrete below 40° F. Do not place concrete over frozen ground.

203-8.1 Use Type III portland cement or Type I with calcium chloride dissolved in the mixing water at the rate of 21 lb/bag of cement. Heat the mixing water (not over 180°) with the aggregates, if necessary, so the mix will be 50°–70°. Keep the concrete at 50° for 7 days with Type I cement or 4 days with Type III. Cover outdoor concrete with 6″–12″ of straw. Use a vented heater indoors.

205 Concrete Masonry Units *(Block)*

205-1 Concrete Masonry Units shall comply with the following:
a. Hollow units, ASTM C-90
b. Solid Units, ASTM C-145

205-2 Grade of Concrete Masonry Units
a. Concrete masonry units used in foundations or for exterior walls shall be grade A.
b. Grade B may be used for back up or interior use.

205-3 Masonry Walls (extracted from Uniform Buildings Code, 1970).

Table 205-3. Minimum Thickness of Masonry Walls

Type of Masonry	Maximum Ratio Unsupported Height or Length to Thickness	Nominal Minimum Thickness (Inches)
Bearing Walls:		
Unburned Clay Masonry	10	16
Stone Masonry	14	16
Cavity Wall Masonry	18	8
Hollow Unit Masonry	18	8
Solid Masonry	20	8
Grouted Masonry	20	6
Reinforced Grouted Masonry	25	6
Reinforced Hollow Unit Masonry	25	6
Nonbearing Walls:		
Exterior Unreinforced Walls	20	2
Exterior Reinforced Walls	30	2
Interior Partitions Unreinforced	36	2
Interior Partitions Reinforced	48	2

Uniform Building Code, 1970.

205-3.1 Cavity Walls

a. The backing must be at least as thick as the facing and both must be at least 4″ thick, except if both are clay or shale brick they may be 3″ thick.

b. The cavity must be at least 1″ but not more than 4″.

c. Bond the wythes with 3/16″ diameter corrosion resistant steel rods, or equivalent, in the horizontal joints.

—1 rod per 4-1/2 sq.ft. for cavities to 3-1/2″; 1 rod per 3 sq. ft. for wider cavities.

—Space rods up to 2′ apart vertically and 3′ horizontally; stagger rods in alternate courses.

—Bend rods to rectangular shape for hollow units with the cells vertical.

—Bend ends of rods to 90° hooks at least 2″ long for other units.

—Around openings, space extra rods up to 3′ apart and within 12″ of the opening.

205-3.2 Hollow Unit Masonry Walls

a. Lay units with full face shell mortar beds and equal width vertical joints.

b. Where 2 or more units make up the wall thickness, bond the stretcher courses with:

—at least a 4″ lap over the unit below up to 34″ apart vertically, or

—units at least 50% thicker than those below up to 17″ apart vertically, or

—rods as for cavity walls for each 4-1/2 sq.ft. of wall up to 1-1/2′ apart vertically and 3′ apart horizontally.

205-3.3 Solid Masonry Walls

a. Lay units in full bed and vertical joints.

b. Unless reinforced for stack bond, units must lap those above and below the greater of 1-1/2″ or 1/2 the height of the units.

c. Bond 2 wythes with

—rods as for cavity walls, or

—solid headers extending at least 4″ into the backing and composing at least 4% of the exposed face area.

205-3.4 Design

Engineering design is required for reinforced masonry walls, columns, etc., and for determining maximum cavity wall height. The following are minimum for low-load conditions:

a. Beams, girders, and other concentrated loads should bear at least 3″ onto solid masonry at least 4″ thick, or on an adequate metal bearing plate.

b. Joists should bear at least 3″ onto solid masonry at least 2-1/4″ thick.

c. Reinforce stack bond walls with at least 2-0.017 sq. in. (#9 steel wire gage) continuous wires in horizontal bed joints up to 16″ apart vertically.

d. Use table 205-3 to determine the minimum thickness of masonry walls.

—Example: 8″ hollow block can be used in unsupported bearing walls up to $18 \times 8″ = 144″ = 12′$ high or long.

—The "thickness" of a cavity wall is the sum of the thicknesses of the 2 wythes.

—For walls of more than one material, use the lesser ratio.

e. Anchor bearing and non-bearing walls against overturn.

206 Mortar

206-1 Recommended Mortar Mixes Proportions by Volume

Type of Service	Cement	Mortar Sand in damp, loose condition
For ordinary service	1 masonry cement°	2-1/4 to 3
Subject to extremely heavy loads, violent winds, earthquakes, or severe frost action. Isolated piers.	1 masonry cement° plus 1 portland cement	4-1/2 to 6

°ASTM Specification C91, Type 11.

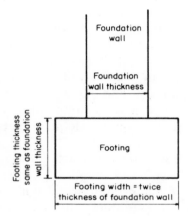

Fig. 207.4 *Dimension for typical farm buildings.*

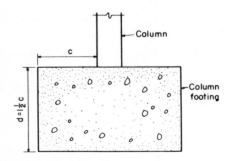

Det. 207-5 *Plain concrete column footings.*

207 Footings

207-1 General. The following recommendations are for light frame, one story farm buildings, only.

207-1.1 Footings shall be of concrete, complying with 203-3 or 203-4.

207-1.2 Use side forms where soil conditions prevent sharpcut trenches. If excavation is too deep, fill with concrete rather than soil.

207-1.3 In freezing weather place concrete as soon as possible after excavation and protect against freezing until hardened.

207-2 Footings are required under all concrete block walls.

207-3 Footings may be integral with a concrete wall poured in a trench with a width of not less than 8″, if the soil is stable and well drained.

207-4 Footing size should be twice as wide as specified on a plan and based on foundation loads and soil types. Dimensions of Det. 207-4 may be used if not specified.

207-5 Pier and Column Footings should be specified on a plan and based on column load and soil type. If not specified, the footing may have a minimum thickness of 8″, and unless reinforced, have a diameter 10″ larger than the column. See Det. 207-5.

210 Foundation Walls

210-1 Concrete foundations

210-1.1 Extend walls supporting wood frame construction at least 8″ above finish grade.

210-1.2 Thickness of foundation walls shall be not less than that of the wall supported. For buildings less than 400 sq.ft. in floor area and superstructure less than 8′ high—minimum 6″. All other buildings 8″ except as provided below.

210-1.3 Foundation walls extending more than 4′ into unstable or poorly drained soils; walls extending more than 7′ into the ground; or foundation and superstructure bearing walls totaling more than 24′ should be planned by an engineer.

210-2 Pilasters (piers forming part of a masonry or concrete wall)

210-2.1 Provide pilasters under girders framing into walls in all 6″ concrete or masonry walls and in all 8″ hollow masonry walls. Cap hollow masonry units used for pilasters in accordance with 211.2.

210-2.2 Minimum size:
Concrete: 2″ × 12″
Masonry: 4″ × 12″

210-2.3 Bond pilasters into the wall.

210-2.4 Girder support
a. Minimum end bearing of girder—4″.
b. When wood girder is used, provide at least 1/2″ clearance around girder unless wood has been pressure-preservative treated.

211 Masonry Walls

211-1 Materials—Block should comply with 205-1 and mortar with 206-1.

211-2 Cap the Top Course with one of the following:
a. 4″ solid blocks or concrete.
b. Cells of top course filled with concrete or grout.
c. Wood Preservative-treated sill minimum 2″ nominal thickness, bearing on both inner and outer shells of block.

211-3 Joints
a. Maximum average thickness of mortar joints, 1/2″. No joint shall be more than 3/4″ thick.
b. Lay solid masonry in full bed and head joints.
c. Lay hollow masonry with mortar applied to bed and head joints of face shells; lay the first course in full mortar bed.

d. Tool or parge *(cement-plaster)* all exposed joints.

212 Concrete Walls

212-1 Concrete shall comply with Par. 203.

214 Reinforcement
Size and spacing of reinforcement for earthquake design or for other foundation walls, when required, shall be in accordance with recognized engineering practice. When size and spacing has not been determined by a structural analysis, the following may be used:
1. Vertical Reinforcement No. 3 Bars @ 24″ o.c. or No. 4 Bars @ 32″ o.c.
2. Horizontal Reinforcement
   a. Concrete: No. 3 Bars @ 32″ o.c.
   b. Masonry: standard joint reinforcing with two 9 gauge or heavier longitudinal wires and No. 12 gauge or heavier cross wires.

216 Sill Anchorage (Det. 216-1)
Wood sills should be pressure-preservative treated, and anchored to exterior walls as follows:

216-1 Masonry walls.
a. 1/2″ bolts with washer or equivalent, imbedded not less than 15″ and full grouted, or
b. 22 3/4″ Anchor clips imbedded and fully grouted.
c. Maximum spacing, 8′ with not less than two bolts in each sill piece. End bolts shall be not more than 12″ from end of piece. Where earthquake design is required, maximum spacing 6′.

216-2 Concrete walls.
a. 1/2″ bolts imbedded not less than 6″, or
b. 14 3/4″ Anchor clips.
c. Spacing same as Masonry walls 216-1c. above.
d. Except where earthquake design is required, hardened steel studs driven by powder actuated tools may be used. Maximum spacing 4′ with not less than two studs in each sill piece.

218 Rigid Frames, Foundations and Anchorages

218-1 Foundations for rigid frames must be carefully constructed to an engineer's specifi-

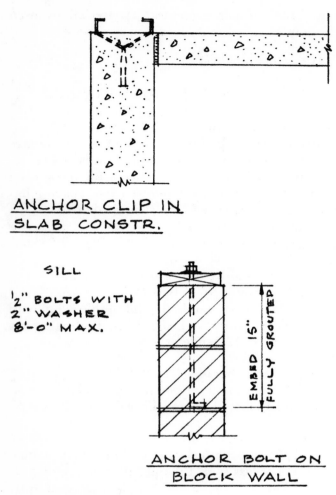

ANCHOR CLIP IN
SLAB CONSTR.

SILL

½" BOLTS WITH
2" WASHER
8'-0" MAX.

EMBED 15" FULLY GROUTED

ANCHOR BOLT ON
BLOCK WALL

Det. 216-1   Sill Anchorage

cations. Besides the normal vertical loads on the foundation that occur with any type of framing, rigid frames place large horizontal loads on the foundation. These loads tend to spread the foundation walls and cause them to overturn.

218-2   Det. 218-2 shows foundation details for one particular type of frame. They are not general, and do not substitute for an engineer's design.

218   Det. 218-3 shows various methods of fastening rigid frames to the plate or foundation, together with safe loads.

220   Grade Beam & Pier Construction

220-1   Extend grade beams and piers supporting wood frame construction at least 6″ above finish grade.

220-2   Extend bottom of grade beam below frost for the area unless:

a.   Soil is of such a nature that moisture will not be retained under grade beam, or

b.   Soil under grade beam is removed to below frost line and replaced with coarse rock or gravel or other material not susceptible to frost action. When trench is excavated in an impervious soil, provide drain tile to a positive outfall.

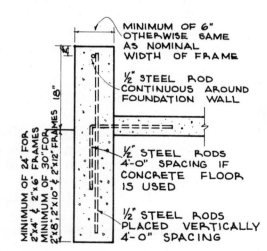

MINIMUM OF 6"
OTHERWISE SAME
AS NOMINAL
WIDTH OF FRAME

½" STEEL ROD
CONTINUOUS AROUND
FOUNDATION WALL

½" STEEL RODS
4'-0" SPACING IF
CONCRETE FLOOR
IS USED

½" STEEL RODS
PLACED VERTICALLY
4'-0" SPACING

MINIMUM OF 24" FOR 2"x4" & 2"x6" FRAMES
MINIMUM OF 30" FOR 2"x8", 2"x10" & 2"x12" FRAMES   18"

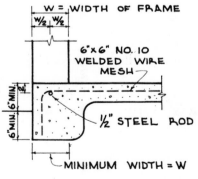

W = WIDTH OF FRAME

W/2 W/2

6"x6" NO. 10
WELDED WIRE
MESH

6" MIN. 6" MIN.

½" STEEL ROD

MINIMUM WIDTH = W

Det. 218-2   (Circ 812, U. of Illinois). Examples of rigid frame foundations for one type of wood rigid frame.

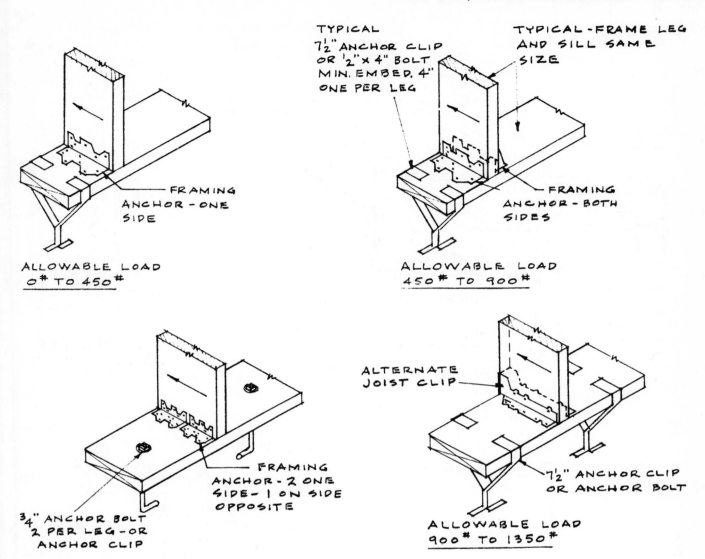

TYPICAL
7½" ANCHOR CLIP
OR ½" x 4" BOLT
MIN. EMBED. 4"
ONE PER LEG

TYPICAL-FRAME LEG
AND SILL SAME
SIZE

—FRAMING
ANCHOR - ONE
SIDE

ALLOWABLE LOAD
0# TO 450#

—FRAMING
ANCHOR - BOTH
SIDES

ALLOWABLE LOAD
450# TO 900#

—FRAMING
ANCHOR - 2 ONE
SIDE - 1 ON SIDE
OPPOSITE

¾" ANCHOR BOLT
2 PER LEG - OR
ANCHOR CLIP

ALTERNATE
JOIST CLIP

7½" ANCHOR CLIP
OR ANCHOR BOLT

ALLOWABLE LOAD
900# TO 1350#

Det. 218-3   Rigid Frame Anchorage.

220-3 Grade beams and piers require engineering design. Where piers and grade beams have not been determined by a structural analysis, the following may be used for one-story structures on average soil.

a. Piers:
1. Maximm pier spacing, 8′ o.c.
2. Minimum size of pier,
   a) Diameter, 10″.
   b) Depth—Bottom of pier below frost line.
   c) Reinforce pier with 2-No. 5 bars for full length of pier and extending into beam.

b. Grade Beam:
1. Minimum width: 6″
2. Minimum depth, 12″.
3. Reinforce with two bars top and bottom of beam as follows:
   a) Four No. 4 bars.
   b) Where grade beam is flared in at top, reinforce with one No. 6 bar instead of two No. 4 bars. See Detail 220-5.

220-4 Sill Plate Anchorage see 218-3.

220-5 See details Det. 220-5

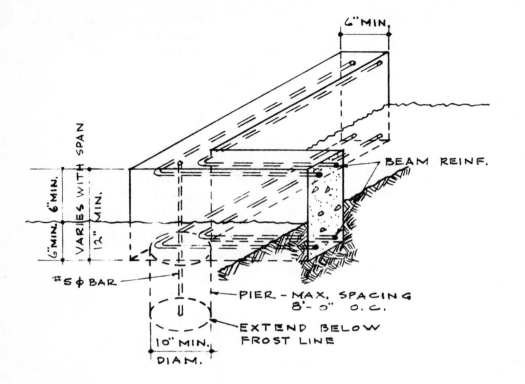

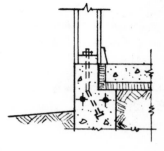

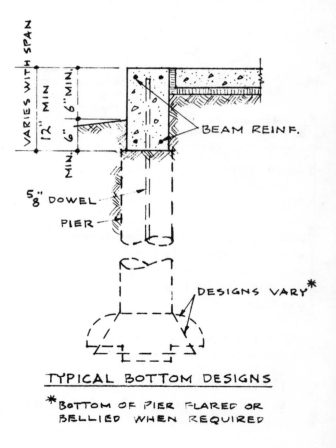

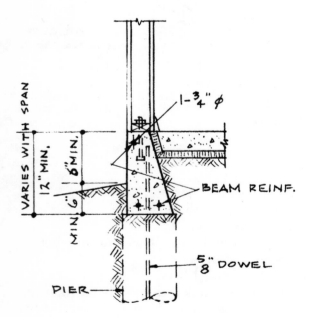

Det. 220-5 Grade Beam & Piers—Ground Supported Slabs

6" MIN.

BEAM REINF.

VARIES WITH SPAN

6" MIN.

12" MIN.

6" MIN.

#5 ⌀ BAR

PIER – MAX. SPACING 8'-0" O.C.

EXTEND BELOW FROST LINE

10" MIN. DIAM.

ALTERNATE EDGE SUPPORT

VARIES WITH SPAN

12" MIN.

6" MIN.

1-¾" ⌀

BEAM REINF.

⅝" DOWEL

PIER

VARIES WITH SPAN

12" MIN.

6" MIN.

BEAM REINF.

⅝" DOWEL

PIER

DESIGNS VARY*

TYPICAL BOTTOM DESIGNS

*BOTTOM OF PIER FLARED OR BELLIED WHEN REQUIRED

223 **Concrete Slotted Floors;** see paragraph 907-6, Chapter 9.

225 **Foundation Drains and Dampproofing**

225-1 Objective: To provide foundation construction that will prevent damage by infiltration of water or moisture.

225-2 Where excessive water may endanger the bearing capacity of the soil or where basement areas are to be in active use, foundation drains and dampproofing may be required.

225-3 **Foundation Drains.**

225-3.1 Install drains below the area to be protected and with gravity discharge to a positive outlet such as a drainage ditch or swale.

225-3.2 Drain tile may be clay, concrete asbestos cement, bituminized fibrepipe, or plastic.

225-3.3 Protect top tile joints with strips of building paper. Cover drain tile with 6″–8″ of coarse gravel, crushed rock or blast furnace slag. Provide about 2″ aggregate material under tile.

225-4 **Dampproofing**
Exterior foundation walls enclosing basements shall be dampproofed. See Detail 225-4.

225-4.1 Masonry Foundation Walls
a. Apply at least one coat of Portland cement plaster parging to wall from footing to finish grade. Minimum thickness, 3/8″.
b. Apply at least one coat of bituminous dampproofing material over parging. Apply in accordance with manufacturer's instructions.

225-4.2 Concrete Foundation Walls.
a. Apply at least one coat of bituminous dampproofing material to wall from footing to finish grade. Apply at rate recommended by manufacturer.

227 **Concrete Floors and Pavements**

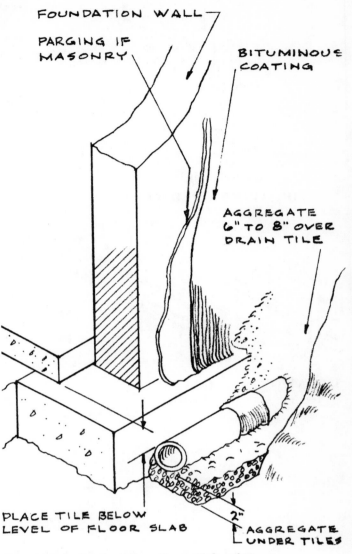

FOUNDATION WALL

PARGING IF MASONRY

BITUMINOUS COATING

AGGREGATE 6″ TO 8″ OVER DRAIN TILE

PLACE TILE BELOW LEVEL OF FLOOR SLAB

2″ AGGREGATE UNDER TILES

Det. 225-4   Drain Tiles Along Side of Footing

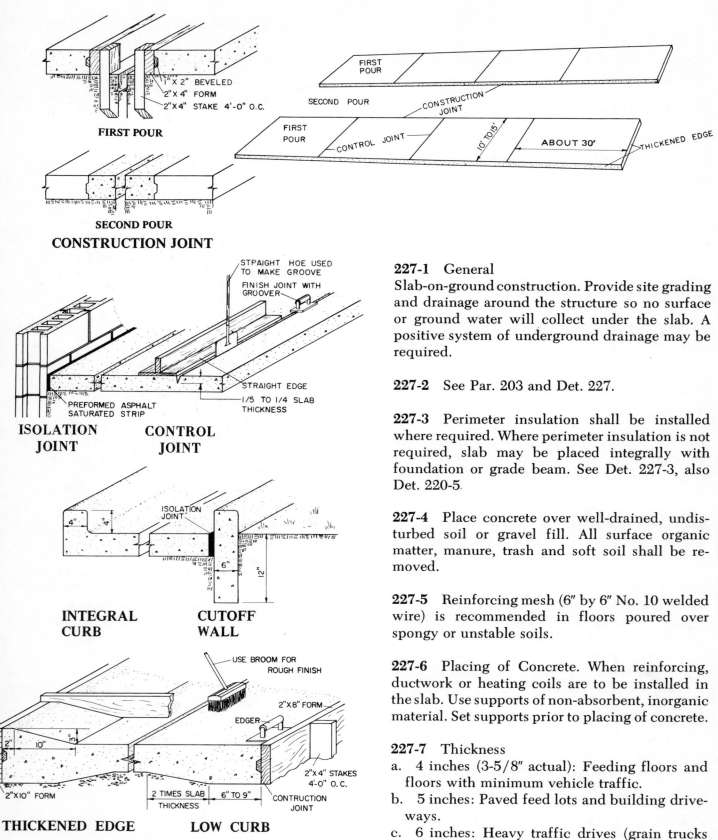

FIRST POUR

1" X 2" BEVELED
2" X 4" FORM
2" X 4" STAKE 4'-0" O.C.

SECOND POUR

CONSTRUCTION JOINT

FIRST POUR
SECOND POUR
CONSTRUCTION JOINT

FIRST POUR
CONTROL JOINT
10' TO 15'
ABOUT 30'
THICKENED EDGE

STRAIGHT HOE USED TO MAKE GROOVE
FINISH JOINT WITH GROOVER
STRAIGHT EDGE
1/5 TO 1/4 SLAB THICKNESS
PREFORMED ASPHALT SATURATED STRIP

ISOLATION JOINT   **CONTROL JOINT**

ISOLATION JOINT
4"
6"
12"

INTEGRAL CURB   **CUTOFF WALL**

USE BROOM FOR ROUGH FINISH
2" X 8" FORM
EDGER
2" X 4" STAKES 4'-0" O.C.
2" 10"
2" X 10" FORM
2 TIMES SLAB THICKNESS
6" TO 9"
CONTRUCTION JOINT

THICKENED EDGE   **LOW CURB**

Det. 227 Concrete Pavement.

227-1 General
Slab-on-ground construction. Provide site grading and drainage around the structure so no surface or ground water will collect under the slab. A positive system of underground drainage may be required.

227-2 See Par. 203 and Det. 227.

227-3 Perimeter insulation shall be installed where required. Where perimeter insulation is not required, slab may be placed integrally with foundation or grade beam. See Det. 227-3, also Det. 220-5.

227-4 Place concrete over well-drained, undisturbed soil or gravel fill. All surface organic matter, manure, trash and soft soil shall be removed.

227-5 Reinforcing mesh (6" by 6" No. 10 welded wire) is recommended in floors poured over spongy or unstable soils.

227-6 Placing of Concrete. When reinforcing, ductwork or heating coils are to be installed in the slab. Use supports of non-absorbent, inorganic material. Set supports prior to placing of concrete.

227-7 Thickness
a.   4 inches (3-5/8" actual): Feeding floors and floors with minimum vehicle traffic.
b.   5 inches: Paved feed lots and building driveways.
c.   6 inches: Heavy traffic drives (grain trucks and wagons).

227-8 Heating coils or reinforcement shall be covered with at least 1-1/2″ of concrete.

227-9 Provide control joints at about 30′ intervals and at offsets.

227-10 Use only clean sand or gravel fill compacted in 4″–6″ layers.

227-11 Finish with wood float or stiff broom.

227-12 Floor Slopes

227-12.1 Floor slopes of 1/8″/ft. or less are not apt to drain well.

227-12.2 Slope paved outdoor lots 1/4″ to 1″/ft, with the steeper slope recommended around feeders and waterers.

227-12.3 Slope indoor floors 1/4″ to 1/2″/ft. in bedded pens, 1/2″ to 3/4″/ft. on feeding floors.

227-12.4 Slope alleys 1/10″ to 1/4″/ft. to drains. Cross slopes to provide a dry crown may be 1/2″/ft.

227-12.5 Gutter and manure pit floors are sloped 1″/25′ to 1″/100′ to drains or pumping stations.

227-12.6 Slotted floors are usually level and 2″–4″ below adjacent aprons or solid floors.

228 Moisture or Vapor Barriers under slabs. Where required by location and type of occupancy barriers shall be polyethylene film complying with C.S. 238-61. Required thicknesses: on sand or tamped earth, 4 mils (.004″); over gravel or under slabs with reinforcing steel, 6 mils (.006″).

232 Termite Protection
See map, Det. 232

232-1 Provide termite protection as follows:
a. Region 1. All areas.
b. Region 2. Generally required in all areas except where specific exceptions can be made because of local experience.

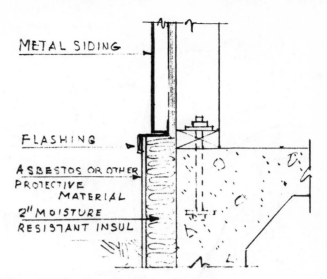

METAL SIDING

FLASHING

ASBESTOS OR OTHER PROTECTIVE MATERIAL

2″ MOISTURE RESISTANT INSUL.

Det. 227-3 Perimeter Insulation.

c. Region 3. Generally not required except in specific areas where infestation has started.
d. Region 4. Termite protection not required.

232-2 Types of Termite Protection.

232-2.1 Pressure treated wood.
a. In frame construction on a slab, use pressure treated wood for all framing to include top plates of walls and partitions.
b. In frame construction on foundation or over a crawl space, use pressure treated wood for sills, joists, and posts.

232-2.2 Metal shield. Galvanized iron or steel, 26 gauge installed continuous under wood sill plate or other wood construction. Shield shall be at least 8 inches above outside or inside finished grade. See Dwg. 232-2.2 for installation.

232-2.3 Chemical soil treatment should be used with great care to avoid contamination of wells or ponds. To be applied only by a licensed soil treatment firm.

232-2.4 Typical pole buildings with treated poles and skirting and with metal siding may be regarded as termite proof if first untreated girt is at least 24″ from finish grade and no other untreated members extend below that line.

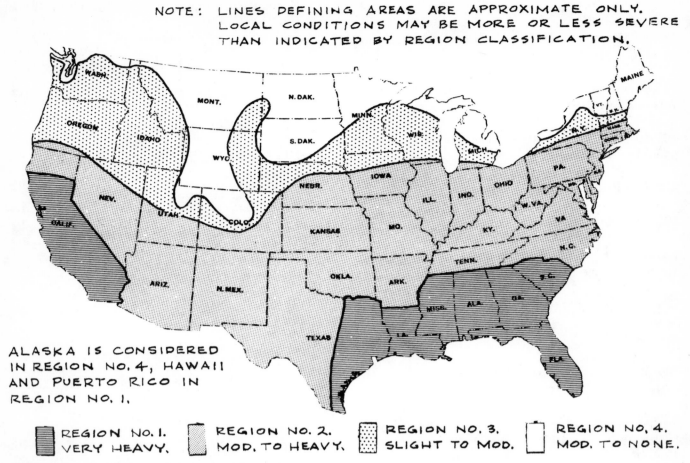

ALASKA IS CONSIDERED IN REGION NO. 4, HAWAII AND PUERTO RICO IN REGION NO. 1.

REGION NO. 1. VERY HEAVY.

REGION NO. 2. MOD. TO HEAVY.

REGION NO. 3. SLIGHT TO MOD.

REGION NO. 4. MOD. TO NONE.

Det. 232   Distribution of Termite Infestation.

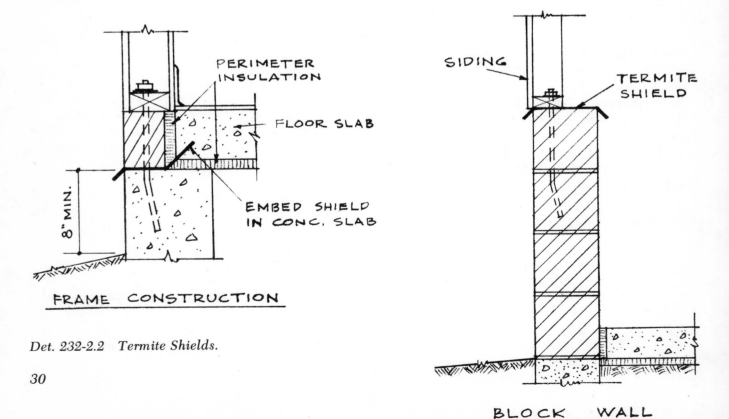

PERIMETER INSULATION

FLOOR SLAB

EMBED SHIELD IN CONC. SLAB

8" MIN.

FRAME CONSTRUCTION

SIDING

TERMITE SHIELD

BLOCK WALL

Det. 232-2.2   Termite Shields.

30

301 Posts and Poles

Poles, as a *structural material,* are superior to sawed rectangular posts:

—The round shape is more efficient in both bending and as a column.

—Knots near the butt of a tree are grown over with complete outer rings and/or are small. The greatest stress—just below the ground-line—is therefore where the material is strongest.

—The natural taper increases the size of the pole where it is needed most.

—Sapwood takes preservative treatment better than heartwood. Poles are encased in sapwood, and therefore well-treated wood.

—A minor advantage is that the natural taper also aids in preventing withdrawal, as when subjected to wind uplift loads. Taper is usually about 1″ change in diameter per 10′ length of pole; or, about 1/2″ even at 5′ depth of set—not a very significant amount.

Posts, as a *construction material,* are superior to poles:

—Despite variations in moisture content, sizes are more uniform and predictable.

—Plane faces at right angles aid in construction of corners; doorways and window openings; and wall-top beams, bracing, and roof connections.

—Sawn lumber is usually straighter.

—Posts are easier to handle, as they will stack without rolling in a warehouse, on a truck, or at the site.

—Posts are more suitable for construction requiring girts or pre-fab panels between the columns.

Between poles, space between poles varies with distance from the ground:.

Slabbed poles are an effective compromise:

—They improve some of the pole's disadvantages above the ground, while maintaining its advantages where strength and durability are most needed, just below the ground.

—Slabbing still leaves a minimum of flat surfaces, some difficulty in determining "vertical," no uniform distance between column faces up a wall.

301-1 Posts or Poles may be of the following species:

Group A Species
    Douglas Fir, Inland
    Douglas Fir, West Coast
    Western Larch
    Southern Pine
Group B Species
    Western Red Cedar
    Ponderosa Pine
    Jack Pine
    Lodge Pole Pine
    Norway Pine *(Red Pine)*

301-2 Preservative Treatment

301-2.1 Posts and Poles. Preservatives should conform to the latest edition of the American Wood Preservers Association Standards.

a. AWPA P 1 Standard for Coal Tar, Creosote for Land and Fresh Water Use. Minimum Retention 8 lbs. *(10 lbs.)* per cu. ft. of gross volume.

b. AWPA P 8, Standard for Oil Borne Preservatives; and AWPA P 9, Standard for Hydrocarbon Solvents for Oil-Borne Preservatives. Minimum retention 0.4 lbs. *(0.5 lbs.)** per cu. ft. of gross volume. *(Minimum retention for western red cedar is 4.5 lbs. per cu. ft. and for the thermal treatment is 20 lbs. of creosote or penta chlorophenol solution in the outer 1/2 inch of the post or pole.)*

***Higher retention is for severe service conditions such as occur in Region No. 1—Map Det. 232, Distribution of termite infestation.*

301-2.2 Non-structural members or ones not expensive to replace may be treated in accordance with the above or one of the following water-borne treatments:

Preservative per AWPA P 5	Min. Retention lbs. per cu. ft. of gross volume
Ammoniacal Copper Arsenite	0.5
Chromated Copper Arsenate (Type A)	0.75
Chromated Copper Arsenate (Type B)	0.42

Note: These preservatives may be desirable where paintability, cleanliness or freedom from odor are required.

301-2.3 Round poles may be modified by slabbing before treatment to provide a continuous flat surface for the attachment of sheathing and framing members, to permit more secure attachment of fasteners, and to facilitate the alignment and setting of intermediate wall and corner poles. The slabbing may be a minimum cut to provide a single continuous flat face from groundline to top of intermediate wall poles, or two continuous flat faces at right angles to one another from groundline to top of corner for doorway poles. Preservative penetration is generally limited in heartwood, so that slabbing, particularly in the groundline area of poles with thin sapwood, may result in somewhat less protection than that of an unslabbed pole.

301-2.4 Posts may be incised *(holes punched in)* before treatment to aid penetration of the preservative.

301-2.5 Round poles shall meet the specifications in ASAE R 299 for rate of growth, allow-

able defects, dimensions, manufacturing, marketing certification, and storage.

301-2.6 Handling: Handle pressure treated material to avoid damage to the original pressure treated surface. As far as practicable, fabricate (such as slabbing or mortising) prior to treatment. Field treat any damage or field fabrication with an appropriate preservative, preferably the type used in the original treatment and obtained from the material supplier. Thoroughly saturate cuts and abrasions; pour holes full of preservative. Horizontal holes may be filled with a bent funnel.

301-3.1 Posts (Square Poles) are rapidly displacing round Poles, particularly in environmentally controlled construction. Equivalent sizes are given in Appendix A.

301-3.2 Posts may be of any of the species listed in 301-1. Posts should be free of evident structural defects, other than sound knots, and growth rate should be not less than 6 rings per inch. Place end of post with least knots down.

302 Lumber—Dimension lumber shall be of species and grade specified in span tables. Dressed sizes as specified in PS-20-71 are assumed.

302-1 Moisture content of lumber should not exceed 19% when incorporated into the building.

302-2 Lumber for trusses should be of the species and grade specified by the fastening manufacturer or other design source.

303 Plywood shall be manufactured in accordance with U.S. Product Standard PS 1-66 and bear the grade stamp of a recognized inspection agency. All plywood used in farm buildings should be made with exterior type glue.

304 Nails. Unless otherwise indicated, all nails specified in this book are to be hardened, deformed shank nails generally described as "pole barn nails."

305 Metal Siding & Roofing

305-1 Steel

a. Formed galvanized steel sheets for roofing and siding are in 26, 28, and 29 gauges. Apply in accord with manufacturer's instructions, using nails and accessories (ridge roll, flashing, etc.) of the same material and as specified by the manufacturer.

b. Girt and Purlin spacing depends on the sheet design and on member size and strength. See Appendix A.

c. Steel roofing and siding shall have a minimum coating class of 1.25 oz/sq ft of zinc coating (total, both sides) per ASTM Specification A-361. For extra long service, heavier coatings are available such as 2 oz "Seal of Quality" sheets. Factory painted sheets will have a longer life than plain galvanized. Periodic painting or repainting can extend life indefinitely.

d. Storage. Life expectancy of galvanized sheets can be reduced considerably should the sheets be exposed to moisture during storage. Never unload unwrapped sheets during rain or snow. When stored on the job for more than 24 hours, provide temporary cover; avoid trapping moisture with tightly wrapped plastic.

305-2 Aluminum

a. Formed, or formed and embossed, aluminum sheets may be used for roofing and siding in weights and/or thicknesses specified by manufacturer. Apply in accord with manufacturer's instructions, using nails and accessories (ridge roll, flashing, etc.) as supplied or specified by the manufacturer.

b. Unless otherwise recommended by manufacturer, limit Purlin or Girt spacing to 36" o.c. See Appendix A.

c. Unless commercial grade alloy sheets are used, aluminum sheets should not contact fertilizer, alkalies, caustic soda or acid. Aluminum is not recommended for buildings used to store them. Keep aluminum 18" off the ground and avoid prolonged, direct contact with animal excretion, wet poultry litter, animal bedding and wet grain or fibrous materials.

d. Do not apply aluminum in direct contact with iron, copper, brass or ungalvanized steel. Coat dissimilar metals with heavy bodied bituminous paint before assembly.

e. Where condensation is expected on the inside of buildings with aluminum siding and roofing, apply vapor barrier under aluminum.

f. Store sheets in a clean, dry area. Avoid trapping moisture between sheets. Use as soon as practicable after delivery.

306 Siding

306-1 Apply siding to affect a weather tight seal and to present a neat and workmanlike appearance.

306-2 Metal Siding

306-2.1 Make sidelaps per manufacturer's recommendations, but of 1 rib or more and nailed at each girt. All exposed edges should finish down and turn away from prevailing winds.

306-2.2 Make endlaps per manufacturer's recommendations but 4 inches or more and supported by a girt.

306-2.3 Use fasteners and accessories as recommended by manufacturer.

306-2.4 Siding may be applied with corrugations or ribs vertical or horizontal. If applied vertically over a stud wall without sheathing, provide 1 × 3 girts spaced not to exceed manufacturer's specifications. If applied over sheathing, use 15 lb. asphalt saturated felt under. Apply metal siding to manufacturer's instructions, using recommended fasteners and accessories.

306-2.5 Install horizontal blocking up to 48" o.c. between studs under metal siding applied horizontally on a wall exceeding 8' in height with no structural sheathing or lining.

306-3 Asbestos—Apply vertically.

306-3.1 Make sidelaps 1 corrugation, with caulking between corrugations and finishing away from prevailing winds.

306-3.2 Make endlaps at least 6″ and supported by a girt.

306-3.3 Use fasteners and accessories as recommended by manufacturer.

306-4 Plywood Siding

306-4.1 Use exterior type plywood. Minimum thickness 3/8″; maximum girt spacing 48″ o.c.

306-4.2 Joints. For draft free construction, use blocking or battens at vertical joints.

306-4.3 Nailing. For 3/8″ plywood use 6d galvanized nails 6″ o.c. at the edges and 12″ o.c. at intermediate supports.

306-4.4 3/8″ exterior type plywood may be applied vertically over studs 24″ o.c. maximum. Recommended: 1 × 2 or plywood batten over vertical joints. Use 6d galvanized common or box nails 6″ o.c. at the panel edges and 12′ o.c. at the intermediate supports.

306-4.5 Texture One Eleven Plywood Siding (exterior type 5/8 inch) is suitable for farm buildings where appearance is a factor. Maximum stud spacing 24″ o.c. Nail with 8d galvanized casing nails 6″ o.c. at panel edges and 12′ o.c. at intermediate studs. Nails on shiplap edges to be 1/2″ from exposed edge and slant driven toward it. Do not set nails.

306-5 Board Siding.
Vertical Board Siding should be free of knot holes, loose knots larger than 1/2″ in diameter, and through checks or splits longer than one half of the width of the piece.

306-5.1 Prevent water from entering Board Siding joints by using shiplapped or matched joints, or vertical wood battens. Minimum thickness 3/4″; maximum width 12″.

306-5.2 Use 7d corrosion-resistant nails to girts not more than 24″ o.c.; 2 nails per bearing.

306-5.3 Vertical Board Siding. Minimum thickness 3/4″; maximum width, 12″.

a. If boards do not have T & G or Shiplap joint, provide batten strips. Nail battens to sheathing or blocking at vertical joint.
b. Over fiber sheathing, nail siding to blocking between studs spaced not more than 32″ o.c. with corrosion resistant nails. Length of nail shall be that which will provide at least 1 inch penetration into blocking.
c. Where sheathing is omitted, vertical siding may be installed to blocking up to 32″ o.c., or to 1 × 3 or 1 × 4 stripping spaced not more than 24″ o.c. applied to face of studs.

306-6 Hardboard Siding. Large sheets, tempered type.
a. Thickness 1/4″—over sheathing with studs or girts 24″ o.c. or, without sheathing, studs 16″ o.c.
b. Thickness 5/16″—without sheathing over studs or girts 24″ o.c.
c. Nail Siding to each bearing with corrosion resistant nails that will penetrate stud at least 1″ if sheathing is used or 1-1/2″ if sheathing is omitted.
d. Nail 4″ o.c. around all edges and 8″ o.c. at intermediate supports. Minimum edge distance 3/8″.
e. Joints need approximately 1/16″ gap filled with mastic unless they are of interlapping type, or battens are installed. Install 2 × 4 or 2 × 3 blocking at horizontal joints if sheathing is omitted.

307 **Insulation.**
Provide insulation as required in Chapter 8.

308 **Vapor Barriers**
Water vapor in air (measured in "relative humidity") tends to move through building materials from warmer indoor air to colder outdoor air. And, when the vapor cools to its "dew point" it condenses, as on a cold glass in summer. If a room is at 70° F and the outdoors is at −20° F, somewhere in a wall between the two—whether insulated or not—a building material will be colder than the dew point and vapor will condense. The condensed water will greatly reduce the effectiveness of bulk or fiber insulation, and may cause decay.

308.1 Provide a good vapor barrier on the warm side of all walls, ceilings, and core doors in confined livestock housing, usually directly under the inside lining material.

308.2 The best barriers are 4 mil polyethylene plastic, aluminum foil or metal siding; somewhat less effective are exterior type plywood, 2 coats of aluminum-in-varnish paint on wood, or kraft-and-asphalt building paper.

308.3 Lap film materials generously at all joints. Vapor seal joints in seams between panels such as plywood or metal siding.

308.4 The vapor barrier on most batt and blanket insulations is not satisfactory because of inadequate seam lapping or sealing.

308.5 Tar and felt building paper and most insulation and insulation boards are inadequate vapor barriers.

308.6 Where construction requires an impermeable outdoor siding (e.g. metal), ventilate the air space between the insulation and the siding. Vapor must be able to move outward from the wall more easily than it can move through the vapor barrier near the warm side of the wall.

308.7 Avoid breaking the barrier at electrical outlets and other openings.

309 Panelized Walls
Suggested construction for insulated, panelized wall which may be applied on the inside of posts is shown in Det. 319.

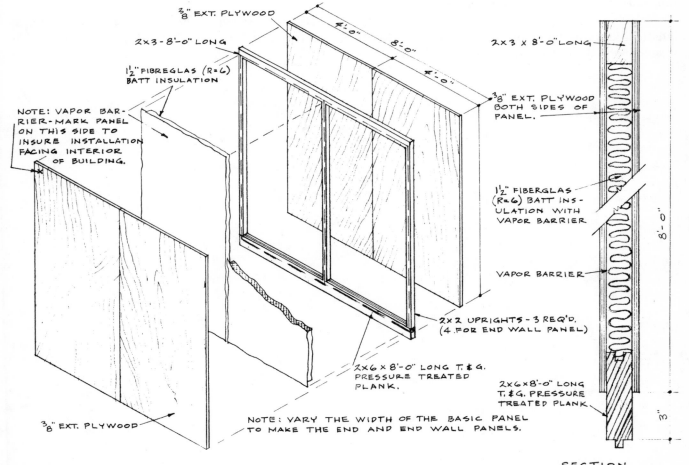

Det. 319   Panelized Walls.

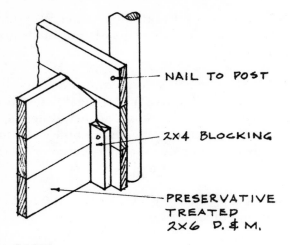

NAIL TO POST

2x4 BLOCKING

PRESERVATIVE TREATED 2x6 D. & M.

Det. 310-5

309-1 Fasten plywood with 6d corrosion resistant nails 6″ o.c. or equivalent staples.

309-2 Mark plywood on vapor barrier side to insure installation facing inside of building.

309-3 Nail panels to posts with 20d nails 18″ o.c.

310 Skirting (Splatter Boards)

310-1 Install skirting on most post and pole buildings. Use 2 × 6 D & M preservative treated per 301-2. Use C or D Group Species lumber.

310-2 Number of courses 2 × 6 skirting will depend on the operation. Minimum 2 courses (10-1/4″).

310-3 Where post or pole spacing exceeds 8′, place short intermediate treated posts or poles at midspan for support.

310-4 Nail to posts with 20d nails. Nail to poles with 40d nails. Two nails at each bearing.

310-5 To prevent the skirt boards from being "pushed off" they may be placed on the inside of the poles. Detail 310-5.

Chapter 4

POST OR
POLE TYPE CONSTRUCTION

400   Post or Pole Type Construction

400-1   Objective:
To provide safe and economical construction that assures adequate support of imposed roof and wind loads and maximum utility in the finished building.

400-2   General
In post or pole type buildings, unlike typical frame or rigid frame construction, all loads are carried to the imbedded section of the posts or poles in the earth. These buildings are "Live" and considerable movement takes place in the building in high or gusty winds. This requires careful attention to joints throughout the building, and particularly connections between posts or poles and roof construction.

403   Posts and Poles
Tables showing the size, spacing, supported span of roof, etc. for post and poles are in Appendix A for the various load zones.

403-1   Posts shall have the wide face perpendicular to the wall.

403-2   Where two or more required posts or poles are omitted in bearing walls for an opening, poles at the edge of the opening shall be increased in size or doubled and securely fastened together with spikes or bolts. See detail 408-5.1.

404   Posts and Poles—Anchorage against wind uplift and overturning.

404-1   Detail 404-1 shows acceptable methods of anchorage. All poles shall be anchored.
a.   Anchor Blocks. Two 2 × 6 or 2 × 8 Blocks, minimum 24 inches securely nailed to opposite sides of the post or pole.
b.   Anchor Pad. This form of anchorage also provides the footing and has the advantage of being poured at the time poles are set. Do not use over 20 inch diameter.
c.   Anchor pad used in conjunction with regular footing at higher spans.
d.   Backfill with gravel.
e.   Backfill with concrete. This method should be used where the orientation of open front buildings exposes them to prevailing winds, and in coastal areas.

404-2   Earth and gravel backfill shall be thoroughly tamped. Concrete backfill shall be thoroughly rodded.

405   Embedment, Posts & Poles *(Soil Classification from Appendix A-13).*

405-1   Posts shall be embedded as follows:

| | Embedment Depth | | |
Post Size	Poor Soil	Average Soil	Good Soil
4 × 4	4'—4"	3'—6"	2'—8"
6 × 6 or			
4 × 6	5'—6"	4'—6"	3'—6"
8 × 8 or			
6 × 8	7'—0"	5'—6"	4'—6"

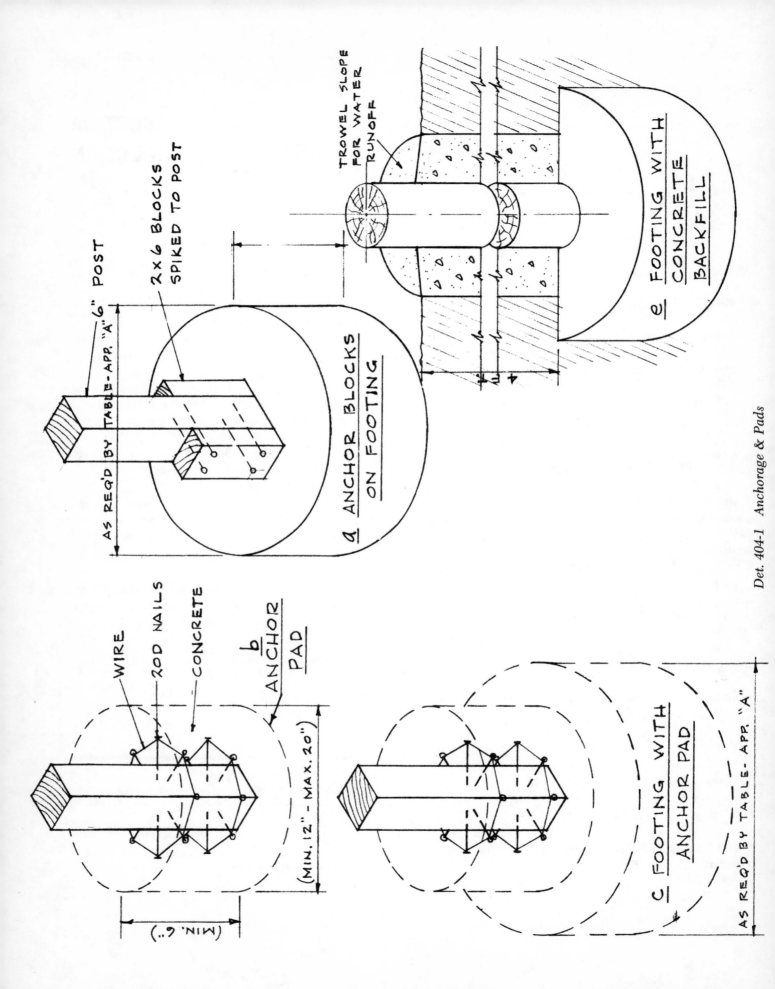

TROWEL SLOPE FOR WATER RUNOFF

2×6 BLOCKS SPIKED TO POST

6" POST

AS REQ'D BY TABLE - APP. "A"

a ANCHOR BLOCKS ON FOOTING

e FOOTING WITH CONCRETE BACKFILL

WIRE

20d NAILS

CONCRETE

b ANCHOR PAD

(MIN. 12" - MAX. 20")

(MIN. 6")

c FOOTING WITH ANCHOR PAD

AS REQ'D BY TABLE - APP. "A"

Det. 404-1 Anchorage & Pads

405-2 Poles shall be embedded as follows:

Pole Dia. (Top)	8'0" Eave			14'0" Eave			20'0" Eave		
	Poor	Average	Good	Poor	Average	Good	Poor	Average	Good
4"	5'5"	4'4"	3'5"	5'11"	4'8"	3'8"	6'4"	5'0"	3'11"
5"	6'4"	5'0"	3'11"	6'7"	5'3"	4'2"	6'11"	5'6"	4'4"
6"	6'11"	5'6"	4'4"	7'3"	5'9"	4'7"	7'7"	6'0"	4'9"
7"	7'7"	6'0"	4'9"	7'11"	6'3"	5'0"	8'3"	6'6"	5'2"
8"	8'3"	6'6"	5'2"	8'6"	6'9"	5'4"	8'10"	7'0"	5'7"

405-3 In no case shall embedment be less than the frost line, par. 202.

407 Pads and Footings, Posts and Poles

407-1 Pads or Footings are required under all post and poles except lightly loaded P-3 Poles, end wall poles or other poles not providing major roof support.

407-2 Precast Pads or Footings are recommended for bearing, but not for anchorage.

407-3 Remove all loose soil from holes before pouring concrete.

407-4 Where required posts or poles are omitted from the structure for door openings, placing the load on adjoining poles, increase the area of the footings on those poles proportionately with a consequent increase in thickness.

408 Plates

408-1 Minimum Size:
a. Where plate does not carry loads from trusses or rafters between poles—2 × 6.
b. Where plates do carry loads from trusses between posts or poles they shall be sized in accordance with tables in Appendix A for the appropriate load zone.

408-2 Vertically built-up beams as specified in tables in Appendix "A" may be constructed as in Detail 408-2 or as designed by an engineer for other fastenings.

408-3 Fasten plates to Posts or Poles as shown in Detail 408-3. Double plate may be on one or both sides of post or pole. Where plate members are on both sides of the post, they should be securely fastened together with blocking or truss ties not to exceed four feet apart.

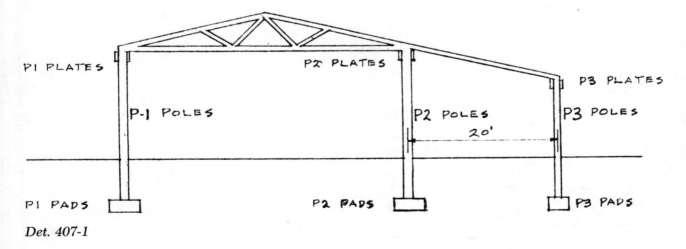

Det. 407-1

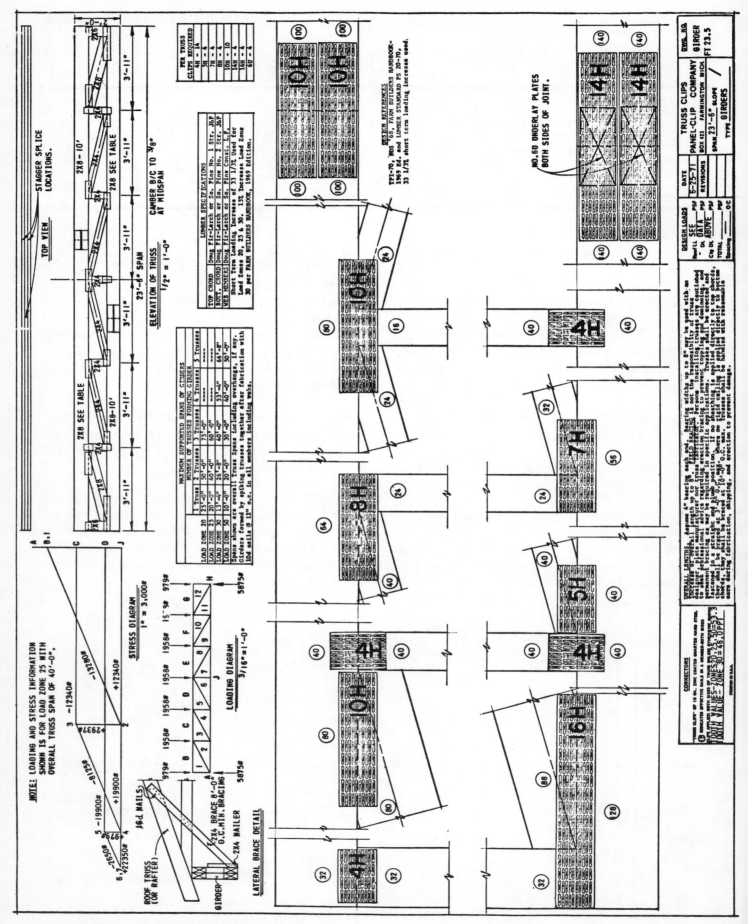

Det. 408-2 *Vertically Built Up Beams*

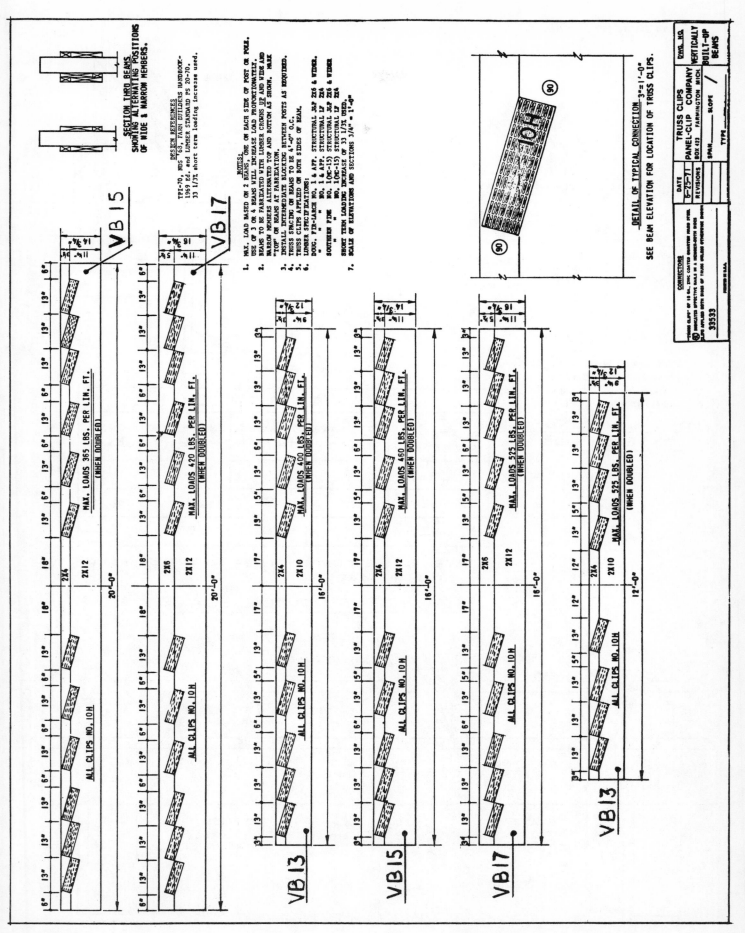

SECTION THRU BEAMS
SHOWING ALTERNATING POSITIONS
OF WIDE & NARROW MEMBERS.

DESIGN REFERENCES
TPI-70, NDS '68, FARM BUILDERS HANDBOOK-
1969 Ed. and LUMBER STANDARD PS 20-70.
33 1/3% short term loading increase used.

NOTES:
1. MAX. LOAD BASED ON 2 BEAMS, ONE ON EACH SIDE OF POST OR POLE.
   USE OF 3 OR 4 BEAMS WILL INCREASE LOAD PROPORTIONATELY.
2. BEAMS TO BE FABRICATED WITH LUMBER CROWNS UP AND WIDE AND
   NARROW MEMBERS ALTERNATED TOP AND BOTTOM AS SHOWN. MARK
   "TOP" ON BEAMS AT FABRICATION.
3. INSTALL INTERMEDIATE BLOCKING BETWEEN POSTS AS REQUIRED.
4. TRUSS SPACING OR BEAMS TO BE 4'-0" O.C.
5. TRUSS CLIPS APPLIED ON BOTH SIDES OF BEAM.
6. LUMBER SPECIFICATIONS:
   DOUG. FIR-LARCH NO. 1 & APP. STRUCTURAL J&P 2X6 & WIDER.
   " " NO. 1 & APP. STRUCTURAL LF 2X4
   SOUTHERN PINE NO. 1(MC-15) STRUCTURAL J&P 2X6 & WIDER
   " " NO. 1(MC-15) STRUCTURAL LF 2X4
7. SHORT TERM LOADING INCREASE OF 33 1/3% USED.
   SCALE OF ELEVATIONS AND SECTIONS 3/4" = 1'-0"

VB15

MAX. LOADS 365 LBS. PER LIN. FT.
(WHEN DOUBLED)
2X4
2X12
20'-0"
ALL CLIPS NO.10H
VB13

VB17

MAX. LOADS 420 LBS. PER LIN. FT.
(WHEN DOUBLED)
2X6
2X12
20'-0"
ALL CLIPS NO.10H
VB15

MAX. LOADS 400 LBS. PER LIN. FT.
(WHEN DOUBLED)
2X4
2X10
16'-0"
ALL CLIPS NO.10H
VB13

MAX. LOADS 460 LBS. PER LIN. FT.
(WHEN DOUBLED)
2X4
2X12
16'-0"
ALL CLIPS NO.10H
VB15

MAX. LOADS 525 LBS. PER LIN. FT.
(WHEN DOUBLED)
2X6
2X12
16'-0"
ALL CLIPS NO.10H
VB17

MAX. LOADS 525 LBS. PER LIN. FT.
(WHEN DOUBLED)
2X4
2X10
12'-0"
VB13

DETAIL OF TYPICAL CONNECTION 3"=1'-0"
SEE BEAM ELEVATION FOR LOCATION OF TRUSS CLIPS.

DATE 6-25-71
REVISIONS
TRUSS CLIPS
PANEL-CLIP COMPANY
BOX 423   FARMINGTON, MICH.
SPAN_____ SLOPE ____/____
TYPE_____
DWG NO
VERTICALLY
BUILT-UP
BEAMS

CONNECTORS
"TRUSS CLIFF" OF 18 GA., ZINC COATED QUARTER HARD STEEL.
90 INDICATES EFFECTIVE NAIL IN A HERRING-BONE ENDS
ALSO APPLIED BOTH ENDS OF TRUSS UNLESS OTHERWISE SHOWN.
33533
PRINTED IN U.S.A.

Det. 408-2

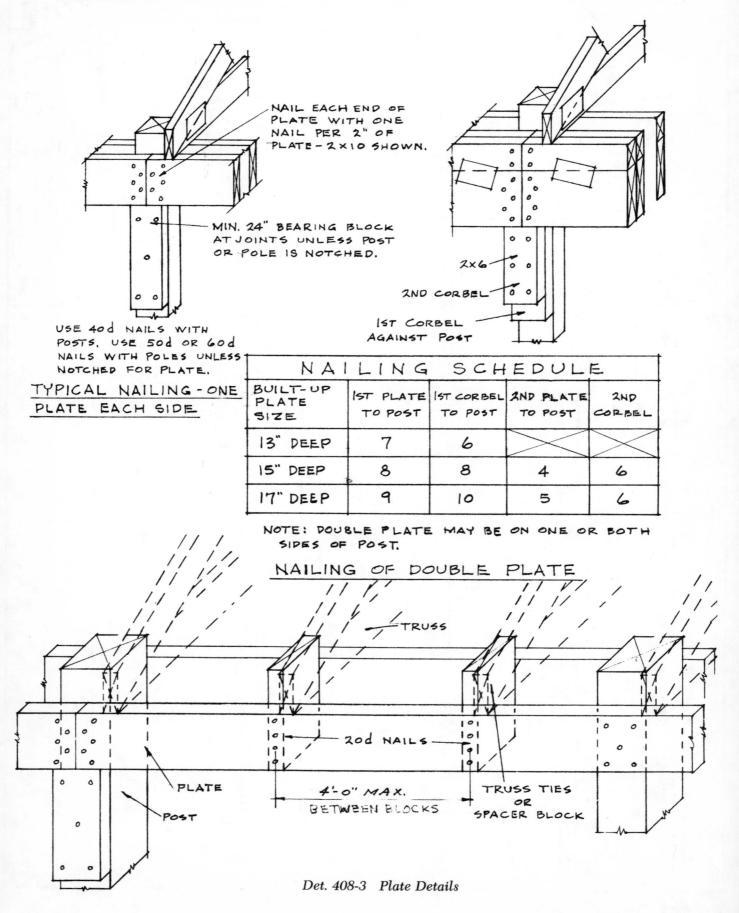

NAIL EACH END OF
PLATE WITH ONE
NAIL PER 2" OF
PLATE - 2×10 SHOWN.

MIN. 24" BEARING BLOCK
AT JOINTS UNLESS POST
OR POLE IS NOTCHED.

USE 40d NAILS WITH
POSTS. USE 50d OR 60d
NAILS WITH POLES UNLESS
NOTCHED FOR PLATE.

TYPICAL NAILING - ONE
PLATE EACH SIDE

2×6

2ND CORBEL

1ST CORBEL
AGAINST POST

NAILING SCHEDULE				
BUILT-UP PLATE SIZE	1ST PLATE TO POST	1ST CORBEL TO POST	2ND PLATE TO POST	2ND CORBEL
13" DEEP	7	6	╳	╳
15" DEEP	8	8	4	6
17" DEEP	9	10	5	6

NOTE: DOUBLE PLATE MAY BE ON ONE OR BOTH
SIDES OF POST.

NAILING OF DOUBLE PLATE

TRUSS

20d NAILS

PLATE

POST

4'-0" MAX.
BETWEEN BLOCKS

TRUSS TIES
OR
SPACER BLOCK

Det. 408-3   Plate Details

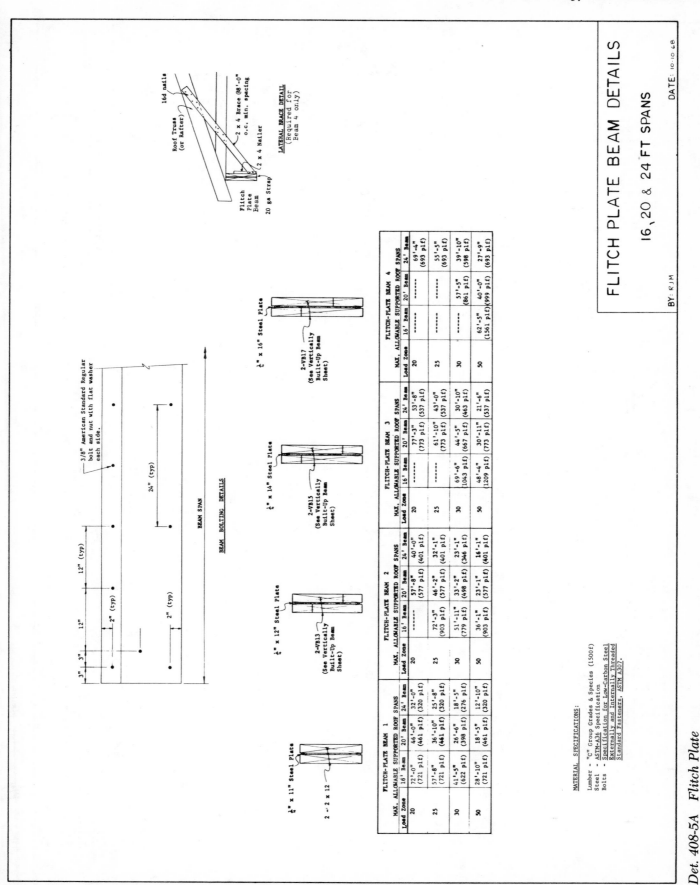

Det. 408-5A Flitch Plate

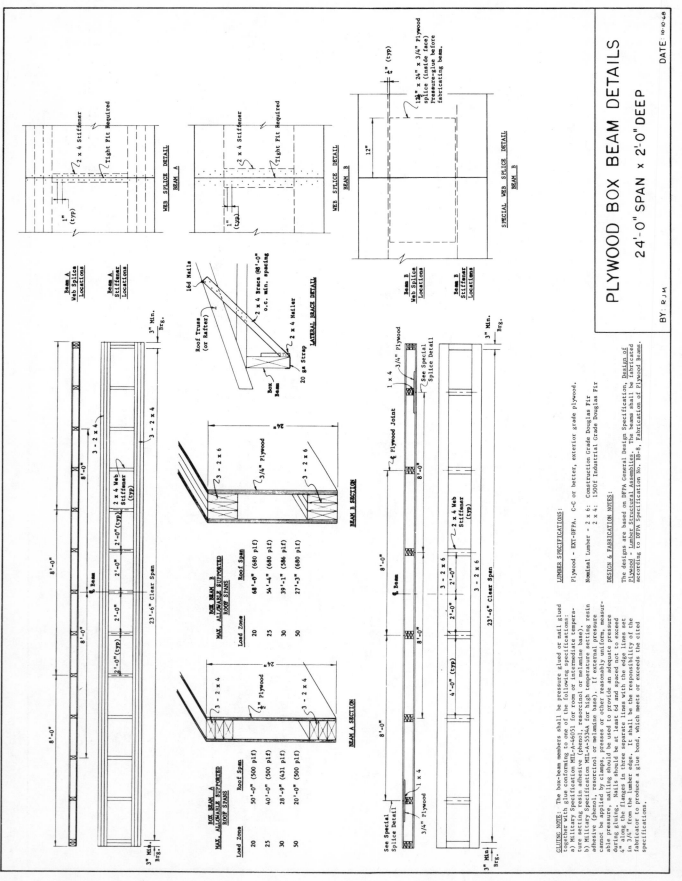

PLYWOOD BOX BEAM DETAILS
24'-0" SPAN x 2'-0" DEEP

BY: RJM   DATE: 10-10-68

WEB SPLICE DETAIL BEAM A

WEB SPLICE DETAIL BEAM B

SPECIAL WEB SPLICE DETAIL BEAM B

1½" x 24" x 3/4" Plywood splice (inside face) Pressure-glue before fabricating beam.

12"

¼" (typ)

2 x 4 Stiffener
Tight Fit Required
1" (typ)

Beam A Web Splice Locations
Beam A Stiffener Locations

Beam B Web Splice Locations
Beam B Stiffener Locations

LATERAL BRACE DETAIL

16d Nails
Roof Truss (or Rafter)
2 x 4 Brace @8'-0" o.c. min. spacing
2 x 4 Nailer
20 ga Strap
Box Beam

BEAM A SECTION

24"
3 - 2 x 4
½" Plywood
3 - 2 x 4

BEAM B SECTION

24"
3 - 2 x 6
3/4" Plywood
2 x 4 Web Stiffener (typ)
3 - 2 x 6

BOX BEAM A
MAX. ALLOWABLE SUPPORTED ROOF SPANS

Load Zone	Roof Span	
20	50'-0"	(500 plf)
25	40'-0"	(500 plf)
30	28'-9"	(431 plf)
50	20'-0"	(500 plf)

BOX BEAM B
MAX. ALLOWABLE SUPPORTED ROOF SPANS

Load Zone	Roof Span	
20	68'-0"	(680 plf)
25	54'-4"	(680 plf)
30	39'-1"	(586 plf)
50	27'-3"	(680 plf)

8'-0" 8'-0" 8'-0"
2'-0"(typ) 2'-0" 2'-0"
¢ Beam
2 x 4 Web Stiffener (typ)
3 - 2 x 4
23'-6" Clear Span
3" Min. Brg.

8'-0" 8'-0" 8'-0"
¢ Plywood Joint
¢ Beam
4'-0" (typ) 2'-0" 2'-0"
2 x 4 Web Stiffener (typ)
3 - 2 x 6
3 - 2 x 6
23'-6" Clear Span
See Special Splice Detail
1 x 4
3/4" Plywood
3" Min. Brg.

See Special Splice Detail
1 x 4
3/4" Plywood
3" Min. Brg.

LUMBER SPECIFICATIONS:

Plywood - EXT-DFPA. C-C or better, exterior grade plywood.

Nominal Lumber - 2 x 6: Construction Grade Douglas Fir
2 x 4: 1500f Industrial Grade Douglas Fir

DESIGN & FABRICATION NOTES:

The designs are based on DFPA General Design Specification, Design of Plywood - Lumber Structural Assemblies. The beams shall be fabricated according to DFPA Specification No. BB-8, Fabrication of Plywood Beams.

GLUING NOTE: The box-beam members shall be pressure glued or nail glued together with glue conforming to one of the following specifications: a) Military Specification MIL-A-46051 for room or intermediate temperature setting resin adhesive (phenol, resorcinol or melamine base). b) Military Specification MIL-A-5534A for high temperature setting resin adhesive (phenol, resorcinol or melamine base). If external pressure cannot be applied by clamps, presses or other reasonably uniform, measurable pressure, nailing should be used to provide an adequate pressure during gluing. Nails should be at least 6d and spaced not to exceed 4" along the flanges in three separate lines with the edge lines set in 3/4" from the lumber edge. It shall be the responsibility of the fabricator to produce a glue bond, which meets or exceeds the cited specifications.

Det. 408-5B Plywood Box Beams

408-4 Nailing. Nail plates at each end and intermediate posts with one 40d *(60d-poles)* per 2" of beam depth. *(5 nails on a 2 × 10, etc.)* Nail double plates to each other or through blocking with the same number of nails.

408-5 Headers. Where opening between posts or poles exceeds that allowable in the plate tables in Appendix "A," use specially-designed headers such as those shown in:

Det. 408-5 a.   Flitch Plate Girder
Det. 408-5 b.   Plywood Box Beams
Det. 408-5 c.   Truss Girder

These may be adapted to other spans or loading situations as described on the drawings. For other situations, obtain special designs.

408-5.1 Support headers in direct bearing on a post or pole. Where two or more required posts or poles are omitted in an opening, double or increase the size of post or pole next to opening. Securely fasten to each other, with bolts or spikes. Det. 408-5.1.

409 End Wall Construction. Construct non-load bearing end walls the same as load bearing side walls except as follows.

409-1 Footings may be reduced in size or eliminated, see Table, Appendix A. Anchorage required.

409-2 Extend posts or poles to the roof line, or to truss lower chords.

409-3 Headers over doors in end walls may be as follows:

OPENING SIZE	HEADER SIZE
8'	1—2 × 6
12'	2—2 × 6
16'	2—2 × 8
20'	2—2 × 10
24'	2—2 × 12

411 Doors

411-1 Construct sliding doors as in 520-2.

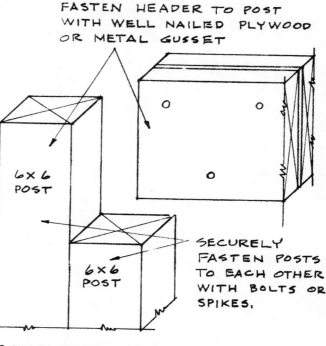

FASTEN HEADER TO POST WITH WELL NAILED PLYWOOD OR METAL GUSSET

6×6 POST

6×6 POST

SECURELY FASTEN POSTS TO EACH OTHER WITH BOLTS OR SPIKES.

DOUBLE POST

Det. 408-5.1   Header Framing

412 Service Doors See Par. 520-1
See Det. 412 for construction in post and pole walls.

413 Windows—See Det. 412

414 Bracing

414-1 Knee Braces See Det. 414.
Install not more than 16' o.c. Minimum length 6'-0"; minimum size 2 × 6. Brace to run from post or pole, across bottom chord of truss, to top chord of truss.

414-1.1 Knee braces in pole buildings may be omitted if:
a. Eave height of buildings is less than 10' or:
b. Exterior knee braces are installed not less than 8' o.c. See Det. 414.

414-2 Plate Braces. See Detail 414.

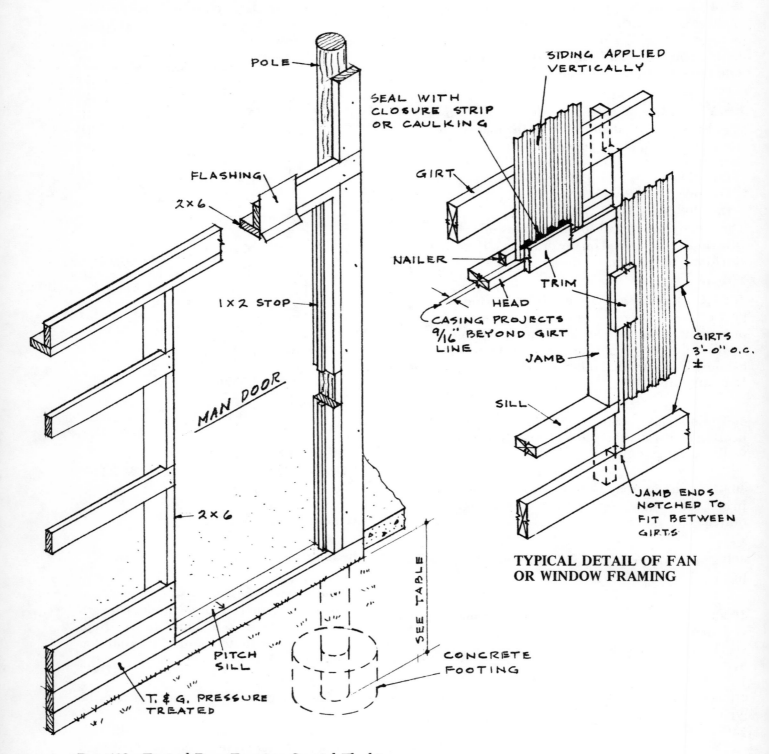

POLE

SEAL WITH
CLOSURE STRIP
OR CAULKING

FLASHING

2×6

1×2 STOP

MAN DOOR

2×6

PITCH
SILL

T. & G. PRESSURE
TREATED

SEE TABLE

CONCRETE
FOOTING

SIDING APPLIED
VERTICALLY

GIRT

NAILER

HEAD

CASING PROJECTS
9/16" BEYOND GIRT
LINE

TRIM

JAMB

SILL

GIRTS
3'-0" O.C.
±

JAMB ENDS
NOTCHED TO
FIT BETWEEN
GIRTS

**TYPICAL DETAIL OF FAN
OR WINDOW FRAMING**

*Det. 412   Typical Door Framing, Special Flashing
and Trim Accessories Match Some Siding Materials,
and Are Recommended to Avoid Caulking and Fit-
ting Problems.*

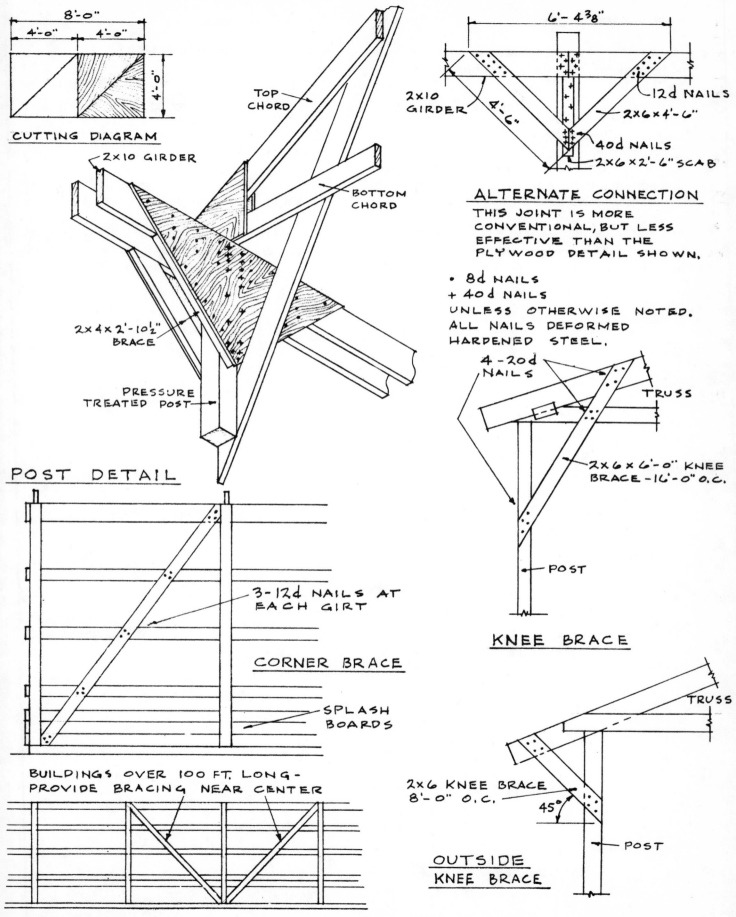

CUTTING DIAGRAM

8'-0"
4'-0" 4'-0"
4'-0"

2x10 GIRDER

TOP CHORD

BOTTOM CHORD

2x4x2'-10½" BRACE

PRESSURE TREATED POST

POST DETAIL

3-12d NAILS AT EACH GIRT

CORNER BRACE

SPLASH BOARDS

BUILDINGS OVER 100 FT. LONG - PROVIDE BRACING NEAR CENTER

6'-4⅜"

2x10 GIRDER

4'-6"

12d NAILS

2x6x4'-6"

40d NAILS

2x6x2'-6" SCAB

ALTERNATE CONNECTION

THIS JOINT IS MORE CONVENTIONAL, BUT LESS EFFECTIVE THAN THE PLYWOOD DETAIL SHOWN.

• 8d NAILS
+ 40d NAILS
UNLESS OTHERWISE NOTED. ALL NAILS DEFORMED HARDENED STEEL.

4-20d NAILS

TRUSS

2x6x6'-0" KNEE BRACE-16'-0" O.C.

POST

KNEE BRACE

TRUSS

2x6 KNEE BRACE 8'-0" O.C.

45°

POST

OUTSIDE KNEE BRACE

Det. 414   Bracing

414-2.1 Plate braces extend the maximum supported truss given in the plate tables in Appendix "A" by 10%.

414-2.2 Install plate braces:
a. On rows of P-2 poles (Fig. 407-1) not less than 16' o.c.
b. On rows of P-1 or P-3 poles where the number of openings in the wall preclude the installation of corner braces described in 414.

414-3 Corner Braces, Det. 414. Install corner braces at all corners permitted by openings, or in nearest panel. Where openings are continuous, install plate braces as in 414-2.2 b.

414-3.1 In buildings over 100' long install opposed braces as in Detail 414 near the center of every 100' of building length.

416 Girts, Pole Walls

416-1 Spacing shall not exceed that recommended by the siding manufacturer.

416-2 Maximum girt span for various spacings, sizes and grades for all areas is given in Appendix A.

Chapter 5

FRAME WALL AND MISCELLANEOUS CONSTRUCTION

500   Frame Wall and Miscellaneous Construction

500-1 Objective: To provide wall and other construction which will assure safe support of design loads.

501   Stud Walls—Size and spacing of studs—Bearing Walls, single story buildings.

2 × 3 Studs: Not over 7' high; max 24" o.c.

2 × 4 Studs: Not over 10' high; max 32" o.c. trusses or rafters over studs. Max 48" o.c. (Double Studs) for 4' or 8' o.c. truss spacing.

2 × 6 Studs: Not over 20" high; max 24" o.c.

501-1 Species and Grades—Group F or better. Appendix A-14.

501-2 Plates

a.   Use sole and top plates the same size as studs.

b.   Single top plate is acceptable where trusses or rafters are spaced same as studs and placed directly over studs.

c.   Double top plate where truss spacing exceeds 24" o.c.

d.   Where trusses are spaced 48" o.c. or more, they shall be placed directly over a stud.

e.   Where trusses are spaced 7'-6" or more, double studs under trusses unless engineering design assures adequate plate stiffness.

f.   Splice single top plate and lower member of double plate over studs.

g.   A single sole plate (sill) is usually adequate; preservative-treated lumber is recommended.

501-3 Nailing

a.   End nail single top plate or lower member of double top plate to studs with two 16d common nails.

b.   Nail studs to sole plate with three 10d or four 8d common toenails, or two 16d end nails.

c.   Nail upper member of top plate with 16d common nails staggered 24" o.c. Splice not less than 24" from splice in lower plate member.

d.   Lap plate members at corners and intersecting partitions, and nail together with two 16d common nails or with 18 gauge galvanized steel ties or clips. If plate members are not lapped, support each double plate with at least 1 stud. See Detail 501-3d.

501-4 Anchorage. Where plywood or board sheathing does not tie sole plate and upper member of top plate to studs, provide additional anchorage as follows:

a.   Where trusses are less than 48" o.c., tie every other stud to sole plate, and upper member of top plate with metal clip. Det. 501-4.

b.   Where trusses are 48" o.c. or more, tie stud under truss to sole plate as above. At truss spacing of 7'-6" or more use two clips on studs under trusses. Similarly tie upper member of top plate to stud.

c.   Where trusses are tied directly to studs as shown in Detail 501-4, clips on top plate may be omitted.

501-5 Wall Bracing shall be accomplished by one of the following:

a.   1 × 4 inch or wider boards nailed to either inner or outer face of studs, sole plate and top

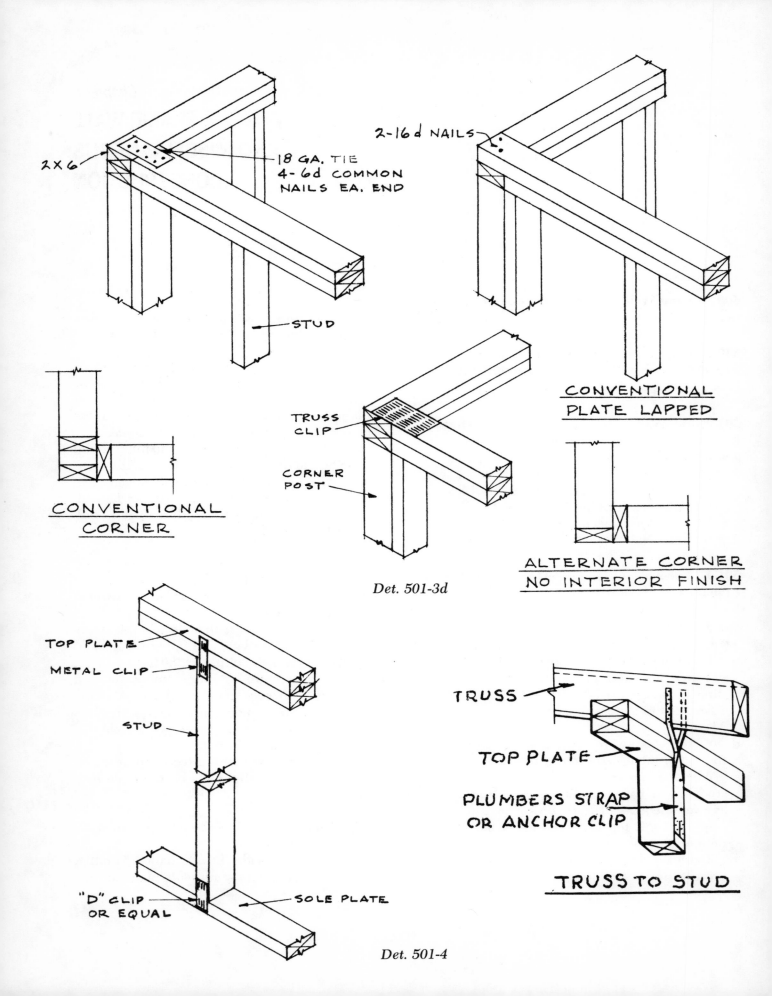

2×6

18 GA. TIE
4- 6d COMMON
NAILS EA. END

STUD

2-16d NAILS

CONVENTIONAL
PLATE LAPPED

CONVENTIONAL
CORNER

TRUSS
CLIP

CORNER
POST

Det. 501-3d

ALTERNATE CORNER
NO INTERIOR FINISH

TOP PLATE

METAL CLIP

STUD

"D" CLIP
OR EQUAL

SOLE PLATE

TRUSS

TOP PLATE

PLUMBERS STRAP
OR ANCHOR CLIP

TRUSS TO STUD

Det. 501-4

plate located near each corner. Set at approximately 45 degree angle. Nail brace to studs and plates with two 8d common nails at each point. When opening is at or near corner install full length brace as close as possible to corner. In walls over 100′ long, brace per 414-3.1. Braces may be let into the face of studs unless they support trusses 4′ or more o.c.

b. Wall is considered braced, if sided, sheathed, or lined with one of the following materials, provided 50% of the 4 × 8 sheets are not cut for openings.

1) Plywood siding or sheathing installed in 4 × 8 sheets.

2) 25/32″ fibreboard in 4 × 8 sheets, installed vertically.

3) 1″ sheathing boards applied diagonally.

4) Other materials where the manufacturer certifies that corner braces may be omitted.

501-6 Framing Openings, Bearing Walls.

501-6.1 Use double studs at all openings exceeding stud spacing in width.

501-6.2 For nailing and framing details see detail 501-6.2.

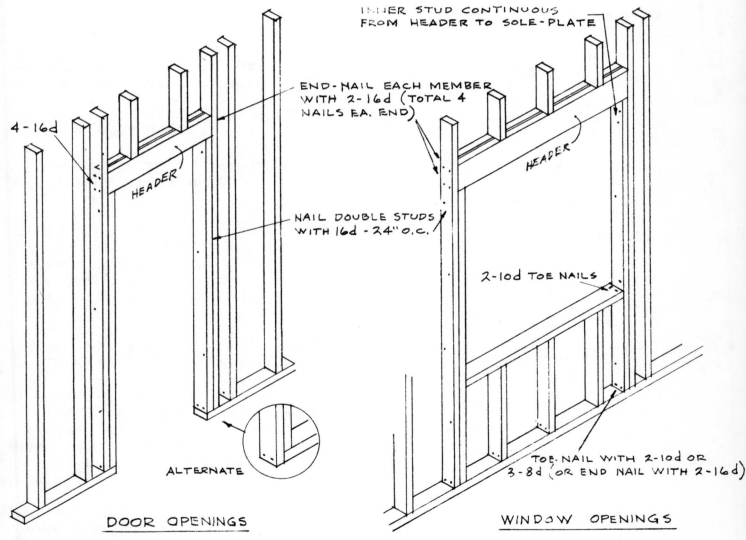

Det. 501-6.2 *Framing Openings in Exterior Walls*

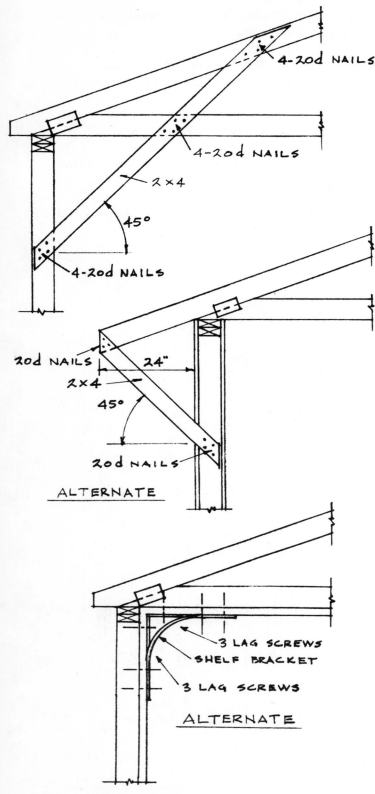

4-20d NAILS

4-20d NAILS

2×4

45°

4-20d NAILS

20d NAILS   24"

2×4

45°

20d NAILS

ALTERNATE

3 LAG SCREWS

SHELF BRACKET

3 LAG SCREWS

ALTERNATE

Det. 506-2   Knee Braces

501-6.3 Header Sizes. "C" Group Lumber (*Appendix* "A").

a. 2–2 × 4's—If no truss occurs over the opening—up to 8'

b. Truss or rafter over opening unless otherwise specified by an engineer:
  2–2 × 6's—3'-6"
  2–2 × 8's—4'-6"
  2–2 × 10's—5'-6"*
  2–2 × 12's—7'0"*
  Triple jamb studs
  ((Note: 2–2 × 12 header often cheaper than smaller header + stub 2 × 4's. Det 501-6.2))

c. Consider full-high doors and windows to avoid header framing.

506 Knee Braces

506-1 Install knee braces in exterior walls without intersecting partitions or other integral bracing.

a. Without solid roof sheathing, where the unbraced wall exceeds 25' in length, install knee braces 8' o.c.

b. With solid roof sheathing, where the unbraced wall exceeds 40' in length, install knee braces 16' o.c.

506-2 Install knee braces as in Detail 506-2; minimum size 2 × 4. Extend interior knee braces from at least 24" below the top plate on the stud at an angle of 45 degrees; nail to both top and bottom chord of truss with four 20d nails at each point.

506-2.1 Where interior knee braces will interfere with building use, the alternate methods in Detail 506-2 may be used.

a. Steel Bracket. Use 12" heavy duty steel shelf bracket or bracket designed for the purpose, lag screwed to the wall stud and truss 48" o.c. Use screws which will penetrate stud and truss at least 2 inches. Do not use over soft wall and ceiling materials like plastic, foam or fibreboard.

b. Exterior knee braces as in Detail 506-2 spaced not more than 8' o.c., provided wall does not exceed 12' high.

508 Wall Sheathing

508-1 Install wall sheathing when exterior finish material requires solid backing or intermediate nailing, or when required for wall bracing. Power driven staples may be used in lieu of nails in accordance with manufacturer's recommendation. See 501-5 for wall bracing.

508-2 Wood Board Sheathing

508-2.1 Minimum thickness, 3/4"; maximum width, 12".

508-2.2 Maximum stud spacing 24" o.c. Wall bracing required unless boards are installed diagonally.

508-2.3 If boards are applied diagonally, extend at approximate 45 degree angle in opposite directions from each corner.

508-2.4 Use T & G, shiplap, or square edge boards with ends cut parallel to and over center of studs with not more than two adjacent boards breaking joints on same stud except at openings and ends. End matched T & G boards may break joints between studs provided two end joints in adjacent boards do not occur in same stud space and each board bears on at least two studs.

508-2.5 Nail sheathing to studs at each bearing with 8d common or 7d threaded nails. Provide two nails in 4, 6 and 8 inch boards and three nails in 10 and 12 inch boards.

508-2.6 Spaced sheathing may be used for shingle type exterior finish materials not requiring solid backing: minimum width, 3"; space sheathing for shingle exposure.

508-3 Plywood Sheathing

508-3.1 Material shall be exterior type.

508-3.2 Minimum thickness = 3/8 inch. Maximum stud spacing 48 inches o.c.

508-3.3 Nail sheathing to studs with 6d common or box nails spaced 6 inches o.c. along all edges and 12 inches o.c. along intermediate members.

508-4 Fibreboard Sheathing

508-4.1 Use material in general construction use; minimum thickness 1/2", maximum stud spacing 24" o.c.

508-4.2 Nail sheathing to studs at each bearing with 1-3/4 inch roofing nails for 25/32 inch and 1-1/2 inch for 1/2 inch thick sheathing as follows:
a. Wall bracing installed: 4 inches o.c. at vertical edges and 8 inches o.c. at intermediate supports.
b. Wall bracing omitted (*Manufacturer's recommendation*) Nail 3 inches o.c. at all edges and 6 inches o.c. at intermediate supports.

509 Sheathing Paper

509-1 Objective: To provide moisture protection for sheathing material and to resist moisture and wind infiltration when sheathing is not used.

509-2 Material: 15# or 30# asphalt saturated felt or other generally acceptable material. Do not use materials which will act as a vapor barrier if wall is insulated and/or enclosed on the inside.

509-3 Application. Apply shingle fashion to sheathing or to stud frame with not less than 4 inch laps.

511 Flashing and Closure Strips.

511-1 Provide metal flashing or asphalt, rubber or plastic closure strips to all critical joints in exterior wall construction. Omit closure strips in walls clad in and out with metal.

511-2 In areas not subject to wind-driven rain, head flashing may be omitted when vertical height between top of opening and bottom of eave is one fourth the eave projection or less.

511-3 See Details 511-3 for flashing of rolling door tracks.
Unless closure strips are used with the rail, corrugations may be cut or crushed when lags

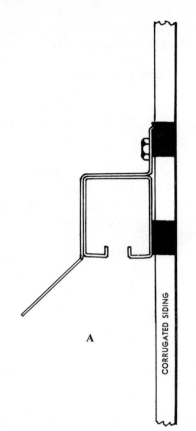

A

CORRUGATED SIDING

Two closure strips must be used, as in A, when mounting trolley rail to corrugated metal-clad building. Cement the closure strips to the rail before mounting.

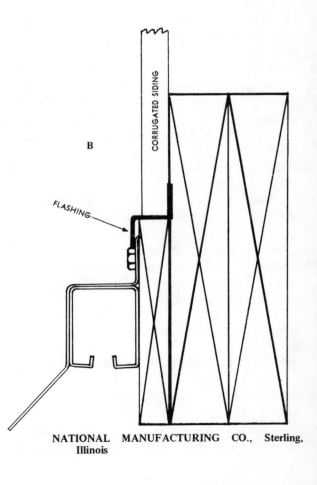

B

CORRUGATED SIDING

FLASHING

B shows rail mounted on 3/4″ board. "Z" flashing is needed under the metal siding and over the mounting board to prevent water from getting behind the board and causing rotting and deterioration.

NATIONAL MANUFACTURING CO., Sterling, Illinois

Det. 511-3

or bolts are tightened. Closure strips also prevent rain or melting snow from running down corrugation valleys behind the rail, and down the inside of door.

513   Wood Floor Framing

513-1   Objective: To provide floor construction assuring safe and adequate support of all design loads.

513-2   Design wood floor framing, including joists, columns, girders and trimmers to support all design loads. See Appendix A for design loads and lumber working stresses.

513-2.1   See Appendix A floor joist tables.
Caution: the floor joist tables in Appendix "A" are for loads not exceeding 50 lbs/sq ft, live and dead, (No ceiling). Agricultural, warehouse, and storage loadings may often exceed 100 lbs/sq ft. These loads should be computed, and floor and supporting construction designed accordingly.

513-2.2   Locate splices only over bearing points.

513-3.2   Support wood columns on concrete or solid masonry base resting on footing. Top of concrete base shall be at least 3 inches above concrete floor or 8 inches above dirt floor. Top of Column shall be fastened to girder. See details 513-3.2 for these methods and alternates.

513-3.3   Columns shall be continuous without splices from base to girder. Squared columns at both ends for level bearing. Unless otherwise specified by the engineer, minimum size as follows:
a.   Supporting first floor girders, 6 × 6.
b.   Supporting other beams, trimmers, etc., 4 × 4.

513-3.4   Where earthquake or uplift design is required, column shall be anchored to base.

513-4   Wood Girders and Beams

513-4.1   Joints of wood girder members shall be made over column supports unless construction follows an engineered plan.

513-4.2   Provide 1/2 inch airspace at ends and sides of wood girders framing into concrete or masonry unless treated wood is used. Untreated wood shims are not acceptable under ends of girders.

513-4.3   Nail built-up wood girders of three or more members from both sides:
a.   Two 20d nails at ends of piece and each splice; and
b.   Two rows of 20d nails in between splices at top and bottom of girder 32 inches o.c. Stagger nails.

513-4.4   For maximum spans of wood girders see table 513-4.4.
Note: Use only with floor loads in Appendix A.

513-5   Sill Construction: Minimum thickness 2″; minimum width as required for full end bearing of studs and not less than 1-1/2″ bearing for ends of joists.

513-5.1   Set sill true and level and provide full bearing on foundation. Set sill in full bed of Portland Cement mortar when necessary to obtain full bearing. Preservative-treated lumber is recommended.

513-5.2   For anchorage of sill see 216-1. For Termite protection, see 232.

514-6   Wood Floor Joists. Span of joists for live loads up to 50 lbs/sq ft are in span table, Appendix A. Design individually for higher loadings. Span of joists is clear distance between supports.

514-6.1   Details 514-6.1 a and b show details of wood joist framing and fastening.

514-7   Bridging. Maximum spacing, 10 feet.

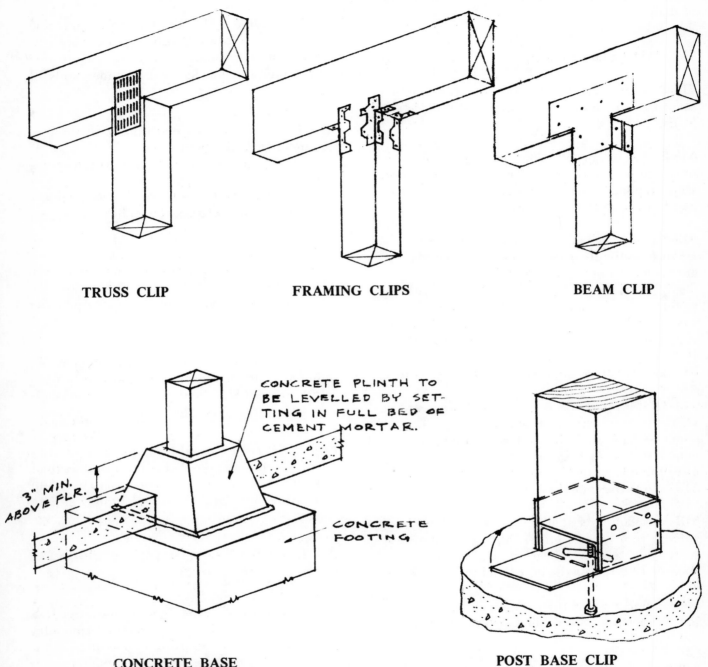

TRUSS CLIP

FRAMING CLIPS

BEAM CLIP

CONCRETE PLINTH TO
BE LEVELLED BY SET-
TING IN FULL BED OF
CEMENT MORTAR.

3" MIN.
ABOVE FLR.

CONCRETE
FOOTING

CONCRETE BASE

POST BASE CLIP

Det. 513-3.2

Table 513-4.4   Maximum Girder Spans

Width of structure	Girder size (solid or built-up)	Supporting Bearing partition		Supporting Non-bearing partition	Intermediate girders (other than main girder)
		1 story	1-1/2 or 2 story		
Up to 26 feet wide	4 × 6	—	—	5'6"	7'6"
	4 × 8	—	—	7'6"	9'6"
	6 × 8	7'0"	6'0"	9'0"	12'0"
	6 × 10	9'0"	7'6"	11'6"	—
	6 × 12	10'6"	9'0"	12'0"	—
26 feet to 32 feet	4 × 6	—	—	—	6'6"
	4 × 8	—	—	7'0"	8'6"
	6 × 8	6'6"	5'6"	8'6"	10'6"
	6 × 10	8'0"	7'0"	10'6"	13'6"
	6 × 12	10'0"	8'0"	11'6"	—

Note: The above spans are based upon "C" Group Lumber. These allowable stresses are average values taking into consideration up-grading for doubling of members in built-up beams. Where conditions vary from these assumptions, design girders in accordance with standard engineering practice.

514-7.1   Bridging may be:
a.   Cross bridging, using 1 × 3 inch boards double nailed with two 6d common nails on each end.
b.   Solid bridging, using member same size as joist, installed in offset fashion to permit toe nailing or end nailing. Solid bridging shall be tightly fitted between joists.
c.   Compression type metal bridging. Install in accordance with manufacturer's instructions.

514-7.2   Bridging may be omitted for clear spans of 15 feet or less when a double floor or plank floor is used and with floor systems with 4' joist spacing.

516   Ceilings
Provide insulation and vapor barriers.

516-1   Where ceiling construction is to carry suspended loads such as cages, feeders, etc. or space above ceiling is to be used for storage, specially designed construction is required.

516-2   Plywood Ceilings

516-2.1   Use exterior grade plywood. An overlaid plywood may be desirable for ease of cleaning.

516-2.2   See Detail 516-2.2 for suggested installations.

516-3   Metal Ceilings: Aluminum or steel roofing may be used for ceilings under trusses 48" o.c.; install to manufacturer's recommendations.

516-4   Other ceiling materials: Fibreboard, plastic faced fibreboard, plastic foam boards and other materials may be used on ceilings at maximum spans and with installation procedures approved by the manufacturer.

517   Stairways

517-1   Headroom. Continuous clear headroom measured vertically from front edge nosing to a

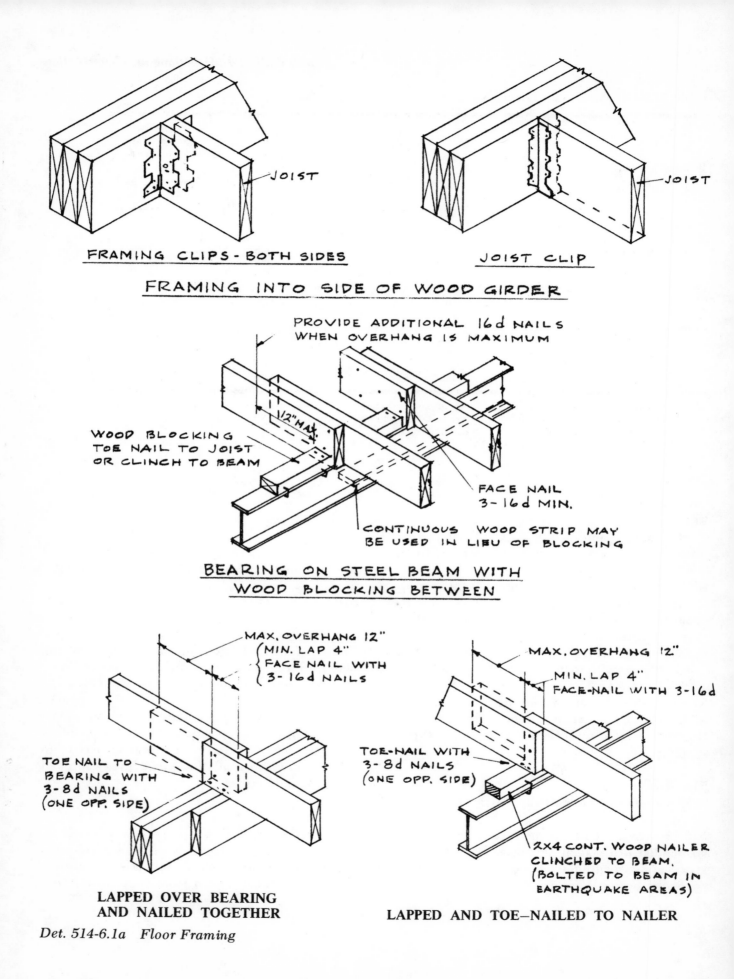

FRAMING CLIPS - BOTH SIDES

JOIST CLIP

JOIST

JOIST

FRAMING INTO SIDE OF WOOD GIRDER

PROVIDE ADDITIONAL 16d NAILS
WHEN OVERHANG IS MAXIMUM

1/2" MAX.

WOOD BLOCKING
TOE NAIL TO JOIST
OR CLINCH TO BEAM

FACE NAIL
3-16d MIN.

CONTINUOUS WOOD STRIP MAY
BE USED IN LIEU OF BLOCKING

BEARING ON STEEL BEAM WITH
WOOD BLOCKING BETWEEN

MAX. OVERHANG 12"
(MIN. LAP 4"
FACE NAIL WITH
3-16d NAILS

TOE NAIL TO
BEARING WITH
3-8d NAILS
(ONE OPP. SIDE)

**LAPPED OVER BEARING
AND NAILED TOGETHER**

MAX. OVERHANG 12"
MIN. LAP 4"
FACE-NAIL WITH 3-16d

TOE-NAIL WITH
3-8d NAILS
(ONE OPP. SIDE)

2X4 CONT. WOOD NAILER
CLINCHED TO BEAM.
(BOLTED TO BEAM IN
EARTHQUAKE AREAS)

LAPPED AND TOE—NAILED TO NAILER

Det. 514-6.1a   Floor Framing

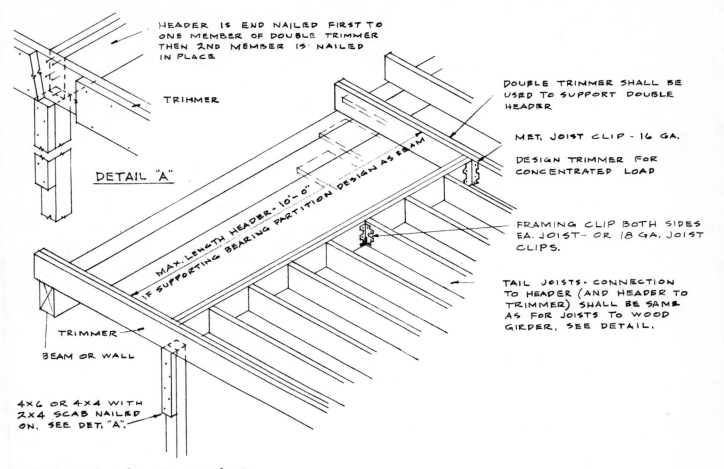

HEADER IS END NAILED FIRST TO
ONE MEMBER OF DOUBLE TRIMMER
THEN 2ND MEMBER IS NAILED
IN PLACE

TRIMMER

DETAIL "A"

MAX. LENGTH HEADER - 10'-0"
IF SUPPORTING BEARING PARTITION DESIGN AS BEAM

TRIMMER

BEAM OR WALL

4X6 OR 4X4 WITH
2X4 SCAB NAILED
ON. SEE DET. "A".

DOUBLE TRIMMER SHALL BE
USED TO SUPPORT DOUBLE
HEADER

MET. JOIST CLIP - 16 GA.

DESIGN TRIMMER FOR
CONCENTRATED LOAD

FRAMING CLIP BOTH SIDES
EA. JOIST - OR 18 GA. JOIST
CLIPS.

TAIL JOISTS. CONNECTION
TO HEADER (AND HEADER TO
TRIMMER) SHALL BE SAME
AS FOR JOISTS TO WOOD
GIRDER, SEE DETAIL.

Det. 514-6.1b   Floor Framing for Large Openings

line parallel with stair pitch; 6', 4" minimum. See Detail 517-6.

517-2   Width, clear of handrail, minimum 2' 6".

517-3   Rise & Run: Maximum rise 8". All rises to be the same in any one flight. Minimum Run: 9" plus 1/2" nosing for open risers, 1-1/8" nosing for closed risers.

517-4   Landings
a.   Provide rectangular landings when stairs change direction.
b.   Provide a landing at the top of any stair run having a door that swings toward the stair.
c.   Minimum dimension 4'.

517-5   Handrails. Install continuous handrail on at least one side of each flight of stairs which exceed 3 risers. Install railing around open sides of all stair wells.

517-6   Where steps occur in walkways, provide at least 2 risers. Provide ramps where change in elevation is less than 10".

517-7   See Detail 517-6 for construction.

518   Ladders

518-1   If stairways are not feasible, provide permanently installed ladders when frequent access is required to locations more than 10' above floor or ground level.

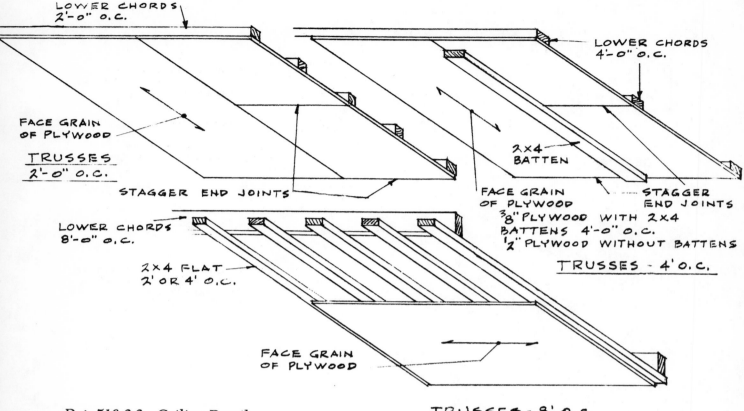

LOWER CHORDS
2'-0" O.C.

FACE GRAIN
OF PLYWOOD

TRUSSES
2'-0" O.C.

STAGGER END JOINTS

LOWER CHORDS
4'-0" O.C.

2×4
BATTEN

FACE GRAIN
OF PLYWOOD

STAGGER
END JOINTS

3/8" PLYWOOD WITH 2×4
BATTENS 4'-0" O.C.
1/2" PLYWOOD WITHOUT BATTENS

TRUSSES - 4' O.C.

LOWER CHORDS
8'-0" O.C.

2×4 FLAT
2' OR 4' O.C.

FACE GRAIN
OF PLYWOOD

TRUSSES - 8' O.C.

Det. 516-2.2   Ceiling Details

518-2   Terminate permanent ladders 5′ above the ground for child safety.

518-3   Extend ladders 3′ above the upper landing, or provide other handholds.

518-4   Provide a clear toe space not less than 5-1/2″ behind all rungs, steps or cleats.

518-5   Space all rungs, steps or cleats of any ladder uniformly and not over 12″.

518-6   The distance between side rails should be not less than 10″.

520   Doors

520-1.1   Service doors (Man). Provide at least one service door to all habitable enclosed areas. Minimum size 2′-6″ by 6′-6″.

520-1.2   Minimum door thickness, 1-3/8″. (Stock Door).

520-1.3   Provide screen doors where required.

520-1.4   Provide all exterior doors opening outward with a safety door check.

520-2   Sliding Doors.

520-2.1   See Appendix B for maximum width and height of projected equipment to be using doors.

520-2.2   See Detail 520-2.2 for typical door construction. See Detail 511-3 for flashing of rolling door heads.

520-3   Hardware—All exterior hardware shall have zinc or other corrosion resistant coating.

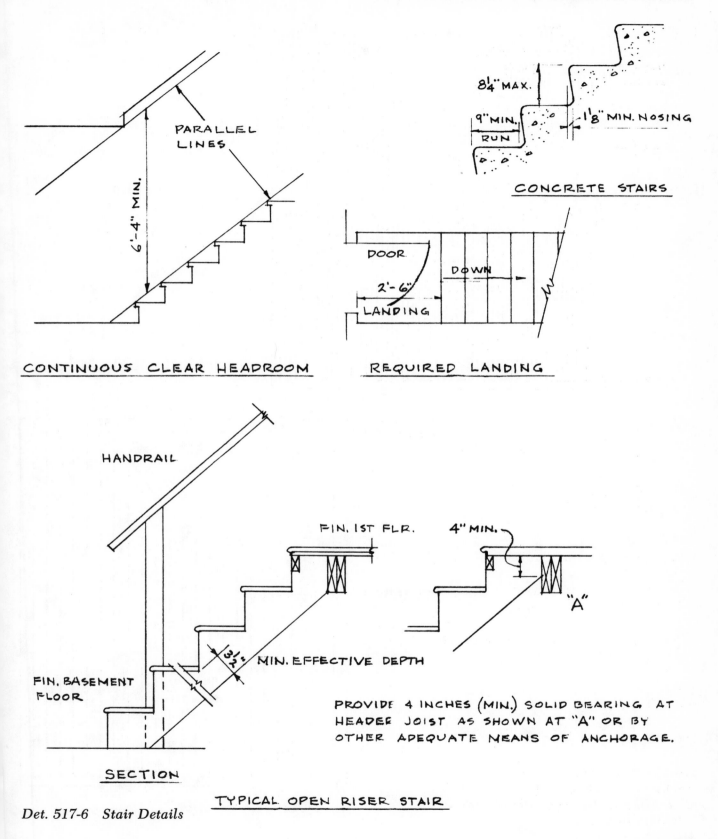

CONTINUOUS CLEAR HEADROOM

CONCRETE STAIRS

REQUIRED LANDING

SECTION

TYPICAL OPEN RISER STAIR

PROVIDE 4 INCHES (MIN.) SOLID BEARING AT HEADER JOIST AS SHOWN AT "A" OR BY OTHER ADEQUATE MEANS OF ANCHORAGE.

Det. 517-6   Stair Details

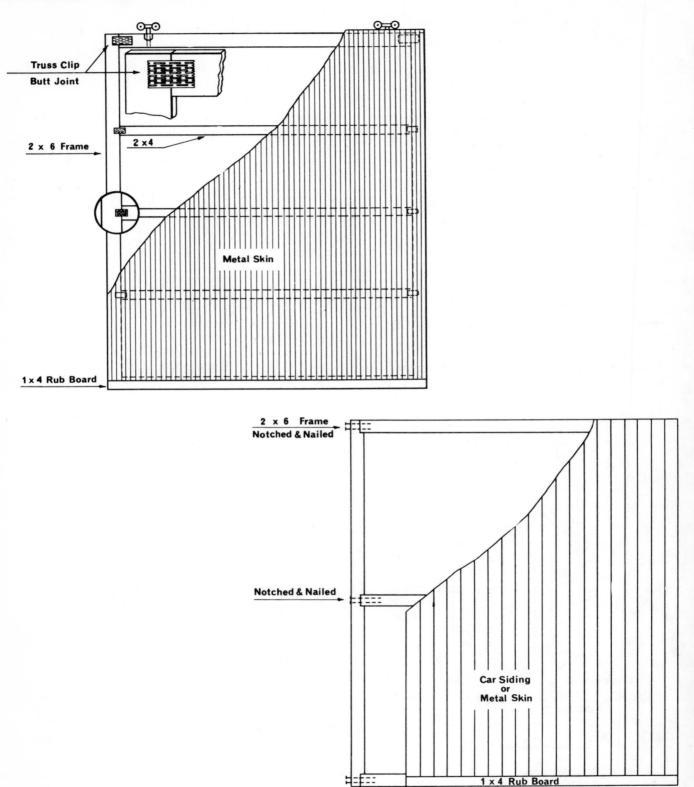

Truss Clip

Butt Joint

2 x 6 Frame

2 x 4

Metal Skin

1 x 4 Rub Board

2 x 6 Frame
Notched & Nailed

Notched & Nailed

Car Siding
or
Metal Skin

1 x 4 Rub Board

Det. 520-2.2   National Manufacturing Co.,
Sterling, Illinois

521 Painting (see "Paints and Coatings Handbook" by Banov, Structures Publishing, 1973)

521-1 Finish all exterior woodwork as follows, except edge grain redwood or red cedar may be left unfinished.

521-2.1 Apply a suitable prime coat to all surfaces to be painted, before or immediately after installation, and at coverage rate recommended by manufacturer.

521-2.2 Apply at least one finish coat at rate of 450–550 sq ft/gal.

521-3 Natural finishes. In lieu of painting, surfaces may be finished with a penetrating oil stain containing 5% pentachlorophenol.

Chapter 6

ROOF CONSTRUCTION

600 Roof Construction

600-1 Objective—To provide roof construction which will assure (a) safe and adequate support of all design loads. (b) Necessary resistance to the elements. (c) Reasonable durability and economy of maintenance, (d) an acceptable quality of workmanship.

600-2 General

600-2.1 Roof framing, including trusses, rafters, joists, purlins and headers shall be designed to support design loads. See Appendix A for design loads and working stresses of materials.

601 Roof Trusses

601-1
- Fink or "W" Trusses. The most common type.
  - King Post Truss—Economical for short spans.
  - Cantilevered Truss—Support is not at the end of the truss on one or both ends. Used to provide sheltered area outside the building. Differs from overhang.
  - Gambrel—Used like the scissors, to increase ceiling height without raising walls. Also to give traditional "barn" look.
  - Umbrella Truss—Roof construction is hung from central pole or poles. Provides sheltered storage area and permits less restricted use of mechanical equipment such as lift trucks.

- Warren Truss—(*Sometimes called a* "double W") used on long spans.
- Howe Truss—Sometimes called a "King Post" truss.
- Single Slope Truss—Used in large buildings from main truss to wall line or use two where a center line of poles is used.
- Scissors Truss—Used to get a higher ceiling height than wall height, for storage of equipment, etc.
- Monopitch Truss—Similar applications to single slope. Also used on additions to existing buildings.
- Girder Truss—Often used in poultry operations with ceiling suspended cages.
- Cambered Fink Truss. See above.
- Rigid Frames—Combines wall and roof construction.
- Flat Top—Used for girder trusses like detail 408-2 and for flat or low slope roofing.
- Arch Frame—Trusses wall and roof construction together.
- Raised Bottom Chord—Not recommended—unsound construction. Use Scissors or Cambered Fink trusses to achieve the same purpose.

601-2 Truss Design—Use trusses designed by an engineer or architect. Sources include the manufacturer of the fastenings used; Agricultural Engineering Departments of one of the colleges providing this service or by Midwest Plan Service.

FINK

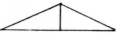

KINGPOST

UMBRELLA

WARREN

SCISSORS

MONOPITCH

RIGID FRAME

FLAT TOP

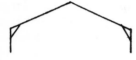

CANTILEVER

GAMBREL

HOWE

SINGLE SLOPE

GIRDER

CAMBERED FINK

ARCH FRAME

RAISED BOTTOM
CHORD

Det. 601   Truss Types

66

See Appendix A for design criteria and reference.

601-2.1 Examples of Truss Design are shown in Figures:
   601-2.1a. *(Glue Nailed Plywood)*
   601-2.1 b. *(Metal Plate)*

601-2.2 Truss Manufacture. All trusses, regardless of type or method of fastening, should be manufactured in strict compliance with designs furnished and using lumber specified in the design. Where substitutions are made in lumber or fastenings they should be approved by the design source.

602   Wind Anchorage
Rafters and trusses. Detail 602.

602-1 Fasten rafters or trusses to Posts, Poles, Tie Down Blocks or top plates at each end as follows:

Uplift Force to be Resisted, in Pounds

Rafter or Truss Spacing	Truss Span				
	24'	32'	40'	50'	60'
2'	288	384	480	600	720
4'	576	768	960	1200	1440
6'	864	1152	1440	1800	2160
8'	1152	1536	1920	2400	2880
10'	1440	1920	2400	3000	3600

Provide any number or combination of the following fastenings to resist the above uplift.

A. 20d Nails into notched pole, post or tie down block (Not Toe Nails) (Use 40d Nails into round pole, no notch),   each 226 lbs.
B. Framing clip,   each 740 lbs.
C. Plumber's strap, wrapped over top of rafter. Nail with 3-8d nails each end and to rafter.
                                        each 800 lbs.
D. 1/2" Diameter Bolt   each 800 lbs.
E. 5/8" Diameter Bolt   each 1200 lbs.
F. 3/4" Diameter Bolt   each 1725 lbs.
G. Anchor Clip   each 1600 lbs.
   Note: Above loads are for wind uplift only.

602-2   For plate to stud anchorage, see 501-4.

602-3   In coastal or other high wind area, increase anchorage proportionately. Above is figured for 85 mph wind. See Map A-8.

602-4   Increase anchorage proportionately for overhangs over 16 inches.

603   Purlins *(Roof Girts)*

603-1   Span Tables, Appendix A, give maximum purlin spans for the four groups of species in the several load zones.

603-1.1   Spacings of purlins should not exceed allowable spans for roofing or sheathing.

603-2   Purlin Fastenings—Alternate methods are shown in detail 603-2.

603-2.1   Purlins on edge: In coastal or other high wind areas and in other areas where trusses are spaced over 4 feet o.c. and purlins spaced 36 inches o.c. or more, use framing clips, plumber's strap or purlin bracket in addition to nails.

603-2.2   Where possible, stagger end joints.

604   Truss Stiffeners—See Det. 604.

604-1   Truss Stiffeners shall be used on bottom chords of all trusses. Except where ceiling is installed.

TRUSS SPAN	Number of Stiffeners
24'	1—at Midspan
30'	2—at 3rd Points
36'	2—at 3rd Points
42'	2—at 3rd Points
50'	3—at 1/4 Points
60'	3—at 1/4 Points

604-2   Minimum size—2 × 4 for 8' or less. Truss Spacing—2 × 6 over 8' spacing.
 Nail 2 × 4 with 2—20d nails and 2 × 6 with 3—20d nails at each truss.

605   Windbracing—See Det. 604.

605-1   Install windbracing on trusses spaced 4' or more o.c. Install for at least 16' each end of building. Space additional 16' braced sections about 32' apart.

605-2   Size of braces—2 × 4 up to 8' truss spacing; 2 × 6 over 8'. If stiffener does not occur at midspan of truss, install extra.

605-3   Nail with three 20d nails at each bearing and at intersection.

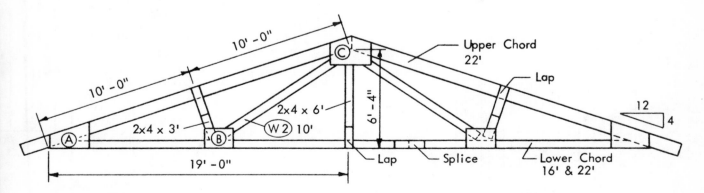

601-2.1a   Typical Glued Truss "Designs for Glued Trusses." Midwest Plan Service.

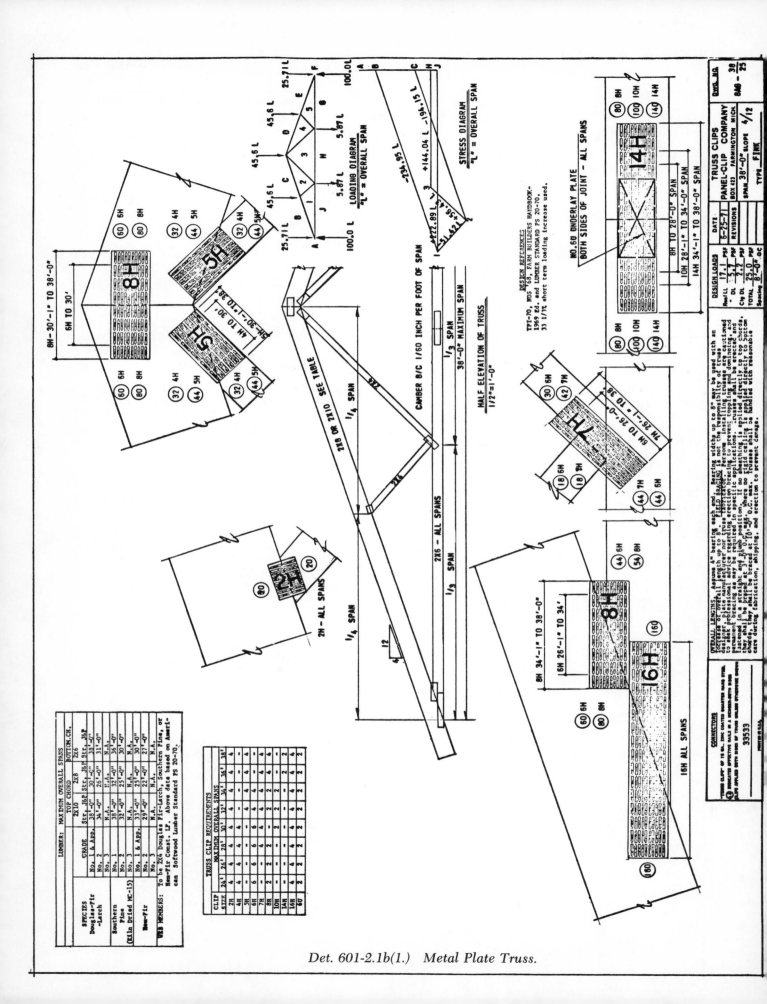

Det. 601-2.1b(1.)   Metal Plate Truss.

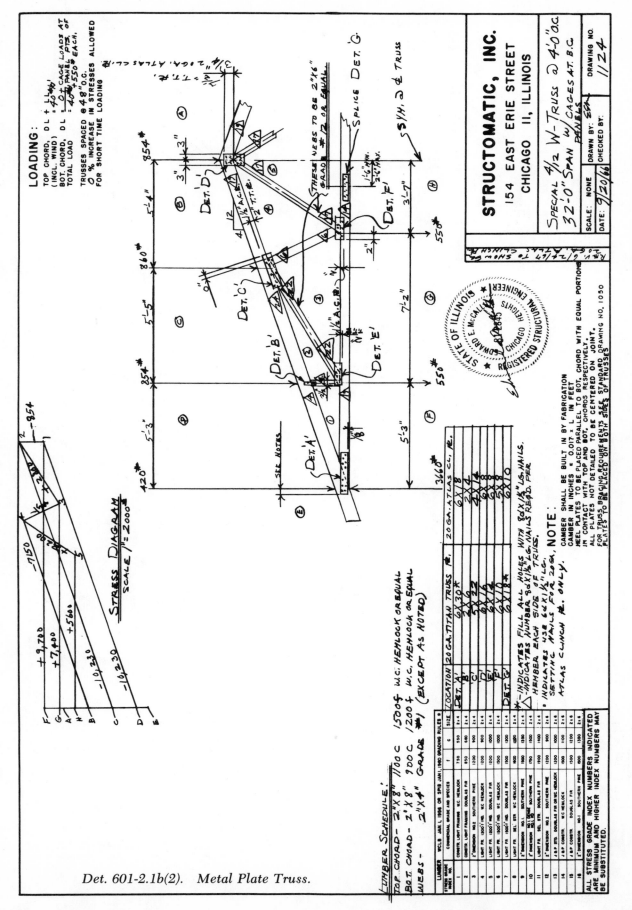

Det. 601-2.1b(2).   Metal Plate Truss.

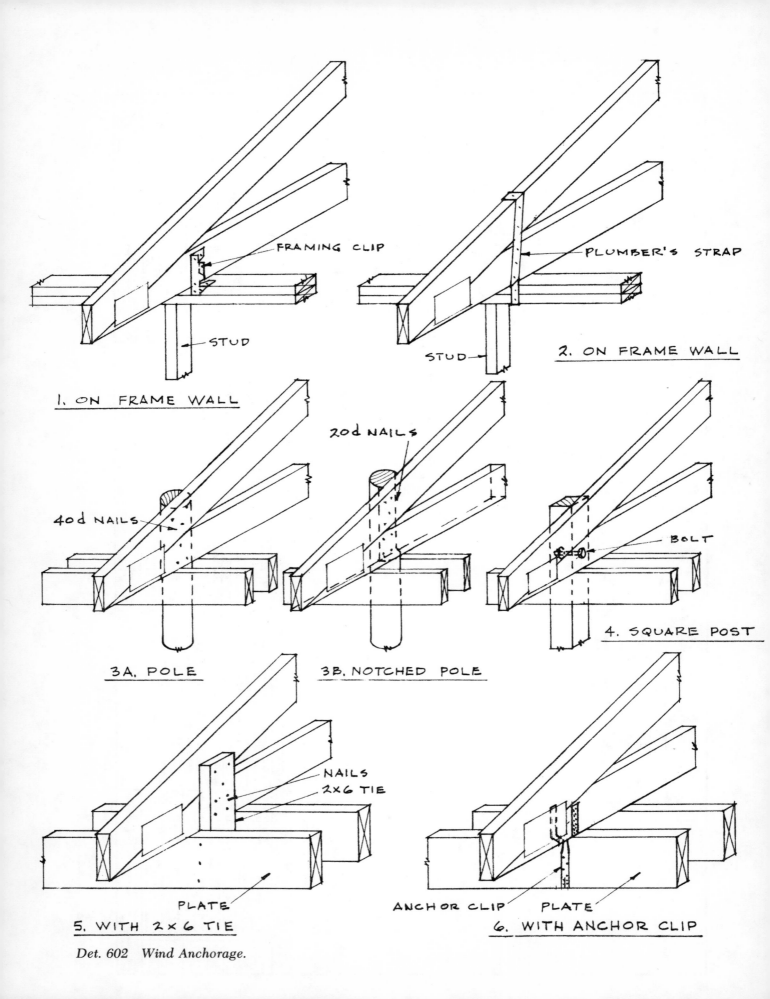

FRAMING CLIP

STUD

1. ON FRAME WALL

PLUMBER'S STRAP

STUD

2. ON FRAME WALL

20d NAILS

40d NAILS

3A. POLE

3B. NOTCHED POLE

BOLT

4. SQUARE POST

NAILS

2×6 TIE

PLATE

5. WITH 2×6 TIE

ANCHOR CLIP   PLATE

6. WITH ANCHOR CLIP

Det. 602   Wind Anchorage.

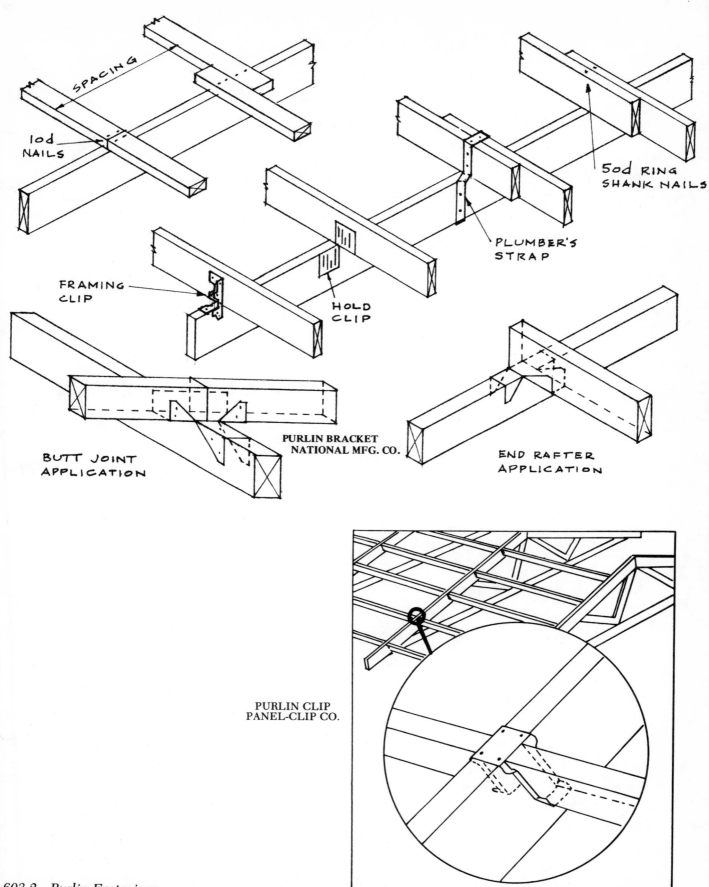

SPACING

IOd NAILS

50d RING SHANK NAILS

PLUMBER'S STRAP

FRAMING CLIP

HOLD CLIP

BUTT JOINT APPLICATION

PURLIN BRACKET NATIONAL MFG. CO.

END RAFTER APPLICATION

PURLIN CLIP PANEL-CLIP CO.

603-2   Purlin Fastenings.

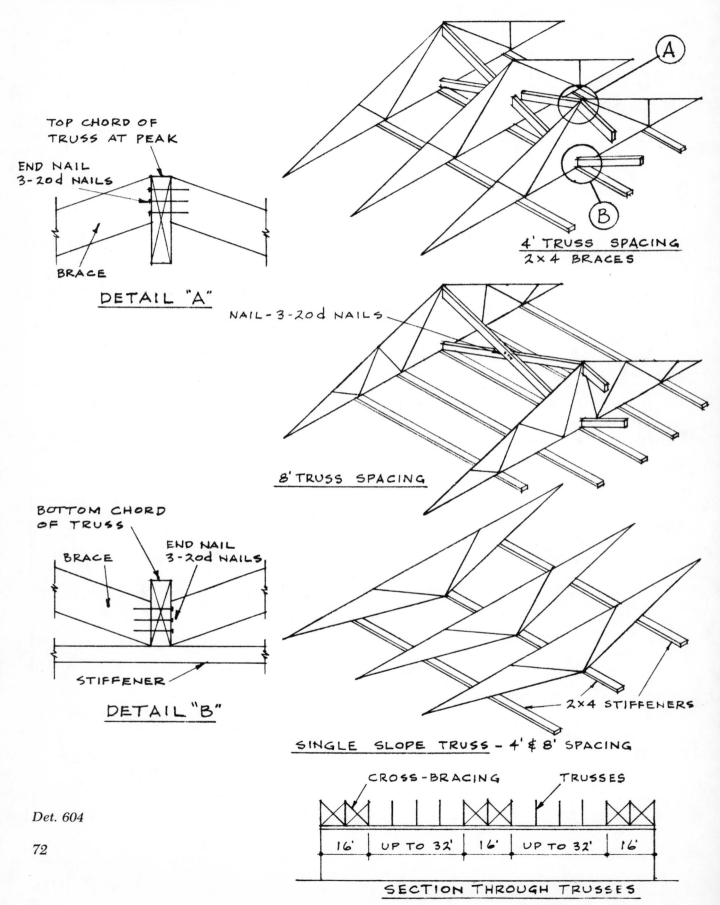

TOP CHORD OF
TRUSS AT PEAK

END NAIL
3-20d NAILS

BRACE

DETAIL "A"

A

B

4' TRUSS SPACING
2×4 BRACES

NAIL - 3-20d NAILS

8' TRUSS SPACING

BOTTOM CHORD
OF TRUSS

BRACE

END NAIL
3-20d NAILS

STIFFENER

DETAIL "B"

2×4 STIFFENERS

SINGLE SLOPE TRUSS - 4' & 8' SPACING

CROSS-BRACING   TRUSSES

16' | UP TO 32' | 16' | UP TO 32' | 16'

SECTION THROUGH TRUSSES

Det. 604

605-4 Windbracing not required on single slope trusses.

606 Rafters—Span tables are given in Appendix A. A rafter span conversion diagram is provided to convert horizontal spans to sloping spans.

606-1 Where rafters frame into a ridge line, roof thrust shall be resisted by:
a. Support ridge line by a row of posts or poles; or
b. Use ceiling joists or tie members across the building and well nailed to each rafter at the plate line and at all splices. For example: with 4/12 pitch rafters 24″ o.c. and a building width of 26′ six 20d nails are required. At 32′, 9 nails are required.
c. Rafters such as those between P-2 and P-3 poles *(Detail 407-1)* need not be tied when securely nailed to trusses or P-2 Plates.

606-2 Provide a rafter tie in the upper third of attic space by one of the following:
a. Gusset at ridge *(no ridge board)* nailed with four 8d nails in each rafter, or
b. Collar beam, 4′ o.c. Minimum size 1 × 6, nailed to rafters with four 8d nails or 2 × 4 inch nailed to each rafter with three 16d nails, or
c. 18 gauge metal strap nailed to every other rafter with four 8d nails in each rafter.

606-3 Anchor rafters against wind as in Table 602-2.

607 Rigid Frames—This type of construction must be carefully designed for span, load and spacing. Design sources include:
a. American Plywood Association
b. University of Illinois
    College of Agriculture
    Circular 812
c. Your truss fastening manufacturer.

607-1 Anchorage; Rigid Frames must be well anchored. See par. 218-3.

607-2 Bracing. Unless solid sheathing is used, rigid frames should be well braced on both the wall sections and the roof sections.

608 Cantilevers—See Detail 607. Consider additional load transmitted to plates, poles and footings.

609 Overhangs—See Detail 607. Consider additional load transferred to plates, poles and footing. See Allowable Overhangs, Appendix A for applicable load zones.

610 Roof Sheathing

610-1 Use solid roof sheathing where required by the type of roofing material.

610-2 Maximum Rafter or Purlin Spacing for Roof Sheathing.

Material Plywood‡	Nails†	Load Zone			
		20	25	30	50
5/16″	6d	24″°	24″°	24″°	16″°
3/8″	6d	32″°	32″°	24″°	24″°
1/2″	6d	48″°	32″°	32″°	32″°
5/8″	8d	48″°	48″°	48″°	42″°
3/4″	8d	48″°	48″°	48″°	48″°
1″ Boards	8d	32″	32″	24″	24″

‡Based on coastal fir, larch or yellow pine plywood.
°Block all edges or use metal plywood clips. Use one clip in spaces 24 inches and under, two on wider spaces.
†Nails for plywood may be common or box nails 6 inches along edges and 12 inches on intermediate members.

610-3 Board sheathing shall be at least 3/4″ actual thickness and not over 12″ wide. Nail 8″ boards with two nails and 10″ or 12″ boards with 3 nails at each support.

610-4 Lay board sheathing close but not driven tight, to permit expansion.

610-5 Plywood in 610-2 is exterior Douglas Fir, Western Larch, Southern Pine and Group 1 of Western Soft woods. For Groups 2 and 3 of Western Soft woods, increase thickness 1/8″ for comparable spacings.

610-6 Install plywood with outer plies at right angles to supports and stagger end joints.

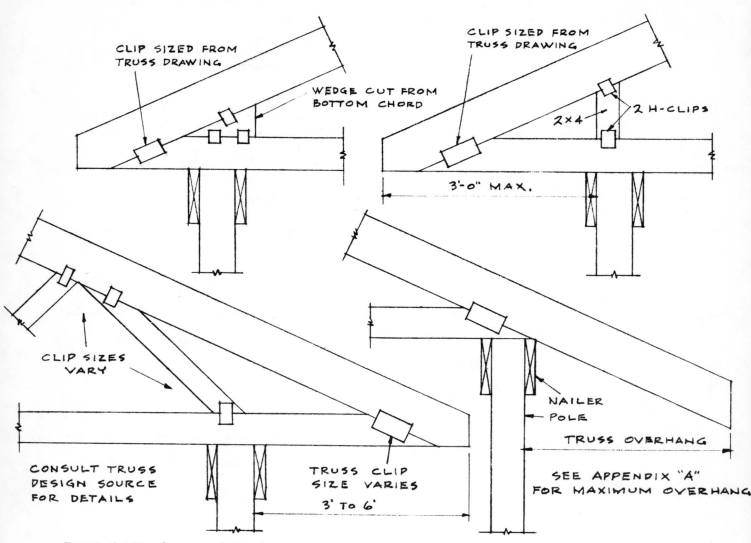

Det. 607 Cantilevers and Overhangs

611   Roofing

611-1   Objective: To provide a roof covering which will prevent entrance of moisture, reflect heat, and which will provide reasonable durability and economy of maintenance.

611-2   Metal Roofings

611-2.1   Roof slope. Follow manufacturer's recommendation for minimum.

611-2.2   Install all sidelaps away from prevailing winds and per manufacturer's recommendations; fasten sheets at each purlin.

611-2.3   Install endlaps per manufacturer's recommendations, but at least 6″ and supported by a purlin.

611-2.5   Allow 2″ to 3″ of overhang at the eaves unless gutters are provided.

611-2.6   Use flashing and closure strips as recommended by manufacturer at ridge, gable roof intersections, etc. See Detail 608-2.7.

74

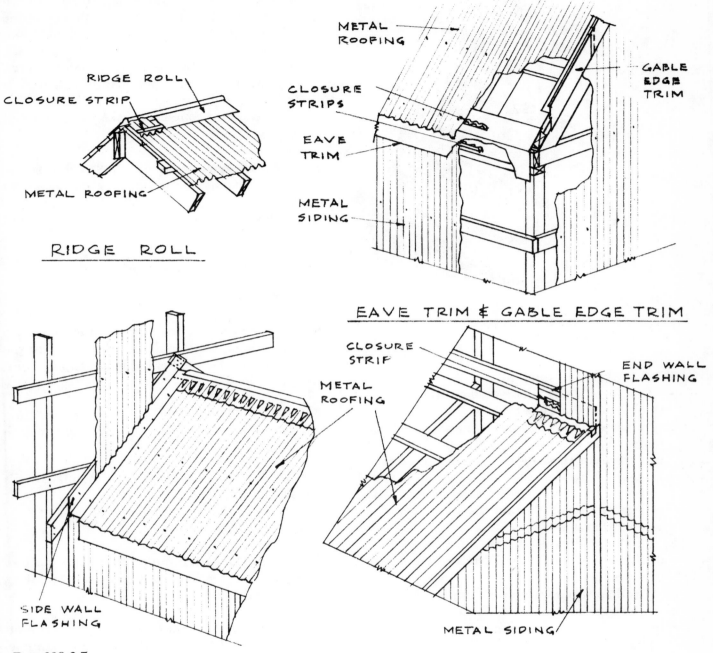

RIDGE ROLL

CLOSURE STRIP

RIDGE ROLL

METAL ROOFING

METAL ROOFING

CLOSURE STRIPS

EAVE TRIM

METAL SIDING

GABLE EDGE TRIM

EAVE TRIM & GABLE EDGE TRIM

SIDE WALL FLASHING

CLOSURE STRIP

METAL ROOFING

END WALL FLASHING

METAL SIDING

Det. 608-2.7

611-2.7 Aluminum Roofing. Use nails or screws with washers as recommended by manufacturer. Copper or bare steel accessories should not be used with aluminum or where water could drip from them onto the aluminum unless painted with asphalt paint at point of contact.

611-2.8 Galvanized Steel Roofing. Use nails or screws with washers as recommended by the manufacturer.

611-3 Asphalt Roofing

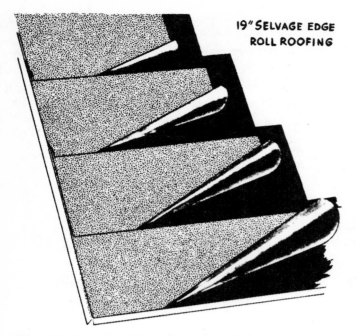

19" SELVAGE EDGE ROLL ROOFING

Det. 611-3.2   Double Coverage Roll Roofing

611-3.1   Asphalt Shingles
a.   Use a starting course providing double thickness at the eave.
b.   In heated buildings where the outside design temperature *(see map 801-2.2)* is 0° F. or colder, provide eave flashing to prevent formation of ice dams. This flashing may be a double application of underlay at eaves extending to a line at least 24 inches inside the interior surface of the exterior wall.
c.   Coverage. Provide at least a double thickness of shingles at all points. Disregard cutouts not in excess of 3/4".
d.   Headlap square tab strip shingles at least 2".
e.   Minimum roof slope 4/12 except that slope may be 3/12 with cemented shingle tabs on square tab shingles.
f.   Use an underlay of 15 or 30 lb. asphalt saturated felt on roofs under 7/12 slope. Headlap—2". Endlap—6".
g.   Spot cement tabs of square tab shingles except in areas with wind velocity under 70 mph; map Appendix A.
h.   Nailing
　　1.   Use corrosion resistant roofing nails, 11 or 12 gauge, with deformed, barbed or threaded shanks, with heads not less than 3/8" in diameter, and long enough to penetrate the sheathing or at least 1" into wood plank decks.
　　2.   Use the number, spacing and pattern of nails recommended by the roofing manufacturer. Use at least 4 nails per strip of square butt or hexagonal shingles.
i.   Extend starter course and rake shingles about 1/2" over the edge.

611-3.2   Selvage edge roofing (19 inch) may be used on roofs having a slope of not less than 1/12.
a.   Follow manufacturer's application directions. See Detail 611-3.2.

611-4   Asbestos-Cement, Corrugated.

611-4.1   Minimum roof slope, 3/12.

611-4.2   When this material is used on farm building roofs, select poles, purlins, etc. for the next higher load zone. For industrial applications, use 50 lb. load zone.

611-4.3   Sidelaps should be away from prevailing winds and be a minimum of one corrugation with caulking.

611-4.4   Apply and fasten per manufacturer's recommendations.

612   Plastic Skylighting

612-1   Glass fibre reinforced plastic may be used with metal roofing for additional light in buildings without ceilings.

612-2   Match panel configuration of metal roofing used. Apply in accordance with manufacturer's instructions. Side and endlaps to be not less than that for the metal roofing used.

612-3   Minimum weight per square foot: 5 ounces.

613   Attic Ventilation—Where attic space is used as part of the ventilation system in confinement housing see Chapter 8.

613-1 Provide cross ventilation for each separate space by ventilation openings protected against the entrance of rain, snow, birds, rodents, or insects.

613-2 Provide a ratio of total net free ventilating area to area of ceiling of not less than 1/150, except that ratio may be 1/300 provided:
a. A vapor barrier is installed on the warm side of the ceiling; or
b. At least 50% of the required ventilating area is provided by ventilators located in the upper portion of the space to be ventilated (at least three feet above eave or cornice vents) with the balance of the required ventilation provided by eave or cornice vents.

613-3 Consider forced ventilation of attics to reduce ceiling temperature.

613-4 Screen Ventilators:
For Birds: 1/2″ hardware cloth.
For Insects: 8 mesh/inch screening.

Chapter 7

SPECIAL PURPOSE BUILDINGS

by MERLE L. ESMAY, Ph.D.
*Professor of Agricultural Engineering,
Michigan State University*

700 Planning and Functional Requirements
Objective: Assure that the structure provides the functional and environmental requirements for the housed livestock, poultry or stored agricultural products.

700-1 Structures Must:
a. Provide optimum environment and controls.
b. Meet space requirements.
c. Permit disease control.
d. Meet sanitary code requirements of Boards of Health.
e. Optimize economic capital investment.
f. Be adaptable to mechanical materials handling equipment.
g. Require minimum labor.
h. Require minimum building maintenance.
i. Provide clear-span shell concept for maximum space utilization.
j. Provide adequate structural strength.
k. Provide desirable aesthetics.

700-2 Confinement: Concept for Livestock and Poultry Production:
a. Animals or birds confined continually in minimum building or lot space *(no pasture).*
b. May or may not be totally under roof shelter.
c. May or may not be in a totally closed insulated structure even if totally under roof.
d. The trend and acceptance is growing towards closed, insulated, mechanically ventilated, environmentally controlled structures for poultry, swine, and dairy enterprises.
e. Reasons for the trend towards confinement and environmental control are:
1. Minimizes management time.

2. Minimizes labor requirement.
3. Maximizes building utilization.
4. Maximizes control of animals and birds.
5. Maximizes genetic potential of animals or birds.
6. Maximizes feed conversion.

700-3 Emergency Power Generation:
A standby generator is required for large confinement-type poultry and livestock enterprises that rely on electricity to provide the necessary air, water, feed and light at all times. In case of power failure a generator can save an operator thousands of dollars in hot weather or during any period when a windowless, mechanically ventilated structure is being used. Removable wall panels or doors can be used to open the building and allow prevailing winds to provide air movement.
Specifications for a generator:
a. The generator may be driven by a stationary engine or tractor powered. An engine driven unit should always be in starting condition. Start and run a few minutes every two weeks.
b. The generator should provide 2 kilowatts for each Hp of electric motor power needed during the power failure. Only essential equipment need be included in sizing a manual standby unit. Some equipment can be shut down while other machines are operated.

700-4 Animal and Bird Waste Disposal Systems Must: *(see Chapter 9)*
a. Minimize air pollution.
b. Minimize water pollution.
c. Maximize handling efficiency.
d. Utilize value of waste material.

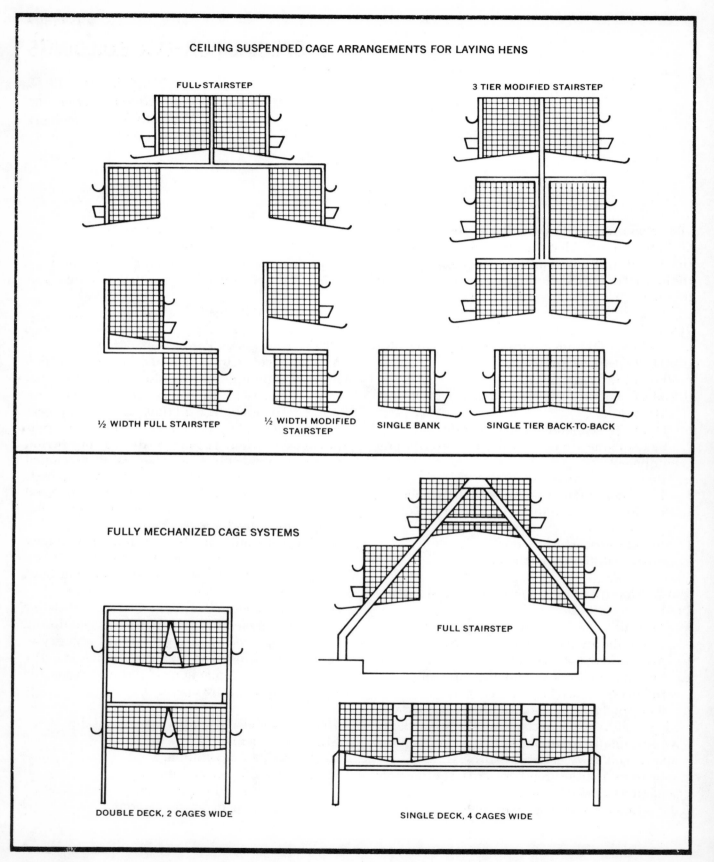

CEILING SUSPENDED CAGE ARRANGEMENTS FOR LAYING HENS

FULL-STAIRSTEP

3 TIER MODIFIED STAIRSTEP

½ WIDTH FULL STAIRSTEP

½ WIDTH MODIFIED STAIRSTEP

SINGLE BANK

SINGLE TIER BACK-TO-BACK

FULLY MECHANIZED CAGE SYSTEMS

FULL STAIRSTEP

DOUBLE DECK, 2 CAGES WIDE

SINGLE DECK, 4 CAGES WIDE

e. Must not spread disease in or out of structure.

f. Must not complicate or make the environmental control system ineffective.

701 Poultry Housing

Types of chicken enterprises and buildings

a. Egg production.

b. Broiler *(meat production)*.

c. Breeder flocks.

d. Pullet growing.

Types of turkey enterprises and buildings

a. Growing.

b. Breeder flocks.

701-1 Chicken Egg Production.

General housing specifications:

a. Wire cages may confine 2 or more birds per cage.

b. One to three decks of cages *(see Det. 701-1)*.

c. Closed, insulated, windowless clear-span structure *(see Det. 701-2)*.

d. Building width of 30 to 40 ft. for optimum ventilation air control.

e. Insulated horizontal ceiling for optimum air and temperature control.

f. Truss strength for supporting cages, birds, feeders and waterers. Provide for 5 to 8 lbs/sq. ft. of ceiling load for each deck of birds.

g. Bird heat is adequate for cold weather environmental control in most of U.S.

701-1.1 Cage Houses.

a. House width is determined by cage row widths, number of cage rows, aisle width and number of aisles. Mechanical ventilation houses may be up to 40 ft. wide for optimum air movement. Practical width limit for natural ventilation is 20 ft.

b. Cage size, type and number of birds per cage is a major management decision based on many factors *(see Table 701-1)*.

c. The stair-step cage arrangements of Det. 701-2 do not use space as efficiently as placing cages directly above each other. Stair-step arrangements have generally been only partially mechanized. Feed distribution was generally with a motorized cart and eggs gathered by hand. Dropping boards below upper deck stair-step

cages are not necessary thus the associated cleaning operation is eliminated.

d. Mechanization of feed distribution and egg gathering is possible and can be economically practical for large units where labor costs are high. (10,000 birds per house and larger).

e. A mechanically-refrigerated egg holding room is a necessity *(see Par. 701-1.2)*.

f. Lighting. Uniform lighting is desired. Place one row of lights down each aisle between cage rows. Caged birds are closer to the lights than floor birds so lower wattage bulbs may be used, however they must be closer together. Light spacing should be no more than 1 1/2 times the distance from the lower deck to the lights. For example, if distance from lower deck to lights is 4-1/2 ft., space lights about 7 ft. apart. Use 15-watt bulbs with bright reflectors. For total light control, ventilation air inlets and outlets must be light trapped.

701-1.2 Egg Handling and Storage

Egg storage facilities depend on egg gathering and marketing practices. If ungraded, uncleaned eggs are marketed in case lots, gathering directly into filler-flats is preferable. Push carts or battery-powered carts are used for gathering. Larger operations that sell washed but ungraded eggs may gather in plastic filler-flats. After washing and drying in these plastic flats they may be transferred to fibre board fillers by means of a vacuum lift. Four-dozen egg flats and 24-dozen egg cases are more efficient under these conditions than the customary 2-1/2 dozen egg flats and 30-dozen egg cases.

Other large operations may use egg gathering belts which deliver eggs directly into a line washer and drier and even into a grader. This eliminates all hand operations until casing.

Egg quality deteriorates rapidly in warm, dry or odorous places. Eggs must be cooled to 55° to 60° F. in less than 6 hours and held at that temperature. A high relative humidity of 75 to 85 percent is also necessary in the egg cool room.

Eggs in open wire baskets cool more rapidly than in flats. Eggs must be placed in a cool room for efficient cooling. If eggs are delivered to market twice a week there must be enough holding

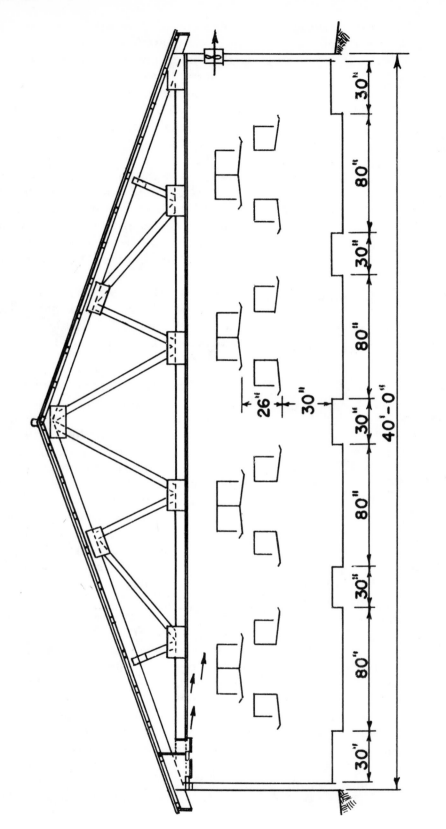

FULL STAIR-STEP CAGE SYSTEM (16 CAGES)

Det. 701-2

Table 701-1. Capacity of Varying Cage Arrangements and Floor Systems of Management.

| | Cage systems | | | | Floor systems | | |
| | | | | | Total birds at various floor space allowances | | |
House size	Cage size	No. of Birds per cage	Total Birds	1 sq. ft.	1 sq. ft.	1 - 1/4 sq. ft.	1 - 1/2 sq. ft.
One deck - 2 cages back to back							
30 x 200	8" x 16"	1	2,850				
Stair step arrangement							
	16" x 16"	4 or 5					
	12" x 16"	3					
30 x 200	10" x 16"	2	5,472	6,000		4,800	4,000
30 x 200	8" x 16"	2	6,840				
32 x 200	10" x 18"	2	5,472	6,400		5,120	4,266
Flat deck arrangement							
40 x 200	12" x 18"	3	9,120	8,000		6,400	5,333
40 x 200	16" x 18"	5	11,680				
Colony cages							
40 x 200	3' x 4'	20	7,680				
Double deck colony							
40 x 200	3' x 4'	20	15,360				

space for four days besides space for cooling each day's eggs. Prefabricated egg holding rooms complete with proper controls and refrigeration are available in many sizes.

Egg cases should not be stacked more than 5 high. The ceiling height should not be less than 8 feet. Fully insulated 2″ × 6″ stud frame construction may be used. Vapor barriers should be used on both sides of fiber insulation. A tight-fitting door should be purchased ready-made or constructed carefully.

The refrigeration unit must be designed to provide the 55° to 65° F. room temperature with high humidities at 75 to 85 percent. The cooling coils must operate without frosting under these conditions.

Automatic humidifiers with thermostatic control should be used to maintain the correct level of humidity with the proper room temperature. The fan on the cooling coil should run continuously.

701-2   Broiler (*Meat*) Production

The broiler industry is now concentrated in southeastern U.S.A.; however other areas are developing production units around processing plants.

General Housing Specifications:

a. A minimum of 5 acres is usually needed for a specialized broiler enterprise; water drainage and air movement should be good.

b. Minimum house with maximum space per bird for 7200 birds is 24 × 300 ft. Normal size is 40 × 300 for 12,000 birds.

c. Birds are grown on the floor, although cages may be used in the future.

d. Space requirements vary from 0.6 to 1.0 sq. ft. of floor area per bird, depending on marketing weight, season and extent of controlled environment.

e. Housing in the south has been open and uninsulated in the past. The trend is towards insulated structures with mechanical environmental control in the summer and winter. At least minimum roof insulation against solar heating should be provided.

f. Clear-span structures 30 to 40 ft. in width are optimum for air movement and economical construction.

g. Closing uninsulated, unventilated broiler structures during cold weather has caused excessive respiratory diseases and subsequent condemnation of birds at the processing plant.

h. Equipment requirements: See Table 701-2.

Table 701-2.   Equipment for Birds with Floor System of Management.

Equipment	Broilers	Pullets	Layers	Breeders Heavy Breeds	Breeders Light Breeds
Feeders, Mechanized Trough type Birds per foot°	12	10–12	8–10	6	8
Pan type (15″ dia.) Birds per pan	40–50	35–40	35–40	20–25	35–40
Pan type (17″ dia.)	50–65	40–50	40–50	30–40	40–50
Waterers Birds per 8′ trough	250	200	200	200	200
Starter Fountains Birds per gallon unit	100	100			
Brooders, unit type Birds per brooder°°	750–1000	500–750			
Nests Birds per nest hole			4–6	5–6	5–7

° Birds per foot of trough means six birds on each side, thus a total of 12 per foot.
°° Bird capacity of brooder varies with brooder diameter and Btu/hr heat output of brooder heater.

Feeders and waterers are generally fully mechanized. See Det. 701-3.

i. Four or five broods can be grown in one building each year due to improved breeding, nutrition, housing and health programs.

j. Houses are generally cleaned and sanitized in the week or so time between each flock of broilers. Building up a compost litter can be practiced in lieu of cleaning.

k. Chicks are usually started under unit brooders with a capacity of 500–1000 chicks. Also hot water or warm air central heat distributors can be used. Temperature under brooders is reduced 5° F. a week to a minimum of 60° F. after an initial 90°–95° F. during the first week. The hover should provide enough continuous light to attract chicks to the heat.

Table 701-3. Broiler Feed and Water Requirements; Approximate Amount per 1000 Chicks

Weeks	Lbs. Feed/Week	Gal. of Water/Week
1	140	7
2	300	11
3	490	15
4	680	20
5	920	24
6	1060	27
7	1250	32
8	1440	41
9	1560	42
10	1550	49

Total Lbs. of Feed—9390 lb. per 1000 Birds.
Source: From University of New Hampshire Bulletin 466.

l. The performance of broilers in the southern states varies with the season. Table 701-4 shows the results of a survey in Georgia.

m. From the third week until marketing, all-night lights should supplement natural lighting. One foot-candle *(about 1/4 watt/sq. ft.)* at feeder height is recommended. In 40-ft. wide houses, two rows of 25-watt bulbs 5 ft. from the sides, 10 ft. on center, and at an 8-ft. height will prove adequate light if bulbs are kept clean or reflectors used.

701-3 Breeder Flocks. These are fertile egg production flocks. Male birds must be housed with the layers in a floor management system. A ratio of one male to ten females is normal.

General Housing Specifications:

a. The basic insulated, windowless, mechanically ventilated house is the same as for a cage laying house *(See paragraph 701-1).*

b. Floor space requirement varies from 1-1/4 sq. ft. for light birds, to 2 sq. ft. for the heavier meat-type birds *(2 to 3 sq. ft. is required for deep litter floor houses).*

c. One-half to two-thirds of the floor area should be covered with a wire mesh covered dropping pit. Feeders, waterers and roosts are placed over the pit area.

d. Equipment requirements: See Table 701-2.

701-4 Pullet Growing. Pullets for laying flocks may be reared under essentially the same management system as broilers except they must be grown

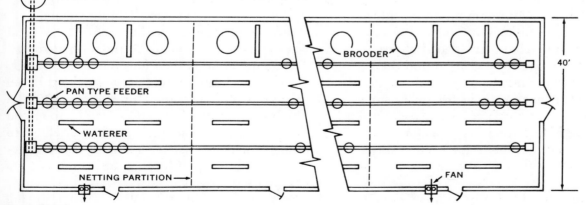

FEED BIN   BROILER HOUSE   BROODER   40'

PAN TYPE FEEDER   WATERER   NETTING PARTITION   FAN

Det. 701-3

701-4.   Broiler Production in Georgia; Average Performance by Season.*

Season	Av. Age Sold	Av. Body Weight	Feed Conversion	Mortality	Condemned
	Days	Pounds	Pounds	Percent	Percent
Winter	62.5	3.45	2.43	4.43	3.03
Spring	62.0	3.42	2.36	4.13	2.85
Summer	62.9	3.40	2.27	3.01	2.34
Fall	62.6	3.40	2.31	2.90	1.92
All	62.5	3.41	2.33	3.57	2.53

*Data obtained from study of records of 283 Georgia contract broiler producers covering over 1,000 flocks and more than 10 million broilers.—from The University of Georgia.

to maturity *(this is about 20 weeks).* Cages may be used from the sixth week on to 20 weeks. Some chicks are also being started in cages. Specially designed cages are necessary.

General Housing Specifications:

a.   The basic insulated, windowless mechanically ventilated house is the same as for an egg production house *(See paragraph 701-1).*

b.   Total light control for regulating the rate of sexual maturity development is necessary in pullet growing houses.

c.   Cages for 6 to 20 week old chickens have level floors of 1″ × 1″ welded wire mesh rather than the standard 1″ × 2″ mesh for laying hens.

d.   Cage-type, chick starting houses require a special heating system. Hot water, hot air or electrical may be used.

701-5   Turkey Raising. Confinement housing for turkeys is still in the early stages of development. In the past it has been maintained as a seasonal operation with the turkey poults hatched during the spring of the year. Minimum brooding equipment is used and the turkeys are grown on open pastures or in completely open sided shelters.

Confinement housing for a year-around turkey industry has the following general requirements:

a.   An insulated, mechanically ventilated breeder hen house for egg production on a year-around basis. This might be a floor management house with a certain ratio of hens for each male or a cage operation utilizing artificial insemination.

b.   An insulated, mechanically ventilated confinement house for growing turkeys on a year-

around basis. The house shell should be basically like the poultry house for layers or growers as described in paragraph 701-1.

701-6   Environment Modification. The main objective of a structure in either meat or egg production is to modify the outside climatic conditions for maximization of the genetic potential of the birds. Det. 701-5 illustrates schematically the various considerations for environmental control.

Major considerations:

a.   The optimum temperature range for chickens by age is shown by Graph. 701-6. Graph 701-7 shows the effect on layers.

b.   Mature chickens are comfortable between 55° to 80° F.

c.   The optimum practical temperature for cold weather housing is 55° F. Heat from the hens may be conserved in an insulated house and used to keep the house warm, heat incoming ventilation air and evaporate excess moisture. Supplemental heat is generally not necessary in the U.S., if the house is fully insulated.

d.   Bird level temperatures for chicks the first week must be from 90° to 95° and with no drafts. The temperature is then lowered 5° each week.

e.   Adult and high production laying hens begin to show stress at temperatures above 80° F. A few hours per day in the 90's may be tolerated if the nights cool to the low 70's or 60's. In climates with persistent above 90° F. temperatures and low humidities, evaporative coolers can be used advantageously.

f.   Relative humidities in the houses during winter months of up to 80% are quite tolerable

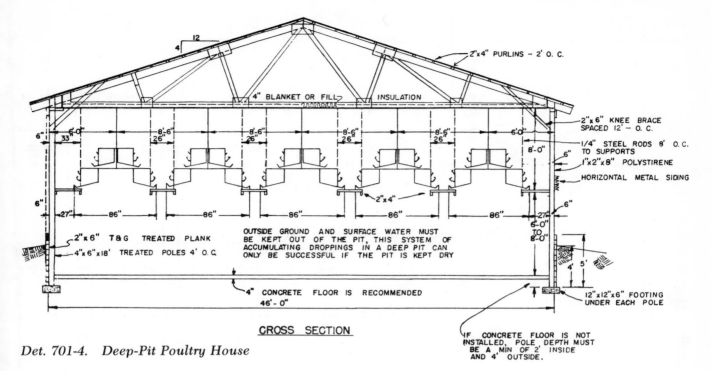

12
4

2"x4" PURLINS - 2' O. C.

4" BLANKET OR FILL INSULATION

2"x 6" KNEE BRACE
SPACED 12' - O. C.

6"
33
6'-0"
8'-6"
26
8'-6"
26
8'-6"
26
8'-5"
26
6'-0"
8'-0"

1/4" STEEL RODS 8' O. C.
TO SUPPORTS

1"x2"x8" POLYSTIRENE

HORIZONTAL METAL SIDING

6"

2"x 4"

6"

6"

27"
86"
86"
86"
86"
86"
27"
6'-0"
TO
8'-0"

2"x 6" T&G TREATED PLANK

4"x 6"x18' TREATED POLES 4' O. C.

OUTSIDE GROUND AND SURFACE WATER MUST
BE KEPT OUT OF THE PIT, THIS SYSTEM OF
ACCUMULATING DROPPINGS IN A DEEP PIT CAN
ONLY BE SUCCESSFUL IF THE PIT IS KEPT DRY

4' 5'

4" CONCRETE FLOOR IS RECOMMENDED
46'- 0"

12"x12"x6" FOOTING
UNDER EACH POLE

IF CONCRETE FLOOR IS NOT
INSTALLED, POLE DEPTH MUST
BE A MIN OF 2' INSIDE
AND 4' OUTSIDE.

CROSS SECTION

Det. 701-4.   *Deep-Pit Poultry House*

and add to the efficiency of the ventilation system in removing moisture from the building.

701-7   Deep-pit Poultry Houses

a.   The deep-pit or high-rise poultry house provides a 6 to 8 ft. lower story below the caged birds for manure storage *(see Det. 701-4).*

b.   The deep-pit house provides ample manure storage capacity for the accumulation of manure for one or more flock laying cycles. (A laying cycle is from 12 to 14 months). Manure is removed from the house at a scheduled time, not more than once a year, when it can be spread on the crop land and plowed under

GOOD HOUSING CREATES FAVORABLE ENVIRONMENT FOR THE CHICKEN

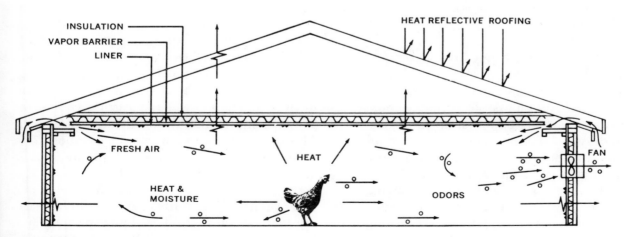

INSULATION

VAPOR BARRIER

LINER

HEAT REFLECTIVE ROOFING

FRESH AIR

HEAT

FAN

HEAT &
MOISTURE

ODORS

Det. 701-5

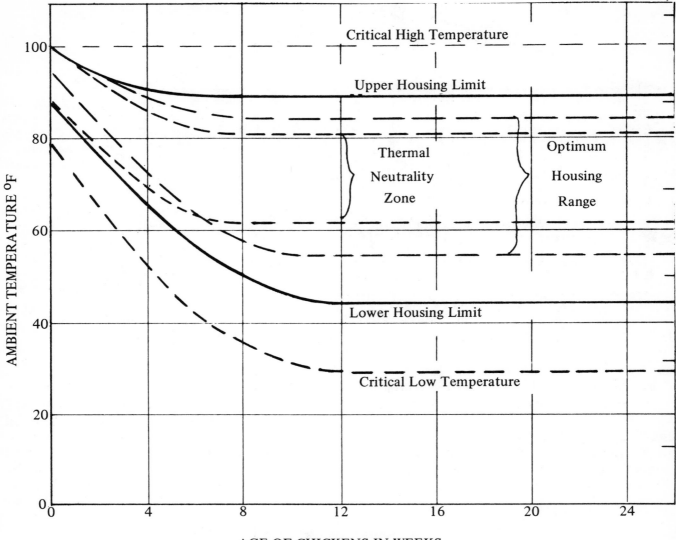

Graph 701-6 Optimum Temperature For White Leghorn Chickens.

immediately to minimize nutritive losses and possible pollution.

c. The concept of in-place manure storage for a year or more is only possible with minimum odor production through the attainment of maximum air drying. Air movement over the surface of the stored manure should be ample to cause the dropping to cone upward directly below the cage rows. This is made possible by placing most of the exhaust fans in the lower story walls and by adding circulating fans where drying is not adequate.

d. Under the described storage conditions some biological degradation occurs and water evaporation accounts for a manure weight reduction of over one-half. Average moisture content of stored manure should approximate 50% w.b. The bulk accumulation should be about one cubic foot per bird per year. If birds are housed at an equivalent floor area of one sq. ft. the depth accumulation would then be one ft. per year. An increase in bird density would increase the depth accordingly. The storage pit must not be subjected to any outside water sources such as from bird watering equipment or ground water.

702 Swine Housing

Types of enterprises and buildings:

a. Farrowing—A warm building where the animal is born and remains until it reaches two to five weeks of age.

b. Nursery *(or growing)*—a warm building used for growing the animals from age two to five weeks up to 40 or 50 lbs.

c. Finishing—An area or building where pigs are grown from nursery age to market weight at 5 to 6 months.

d. Breeding Stock Housing—The area or areas where the sows, gilts and boars may be fed and managed.

702-1 Two or more of these areas may be combined in one house.

a. Farrowing—Nursery

b. Nursery—Finishing

c. Farrowing—Nursery—Finishing *(See Det. 702-1)*. The breeding stock should always be housed in a separate building.

702-2 Housing Systems in the past have featured open buildings with yards or pastures. Present trend is towards confinement, either cold or warm. The confinement systems have the following advantages:

a. More profitable use of land for other crops rather than hog grazing.

b. Building conveniently located on the farmstead and more easily designed for temperature control.

c. Better control of herd health and disease by reducing outside contacts with disease carriers.

d. Less labor and chore time by permitting use of mechanical feeding and watering.

702-3 Controlled-Environment Housing designed to control extreme fluctuations of temperature, humidity, air velocities, air purity and solar radiation; by providing insulated side walls and ceiling and mechanical ventilation are reported to have the following benefits:

a. Less feed per pound of grain *(See Det. 702-2)*.

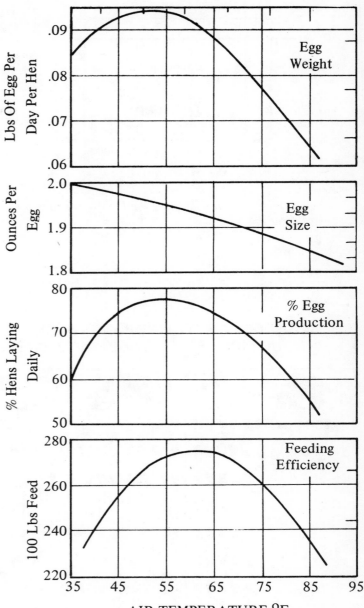

Graph 701-7 The Effects of Temperature on Egg Weight, Egg Size, Production, and Feeding Efficiency for Hens.

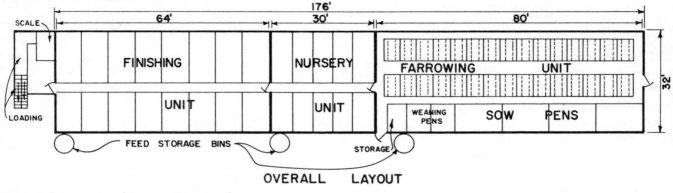

Det. 702-1.   *A Production-Line Confinement Swine Building.*

EFFECT OF TEMPERATURE ON PRODUCTION EFFICIENCY OF SWINE

100 LB.		200 LB.
750	100	
470	90	1100
310	80	500
255	70	400
320	60	360
410	50	500
530	40	1100

FEED REQUIRED PER CWT. GAIN	EACH SACK = 100 LB. FEED

Det. 702-2   *It Takes More Feed at High or Low Temperatures to Produce 100 Pounds of Pork.*

b.   Less back fat—a leaner carcass which may command premium prices.

c.   Better herd health, due to sanitation control, exclusion of birds, rodents and other disease carriers; and freedom from quick temperature changes which often lead to respiratory trouble.

d.   Provides more time for management since less time is required for routine chore labor.

e.   Permits scheduling multiple farrowing for any month in the year independent of outside weather conditions.

f.   More pleasant working conditions.

g.   Personal satisfaction from seeing hogs respond to good care.

702-4   Planning the Farrowing House.

The gestation period for sows is 114 days and approximately 160 days are needed to grow the 2-1/2 pound pig to a 220 lb. market hog. Sows can produce two litters a year. The breeding herd may be managed so litters will arrive 2, 3, 4, 6 or 12 times a year.

A closed building for farrowing is recommended as small pigs must be kept warm, dry and free from drafts. Farrowing crates (*also called stalls*) are usually arranged in parallel rows with access aisles in both the front and rear (*See Det. 702-3*).

Supplemental heat must be supplied in the pig brooder or creep area. If no separate nursery is provided the pigs can be kept in litters or groups of litters in the crates or pen area. They may be moved to a nursery area at one end or side of the building.

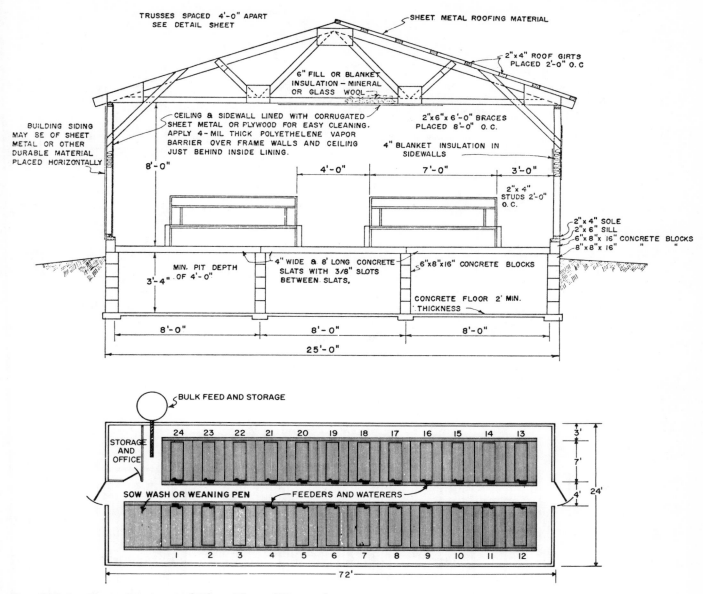

Det. 702-3   Cross-Section and Floor Plan of Typical Slotted-Floor Farrowing House.

702-5   Planning the Nursery.

A separate nursery building is part of a three building system and provides housing for the pigs from weaning age until ready to move to the finishing house at 7 to 10 weeks of age or 40 to 60 pounds weight *(See Det. 702-4)*. This house like the farrowing house should be enclosed, insulated and ventilated. The house should provide supplemental heat and be free of drafts.

702-6   Planning the Finishing House.

Provide for temperature control with the ventilation system. Controlled environment is recommended for the north central states. *(Zones 1 and 2 of U.S.A. map, Det. 801-2)*. Save labor by including an effective materials handling system. Bulk feed storage and a mechanical conveying system for delivering feed to pen feeders is desired. Slotted floors or partially slotted floors

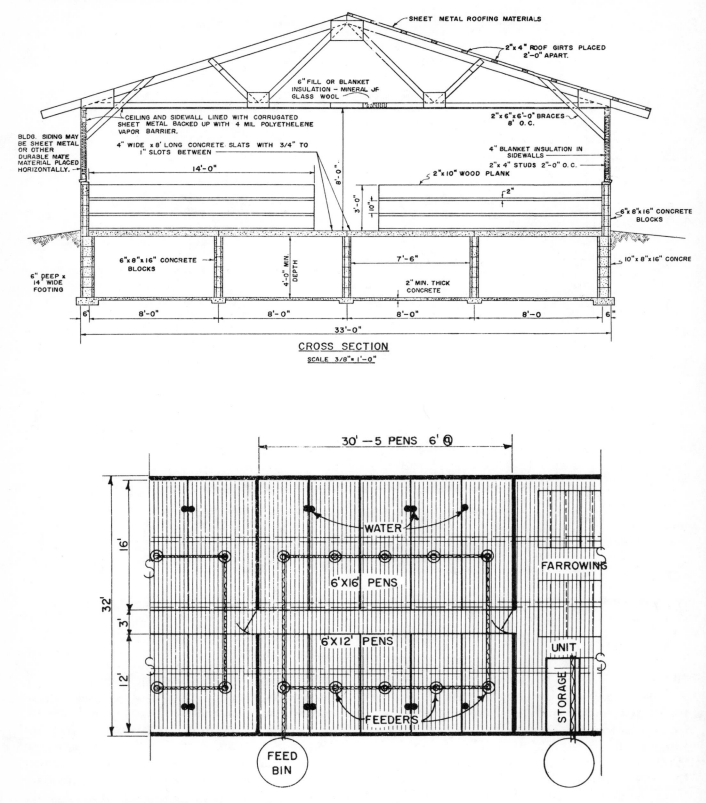

SHEET METAL ROOFING MATERIALS

2"x4" ROOF GIRTS PLACED 2'-0" APART.

6" FILL OR BLANKET INSULATION – MINERAL OF GLASS WOOL

CEILING AND SIDEWALL LINED WITH CORRUGATED SHEET METAL BACKED UP WITH 4 MIL POLYETHELENE VAPOR BARRIER.

2"x6"x6'-0" BRACES 8' O.C.

BLDG. SIDING MAY BE SHEET METAL OR OTHER DURABLE MATE MATERIAL PLACED HORIZONTALLY.

4" WIDE x 8' LONG CONCRETE SLATS WITH 3/4" TO 1" SLOTS BETWEEN

4" BLANKET INSULATION IN SIDEWALLS

2"x4" STUDS 2'-0" O.C.

2"x10" WOOD PLANK

14'-0"

8'-0"

3'-0"

1'-0"

2"

6"x8"x16" CONCRETE BLOCKS

6" DEEP x 14" WIDE FOOTING

6"x8"x16" CONCRETE BLOCKS

4'-0" MIN DEPTH

7'-6"

2" MIN. THICK CONCRETE

10"x8"x16" CONCRE

6" 8'-0" 8'-0" 8'-0" 8'-0 6"

33'-0"

CROSS SECTION

SCALE 3/8"= 1'-0"

30' – 5 PENS 6' @

16'

32'

3'

12'

WATER

6'X16' PENS

6'X12' PENS

FEEDERS

FARROWING

UNIT

STORAGE

FEED BIN

Det. 702-4   Combination Nursery-Finishing House

practically eliminate daily manure cleaning *(See Chapter 9)*. One watering cup should be provided for each pen near the dunging area. Supplemental heat may be required in sub-freezing weather if all pigs are small *(In the 40 to 60 lb. range)*. Common pen sizes are 6′ × 16′ to 4′ × 12′. See Det. 702-4.

702-7 Facilities for the Breeding Herd.
The importance of good care, feeding and management in breeding herds is becoming better recognized, particularly for intensified hog operations. Conception rates and embryo survival are much lower in sows bred during hot weather than during cooler months of the year. Water sprays which wet and cool the hogs during hot weather are beneficial.

702-8 Space Requirements for Total Confinement Houses. Growing and Finishing Houses:

	Under 100 lbs.	Over 100 lbs.
Slotted Floor	3–5 ft²	7 ft²
Concrete Floor	5–6 ft²	10–12 ft²
Farrowing Sows	Under 400 lbs.	Over 400 lbs.
Farrowing Crate	22″ × 7′	24″ × 7′ to 8′
Pen Type	7′ × 8′	7′ × 9′ to 8′ × 9′
Nursery	20 to 30 lbs.	40 to 60 lbs.
Slotted Floors	3 ft²	4 ft²

702-9 Optimum Temperatures

	Closed Buildings	Open Buildings
Farrowing	Pigs—80 to 90° F Sows—50 to 60° F Building—50 to 60° F*	Not Recommended
Nursery	Pigs—60 to 80° F Building—60 to 65° F	Not Recommended Below 40 lb. weight
Finishing	Pigs—55 to 65° F Building—55 to 65° F	Dry, No-draft, Bedded Area, Cross Ventilation in Summer.

*Sometimes maintained at 80° F without floor and brooder heat over fully slotted floors.

702-10 Feed and Water Requirements

Animal Weight	Full Feed Lbs.	Water Gal./Day
50	2.7	1
100	4.7	1 1/2
150	6.3	2
200	7.6	2 1/2
250	8.2	3

703 Dairy Cattle Housing.
Types of Buildings:
a. The stall barn is closed, insulated and mechanically ventilated.
b. Free-stall barn may be either warm or cold design.
c. Loose housing, resting barn is cold with built-up manure pack.
d. Dry cow housing is normally open and cold.
e. Calf and young stock housing should be warm, insulated and mechanically ventilated.
f. Milking parlor and milk room.

703-1 The distribution of animals in typical dairy herds including replacements are as follows:

Milking Cows	45%
Dry Cows	10%
Young Stock	
10 months to freshening	24%
6 weeks to 10 months	13%
Under 6 weeks	8%
TOTAL	100%

703-2 Critical Factors In Planning Dairy Enterprise Facilities:
a. Must meet sanitary regulations of Public Health Agencies.
b. Provide a system to handle each material from harvest to animal.
c. Provide a system to handle all animals, not just the milking cows. Separate dry cow, young stock and calf facilities are required.
d. Excess moisture removal from both cold and warm buildings must be provided. Cold housing must have 4″ to 8″ above plate openings plus 2″ to 3″ continuous ridge opening plus doors for summer air movement. Supplemental mechanical ventilation is required in wide com-

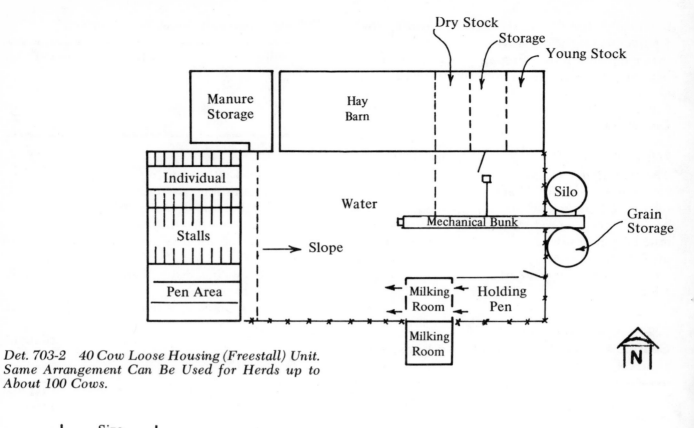

Dry Stock
Storage
Young Stock

Manure Storage

Hay Barn

Individual

Stalls

Water

Silo

Pen Area

Slope

Mechanical Bunk

Grain Storage

Milking Room

Holding Pen

Milking Room

N

Det. 703-2   40 Cow Loose Housing (Freestall) Unit.
Same Arrangement Can Be Used for Herds up to
About 100 Cows.

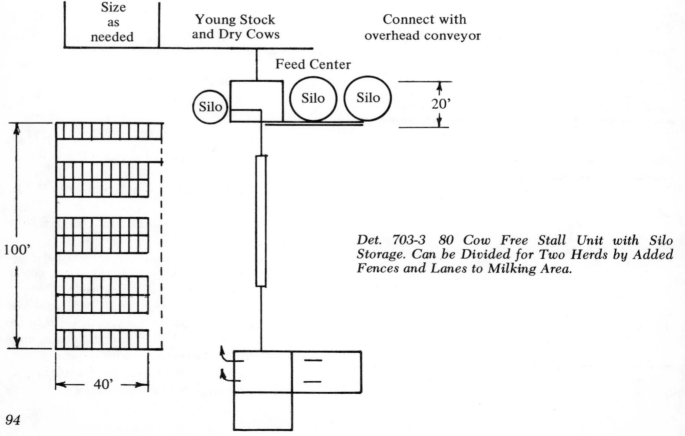

Size as needed

Young Stock and Dry Cows

Connect with overhead conveyor

Feed Center

Silo

Silo

Silo

20'

100'

40'

Det. 703-3 80 Cow Free Stall Unit with Silo
Storage. Can be Divided for Two Herds by Added
Fences and Lanes to Milking Area.

SIDE VIEW OF STALL (post inside curb)

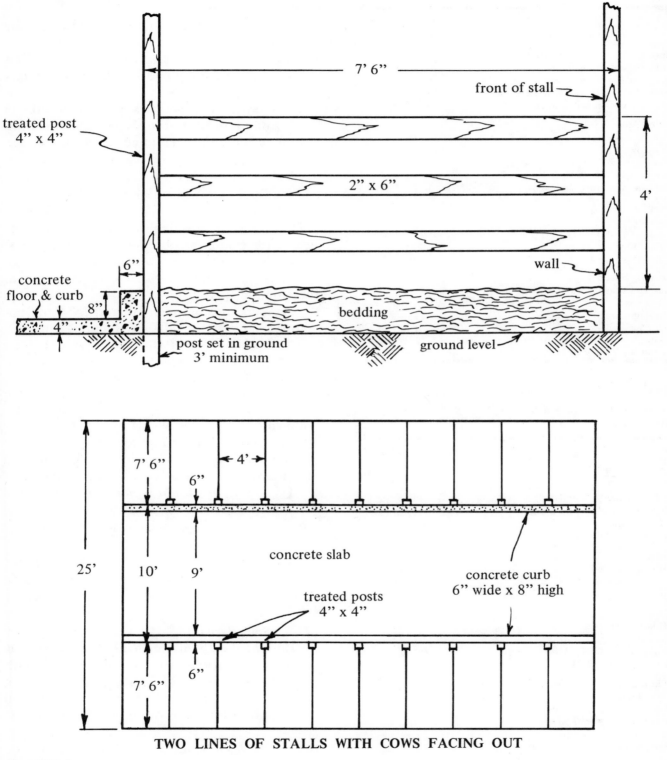

treated post
4" x 4"

7' 6"

front of stall

2" x 6"

4'

6"

wall

concrete
floor & curb

8"

bedding

4"

post set in ground
3' minimum

ground level

25'

7' 6"

6"

4'

10'

9'

concrete slab

concrete curb
6" wide x 8" high

treated posts
4" x 4"

7' 6"

6"

TWO LINES OF STALLS WITH COWS FACING OUT

Det. 703-4

Table 703-1   Space Requirements for Loose Housing.

Area and Animal Class	Min. Space Per Head or Unit
Resting Area *(Individual Stalls)*	
Milking cow *(Built-up pack)*	50 sq. ft.
Dry Cow *(Built-up pack)*	60 sq. ft.
Young Stock—10 month to Freshen	60 sq. ft.
Young Stock—6 weeks to 10 months	30 sq. ft.
	30 sq. ft.
Paved Area	
Milking Cow	100 sq. ft.
Dry Cow	100 sq. ft.
Young stock—10 month to Freshen	40 sq. ft.
Young stock—6 weeks to 10 months	40 sq. ft.
Holding Area for milking cows	15 sq. ft.
Hospital	
Maternity-isolation	
1 pen/10 milking cows	100 sq. ft./pen
Calves under 6 weeks	
individual pens	25 sq. ft./pen
Feeding Space	
Hay and silage fed twice a day if oftener use	
1/2 space	
Milking cow	24 in./hd.
Dry cow	24 in./hd.
Young stock—10 months to Freshen	12 in./hd.
Young stock—6 weeks to 10 months	12 in./hd.

Table 703-2.   Materials Requirement for a Loose Housing System for Sizing Storage Structures.

Material and Animal Class	Amount/Year/ Head or Unit
Hay	
Milking cow *(50% of Total)*	3-1/2 tons
Dry cow *(roughage dry matter)*	3-1/2 tons
Young stock—10 months to Freshen	2-1/2 tons
Young stock—6 weeks to 10 months	1 ton
Silage	
Milking cow *(50% of Total)*	10 tons
Dry cow *(roughage dry matter)*	10 tons
Young stock—10 months to Freshen	3 tons
Grain	
Milking cow	1-1/2 tons
Dry cow	1-1/2 tons
Young stock—6 week to 10 months	1/3 ton
Calves under 6 weeks	1/10 ton
Bedding *(Straw, sawdust, ground corn cobs or shavings)*	
Milk cow *(Built-up pack)*	1-1/2 tons
Milk cow *(Free-stall barn)*	1/2 ton
Dry cow *(Loose housing)*	1-1/2 tons
Young stock—10 months to Freshen	1/2 ton
Young stock—6 weeks to 10 months	1/2 ton

pletely covered buildings. Provide insulation and mechanical ventilation in warm housing *(See Table 800-2)*.

e.   Labor and traffic patterns must be laid out for efficiency.

f.   Allow for expansion. A good plan should allow for doubling the size of all buildings and facilities.

g.   The layout and facilities must be capable of returning a profit to the owner. Electrical service, water supply, silo and harvesting equipment must be paid from the enterprise returns.

703-3   Some Non-Critical Factors which influence the amount of investment in a dairy facility:

They do not alter milk production or make any substantial change in labor requirements for most farms. These factors must be considered in design since decisions must be made at the time of construction.

a.   Temperatures between 10° and 75° F. do not appreciably affect milk production, thus this is a non-critical factor. However, periods of high temperature will depress milk production, so summer ventilation is a concern in the warmer regions. About 75% of labor is in the milking area which should be heated in all colder climates.

b.   The choice of construction materials such as wood, steel or masonry and combinations are non-critical as long as ventilation is provided.

c.   Type and size of silo is non-critical as is the manure handling system. They must, of course, be adequate and approved by milk code inspectors.

703-4   Roughage   Requirements—*(see   Table 703-4)*

703-5   Stall Barns.

a.   Dairymen with milking herds of over 50 cows frequently consider using a milking parlor with a stall barn. Det. 703-5 shows the floor plan for a two-row barn. If the herd exceeds 100 cows a four-row barn should be considered.

703-5.1   Sizes of Cow Stalls when using electric cow trainers.

703-4 Roughage Requirements Based on 30 lbs. of Dry Matter Daily per 1000 lb. of Animal Weight.

| | *60% Moisture Silage Only* | *1/2 Silage, 1/2 Hay* | | *Hay Only* |
		Silage	*Hay*	
1000 lb. cow—365 days	13.7 tons	6.25 tons	2.7 tons	5.4 tons
Example: 50 cows × 1250 lb each ──────── 1000	= 62.5	62.5	62.5	62.5
Total required 240 ─── days 360	856 tons = 66.7%	428 tons 66.7%	169 tons 66.7%	338 tons 66.7%
Total req'd., 50 cows, 240 days	571 tons	286 tons	113 tons	226 tons
Storage per ton	50 cu. ft.	50 cu. ft.	300 cu. ft.	300 cu. ft.
Volume of storage	28,550 cu. ft.	14,300 cu. ft.	33,900 cu. ft.	67,800 cu. ft.

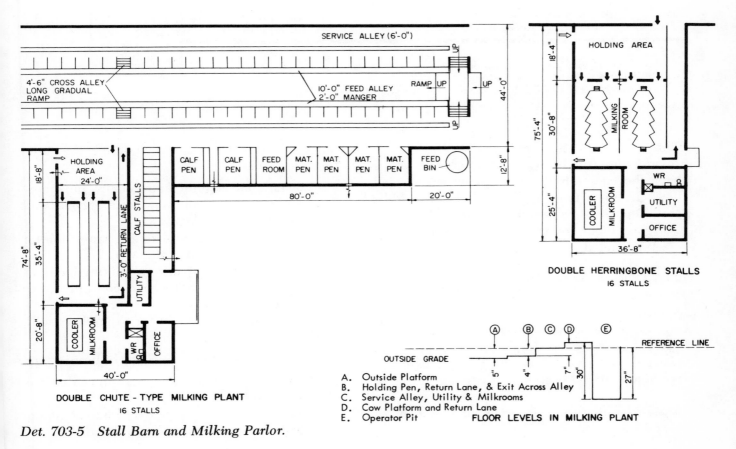

SERVICE ALLEY (6'-0")

4'-6" CROSS ALLEY LONG GRADUAL RAMP

10'-0" FEED ALLEY 2'-0" MANGER

RAMP UP · UP

44'-0"

HOLDING AREA 24'-0"

18'-8"

74'-8" 35'-4"

20'-8"

3'-0" RETURN LANE · CALF STALLS

CALF PEN · CALF PEN · FEED ROOM · MAT. PEN · MAT. PEN · MAT. PEN · MAT. PEN · FEED BIN

80'-0" · 20'-0"

12'-8"

UTILITY

COOLER · MILKROOM · WR · OFFICE

40'-0"

DOUBLE CHUTE - TYPE MILKING PLANT
16 STALLS

HOLDING AREA

18'-4"

75'-4" · 30'-8"

25'-4"

MILKING ROOM

COOLER MILKROOM · WR · UTILITY · OFFICE

36'-8"

DOUBLE HERRINGBONE STALLS
16 STALLS

REFERENCE LINE

OUTSIDE GRADE

Ⓐ Ⓑ Ⓒ Ⓓ Ⓔ

5" · 4" · 7" · 30" · 27"

A. Outside Platform
B. Holding Pen, Return Lane, & Exit Across Alley
C. Service Alley, Utility & Milkrooms
D. Cow Platform and Return Lane
E. Operator Pit

FLOOR LEVELS IN MILKING PLANT

Det. 703-5 Stall Barn and Milking Parlor.

703-5.1 Sizes of Cow Stalls When Using Electric Cow Trainers:

Weight of Cows Lbs.	Girth of Cows In.	Stanchion Stalls		Comfort Stalls		Tie Stalls	
		Width	Length	Width	Length	Width	Length
800	65	3'-6"	4'-8"	3'-9"	4'-11"	4'-0"	5'-2"
1000	70-1/2	3'-9"	5'-0"	4'-0"	5'-3"	4'-3"	5'-6"
1200	75	4'-0"	5'-4"	4'-3"	5'-7"	4'-6"	5'-10"
1400	79-1/2	4'-3"	5'-8"	4'-6"	5'-11"	4'-9"	6'-2"
1600	84+	4'-6"+	6'-0"	4'-9"	6'-3"	5'-0"	6'-6"

703-5.2 Stall Barn Dimensions:

		Dimensions		Note No.
		Minimum	Recommended	
Alleys	Feed Alleys—Sweep Mangers	3'-6"	4' to 5'	1
	Cross Alleys	3'-6"	4'-6"	1
	Service Alley with Barn Cleaner	5'-0"	6'-0"	
	Service Alley for Spreader	7'-6"	8'-0"	
Gutters:	Width	16"	16"	2
	Depth—Stall Side	10"	11" to 12"	
	Depth—Alley Side	8"	11" to 12"	3
Mangers:	Width—Cows under 1200 lb.	20"	22" to 27"	
	Cows over 1200 lb.	22"	24" to 27"	

Note:
1. Where large carts are used, a 5-foot wide cross alley is desirable.
2. Or as required for barn cleaner.
3. Where barn cleaners are used, have the service alley level with the stall floor.

703-5.3 Lighting the Stall Barn.
Provide rows of 100-watt incandescent lamps above the center lines of the service and feed alleys. Lamps should be spaced 3-stall widths apart. One sq. ft. of window glass or 1-1/4 sq. ft. of glass block for each 15 sq. ft. of floor area is recommended.

703-5.4 Environmental Control of the Stall Barn.
The structure must be insulated and ventilated according to information given in Chapter 8. Uniform winter minimum temperature is 50–55° F. Heat from the cows should provide ample heat to keep the stall barn above 50° F., heat incoming ventilation air and evaporate excess moisture.

703-6 Planning the Loose Housing System for Dairy Cows.

Some of the reasons for considering the loose housing system are:

a. Lower labor requirements per cow plus more flexibility in use of manpower during peak labor periods and on weekends.

b. Easier and more complete mechanization for handling large volumes of materials.

c. A lower cost for expansion: milking facilities usually do not have to be changed—only lower cost buildings added.

d. Less investment per cow for a complete facility for 60 or more cows.

Other characteristics which may be limiting are:

a. Group handling of cattle, both in feedlot and milking unit.

b. Less convenient arrangement for treatment of animals, unless a hospital area is built.

703-6.1   Some Important Considerations for the Layout are:

a.   Drainage should be away from structures and lots with a slope of 1/4″ to 1/2″ a foot.

b.   Protect animals from wind and snow. Open resting barns away from prevailing winds. Avoid long narrow open buildings. Keep taller structures on leeward side of yard to minimize snow drop out in lots.

c.   Pen lots should open to south and east for maximum winter sun and best protection from stormy winds in cold regions.

d.   Allow for expansion. Silos should not cut off building extension.

e.   Provide separate areas for milking, feeding and resting.

f.   Separate young stock and dry cows from cows in milk.

g.   All weather drives are needed to the milking unit and feed area. Do not let drives block the surface drainage system.

703-6.2   Layouts for 40 and 80 Milking Cow Loose Housing systems are shown in Details 703-2 and 703-3. When herds near 100 milking cows it is desirable to consider separation of young stock from the main unit. A separate calf and maternity building also becomes economical. See Tables 703-1 and 703-2 for space requirements.

703-6.3   Free Stalls are Recommended in the Resting Area for these Reasons:

a.   Cows stay cleaner than when kept on built-up manure packs.

b.   Bedding requirements are reduced to 1/4 to 1/2 ton per cow per year.

c.   Damage to udders and teats is reduced.

d.   Milking time may be reduced as less washing of cows is necessary.

e.   Less hand labor may be needed to clean manure from resting area.

f.   Less area per cow is needed than for built-up packs.

Some Limitations:

a.   Older animals may tend to lie in the alleys.

b.   Alleys must be cleaned daily.

c.   Some hand cleaning of stalls may be necessary.

703-6.4   Recommended free-stall sizes:

Large cows *(1200 to 1500 lbs.)* 45″ to 48″ × 7′6″.
Med. cows *(800 to 1200 lbs.)* 40″ to 42″ × 7′0″.
Small cows *(500 to 800 lbs.)* 36″ to 38″ × 6′6″.
Calves *(300 to 500 lbs.)* 32″ to 26″ × 60″.

a.   Stall floors are dirt, sand or gravel, plus bedding, not paved.

b.   Alleys should be 9′ to 10′ wide.

c.   Alleys should be of concrete for easy cleaning with a tractor scraper.

d.   Stall construction is shown by Detail 703-4.

703-6.5   Ventilation is a key factor in the successful operation of free-stall resting building.

a.   A minimum of 50% of building front should be open—more is desirable.

b.   A 2″ to 4″ opening between eaves and roof is necessary.

c.   Use ridge ventilators 18′ to 20′ apart, or leave off ridge roll.

d.   Two to three air changes per hour is minimum required for ventilation of the open building.

703-6.6   Free Stall Housing May Be Enclosed, Insulated and Mechanically Ventilated. In this case the feeding area must also be enclosed and the cows must be kept inside all of the time. See Det. 703-6.6. Ventilation requirements would be similar to those for a stall type barn.

703-7   The Milking Plant.

a.   The bulk milk tank should hold three milkings if milk is picked up every day *(E.D.)* and five milkings with every other day *(E.O.D.)* pickup.

b.   Suggested floor area for milk room:

Milk Production	Floor Area Sq. Ft.	
Gal. Per Day	E.D. Bulk	E.O.D. Bulk
50 or Less	168	168
50 to 100	192	216
100 to 160	208	240
Over 160	Provide Adequate Space	
Provide 24″ to 36″ clearance around bulk tank		

c.   Check sanitation regulations with local health authorities before building.

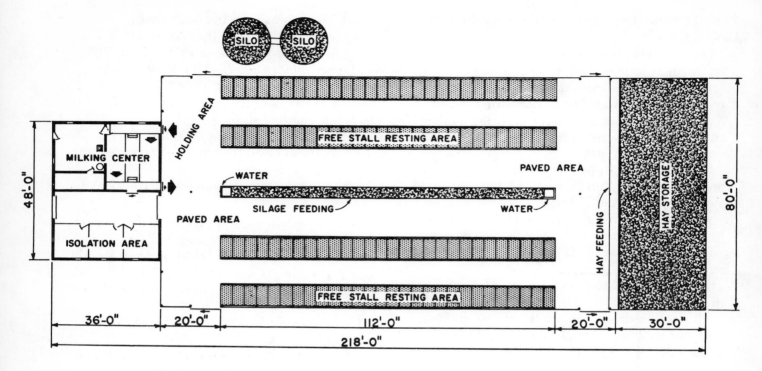

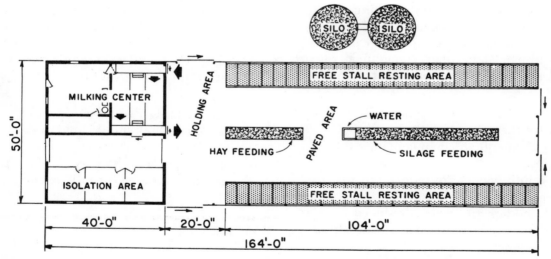

Det. 703-6.6

703-7.1 The milking parlor should be designed for top labor efficiency, comfort and sanitation. With a given number of milking units and opera- tors for various types of milking systems the following number of cows can be milked each hour:

Type of Milking Room and Stalls	No. of Operators	Milking Units	Cows/ Hour
Side Opening and Stalls			
3 Stalls on one side	1	3	25–30
4 Stalls on one side	1	4*	25–30
2 Stalls on each side	1	4*	30–35
3 Stalls on each side	2	6	45–55
4 Stalls on each side	2	8*	55–65
Chute or Lane Type			
2 Stalls on each side	1	2	25–30
3 Stalls on each side	1	3	30–35
Herringbone Stalls			
4 Stalls on each side	1	4	35–45
8 Stalls on each side	2	8	70–80

*Only three units per man will operate at any one time.

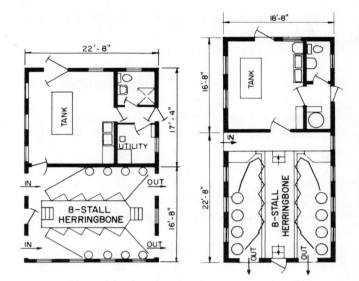

Det. 703-7.2   *Eight-Stall Herringbone Milking Plant Layouts.*

703-7.2   The Herringbone parlor is the most efficient and requires the least building space for construction. Det. 707-7.2 shows two layouts for the double four-parlors.

703-8   Calf and Youngstock Housing.
The mortality rate for young calves has been high because of haphazard planning and poor buildings.

Calves may be cared for:
a.   In a cold, draft-free cubicle.
b.   In an artificially heated calf barn.
The warm barn is recommended in the northern states.

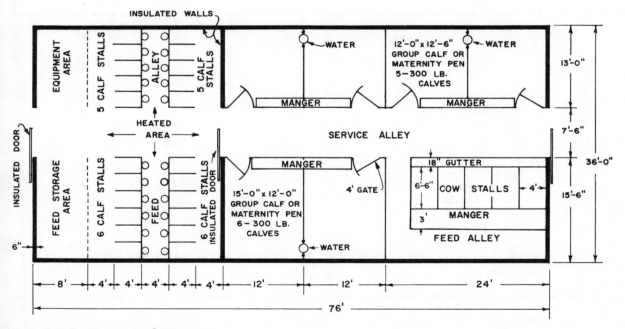

Det. 703-8   *Youngstock Housing.*

703-8.1 The Warm Youngstock Housing Facility should contain the following:

a. Warm, draft-free individual calf stalls for youngest calves.
b. Group pens to handle young animals until they are on solid feed.
c. Maternity pens for use in cold weather.
d. Storage space for limited amounts of feed.
e. Running water, water heater and storage for cleaning solutions.
f. Building must be weather-tight and insulated.
g. Thermostatically controlled fan.
h. Oil, gas or electric heat must be provided.

704 Beef Cattle Housing and Facilities.

There are four basic systems defined as follows:

a. Drylot system consists of open front buildings with an outside lot for feeding. Lot is preferably paved. Feeding is done in auger bunks in fenceline bunks or self-feeders.
b. Open-lot system uses no sheds. Weather protection is limited to windbreak fences in winter and sun shades in summer. Most lots are dirt except for a strip of concrete along the bunks.

Feed is generally delivered by self-unloading wagons to fenceline bunks.

c. Cold confinement systems feature a building with one side open in winter and both sides open in summer. Cattle are kept under shelter but temperature fluctuates with outside conditions.
d. Warm confinement system is enclosed, insulated and fan-ventilated. Inside temperatures during the winter are kept at 50° F. or above with heat from animals. Most of the closed buildings are equipped with slotted floors, manure storage pits and a liquid manure-handling system.

704-1 The Drylot System has been conventional for beef in the midwest and the open lot in the west and southwest. There now is some trend towards confinement. However, at the same time, there is some movement to open-lots in the midwest. Open lots are the choice of corporation feeding while confinement appears to be the choice of owner operated farms.

Table 704-1 Approximate Feed Storage Requirements for Several Selected Drylot Beef Feeding Programs.

	Purchase Weight Lbs.	Market Weight Lbs.	Feeding Period Months	Corn Bu[1]	With Corn Silage Protein Lbs.[1]	Silage Ton[1]	Hay Ton[1]	With Hay Corn Bu[1]	Protein Lbs.[1]	Hay Ton[1]
Steer Calves										
Liberal Grain	400	1000	9					60	300	0.8
Liberal Roughage	400	950	11	35	450	3.1	0.4	50	200	1.0
Heifer Calves										
Liberal Grain	400	850	9					44	200	0.8
Liberal Roughage	400	850	10	33	300	1.5	0.5			
Yearling Steers										
Liberal Grain	650	1150	7					60	250	0.9
Liberal Roughage	650	1150	8	30	300	3.5	0.8	39	100	1.8
Maximum Roughage	700	1050	6	10	300	3.0	0.3			
Heavy Steers										
Short Fed										
Liberal Grain	950	1150	3.5	28	180	1.0	0.2	34	100	0.4
Liberal Roughage	850	1100	4	5	300	3.5	0.1			
Long Fed										
Liberal Grain	850	1200	5					49	200	0.7

[1] Feed Requirement Per Head

1-Ton Alfalfa grass silage = 1/3 ton hay; 1-ton haylage = 1/2 ton hay; 1-ton corn silage + 70 lbs. protein = 0.3 ton hay + 5 bu. corn; 1-ton oat silage + 50 lbs. protein = 1/3 ton hay.

704-2 Confinement Systems For Beef.
Both types of confinement systems have these advantages over drylot or open-lot systems:
a. Surface runoff of waste products may be eliminated to minimize air and water pollution.
b. Protecting manure from sun and rain increases its fertilizer value.
c. Less labor required to handle manure.
d. Flies and odors are reduced.
e. Cattle are more docile and easier to handle when sorted and treated.
f. Herdsman can observe cattle better.
g. Less land and skill needed to lay out a good system.
Warm Confinement has these additional advantages:
a. Use of a slotted floor eliminates cost of bedding and the associated labor.
b. A controlled environment usually improves feed efficiency and rate of gain.
c. Feed handling can be more easily mechanized in a non-freezing environment.
Disadvantages of confinement:
a. Greater first cost.
b. Higher property tax.
c. Limited research and experience with the system with few tested layouts and construction plans.

704-3 Beef Housing Requirement Factors:

	Open-Front Sheds	Sun Shades	Confined In Shed
Space per Animal	20 to 30 sq. ft.	30–40 sq. ft.	30–40 sq. ft.
Building Width	30 to 40 ft.	16–20 ft.	60–70 ft.

704-4 Beef Feed Lot Space Requirement Factors:

Type of Lot	Space Per Head Sq. Ft.
Paved	35–50
Partially Paved (Good Drainage)	100–150
Partially Paved (Average Drainage)	150–200
Unsurfaced (Good Drainage)	200–300
Unsurfaced (Average Drainage)	300–400

704-5 Beef Feed Bunk Space Requirements:

Feeding Method	Feeding Space Per Head (In.)
All animals fed at one time	20-24
3 or more feedings per day	12
Self-feeding grain	3–4
Self-feeding roughage	4–6

Fenceline bunk should be 30 inches wide. Mechanical or auger bunk should be 52 inches wide for feeding on both sides, and 60 inches wide for feeding separate rations on each side.

704-6 Feed Storage Requirements (*See Table 704-1; also Appendix "B"*).

704-7 Suggested Drylot Layouts are shown in Det. 704-1.
Note that the small unit and the larger, fan-shaped unit have mechanical feed bunks. The other has a fenceline bunk which must be filled with a self-unloading wagon or truck. A typical resting shed and feeding center is shown in 704-2. Other feed center layouts are shown by Det. 704-3.

704-8 Shades for Beef Cattle. Shades are a good investment where summer temperatures exceed 75° F. In Yuma, Arizona, the following results were obtained with beef cattle:

Types of Shade and Daily Gains

	Aluminum Roof	Straw Thatch	Double Snow Fence	No Shade
Heifers	1.83 lb.	1.69 lb.	1.52 lb.	1.28 lb.
Steers	2.00 lb.	1.77 lb.	1.77 lb.	1.64 lb.

Good shades increased gains by 1/2 lb. a day at El Central, Calif. Shades should be 12 ft. high.
Allow 35 to 40 sq. ft. of shade per animal.

704-9 Corral Design For Beef Feed Lots.
a. Wire or cable fences around corrals in areas of hot weather will provide maximum natural air circulation.
b. Water sprays in hot climates will also increase beef cattle rates of gain. Use coarse sprays, not fine mists.
c. Cooled drinking water is beneficial during hot weather.

103

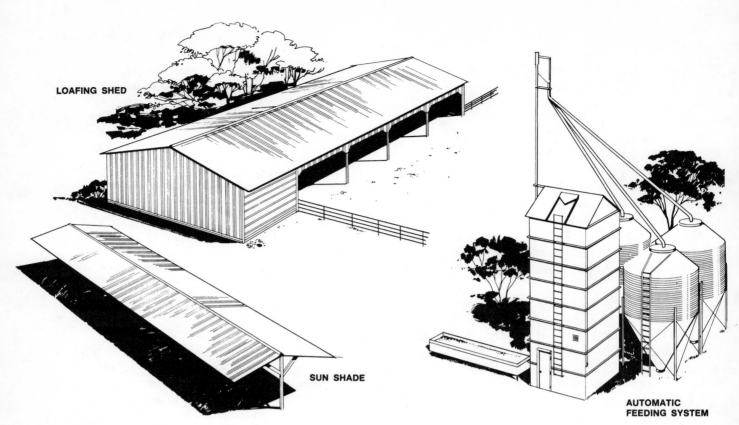

LOAFING SHED

SUN SHADE

AUTOMATIC
FEEDING SYSTEM

*Det. 704-1   Exterior Typical Feedlot Buildings and
Shade.*

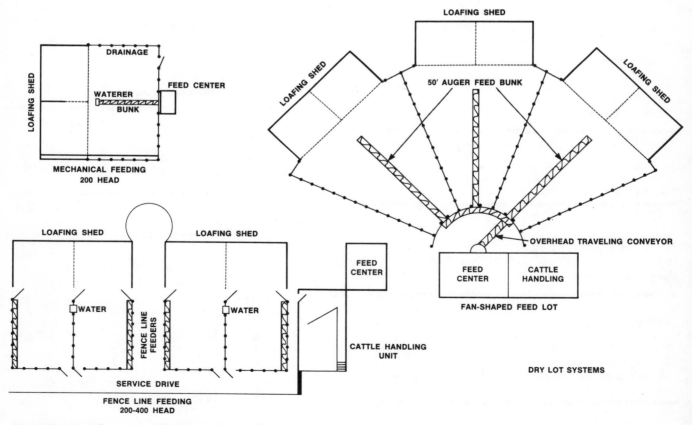

LOAFING SHED

DRAINAGE

WATERER

FEED CENTER

BUNK

MECHANICAL FEEDING
200 HEAD

LOAFING SHED

LOAFING SHED

50' AUGER FEED BUNK

LOAFING SHED

OVERHEAD TRAVELING CONVEYOR

FEED
CENTER

CATTLE
HANDLING

FAN-SHAPED FEED LOT

LOAFING SHED

LOAFING SHED

WATER

WATER

FENCE LINE FEEDERS

FEED
CENTER

CATTLE HANDLING
UNIT

SERVICE DRIVE

FENCE LINE FEEDING
200-400 HEAD

DRY LOT SYSTEMS

Det. 704-2   Blueprint of 3 Typical Feedlot Systems

COMPLETE RATIONS are mixed in metered amounts in the examples on this page. Delivery may be to a MECHANICAL BUNK or a WAGON or TRUCK.

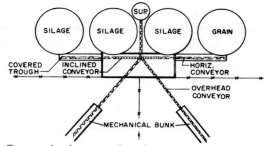

One swinging overhead conveyor can serve both bunks. Lot drainage may be a problem with this bunk arrangement.

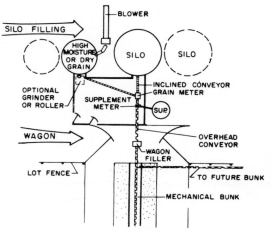

Good access and easy expansion are provided in this layout.

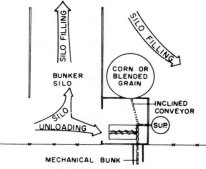

A live-bottom box, filled with a tractor scoop, permits mechanized feeding from a horizontal silo.

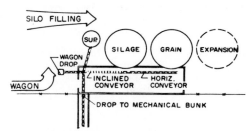

A convenient wagon drop can be added to many existing centers. Access to storages is good.

Det. 704-3   Feed Centers.

d.   Evaporative cooling is economical and feasible in hot dry climates.

705   Horse Housing.
(Extracted from Midwest Plan Service Handbook MWPS-15).

705-1   Site Selection
a.   The building site should be well drained, accessible, and have a slope of about 5'/100' away from the building in all directions to assure good surface drainage.

b.   In addition to room for the planned buildings, provide space for other planned facilities and areas, and for future expansion.

c.   Zoning regulations, building codes, sanitary regulations, deed restrictions, easements, and covenants may affect or limit the development and use of property at a specific location.

d.   Avoid sites that have serious drainage problems.

705-2   Space Requirements
Tables 705-2A and 705-2B list dimensions for basic facilities.

Table 705-2a Space Requirements for Horses in Buildings

	Dimensions of Stalls including Manger		
	Box Stall Size		Tie Stall Size
Mature Animal (Mare or Gelding)	10' × 10'	small	
	10' × 12'	medium	5' × 9'
	12' × 12'	large	5' × 12'
Brood Mare	12' × 12'	or larger	
Foal to 2-year old	10' × 10'	average	4-1/2' × 9'
	12' × 12'	large	5' × 9'
Stallion[1]	14' × 14'	or larger	
Pony	9' × 9'	average	3' × 6'

[1]Work stallions daily or provide a 2-4 acre paddock for exercise.

Table 705-2b Hay Manger and Grain Box Dimensions (dimensioning inside the stall)

	Hay Manger[1]	Dimensions[2]	Grain Box
All Mature Animals (Mares, Geldings, Brood Mares, Stallions)	30"–36"	Length	20"–24"
	38"–42"	Throat Height	38"–42"
	20"–24"	Width	12"–16"
	24"–30"	Depth	8"–12"
Foals and 2-year olds	24"–30"	Length	16"–20"
	32"–36"	Throat Height	32"–36"
	16"–20"	Width	10"–16"
	20"–24"	Depth	6"–8"
Ponies	24"	Length	18"
	32"	Throat Height	32"
	18"	Width	10"
	20"	Depth	6"–8"

[1]Wall corner hay racks are often used instead of mangers. Five feet is the usual distance between the floor and bottom of the rack. Many horsemen feed hay on the stall floor in both box and tie stalls and use a wall-mounted grain box in the corner of the stall.

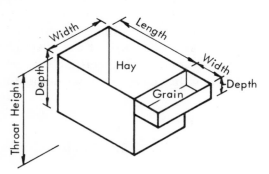

An open-front shelter is usually planned for 60 to 80 sq ft/1000 lbs of animals housed.

Minimum ceiling height is 8' for a horse, 12' for a horse and rider.

Doors are commonly:	width × height
Stalls	4' × 8'
Small wheeled equipment	10' × 10'
Horse and rider	12' × 12'
Large equipment, horse + rider	16' × 14'

A single heated water bowl will serve 8 to 10 horses.

Ceiling Height

Commonly used ceiling heights are 9'–10' and for riding areas 14'–16'.

Alleys

10' or wider litter and work alleys between stalls; a 6' litter alley when it is back of a single row of stalls; 4' minimum feed alleys and cross alleys.

705-3 Layouts for Box Stalls

The width of a structure for box stalls is determined by stall size and alley width. The most often used width increment is 12'. Clear distances inside stalls and alleys will then be about 11'-11'-6".

705-4 Layouts for Tie Stalls

The width of a structure for tie stalls is determined by stall length and alley width. If the building has both box stalls and tie stalls, the size of the box stalls usually determines barn width.

705-5 Feed Room

The feed room is seldom larger than a box stall. Plan storage for feed materials, equipment, and tools.

Provide at least 150 watts of light, at least two convenience outlets and a door at least 4' wide and equipped with a latch.

Provide space for feed storage: 1-3/4 lb of hay and 1 lb of grain per day per 100 lb of the horses' weight.

705-6 Tack Room

In larger stables the tack room has traditionally been the horseman's headquarters for essential equipment and activities associated with horse owners. In addition to storing riding equipment, it can be large enough to serve as office, service shop, and meeting and lounging room.

705-7 Floors

Packed or puddled rock-free clay on a well-drained base makes one of the best floors for stables. Wood plank stall floors or wood block floors on concrete are preferred by some but are difficult to keep dry and free of odors. Concrete floors are the least desirable. Raise the floor 8″–12″ above outside ground level. Use concrete floors in the wash area, feed room feed alleys, and tack room.

705-8 Windows

Provide an adjustable 2′ × 2′ window in each box. Put window sills at least 6′ above the stall floor. Protect all windows that can be reached by horses with welded wire or a steel grating.

705-9 Ventilation

Horses in mild or moderate climates are usually housed in uninsulated buildings. Wood or masonry sidewalls and tight sheathing under the roof are desirable.

In northern regions, insulated buildings and supplemental heat are more common. Heated barns are also used for show horses.

a. Provide a ventilating fan capacity of 100 cfm/1000 lb of animal weight for temperatures below 60° F outside. During extremely cold weather only about 1/4 of the fan capacity is needed. Set the thermostat at about 45° F.

b. Supplemental Heat. Supply heat to control moisture and maintain indoor temperatures above freezing when outside temperatures fall below about 15° F. The approximate supplemental heat needed can be determined by adding the "building heat loss" and the "ventilation heat loss."

"Building heat loss" (Btu/hr): Multiply the inside wall and ceiling areas (sq ft) by the indicated multiplier for the zone.

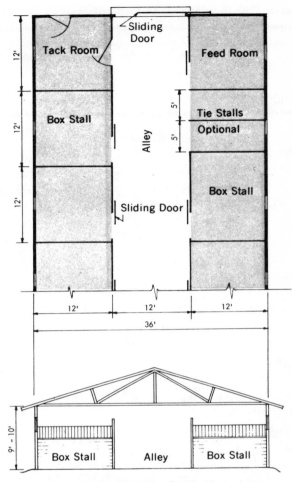

Two rows of stalls, center alley (inside service)

Fig. 705-3   Box Stall Layout.

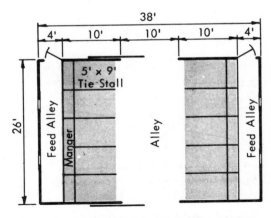

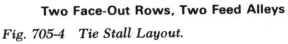

Two Face-Out Rows, Two Feed Alleys

Fig. 705-4   Tie Stall Layout.

Table 705-9. Heat loss multipliers

| | 35° F inside | | | 45°–50° F inside | | |
	cold	moderate	mild	cold	moderate	mild
Ceiling	2.4	2.8	2.9	3.0	3.7	4.2
Wall	3.9	3.8	3.9	5.0	5.0	5.5
Ventilation	3.0	2.4	1.9	3.9	3.2	2.7

"Ventilation heat loss" (Btu/hr): Multiply the weight of the animals by the multiplier for the appropriate climate. Ventilation head loss will increase about another 10% for each 5 cfm increase in ventilation rate over 100 cfm/1000 lb. at the following insulation levels:

Recommended Insulation		
Climate	Resistance (R)1	
Zone	Walls	Ceilings
Mild	9	12
Moderate	12	16
Cold	14	23

1Total of resistances of insulation, lining and siding, surfaces, and air spaces.

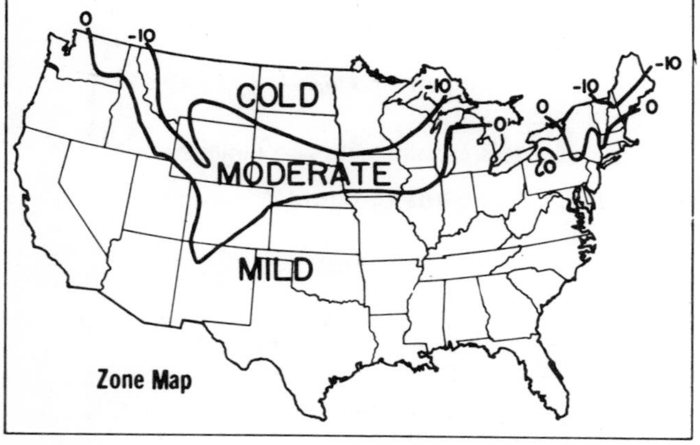

Zone Map

Fig. 705-9

706   Green House Facilities.

Green Houses must be designed to withstand the snow and wind loads of the local area and provide the space, light and environment required by the plants to be housed. Covering materials can be glass, rigid plastic or plastic films.

706-1   Glass-Covered Green Houses.
Glass Houses have been supplied by reputable commercial companies for many years. Structural and environmental requirements have been established, tried and accepted.

706-2   Plastic Green Houses. Although they may not replace glass houses, they have the following uses:
a.   As extra space beyond that of a permanent building.
b.   As temporary space for starting plant sets.
c.   As a seasonal unit for flowers or vegetables.
d.   As a hobby house for the home.

706-2.1   When designing heating units in the plastic green house assume a U-value of 0.69 Btu/(hr) (ft^2) (° F) for the double film wall with air space. This is an R-value of 1.45. Two air changes per hour should be provided during winter. Capacity for one air change per minute should be provided for summer weather.

706-3   Rigid-frame and reinforced plastics are being used some for green houses. The plant response appears satisfactory, since the glass fiber reinforced plastics have high light transmission qualities.

707   Storage Structures. Space, proper environment, handling facilities and structural strength must be provided (see also Chapter 10).

707-1   Grain Storage Bins for on the farm storage may be constructed with wood framing in accordance with Table 707-1.

707-2   Pole Structures may be used for grain and fertilizer storage if adequate strength is provided. Graph 707-1 provides a graphical solution for determining pole spacing.

707-3   Tower silo capacities for corn and grass silage storage may be determined from Appendix B.

Table 707-1 Sizes of Studs, Rods, and Walers for Grain Storage Bins.

| Grain Depth | Studs | Ties—Distance From Top | | | Walers | | | Bin Lining Plywood |
		Top	2nd	Bottom Row	Top	2nd	3rd	
		1/2″ Rod 4′ o.c.						
12′	2″ × 6″—12″ o.c.							3/8″
	2″ × 8″—18″ o.c.	9′			4″ × 6″			3/8″
14′	2″ × 6″—12″ o.c.							3/8″
	2″ × 8″—18″ o.c.	9′			4″ × 6″			3/8″
16′	2″ × 6″—12″ o.c.							3/8″
	2″ × 8″—18″ o.c.	8′	12′		4″ × 6″	4″ × 6″		1/2″
		5/8″ Rod 4′ o.c.						
16′	2″ × 8″—12″ o.c.							3/8″
	2″ × 10″—18″ o.c.	11′			6″ × 6″			1/2″
18′	2″ × 8″—16″ o.c.	10′	14′		4″ × 6″	6″ × 6″		1/2″
20′	2″ × 8″—12″ o.c.							1/2″
	2″ × 10″—18″ o.c.	11′	16′		6″ × 6″	6″ × 6″		5/8″
24′	2″ × 6″—12″ o.c.							5/8″
	2″ × 8″—18″ o.c.	9′	14′	19′	4″ × 6″	6″ × 6″	6″ × 6″	3/4″

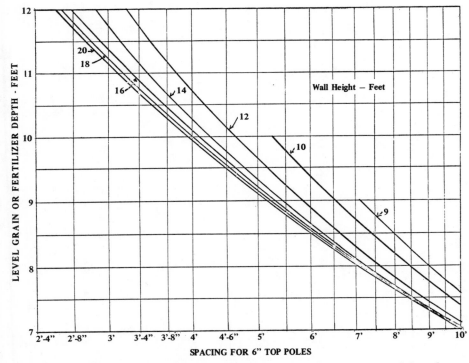

This chart may be used to help estimate the cost of grain and fertilizer bins. It assumes that the poles are held at the top of the wall by a rafter or a tie-rod. For heaped bins the pole spacing may be only half the chart values. For deeper bins larger poles and/or intermediate tie-rods may be used.

Graph 707-1 Pole Spacing for Grain & Fertilizer Bins

Chapter 8

CONTROLLED ENVIRONMENTAL HOUSING.

by MERLE L. ESMAY, Ph.D.
Professor of Agricultural Engineering
Michigan State University

800 Controlled Environmental Housing refers to structures designed to modify extreme climatic conditions. Undesirable large fluctuations in the following controllable environmental factors should be minimized within the limitations of economics:
a. Dry-bulb temperature.
b. Wet-bulb temperature *(humidity)*.
c. Air velocities *(drafts and wind)*.
d. Solar radiation *(sun heat)*.
e. Evaporation of water.
f. Air composition; O_2, CO_2, odors.

800-1 Structures May Provide the Optimum Controlled environment in the following ways:
a. For Temperature Control:
  1. Building insulation.
  2. Mechanical heating or cooling
  3. Air velocity *(convective cooling)*.
  4. Ventilation air exchange control.
  5. Utilization, absorption or reflection of solar radiation.
  6. Evaporative cooling.
  7. Maximum utilization of animal or bird heat.
b. For Humidity control in cold weather:
  1. Adequate ventilation air exchange.
  2. Sufficient heat for evaporating excess moisture for removal by ventilation.
  3. Minimize water in building and wetted surfaces.
c. For Air Velocities:
  1. Well distributed cold air when brought into the building during winter weather.
  2. High velocities for convective cooling in hot weather may be created with fans and/or by opening sidewalls for natural winds.

d. For Solar Heat:
  1. Reflective *(white)* roofing materials along with roof and/or ceiling insulation for minimizing heat transfer in summer.
  2. Absorptive *(black)* roofing materials and solar *(insulated glass)* windows on side-walls oriented for maximizing solar heat utilization in winter.
e. For Evaporation of Water:
  1. A continually wetted fibrous pad through which outside air is drawn into the building may be used for evaporative cooling. This works well in climates that are hot and dry such as southwestern U.S.A.
  2. Evaporation must be used to carry excess respired moisture and waste liquids from live-stock and poultry structures during winter as well as summer.
f. For Air Purification:
  1. Sufficient fresh air must be brought into building and the stale air must be removed.
  2. Minimization of toxic gas formation from accumulated animal wastes is necessary in buildings.

800-2 Optimum Environmental Conditions must be provided for maximum production by poultry and livestock. Today, with genetically superior animals and birds and scientifically balanced feed rations, it is only with an optimum environment that their genetic potential and maximum feed conversion can be realized. Graph 800-1 illustrates schematically the effect temperature can have on production.

See Chapter 7 for specific temperature require-

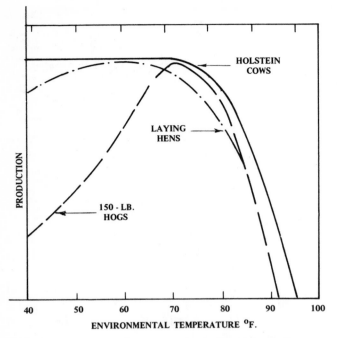

Graph 800-1 A Schematic Diagram of the Influence of Environmental Temperature of Animal Production Trends (from Bond of U. of Calif.).

ments for each type of poultry and livestock housing.

801-1 Ventilation Air Exchange
a. Must provide adequate fresh air at all times.
b. Must remove toxic gases. *(Carbon dioxide, ammonia, methane and others).*
c. Must remove excess moisture in winter. *(A minimum requirement is the removal of moisture vaporized directly by birds or animals.)*
d. Must remove excess heat in summer to minimize a temperature rise in the structure. A maximum conversion of sensible heat* to latent heat* by evaporization of moisture in the house is beneficial in avoiding temperature build-up.
e. During summer weather a minimum of one air change per minute is required in all full poultry and livestock housing to minimize temperature build-up and heat stress on housed birds or animals.

*Note: Sensible heat is the heat that affects the temperature of the air and surroundings and latent heat is heat consumed in vaporizing water.

f. During winter weather, minimum air flow may be only 1/25th of summer air flow. This is in the range of two air changes per hour or one quarter cfm/sq. ft. of floor area.
g. Air exchange is limited in cold weather by the heat available from the housed animals or birds, or by the economics of providing artificial supplemental heat. Graphs 800-2, 800-3, and 800-4 show heat requirements for various rates of airflow during cold weather while the inside condition is kept at 50° F. and 80%. Graph 800-5 shows the air exchange necessary to remove one pound of water.
h. Heat and moisture produced by animals are presented in Graphs 800-6 through 800-10. Not all heat produced by animals is available for warming air and evaporating moisture as some is lost through walls and ceilings.

801-1.1 Temperature Control:
a. Heat loss through the exposed surfaces of the house must be accounted for first when designing ventilation systems.
b. The overall heat transfer coefficient U is calculated from the insulation values of the materials in the exposed walls, ceiling and/or roof. R is the resistance or insulation value of materials. $R = 1/U = r_1 + r_2 + r_3$ etc. The heat loss units of $U = Btu/(hr)(FT^2)(°F.)$ and R has the reciprocal units of this. These insulation R-values may be obtained from Table 800.

Once the overall R-value is calculated, the total heat loss for a given wall or ceiling may be calculated from the equation *(See Det. 800-11 for overall R-values of wall sections)*

$Q = A(t_i - t_o)/R$

Where $Q = A(t_i - t_o)/R$
Q = heat loss in Btu/hour.
R = Total resistance or insulation.
A = Area of wall or ceiling in square feet.
t_i = Inside temperature in °F.
t_o = Outside temperature in °F.
Once having design inside and outside temperatures and the wall and ceiling insulation values and areas, total heat loss through the exposed surfaces may be calculated. This heat loss subtracted from the total heat produced gives the

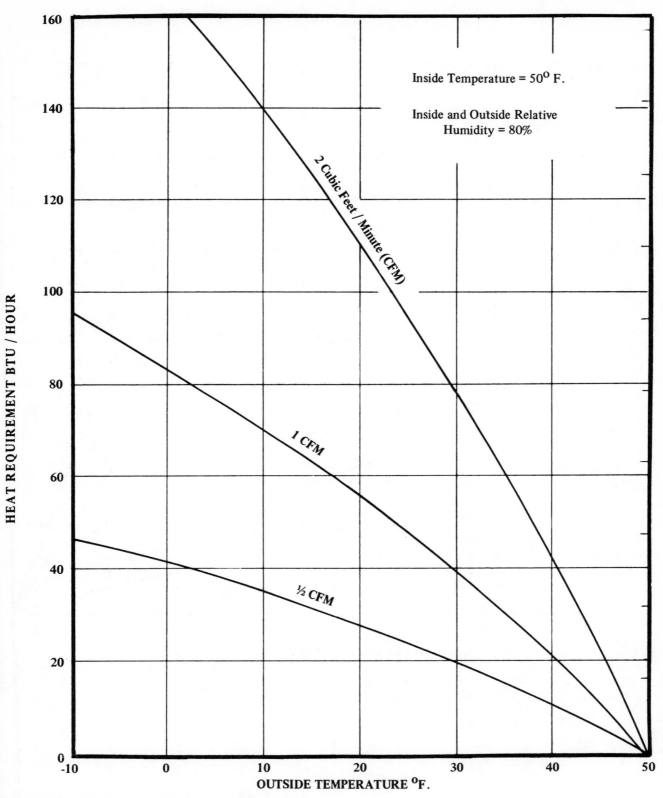

*Graph 800-2 Heat Required Per Hour for Low
Rates of Ventilation During Winter Operations.*

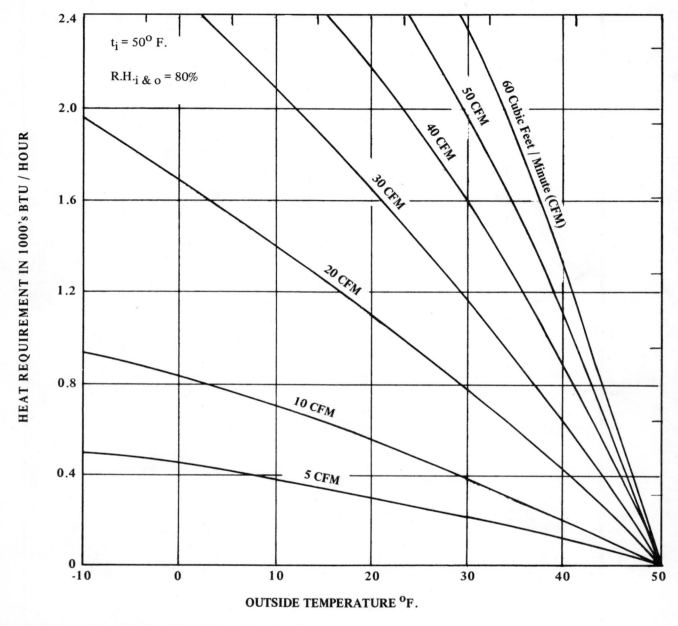

Graph 800-3 Heat Required Per Hour for Ventilation Air Exchange at Various Outside Temperatures.

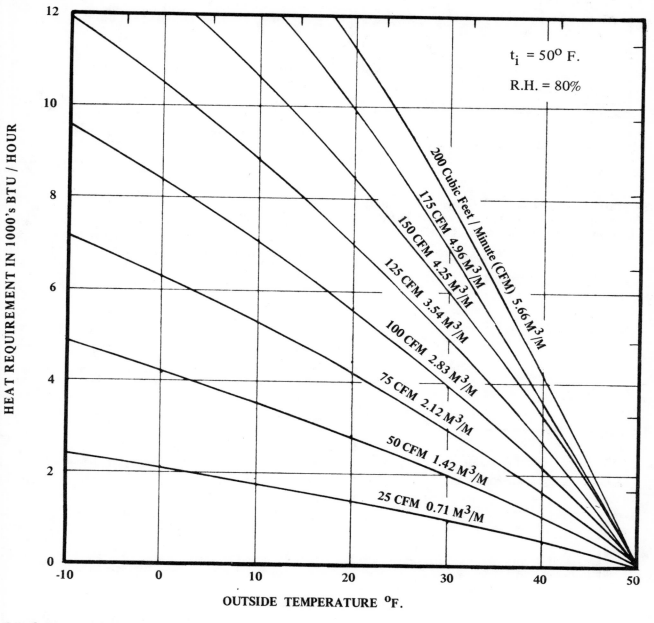

Graph 800-4   *Heat Required Per Hour for Ventilation Air Exchange for Cattle at Various Outside Temperatures.*

115

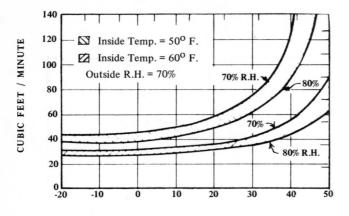

Graph 800-5 Air Exchange Required to Remove One Pound of Water Vapor Per Hour With Different Outside Temperature Conditions. (Dale)

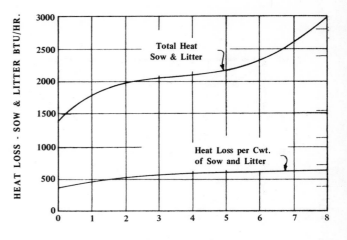

Graph 800-6 Total Heat Loss from Sow and Litter During First Weeks. Litters Averaged 6 Pigs. Temperature from 60–80° F. (15.5–26.6° C.) Sows weighed 335, 382 and 390 Lbs. (Adapted from Bond).

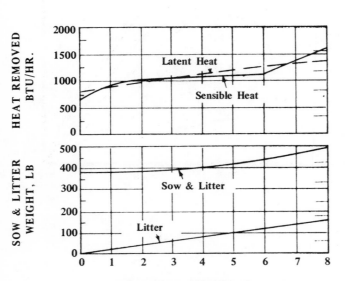

Graph 800-7 Building Sensible and Latent Heat, and Animal Weight for Sows and Litters. (Solid concrete floor, scraped daily, no bedding used; average of observations for three sows and litters). (Adapted from Bond).

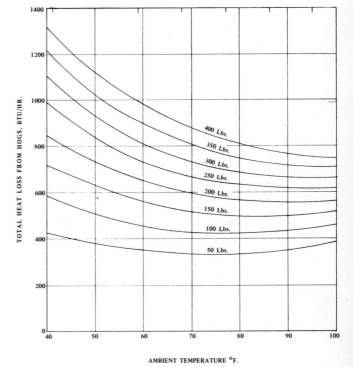

Graph 800-8 Heat Production of Growing, Fattening and Mature Swine. Air Velocity 20 to 30 FPM. Relative humidity 50%, Air and Surface Temperatures Were the Same. (Adapted from Bond).

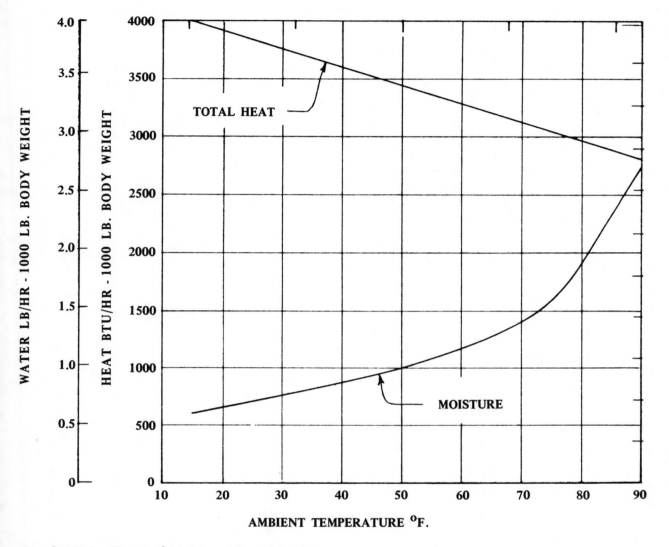

Graph 800-9   Heat and Moisture Dissipation Rates by Stanchioned Dairy Cows, Including Moisture Evaporation from Stall Surfaces Not Including Heat from Lights, Men or Equipment. Data were Taken at 55 to 70 Percent Relative Humidity, Except the 90° F. Points. (From Yeck)

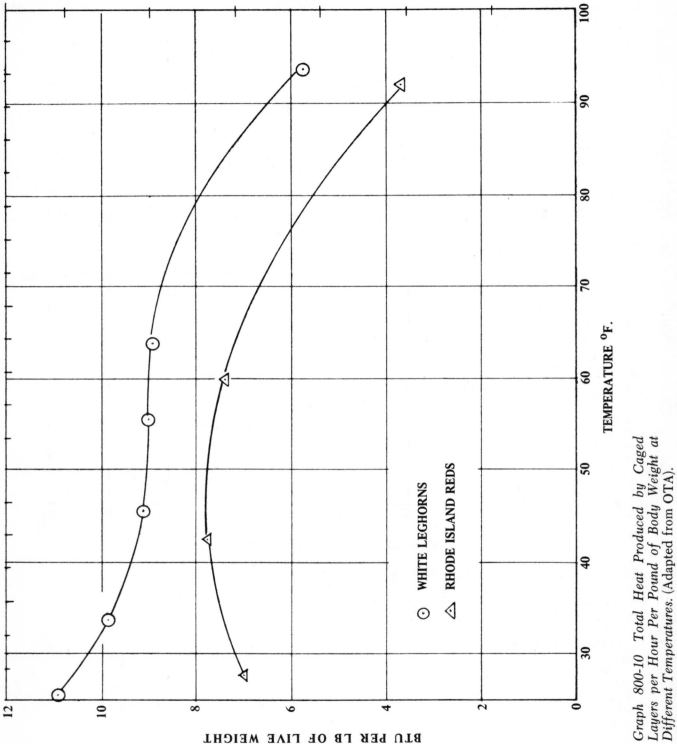

Graph 800-10 Total Heat Produced by Caged Layers per Hour Per Pound of Body Weight at Different Temperatures. (Adapted from OTA).

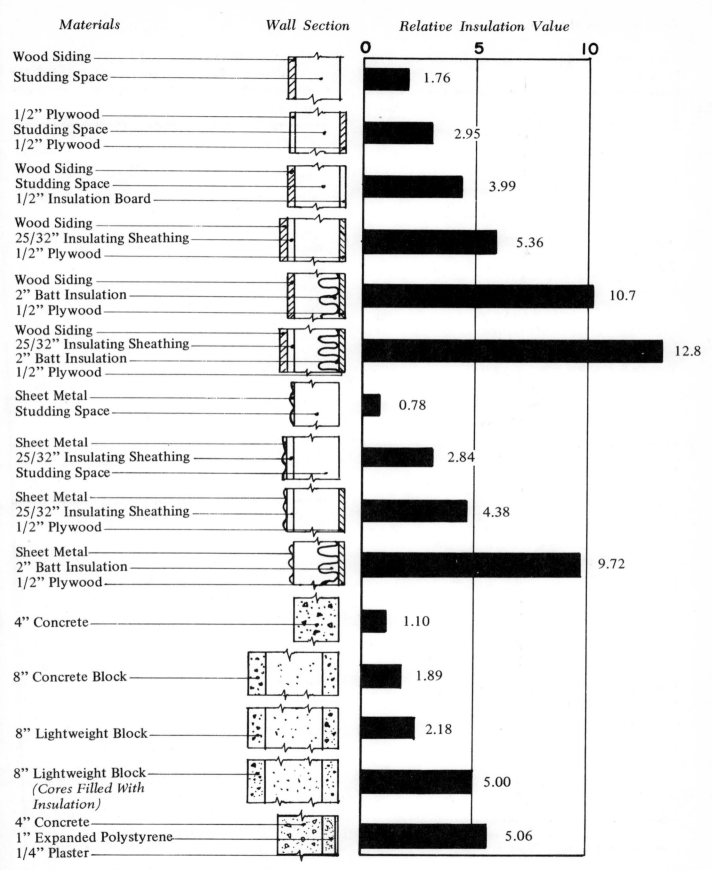

Materials	Wall Section	Relative Insulation Value

Wood Siding — 1.76
Studding Space

1/2" Plywood — 2.95
Studding Space
1/2" Plywood

Wood Siding — 3.99
Studding Space
1/2" Insulation Board

Wood Siding — 5.36
25/32" Insulating Sheathing
1/2" Plywood

Wood Siding — 10.7
2" Batt Insulation
1/2" Plywood

Wood Siding — 12.8
25/32" Insulating Sheathing
2" Batt Insulation
1/2" Plywood

Sheet Metal — 0.78
Studding Space

Sheet Metal — 2.84
25/32" Insulating Sheathing
Studding Space

Sheet Metal — 4.38
25/32" Insulating Sheathing
1/2" Plywood

Sheet Metal — 9.72
2" Batt Insulation
1/2" Plywood

4" Concrete — 1.10

8" Concrete Block — 1.89

8" Lightweight Block — 2.18

8" Lightweight Block — 5.00
(Cores Filled With Insulation)

4" Concrete — 5.06
1" Expanded Polystyrene
1/4" Plaster

Det. 800-11   Relative Insulation Values of Common Wall Sections for Livestock Shelters.

Table 800 R-values of Various Insulating Materials.

Material—Thickness—Density	R-Value
Plywood 1/2″ *(34 lb./cu. ft.)*	0.63
Wood—Fir or Pine sheathing 25/32″	0.98
Asbestos—cement board 1/8″	0.03
Gypsum or Plastic Lath 1/2″ *(50 lb./cu. ft.)*	0.45
Wood Fiber Board 1″ *(31 lb./cu. ft.)*	2.00
Mineral Wool Blanket Fibrous form, processed from rock, slag or glass, 1″	
Rigid polystyrene *(extruded)* 1″ *(2.2 lb./cu. ft.)* @ 0° F. = 5.88, @ 75° F. = 5.00	
Rigid polystyrene *(extruded)* 1″ *(1.8 lb./cu. ft.)* @ 0° F. = 4.77, @ 75° F. = 4.00	
Rigid polystyrene *(molded beads)* 1″ *(1.0 lb./cu. ft.)* @ 0° F. = 4.17, @ 75° F. = 3.57	
Polyurethane *(aged board stock)* 1″ *(1.5 to 2.5 lb./cu. ft.)* @ 0° F. = 5.55, @ 75° F. = 6.25	
Mineral Wool, fill type, 1″ *(2.0-5.0 lb./cu. ft.)*	3.33
Vermiculite *(expanded)* 1″ *(7.0 lb./cu. ft.)*	2.08
Concrete, stone aggregate, 1″ *(140 lb./cu. ft.)*	0.08
Concrete Blocks, stone aggregate, 8″	1.11
Concrete Blocks, light weight aggregate, 8″	2.00
Air space *(3/4 to 4 in.)*	1.00
Air space with one reflective surface	2.00
Air space with two reflective surfaces	2.50
Outside surface film *(15 mph wind)*	0.17
Inside surface film	0.68

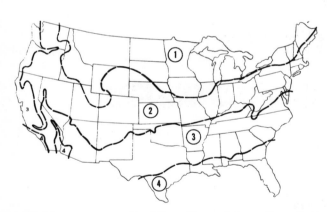

Det. 801-2 Farm Building-Zone Map, Based on January Temperatures.

	Insulation R-values	
	Walls	Ceiling
Zone 1	8	12
Zone 2	6	10
Zone 3	4	8
Zone 4	4	8

The fairly high ceiling insulation in the warmer zones is for protection from sun radiation heat.

Table 800-2 Recommended Ventilation Rates for Poultry and Livestock in Closed, Insulated, Confinement Housing. In cubic feet per minute *(cfm)* per bird or animal:

Animals or Birds Housed	At Minimum Cold Temperature (Fig. 800-17)	At Average Jan. Temperature (Fig. 800-15)	Summer Minimum Ventilation*
Layers (Light)	1/4	1/2	6
Layers (Heavy)	1/3	2/3	8
Broilers	1/10	1/4	5
Pullets	1/10	1/4	5
Turkey Breeders	3/4	2	25
Turkey, Hens	1/2	1-1/2	20
Turkey, Toms	1/2	2	25
Sow and Litter	10	30	500
Hog @ 200 lbs.	5	20	50
Hog @ 50 lbs.	1	5	25
Dairy Cow @ 1000 lbs.	20	50	600
Dairy Calf @ 100 lbs.	5	10	100
Beef Animal @ 1000 lbs.	25	50	500
Beef Animal @ 500 lbs.	15	30	300
Beef Calf @ 100 lbs.	5	10	100
Sheep @ 200 lbs.	5	20	50
Sheep @ 50 lbs.	1	5	25

*Or at least one air change per minute.

heat available for heating ventilation air and evaporating moisture.

Insulation recommendations are regional in accordance with Det. 801-2 and the four zones. Recommended minimum R-values are indicated.

801-2 Design Temperature for Cold Weather. The average temperature for the month of January can be used when designing for adult bird and animal housing. All vaporized moisture from birds or animals must be removable by ventilation air at this coldest monthly average temperature. Detail 801·2.1 gives the average daily temperature for the month of January in the United States. For example, in lower Michigan the design temperature is 20° F. At this temperature outside and 50 to 55° F. inside at 80% relative humidity, 1/2 cfm per laying hen will remove all vaporized moisture. At the extreme low design temperature, as shown by Det. 801-2.2, one-half of the possible airflow at the average design temperature should be provided to remove moisture directly vaporized by hens. For laying hens this would be 1/4 cfm per bird. One fan in the house should be sized to provide this on a continuous basis.

801-3 Fan and Air Exchange Control:
Each fan must have a separate thermostat. Det. 801-3 shows a possible fan control system. One small fan, sized to provide the minimum ventilation for laying hens of 1/4 cfm each is set thermostatically to shut off only at the lowest desirable temperature in the house. Two large fans are set to provide additional cold weather ventilation when warmer weather permits. The other two fans turn on only during hot weather to provide maximum air exchange.

801-4 Example Air Exchange Calculation for Winter Operation.
Assume a poultry house as shown in Det. 801-3 *(8000 sq. ft. of floor space for 10,000 5-lb. laying hens).* Let it also be assumed that it is located in zone 1 *(Central Iowa)* and has wall insulation of R = 8 and ceiling insulation of R = 10. Solution as Follows:
a. Heat available from birds at 55° F. *(Graph 800-10)* 9 Btu/lb. or 5 × 9 = 45 Btu/bird.
    Total Heat = 45 × 10,000 = 450,000 Btu/hr.
b. Heat loss through walls and ceiling at average outside Jan. Temp. and Min. Temp. Details 801-2.1 and 801-2.2.
    Outside Temperatures = 20° F. and 0° F.
    R_1 for walls = 8
    R_2 for ceiling = 10
    A_1 for walls = [40 + 40 + 200 + 200] × 8
       = 3840 ft.^{2}
    A_2 for ceiling = 40 × 200 = 8000 ft.^{2}
    From Par. 801-1

$$A_1/R_1 = \frac{3840}{8} = q_1 = 480 \text{ Btu}$$

$$A_2/R_2 = \frac{8000}{10} = q_2 = 800 \text{ Btu}$$

Total Q   = 1280 Btu/°F.
Total Area = 11840 ft.^{2}

$$U_{av} \text{ or } 1/R_{av} = \frac{1280}{11840} = .108 \text{ Btu/}$$
$$(\text{ft}^2)(\text{hr})(° \text{ F})$$
$$R_{av} = 1/U_{av} = \frac{1}{.108} = 9.25$$

c. Heat Loss For 35° F. and 55° F.
    Temperature Differences between inside and outside are:

$$Q \, 35° \text{ F.} = \frac{11840}{9.25} \, (35) = 44800 \text{ Btu}$$

$$Q \, 55° \text{ F.} = \frac{11840}{9.25} \, (55) = 70400 \text{ Btu}$$

d. Heat available for heating ventilation air = total heat available minus heat loss through walls and ceiling.
    At outside 20° F. = 450,000 − 44,800 = 405,200 Btu
    At outside 0° F. = 450,000 − 70,400 = 379,600 Btu
    On a per bird basis this is
    At 20° F. 405,200/10,000 = 40.52 Btu/bird
    At 0° F. 379,600/10,000 = 37.96 Btu/bird.
e. Ventilation air possible *(Fig. 800-2)*
    At 20° F. outside = .75 cfm/bird
    At 0° F. outside = .45 cfm/bird.
f. Conclusion: This amount of ventilation air possible is above the recommended rates of Table 800-2, thus satisfactory.

801-5 The mechanized ventilation system consists of three principle parts:
a. Two or more electrically-powered fans to move air in or out of building.
b. Suitable devices to automatically control fan operation and thus temperature *(See Detail 801-3).*
c. Adjustable openings to admit or exhaust the air from the building.

801-5.1 Certain General Design Criteria have been established for ventilation systems:
a. Each fan or pair of fans should have a separate thermostat so the fans may be set to provide suitable air flow from minimum to maximum required depending on climatic conditions.

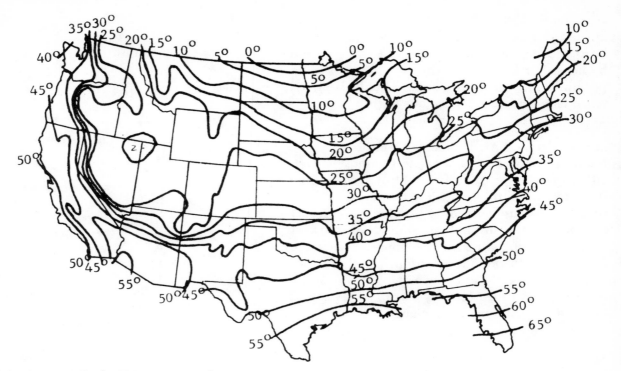

Det. 801-2.1   Average Daily Temperatures for January in the United States. (U.S. Weather Bureau)

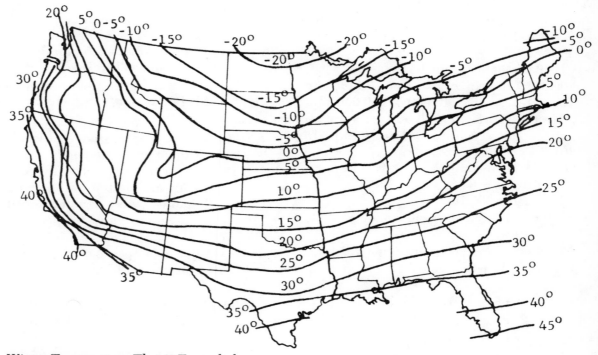

Det. 801-2.2   Winter Temperature That is Exceeded Less than 2-1/2% of the Time in the United States. (ASHRAE Guide)

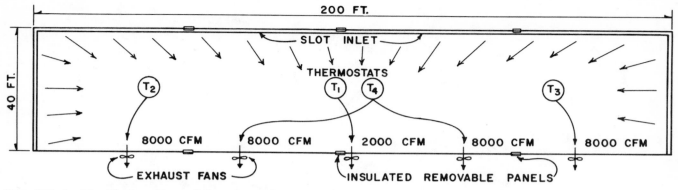

Det. 801-3   Ventilation Control System.

b. There should be continuous positive flow of air at all times. The minimum cold-weather air flow should thus be continuous.

c. An exhaust ventilation system with fans removing air from the building requires no ducts and is recommended for winter time operation.

d. The exhaust ventilation system with fans on one side wall and the slot-inlet in the opposite wall is satisfactory for buildings up to 40 ft. in width *(See Details 801-4.1 and 801-4.2).*

e. Continuous operation of slot-inlet designed to take air from the attic is recommended in winter. The slot-inlet should be adjusted down to 1/2″ in width and direct air horizontally below the ceiling.

f. Summer air-inlet should be not less than 6 inches wide and draw air over the plate directly from outside *(Summer inlet air should not be drawn directly from the attic under any circumstances).* Summer inlet air should be directed towards the floor for maximum effectiveness.

g. Summer air movement for confined housing, where there is a high density of animals such as a swine finishing house may use natural winds by providing large openings along each sidewall.

h. Buildings wider than 40 ft. must provide an inlet or outlet for air in the center of the building. Exhaust fans may be provided in both sidewalls with a continuous air inlet in the center. With

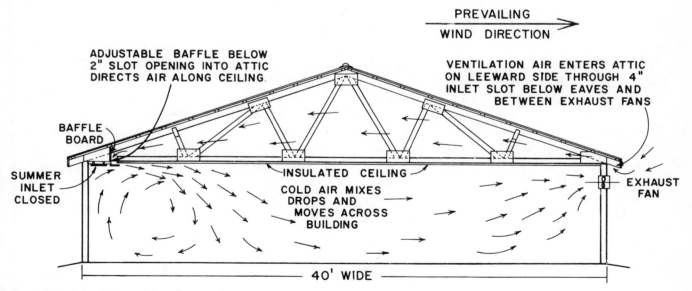

Det. 801-4.1   Winter Ventilation System.

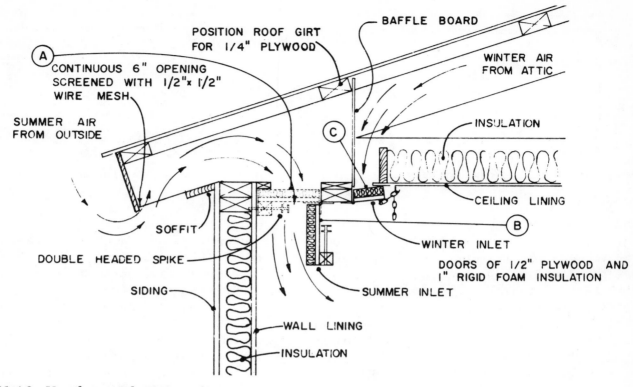

Det. 801-4.2   Ventilation Inlet System for Window-less Buildings.

an insulated horizontal ceiling, which is recommended, the summer inlet must bring air down through the attic but not out of it as the attic air is superheated. Exhaust outlet fans may be provided in the center of a wide building with inlets in both outside walls. Ceiling or roof fans are inconvenient to maintain, however.

i.   Slot inlets should never be narrowed enough to force inlet air velocities above 500 ft/min. This increases the pressure difference between inside and outside of house undesirably and cuts down on air delivery capability of the fans. Pressure difference should not be above 0.06 inches of water.

j.   Fans should be selected for dependability, durability, air delivery and economy. Fans should be certified as to air delivery capacities by AMCA. Large fans of the 10,000 cfm range of air delivery should be used in large buildings. Smaller fans are more expensive to purchase and operate on the basis of each cfm of air delivered.

k.   Pressure ventilation systems have an advantage in that the fans handle only clean air. The pressure system is used successfully in mild climates. The incoming air is forced in through centrally located ceiling openings with horizontally mounted pressure fans. A horizontally mounted baffle board is placed below each fan to deflect the air horizontally in all directions. This system is particularly adapted for houses with fairly open walls in summer and untight walls in winter.

Chapter 9

LIVESTOCK WASTE MANAGEMENT.

by ARTHUR J. MUEHLING

*Associate Professor and
Farm Buildings Extension Specialist,
Agricultural Engineering Department
University of Illinois*

900 Livestock Waste Management

900-1 Disposing of livestock wastes has rapidly become a major problem because of the rapid trend toward high density animal population in confinement housing and total drylot feeding. Livestock wastes must be disposed of in such a way that the health, safety, and sanitation of the public and livestock is maintained.

900-2 Recent public interest and legislation has focused much attention on the handling of livestock wastes and its contribution to water pollution. Increased attention in this area will be followed by the passage of stronger legislation in many states.

900-3 Livestock producers must take positive steps to satisfactorily handle the wastes on their farm. State Public Health personnel have been forced to investigate individual waste handling systems because of formal complaints from neighbors. Every producer must constantly be aware of his responsibilities to his neighbors and do all he can to minimize odors and pollution.

901 Amounts and Concentrations

901-1 The amounts of manure by different types of livestock are shown in Table 901-1A. Table 901-1B will help calculate volume capacities required. The properties of confined livestock wastes are given in Table 901-1C.

901-3 *Concentrations* of livestock wastes are very high. Table 901-3 shows the average BOD concentrations for different types of wastes. Undiluted livestock wastes have a BOD concentration

Table 901-1a Approximate Daily Manure Production (Midwest Plan Service)

Animal	Cu. Ft. per day (Solids and liquid)	Percent Water	Gallons per day
1000 lb. horse	3/4	65	5 1/2
1000 lb. cow	1 1/2	80–90	11
1000 lb. steer	1	70	7 1/2
10 head of sheep	1/2	75	5
10 head of hogs, 50 lbs.	2/3	75	5
10 head of hogs, 100 lbs.	1 1/3	75	10
10 head of hogs, 150 lbs.	2 1/4	75	17
10 head of hogs, 200 lbs.	2 3/4	75	20 1/2
10 head of hogs, 250 lbs.	3 1/2	75	26
Bred Sows	1/8	75	1
Lactating Sows	1/2	75	3.5
1000—5 lb. layer	3	55–75	22 1/2

Table 901-1b Liquid Manure Capacity Conversion Guides

Volume *(Cu. Ft.)* = Length *(ft.)* × width *(ft.)* × depth *(ft.)*
1 Cu. Ft. = 7.5 gal.
1 Gal. = 8.3 lbs
1 Cu. Ft. = 62.5 lbs.
1 Ton = 32 Cu. Ft.
1 Cu. Yd. = 27 Cu. Ft.

Table 901-1c Values for Manure Production and Properties of Confined Livestock per 1,000 Pounds Live Weight

	Dairy cattle	Beef cattle	Hens	Pigs	Sheep
Raw manure (RM), lb. per day	88	60	59	50	37
Total solids (TS), lb. per day	9	6	17.4	7.2	8.4
Total solids, percent RM	10	10	30	14.4	22.7
Volatile solids (VS), lb. per day	7.2	4.8	12.9	5.9	6.9
Volatile solids, percent TS	80	80	74	82	82
BOD_5, lb. per day	1.7	1.5	4.4	2.1	.7
BOD_5, lb. per lb. VS	.233	.252	.338	.363	.101
BOD_5 per COD, percent	16	17	28	33	8
Nitrogen, percent TS	4	7.8	5.7	5.6	4
Phosphoric acid, percent TS	1.1	1.2	4.6	2.5	1.4
Potassium, percent TS	1.7	1.8	2.1	1.4	2.9

Table 901-3 Typical BOD Concentrations for Wastes

Type of Waste	Biochemical Oxygen Demand (BOD), mg./liter
Concentrated livestock wastes	35,000
Runoff from concentrated feedlot	1,000
Anaerobic lagoon effluent	700
Oxidation ditch effluent	150
Untreated municipal sewage	250
Treated municipal sewage (after secondary treatment)	20

over 100 times greater than the BOD of untreated municipal sewage. These very high concentrations usually make it uneconomical and unrealistic to directly apply municipal sewage treatment practices to the treatment of livestock wastes. Recent effluent standards almost eliminate the possibility of adequately treating livestock wastes so the effluent can be returned to a natural watercourse.

902 Methods of Handling Livestock Waste

902-1 Solid—Scrape floors and lots and handle as solid.
a. Stockpile and haul with conventional spreader (most common).
b. Composting (limited application).
c. Dehydration (costly with limited market for by-product).
d. Incineration (costly).

902-2 Liquid—Wash and scrape floors or use slotted floors and handle as liquid.
a. Haul to the field.
  1. Haul with tank wagon and spread on land (most common).
  2. Place in plow furrow and cover (controls odors in the field).
b. Aerobic treatment.
  1. Oxidation ponds.
  2. Aerated lagoons.
  3. Oxidation ditch.
c. Anaerobic treatment.
  1. Anaerobic lagoons.
  2. Septic tanks.
  3. Anaerobic digester.
d. Combination.
  1. Haul solids and let liquids run into lagoon (common with large unit).
  2. Use Oxidation ditch and let overflow run into lagoon.
e. Pump through irrigation system.
  1. Spread with sprinkler nozzle (must dilute to prevent burning crops).
  2. Run down crop rows.

903 Aerobic Treatment

Aerobic treatment requires free oxygen and makes livestock wastes odorless. This method is not widely accepted by livestock producers because of the costs involved. The main purpose of treating municipal waste is to reduce the amounts of suspended solids, bacteria, and oxygen-demanding material to an acceptable level for discharging waste water into streams and lakes. It does not seem economically feasible to treat livestock wastes to have an effluent acceptable for discharging into streams and lakes. Treatment for odor control is the main objective. Aerobic lagoons may be divided into two classifications, depending on method of aeration: oxidation ponds (naturally aerated lagoons) and aerated lagoons (mechanically aerated lagoons).

903-1 *Oxidation ponds* are usually a shallow basin 3 to 5 ft. deep. Loadings of 30 to 45 pounds of BOD per surface acre per day are generally acceptable in the mid-latitudes of the United States. Recommended sizes for oxidation ponds for livestock are given in Table 903-1 (assuming there is no effluent).

Because of the large surface area required, oxidation ponds have not found favor with livestock producers. Their use has been essentially limited to receiving effluent from anaerobic lagoons, oxidation ditches, and other treatment units.

903-2 *Aerated lagoons* have a mechanical device that beats or blows air into the water with a portion

Table 903-1   Capacities of Oxidation Ponds for Livestock Wastes[a]

	BOD (pounds per day)	Oxidation pond[b] surface area (square feet per animal)	Oxidation pond[c] volume (cubic feet per animal)
Dairy Cow (1400 pounds)	2.4	2,320	9,280
Beef Animal (800 pounds)	1.2	1,160	4,640
Swine (100 pounds)	0.21	204	816
Poultry (4 pounds)	0.0176	17	68

[a]Assuming all the manure goes to the facility at a uniform rate, corrections to be made for other situations and for other animal sizes.
[b]Based on 45 pounds daily BOD per surface acre.
[c]Based on 4-foot depth.

of the oxygen being dissolved. Because the lagoon is not dependent on wind or algae for the oxygen supply, the surface area can be made smaller than that of the oxidation pond and the depth can be greater, which reduces temperature fluctuations.

A mechanically aerated lagoon should be aerated continuously. Floating aerators (Detail 903-2) appear to be satisfactory, but other schemes such as compressed air entering through diffusers (per-

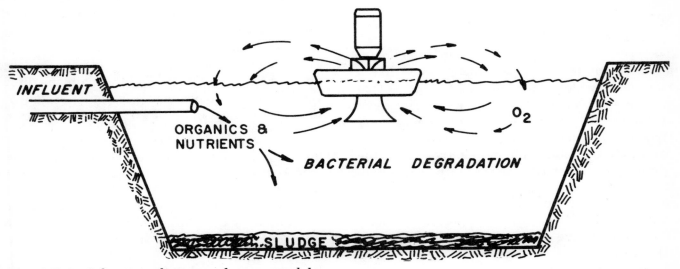

INFLUENT

ORGANICS & NUTRIENTS

BACTERIAL DEGRADATION

O₂

SLUDGE

Det. 903-2   Schematic diagram of an aerated lagoon with a floating surface aerator. (D. L. Day, University of Illinois)

Table 903-2   Aerated Lagoons for Livestock Wastes for Long Term Storage[a]

	Manure[b] produced (cubic feet per day)	BOD produced (pounds per day)	Pond[c] volume (cubic feet per animal)	Aerator[d] power (animals per horsepower)
Dairy Cow (1400 lbs.)	1.96	2.4	1,760	17
Beef Animal (800 lbs.)	.76	1.2	680	33
Swine (100 lbs.)	.078	.21	70	191
Poultry (4 lbs.)	.00375	.0176	3.4	2,270

[a] Assuming that all the manure goes to the pond at a uniform rate and is aerated continuously. Corrections to be made for other situations and for other animal sizes.

[b] Excrement only.

[c] Based on 900 times daily excrement.

[d] Based on an aerator output of 2.5 pounds of oxygen per horsepower hour supplying oxygen equal to 1.5 times the daily BOD produced.

forated pipes), rotating aerators, and rotary blowers may also work satisfactorily.

The rate of decomposition is slowed as the temperature decreases and is greatly reduced below 40° F. It appears that little decomposition is accomplished by operating the unit in cold weather. Start the aerator as soon as the temperature warms up in the Spring. Some objectionable odors can be expected during the start-up period. Recommended sizes for aerated lagoons are given in Table 903-2.

903-3   *Oxidation ditches* were developed as a low-cost sewage treatment for small communities. The principal parts of the oxidation ditch are (a) a continuous open-channel ditch shaped like a race track, which holds the waste, and (b) an aeration rotor for supplying the necessary oxygen and keeping the ditch contents circulating (*Detail 904*). The mixture of sewage and activated sludge passes the aeration rotor frequently, where the spinning of the rotor churns air with oxygen into it. The intense, prolonged aeration and mixing of fresh and aerated sewage reduced BOD (*Biological Oxygen Demand*) by 90 percent or more. The liquid in the ditch becomes a deep-brown flocculent typical of activated sludge. Surplus sludge separated from the treated effluent in a settling tank dries to a dark brown stable and odorless cake. During winter operation, ice may cover the ditch and cause some decrease in efficiency, but the operation still remains satisfactory.

903-4   *Design* of the in-the-building oxidation ditch for livestock wastes is for a completely mixed aerobic method of having a detention time of about 50 days. It differs from a municipal ditch in that (a) it is located beneath self-cleaning slotted floors; (b) the liquid volume is about 30 cu. ft. per pound of BOD, or less than half that of municipal ditches, and the loading is a much more concentrated form (30,000 to 50,000 milligrams per liter instead of 300 to 500 milligrams per liter); (c) the liquid depth is shallow (usually less than 2 feet) so there is sufficient velocity to keep solids suspended; and, (d) a constant rotor height is maintained for the operator's convenience. Design recommendations are given in Table 903-4.

903-5   *Start-up* procedure for the in-the-building oxidation ditch with continuous effluent overflow is as follows:

(a) Fill the ditch with the volume of water required by the ditch loading rate. Do not try to start with anaerobic liquid manure in the ditch.

(b) Adjust the height of the rotor for the desired immersion depth (usually 4 to 6 inches). This should not require further adjustment for a

Table 903-4   Design Recommendations for In-the-Building Oxidation Ditches

Animal unit	Weight, lb. per unit	Daily BOD_5, lb. per unit[a]	Daily reg. oxygenation cap., lb. per unit[b]	No. of animals per ft. of rotor, units per foot[c]	Ditch vol., cubic ft. per unit[d]	Daily power reqmt., KWH per unit[e]	Daily cost, cents per unit[f]
Swine							
Sow with liter	375	.79	1.58	16	23.7	.83	1.66
Growing pig	65	.14	.28	91	4.2	.15	.30
Finishing hog	150	.32	.62	41	9.6	.33	.66
Dairy Cattle							
Dairy cow	1,300	2.21	4.42	6	66	2.33	4.66
Beef Cattle							
Beef feeder	900	1.35	2.70	10	40	1.42	2.84
Sheep							
Sheep feeder	75	.053	.11	230	1.6	.06	.12
Poultry							
Laying hen	4.5	.0198	.0396	650	.6	.021	.042

[a] From Table 901-1c. Use specific production data when known.
[b] Twice the daily BOD.
[c] Based on 25.5 lb. of O_2 per ft. of rotor per day.
[d] Based on 30 ft.^{3} per lb. of daily BOD.
[e] Based on 1.9 lb. of O_2 per KWH.
[f] Based on electricity at 2 cents per KWH.

continuous-effluent system because the liquid depth will remain constant.

(c)   Put animals into the building and start the rotor. It is best to put the animals in gradually if possible so that the full load will not be applied until the bio-oxidation system becomes established.

(d)   Monitor the ditch for foam. Some foaming is likely at start-up. It may be controlled with the anti-foaming agents if the condition exists; even a quart of engine oil applied a time or two during the foaming period will usually suffice.

Keep the motor running and do not upset the system by sudden excessive changes in the loading rate. After a few months of operation, the concentration of suspended solids may get too high for good circulation to continue. This is partly due to evaporation at the rotor. Solids can be diluted by allowing water to run into the ditch. After the oxidation system comes to equilibrium, the mixed liquor BOD will typically be 3,000 to 5,000 milligrams per liter, resulting in BOD reductions to about 90 percent. Also, total volatile solids are reduced about 50 percent.

904   Anaerobic Treatment
Anaerobic treatment takes place without free oxygen but does produce objectionable gases and odors such as hydrogen sulfide and ammonia. It is the most common treatment of livestock wastes. The major anaerobic system of interest in livestock waste treatment is the anaerobic lagoon. Septic tanks and anaerobic digesters are also considered.

904-1   *Anaerobic lagoons* have found widespread application in the treatment of animal wastes because of their low initial cost, ease of operation, and convenience of loading by gravity flow from livestock buildings. The main disadvantage is the release of odors from the surface of the lagoon, especially during the Spring warmup. Mosquitoes can also be a serious problem.

A wide range of loading rates from 0.001 to 0.01 pound of daily volatile solids per cubic foot

Table 904-1   Minimum Capacities of Anaerobic Lagoons, Septic Tanks, and Digesters for Livestock Wastes[a]

	VS (pounds/day)	Lagoon[b] volume (cubic feet per animal)	Septic tank[c] volume (cubic feet per animal)	Digester[d] volume (cubic feet per animal)
Dairy Cow (1400 pounds)	10.1	2,020	337	51
Beef Animal (800 pounds)	3.8	760	127	19
Swine (100 pounds)	.59	118	20	3
Poultry (4 pounds)	.052	10.4	1.7	.26

[a]Assuming all the manure goes to the facility at a uniform rate and is uniformly distributed, corrections to be made for other situations and for other animal sizes.
[b]Based on 0.005 pound daily VS per cubic foot.
[c]Based on 0.03 pound daily VS per cubic foot.
[d]Based on 0.2 pound daily VS per cubic foot.

has been used in the United States. A loading rate of 0.005 pound of volatile solids (VS) per cubic foot of lagoon volume is recommended for moderate midwestern climates. Table 904-1 gives lagoon volumes for livestock based on this loading rate.

904-2 *Septic tanks* have been considered as a treatment method of livestock wastes with effluent going to a soil adsorption field or to a lagoon. In practice, septic tanks for livestock wastes appear to operate mainly as sedimentation tanks and adsorption fields have been inadequate except for very small livestock facilities. Septic tanks for home sewage are sized on loading rates of approximately 0.03 to 0.05 pounds daily volatile solids per cubic foot. Table 904-1 gives septic tank volume required for livestock based on 0.05 pound volatile solids per cubic foot.

904-3 *Anaerobic digesters* decompose more organic matter per unit volume than an aerobic counterpart. Also, continuous operating power is not required as in the case of aerated processes and harvesting methane gas is possible. The obvious disadvantages are the initial cost of the digester and the high degree of operational management required. A loading rate of approximately 0.2 pound of daily volatile solids per cubic foot at

95° F. The gas produced by a properly operating anaerobic digester is about 60 percent methane and 40 percent carbon dioxide. Table 904-1 gives the digester volume for livestock. A schematic diagram of a digester is shown in Detail 904-3.

905   Handling Hog Wastes from Solid Floors

905-1   The most common method of handling hog wastes has been to use bedding, scrape the floors periodically, and haul manure to the field in a conventional spreader.

905-2   Farrowing House—Follow these recommendations when using solid floors for farrowing (*see Detail 905-2*).
a.   Slope floor 1/2 inch per ft. for drainage.
b.   Form 2 inch drop for small gutter at alleyway.
c.   Feed and water sow outside.

905-3   Growing and Finishing Pens—For minimum floor cleaning: a. Slope floor 1/2 inch per ft. for drainage. b. Keep pen full of pigs—start with pen full and divide pigs as they grow. c. Feed at the top of slope (*where you want it to remain clean*) and water near the bottom of the slope or outside (*where you want the manure deposited*).

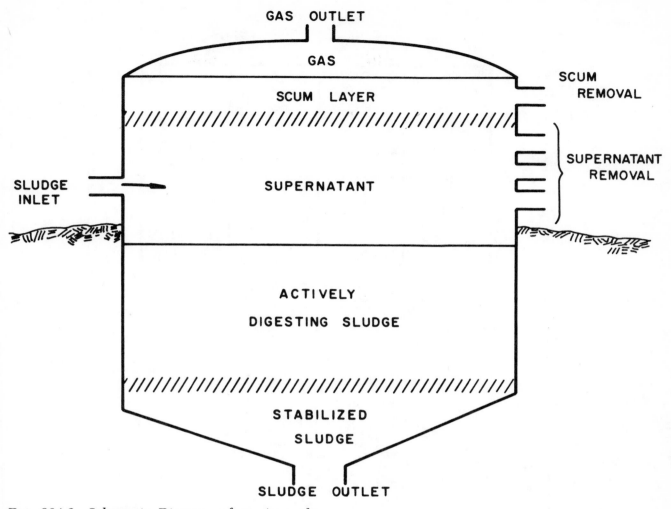

GAS OUTLET

GAS

SCUM LAYER

SCUM REMOVAL

SLUDGE INLET

SUPERNATANT

SUPERNATANT REMOVAL

ACTIVELY

DIGESTING SLUDGE

STABILIZED

SLUDGE

SLUDGE OUTLET

Det. 904-3 Schematic Diagram of an Anaerobic Digester (D. L. Day, University of Illinois)

906 Slotted Floor Arrangements for Hogs

The adoption of slotted floors has done more to reduce the labor required to raise hogs than any other development for many years.

906-1 Farrowing—Two rows of farrowing crates located over 8 ft. wide manure pits fit a 24 ft. building *(see Detail 702-3, Chapter 7)*. Run the slats with the sow and space them 3/8 inches apart. For a detailed plan ask for Midwest Plan Service plan No. 72677.

906-2 Nursery—Since a small pig does a poor job of keeping his pen clean, it is best to use

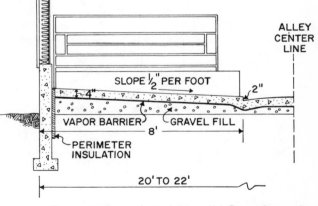

ALLEY CENTER LINE

SLOPE ½" PER FOOT

1'-4"

2"

VAPOR BARRIER

GRAVEL FILL

8'

PERIMETER INSULATION

20' TO 22'

Cross-section of typical solid-floor farrowing

Det. 905-2

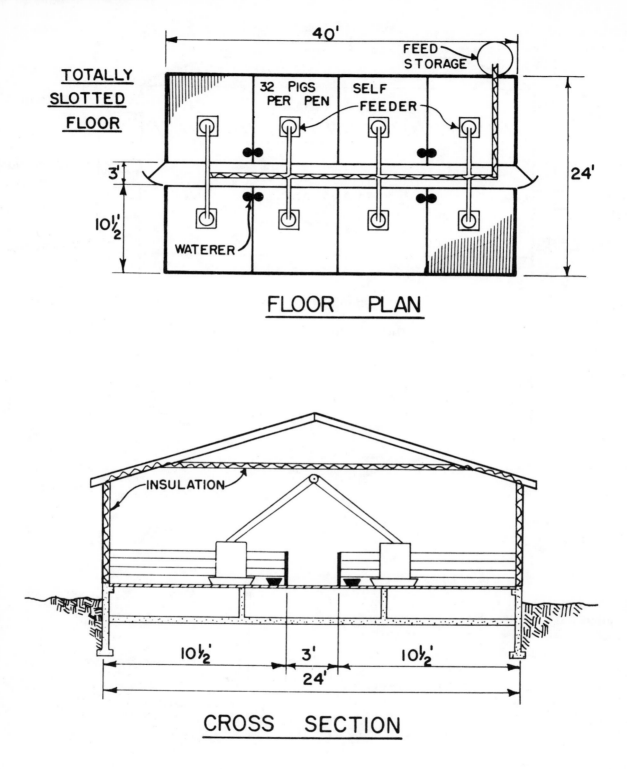

FLOOR PLAN

CROSS SECTION

*Det. 906-2 Cross-Section and Floor Plan of Totally
Slotted Floor Nursery.*

a totally slotted pen for a nursery *(see Detail 906-2)*. For plans ask your Agricultural Extension Service for Midwest Plan Service plan No. 72678.

906-3 Partially slotted—floor buildings were the earliest use of slotted floors for hogs *(see Detail 906-3)*. These pens have primarily been used for growing and finishing hogs but can also be used for sows with small pigs and for confined sows. This arrangement works well but normally some pens get dirty. You can limit feed on the floor or use a self-feeder. Floor feeding encourages cleaner pens. Slope the floor to the pits, keep the pens full of pigs, and locate waterer over the slotted floors for cleanest pens.

906-4 Remodeling—A partially slotted-floor arrangement with one central gutter *(see Detail 906-4)* works best when remodeling an existing building. All excavating is done in the center of the building and not next to the often shallow foundation.

906-5 Open-Front, Partially Slotted finishing buildings can be used for growing pigs or for gestating sows *(see Detail 906-5)*. This open arrangement is better adapted to milder climates than to the northern states with extremely cold winters. Heat in the floor will provide some heat for small pigs and will assure that all pigs lie in the front of the pen, resulting in cleaner floors. Provide a wall every 40 ft. to eliminate longitudinal drafts during cold weather. Open this wall for circulation during hot weather.

906-6 Totally slotted floors for finishing are becoming quite popular *(see Detail 906-6)*. Essentially, no floor cleaning is required and maximum storage is provided for liquid manure.

907   Slotted-Floors

907-1 Types of slotted floors must be made of the proper material and be installed properly.

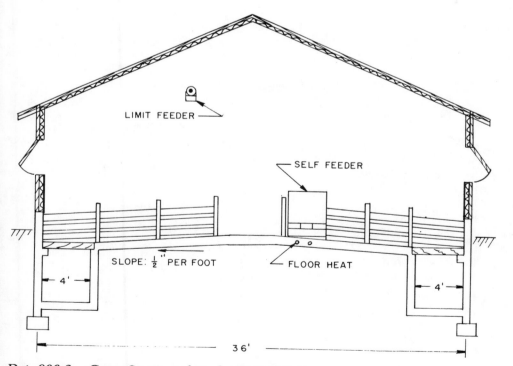

LIMIT FEEDER

SELF FEEDER

SLOPE: ½" PER FOOT

FLOOR HEAT

4'

4'

36'

Det. 906-3. Cross-Section of Early Partially Slotted-Floor Hog Buildings.

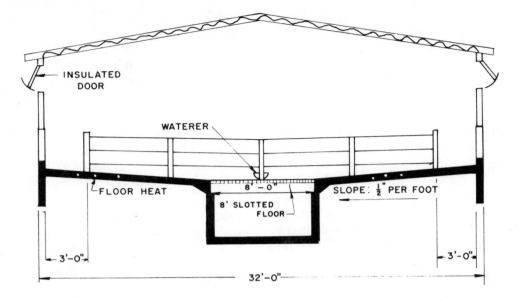

INSULATED
DOOR

WATERER

FLOOR HEAT

8' - 0"   SLOPE: ½" PER FOOT

8' SLOTTED
FLOOR

3'-0"

3'-0"

32'-0"

*Det. 906-4.   Partially Slotted-Floor Hog Building
with Single Center Gutter.*

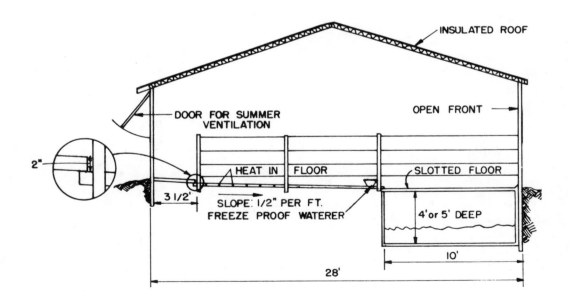

INSULATED ROOF

DOOR FOR SUMMER
VENTILATION

OPEN FRONT

2"

HEAT IN FLOOR

SLOTTED FLOOR

3 1/2'

SLOPE: 1/2" PER FT.
FREEZE PROOF WATERER

4' or 5' DEEP

10'

28'

*Det. 906-5   Open-Front,   Partially   Slotted-Floor
Finishing Building.*

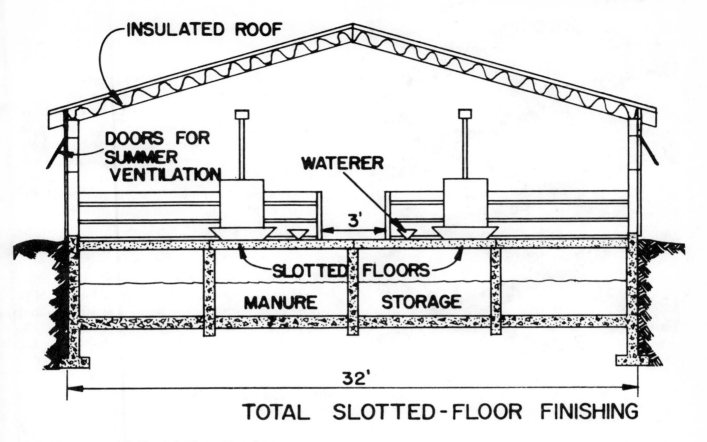

INSULATED ROOF

DOORS FOR SUMMER VENTILATION

WATERER

3'

SLOTTED FLOORS

MANURE STORAGE

32'

TOTAL SLOTTED-FLOOR FINISHING

Det. 906-6.   Total Slotted-Floor Finishing

Table 907-1

Material	Expected Life	Advantages	Disadvantages
Wood	2–4 years	Lowest initial cost	Difficult to maintain spacing.
Concrete	10–15 years	Longest life	Quality control difficult when poured at site.
Steel	4–8 years	Easiest cleaned	Highest cost

Table 907-2

Use of Slat	Slat Width	Spacing
Farrowing	4"–5"	3/8"*
Nursery (over 3 weeks of age)	3"–5"	1"
Finishing	4"–6"	1"
Sows	4"–6"	1 1/4"

*Widen spacing to 1-inch at rear of sow and cover with grate while farrowing.

907-3 Expanded metal works well for farrowing and nursery units *(see Detail 907-3)*. Use 3/4 inch, 9–11 gauge, flattened, expanded metal. Supports under mesh should be on 1 ft. centers. Run the opening lengthwise with sows in farrowing crates.

907-4 Steel Straps spaced 3/8-inches apart have worked well for farrowing *(see Detail 907-4)*. These sections can be used for the 2 ft. in front and rear of the farrowing crate *(running across the crate)* with a solid concrete or wood center or can be run lengthwise over the entire floor of the crate. The 3/16 or 1/4-inch thick straps can be epoxy coated for longer life.

907-5 Wood slats should be made from white oak or some other equally hard wood to resist wear. Normally, the wood must be worked green

135

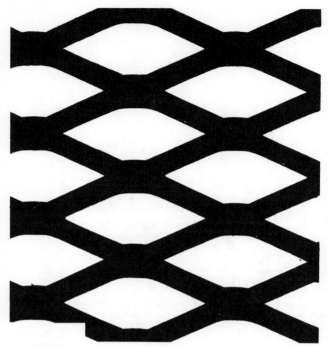

Det. 907-3.

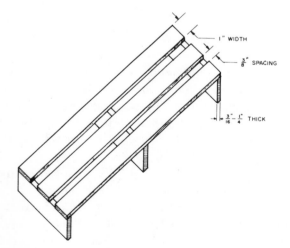

Det. 907-4.

and then fastened securely to resist warping. The design of wood slats is shown in Detail 907-5.

907-6 Concrete Slats can be cast-in-place *(commercial forms are available)* or precast. Use a rich concrete mix *(7-1/2 bag mix of air entrained cement)* with a 3/4 inch maximum size aggregate. The surface of farrowing slats must be smooth and spacing must be uniform. Many builders use a saw to grind out the exact 3/8-inch spacing for farrowing. A wooden plug is placed in the form to provide the 1-inch spacing behind the sow. The design of concrete slats is shown in Table 907.5.

907-7 Joists for supporting slotted floors must be sufficiently strong. Pressure treated wood joists can be used for wood or light-gage steel slotted floors. Use concrete joists to support concrete slats. Detail 907-7 gives the recommended sizes for wood and concrete joists.

908 Dead Animal Disposal
Disposal of dead animals has become a serious problem on large commercial hog farms. Many states have a law that requires all dead animals to be disposed of within 24 hours of death. The dead animals can either be buried or burned in an incinerator, or hauled away by a licensed rendering plant.

909 Handling Beef and Dairy Cattle Manure
The manure from beef and dairy cattle can either be handled as a solid or a liquid. Confined feeding on drylot and the reduced use of bedding with free stalls has created new manure handling problems.

909-1 When scraping floors and paved lots, provide a definite storage area if manure can't be taken to the fields daily *(see Detail 909-1).* Locate this fenced storage area so it can be unloaded from outside the lot. Clean at least weekly in fly breeding season *(above 70° F.).*

909-2 A loading ramp for scraping manure directly into a spreader can be used. An area for

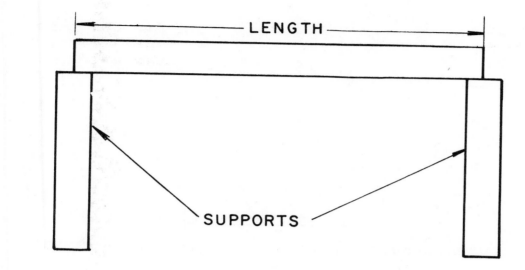

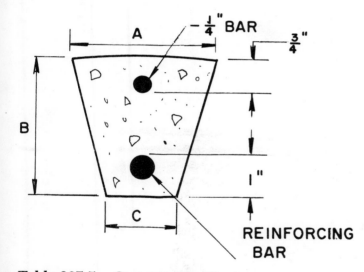

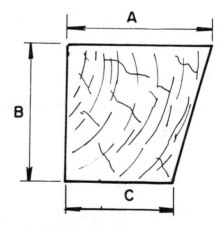

Table 907-5. Concrete Slat Design.

Length, ft.	A	B	C	Reinforcing Bar
4	4″	3 1/2″	3″	No. 3 (3/8″)
6	4″	4″	3″	No. 3 (3/8″)
8	5″	4 1/2″	—	No. 4 (4/8″)
10	5″	5″	—	No. 5 (5/8″)

Wood Slat Design.

Length, ft.	A	B	C
4	4″	3″	2 1/2″
6	4″	3″	3″
8	5″	4″	3 1/2″
10	5″	4″	4″

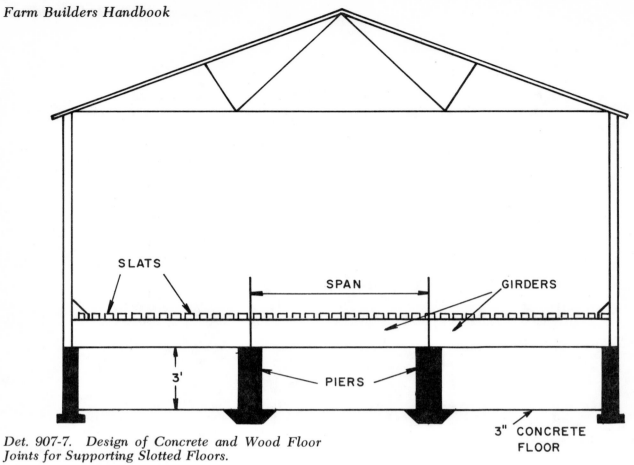

SLATS

SPAN

GIRDERS

PIERS

3'

3" CONCRETE FLOOR

Det. 907-7.   Design of Concrete and Wood Floor Joints for Supporting Slotted Floors.

Reinforced Concrete Joist Sizes for Concrete Slotted Floors [1]

Slat Length Between Joists	Joist sizes [2] for Spans of		
	8'	10'	12'
4'	7 1/2 × 7 1/2 2-#4	7 1/2 × 9 3-#4	9 1/2 × 9 1/2 3-#5
5'	7 1/2 × 8 2-#4	7 1/2 × 10 3-#5	9 1/2 × 10 3-#6
6'	7 1/2 × 9 3-#4	7 1/2 × 10 1/2 3-#5	9 1/2 × 11 3-#6
8'	7 1/2 × 10 3-#5	7 1/2 × 11 1/2 3-#5	9 1/2 × 12 1/2 3-#6
10'	7 1/2 × 10 1/2 3-#5	7 1/2 × 12 1/2 3-#6	9 1/2 × 13 1/2 3-#7
12'	7 1/2 × 11 1/2 3-#5	7 1/2 × 13 1/2 3-#6	9 1/2 × 14 1/2 3-#7

[1] Approximately 125 psf dead-live design load.
[2] Dimensions listed are:
Width by Depth
Number of Reinforcing
Bars and their size.

Joists Sizes [1] for Wood or Light-Gage Steel Slat Floors [2]

Slat Length Between Joists	Joist Sizes for Spans of		
	8'	10'	12'
4'	2" × 8"	2" × 10"	2" × 12"
5'	2" × 8"	2" × 10"	2" × 12"
6'	2" × 10"	2" × 12"	3" × 12"
8'	2" × 10"	3" × 12"	3" × 12"
10'	2" × 12"	3" × 12"	4" × 12"
12'	2" × 12"	3" × 12"	4" × 12"

[1] Use pressure-treated lumber for joists.
[2] Approximately 55 psf dead + live design load (do not drive trucks or tractors on these floors).

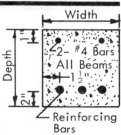

Width
Depth
2- #4 Bars
All Beams
1 1/2"
Reinforcing Bars

stockpiling manure is still required if manure can't be hauled to the fields daily.

909-3 *Runoff* from concentrated feedlots cannot be allowed to drain into waterways causing pollution. State laws require that polluted runoff must be intercepted and collected. To collect and control feedlot runoff (see Detail 909-3):

a. First, divert any water falling outside the feedlot so it will not flow across the lot. This means installing gutters on roofs and constructing conversion terraces to channel all surface drainage around the feedlot. That will minimize the polluted runoff to be handled.

b. Provide a collection and impoundment system that will prevent the entry of the polluted runoff into a stream or other natural watercourse. This collected runoff is normally directed through a settling basin to remove the solids, with the

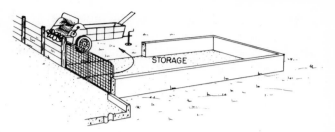

Det. 909-1. Manure Storage Area with Bumper Wall for Easy Loading. (Midwest Plan Service)

liquids draining into a holding pond. The solids are settled out when the velocity of the runoff is reduced.

c. Provide a method of cleaning out the solids from the settling basin. Normally, the solids can be loaded with a tractor front-end loader and spread on the land.

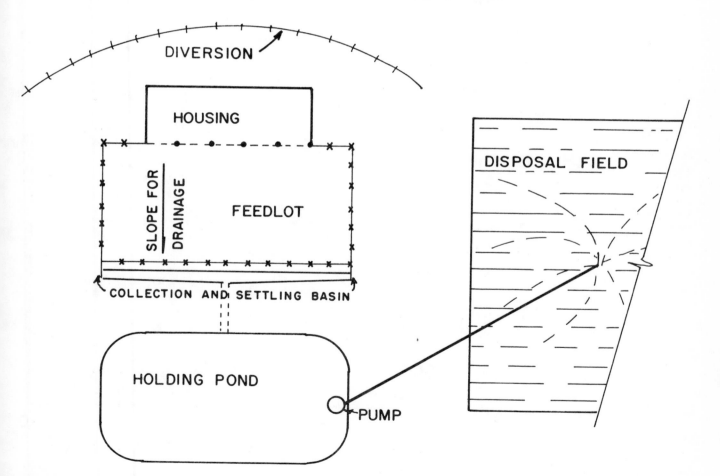

Det. 909-3 Feedlot Runoff Control.

d. The collected liquids in the holding pond must also be returned to the land in such a manner that runoff will be avoided. The liquids are usually pumped with a small, irrigation-type pump and spread on the land. The pond should be emptied as soon after a rain as possible to provide storage for future rains.

909-4 Liquid Manure. A liquid manure system for dairy and beef cattle requires the following parts:
a. Manure storage tank.
b. Chopper manure pump.
c. Agitation—The manure must be agitated, mixing the solids and liquids before pumping is started or only the liquids will be pumped leaving the solids settled on the bottom. The chopper-manure pump is normally used for agitation.
d. Tank wagon for hauling and spreading. *(For dairy operations, check any liquid manure plans with your local dairy inspector).*

909-5 Capacity Needs of storage tanks depend on:
a. Number of cattle.
b. Length of time land is not available in bad weather.

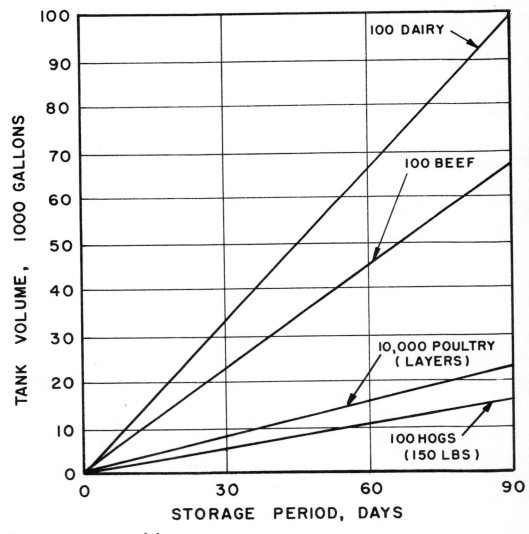

Det. 909-5 Storage Tank Capacities Required for Various Storage Periods.

c. Availability of land during the growing season.

d. The seasonal labor demand during cropping.

e. Amount of water that will be added from surface runoff, roof gutters, milking parlors, etc.

The graph in Detail 909-5 will help you determine the size of storage tank you require. Remember that you must add to this amount any water that will be added from surface runoff, roof gutters, or wash water from milking parlors.

909-6 Construction of Storage Tanks:

Because of rapid changes in livestock production and waste handling systems, and with growing interest in pollution control, plans for facilities are frequently revised. Contact your County Extension Office or the Extension Agricultural Engineer at your state University for the most recent edition of the following, and related, publications:

a. *USDA Plan 5981,* Rectangular, 6′ and 10′ deep, 20′ wide, any length. (see Detail 909-6A).

b. *Midwest Plan Service plan no. 74303* gives materials specifications and construction requirements for concrete tanks up to 12′ deep, 24′ wide, and any length. Reinforcing schedules are included for walls, lids, and around openings. Tables give capacities in cubic feet and gallons, and estimate cubic yards of concrete and pounds of steel.

c. *Midwest Plan Service report TR-3* is intended primarily for design engineers. It includes design criteria and reinforcing for selected sections, but many essential construction details are not included. Reinforcing requirements are included for tanks up to 16′ deep subjected to loads up to 60 pcf; tops up to 24′ wide for loads up to 150 psf and for 10,000 lb axle load; and for walls not supported by an adequate top. Also included are tables of allowable superimposable loads/foot on slats and beams up to 10″ wide by 15″ deep with up to 3 bars per beam.

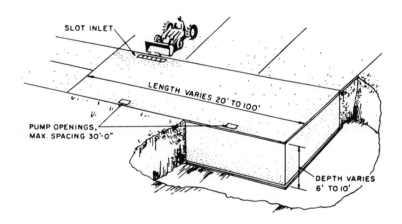

Detail 909-6A.   USDA Plan No. 5981, Rectangular Concrete Manure Tank 20 ft. Wide Approximate Capacities in Gallons—20 ft. Inside Width

Depth, Ft.	Length, Ft.				
	20	40	60	80	100
6	18,000	36,000	54,000	72,000	90,000
8	24,000	48,000	72,000	96,000	120,000
10	30,000	60,000	90,000	120,000	150,000

909-7 Agitation—Achieving adequate agitation can be a problem in some manure storage tanks. A liquid manure storage tank with a center partition (*see Detail 909-7*) can be used to circulate the manure around the center partition resulting in complete agitation and mixing of solids.

909-8 Pit Size—Do not make size of single pit or compartment too large. Most pumps will not agitate further than 30 ft. in one direction. It is better to use partitions and make smaller compartments than to have one large compartment. Pit partitions should be designed to withstand the pressure when one compartment is full and adjacent compartment is empty.

In deciding the pit depth, you must consider the length of pumps available. The most common pit depths are 8' and 10'.

909-9 Manure Gasses from liquid wastes stored inside a building can create a hazard and undesirable odors. Provide proper ventilation if manure is stored inside a building. Most gasses are released during agitation so check ventilation at this time. Never climb into a manure storage pit without another person knowing of your whereabouts. Provide a means of easy exit from pits such as a ladder.

909-10 Slotted Floors for beef and dairy reduce the labor and time needed for cleaning pens and removing manure. They eliminate most bedding and help maintain dry conditions. Totally slotted floors have worked best for beef in confinement (*see Detail 909-10A*).

Free stalls with a slotted alleyway (*see Detail 909-10B*) work best for dairy. Get plans approved from your local dairy inspector before starting any construction.

909-11 Concrete Slats can be made on the farm or purchased precast. Forms for cast-in-place are available. Detail 909-11 shows the recommended design for concrete slats. Follow concrete practices in paragraph 907-6. Use a 7-1/2 bag mix with 3/4 inch maximum aggregate.

909-12 Floor Supports for the slats must also be designed properly. Detail 909-12 shows the recommended design for concrete beams and columns for supporting concrete slats.

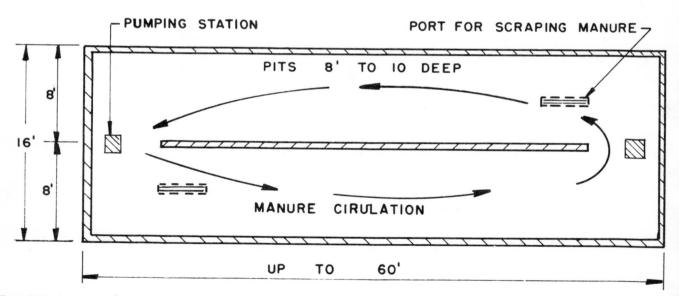

Det. 909-7. Liquid Manure Tank with Center Partition for Circulating Manure for Agitation.

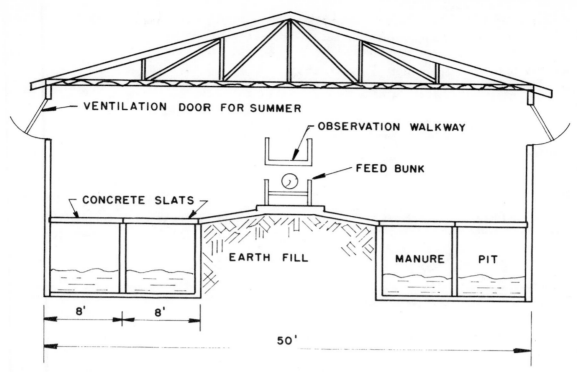

Det. 909-10A. *Slotted-Floor Arrangement for Confinement Beef.*

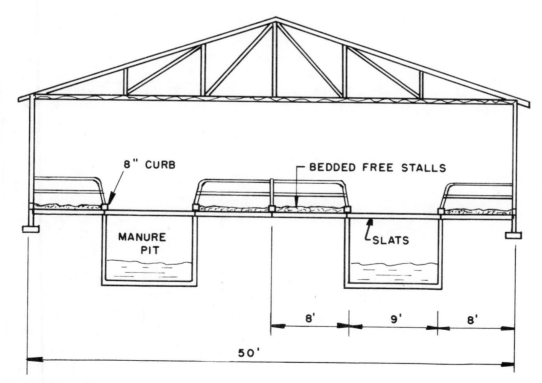

Det. 909-10B. *Slotted-Floor Arrangement for Dairy Free Stall Barn.*

SIZES OF CONCRETE SLATS*

Length	A	Reinforcing Bar
6'	6"	No 4 ($\frac{1}{2}$")
8'	6"	No 6 ($\frac{3}{4}$")
10'	7$\frac{1}{2}$"	No 7 ($\frac{7}{8}$")

* Approx. 250 lbs per linear ft design live load.

Space slats 1$\frac{1}{4}$" apart for calves, 1$\frac{1}{2}$" to 1$\frac{3}{4}$" apart for steers to market weight.

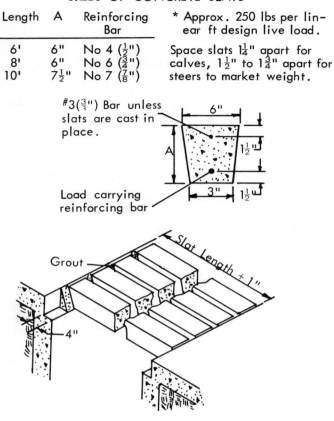

#3($\frac{3}{8}$") Bar unless slats are cast in place.

Load carrying reinforcing bar

Det. 909-11   Design of Concrete Slats for Dairy and Beef Cattle. (Midwest Plan Service).

REINFORCED CONCRETE BEAMS FOR CONCRETE SLOTTED FLOORS

Slat Length Between Beams	Beam Sizes for Spans Of: 8'	10'
6'	8"x12" (w x d) 2-#6 (Bars)	8"x14" 3-#6
8'	10"x12" 2-#6	10"x14" 3-#6

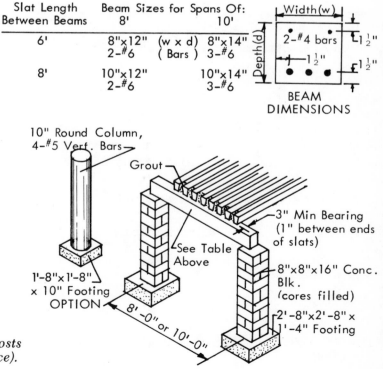

Width (w)

2-#4 bars

1$\frac{1}{2}$"

1$\frac{1}{2}$"

1$\frac{1}{2}$"

Depth (d)

BEAM DIMENSIONS

10" Round Column, 4-#5 Vert. Bars

Grout

1'-8"x1'-8" x 10" Footing OPTION

See Table Above

8'-0" or 10'-0"

3" Min Bearing (1" between ends of slats)

8"x8"x16" Conc. Blk. (cores filled)

2'-8"x2'-8" x 1'-4" Footing

Det. 909-12.   Design of Concrete Beams and Posts for Dairy and Beef Cattle. (Midwest Plan Service).

909-13 When possible, provide a manure port *(Detail 909-13)* every 20 feet for agitating and unloading pits along outside walls.

910 Handling Poultry Manure

Poultry manure can be handled as a solid or a liquid from both floor flocks or caged flocks.

910-1 Solid—Most all poultry manure handled as a solid is hauled to the field with the conventional spreader or with a flail-type spreader. The flail-type spreader with tank body works well with manure which is quite thin. A very small amount of poultry manure is dehydrated and sold as fertilizer. The major difference in handling poultry manure as a solid is how the manure is removed from the house.

a. Many floor houses allow manure pack to build up and then use tractor with front-end loader to clean periodically.
b. Many cage operations are arranged to use a small tractor with side scrapers to scrape manure to end of house into a cross conveyor.
c. A small tractor with special loader can be used with many cage houses. The loader empties directly into a spreader.
d. Some houses *(both floor and caged flocks)* are equipped with a mechanical cleaner to drag the manure to a cross conveyor which loads it into a spreader.

910-2 Liquid—Some of the large producers have gone to liquid manure for ease of handling. A vacuum tank wagon is used for agitation and hauling to the field. Some producers discharge liquid manure in plow furrow and cover immediately reducing odors in the field to a minimum.

a. Slotted floors with storage tank beneath. Haul out every 1 to 3 years.

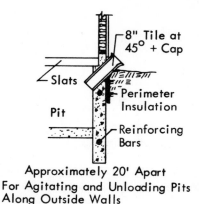

Approximately 20' Apart
For Agitating and Unloading Pits
Along Outside Walls

Det. 909-13. Detail of Manure Port for Access to Manure Pits. (Midwest Plan Service).

b. Clean into outside storage tank
 1. Flush manure into tank.
 2. Use mechanical cleaner with water to clean shallow pits into tank.
c. Lagoon—A few lagoons are used for poultry—see par. 903-2.
d. Combination of hauling and lagoon.

911 Dead Bird Disposal

911-1 Disposal Pits *(Detail 911-1)* for dead birds should be based on flock size. For broilers—allow 20 cu. ft. per 1000 birds in flock. For layers—allow 80 cu. ft. per 1000 birds in flock.

911-2 Incinerators do an efficient job of disposing of dead birds. Objectionable fumes can be reduced by using burners which produce extreme heat resulting in combustion of most gases. Most commercial incinerators have proven more satisfactory than any home made units.

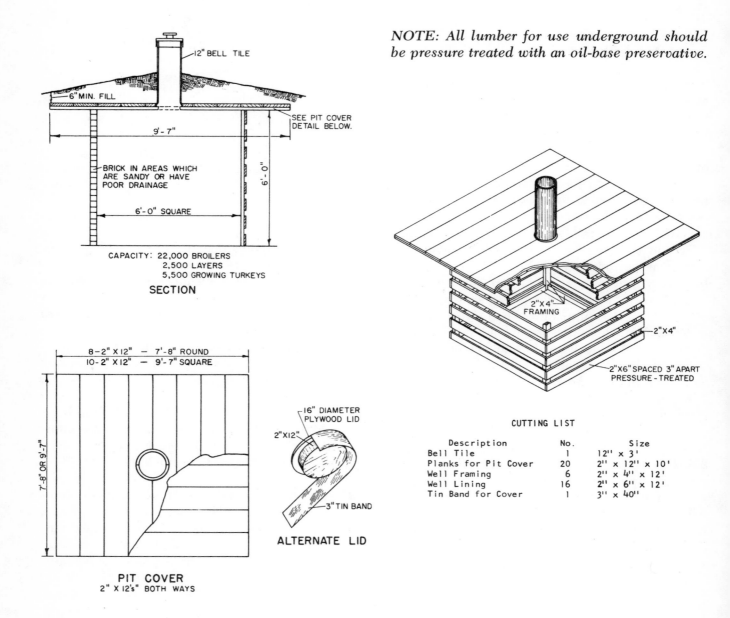

NOTE: All lumber for use underground should be pressure treated with an oil-base preservative.

12" BELL TILE

6" MIN. FILL

SEE PIT COVER
DETAIL BELOW.

9'-7"

BRICK IN AREAS WHICH
ARE SANDY OR HAVE
POOR DRAINAGE

6'-0"

6'-0" SQUARE

CAPACITY: 22,000 BROILERS
2,500 LAYERS
5,500 GROWING TURKEYS

SECTION

2"X4"
FRAMING

2"X4"

2"X6" SPACED 3" APART
PRESSURE - TREATED

8- 2" X 12" — 7'- 8" ROUND
10- 2" X 12" — 9'- 7" SQUARE

7'-8" OR 9'-7"

16" DIAMETER
PLYWOOD LID

2"X12"

3" TIN BAND

ALTERNATE LID

PIT COVER
2" X 12's" BOTH WAYS

CUTTING LIST

Description	No.	Size
Bell Tile	1	12" x 3'
Planks for Pit Cover	20	2" x 12" x 10'
Well Framing	6	2" x 4" x 12'
Well Lining	16	2" x 6" x 12'
Tin Band for Cover	1	3" x 40"

Det. 911-1.   Detail of Disposal Pit for Dead Poultry.

Chapter 10

GRAIN AND SILAGE STORAGE

by LARRY VAN FOSSEN
Extension Agricultural Engineer
Iowa State University

1000   There are many alternate methods to store grain. The following will briefly point out the main advantages of each method, suggest what type and size of farming operation each method commonly fits into, and present data on structural requirements. This will enable you to better advise your clients.

1000-1   Plan a System. Grain storage structures must be part of a system designed for a specific farm enterprise. The system must provide for not only storage; but for a flow of materials between storage, drying and processing units. Buildings and/or equipment may be added one at a time but should fit a master plan. The flow pattern must allow for a drying unit with a capacity geared to the harvesting rate of the grain crops. Space for on-farm processing and feed preparation should be allowed for. And above all, flexibility for growth should be provided for with room for alternative handling methods and storage facilities.

The primary function of grain storage structures is a simple one—to store grain safely at or as near to its original quality as possible. Use of an efficient grain storage and conditioning system enables the farmer to realize a larger profit margin as he can market at favorable prices or feed as required. For a livestock operation requiring feed grains more or less continually, it makes little logic to transport the harvested grains to the elevator from the farm and then back again to feed. For livestock feeding, additional storage and drying facilities will most likely provide the most economical and flexible solution.

Selecting the appropriate on-the-farm drying and storage system can save several cents per bushel as compared to having it done commercially. Besides, the inconvenience and cost of hauling the grain at a busy time is avoided. The possible economic benefit of your system depends on local drying and storage costs, discount rates, the normal seasonal fluctuation of market prices and how long you may have to wait at your local elevator to unload. Seldom is it a good choice to sell corn at harvest if the discount rate exceeds 2¢ a percentage point of moisture content above 15-1/2%.

Grain storage and handling systems must be economical—they must pay off in one way or another for the farmer. Some of the possible benefits are:
1.   Probably the main advantage—good storage facilities allow for holding top quality grain until the best market price may be obtained.
2.   Mechanical handling of materials reduces total labor and may help keep a good hired helper.
3.   A labor-saving grain system allows more time to manage.
4.   A properly designed drying system will permit harvesting early. This minimizes the time the crop is subject to damaging storms, lowers field losses and gives more time for fall field tillage.

1001   Corn Storage
Corn stored dry will give maximum flexibility. It can be fed or marketed. But wet storage is the easiest way to store corn to be fed on the farm.

Shelled corn harvested in the fall must be artificially dried to store as dry corn. There are three basic methods of drying: (1) dry and store the corn in a bin; (2) dry the corn in a bin and move it to another storage structure; and (3) dry the corn in a heated-air dryer and convey it to another storage structure for storing.

1001-1a *Dry and Store in the Same Bin* Multiple-layer or in-storage drying in a bin is a good system for drying from 4,000 to 5,000 bushels up to about 20,000 to 25,000 bushels.

Successful drying by this method requires a correctly controlled supplemental heater, usually with a humidistat. A humidistat must be accurately calibrated and correctly adjusted to dry corn to the desired moisture content. There is no need for overdrying. Humidistats should be cleaned and calibrated at least once a year—before drying starts in the fall.

An accurately calibrated humidistat set according to the following table will dry the corn to approximately 13% moisture.

Average 24-hour temperature	Humidistat setting to dry to approximately 13%
Below 40° F	50%
41–50° F	55%
51–60° F	60%
61–75° F	70%
Above 75° F	75%

The main advantage for multiple-layer drying is low labor requirement. But the system does require maximum know-how. Satisfied users know how to operate the system and they have not been oversold on its drying capacity.

Multiple-layer drying is a warm weather drying system—for the farmer who harvests early. If he does not plan to harvest until late October, he probably will not be satisfied with the system.

Drying bins must not be filled too fast; the corn might spoil before it is dried. As a rule of thumb, a bin with total drying grain depth of 12 feet can be filled in a week; 16-foot grain depth in 2 weeks; and 19-foot grain depth in 3 weeks. Several more days will be needed to dry the corn after the bin is full. If it is desired to harvest in a short period of time, he should select larger diameter and shorter bins.

1001-1b *Continuous Filling In-Storage Drying Bins* This is a new approach for in-storage drying. Constant heat to increase the drying air temperature a few degrees (less than 10° F) is used. Electric heat is most common. This method is safest if the corn has not more than 22% moisture and it is loaded into the bin when daily temperatures are 50° F or lower. The drier the corn and the lower the outside temperature when the corn is loaded into the bin, the less chance of spoilage. If temperatures are unseasonably high, the corn can deteriorate before it is dried. If the season is abnormally cold, drying costs will be high.

1001-2a *Bin Dry and Move to Storage* A second basic method of bin drying is to dry in one bin and move to another for storage. Three such systems—conventional batch drying, stir drying, and recirculating or continuous-flow drying—have many similar traits. All are high-temperature (up to 160° F), high-capacity drying systems.

They require liquid withdrawal burners to satisfactorily operate at high temperatures. Humidistats are not used. But a high limit thermostat is a desirable safety feature.

The following points out the characteristics of these systems in more detail. A range of annual capacities where each method is most common is given. There will be exceptions, particularly for the upper size suggested.

1001-2b *Conventional Bin-Batch Drying* With this system, corn is dried in a 2-1/2- to 4-foot layer with temperatures up to 160° F, then moved to another storage bin. The common practice is to dry and cool one batch per day. Batch size depends on the diameter of the bin.

Batch drying is usually the least-cost drying method. But it requires more labor than an in-storage system because the corn must be moved out of the bin.

Bin batch drying is one of the most common methods when a drying capacity is needed for as little as 5,000 to 6,000 bushels and up to about 30,000 bushels per year.

1001-3 *Batch Drying with Stirring Equipment* Use of stirring equipment in a bin is similar to conventional batch drying, but the batch depths

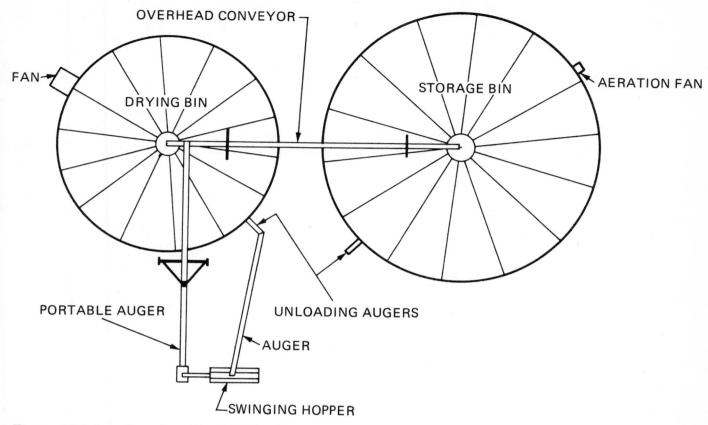

Figure 1001-2A   Complete Circuit Grain Conveying.

are commonly 6 to 9 feet deep. With adequate capacity fans, a batch can be dried, cooled and unloaded within 24 hours.

Grain stirring equipment does not greatly increase the hourly drying capacity of conventional bin-batch dryers, but the bin can be loaded 2-1/2 to 3 times deeper; therefore, the daily drying capacity is increased.

One of the major problems with stir drying is wet grain next to the wall. This does not cause a serious problem when the grain is dried in the bin and moved to other storage. The wet grain mixes with the dry grain. When the grain is dried and stored in the bin, the wet grain can spoil. Vertical, perforated tubes spaced about every 9 inches or perforated wall liners installed on the inside of the wall lessen the potential problem of wet corn next to the walls.

Stir drying usually is most appropriate for farmers who dry as little as 10,000 bushels up to about 50,000 bushels of corn per year.

1001-4 *Bin-Batch and Batch Drying with Stirring Equipment* The greatest bottleneck for this type of drying is normally inadequate dry grain conveying equipment. New bins to be used for either method of batch drying should be equipped with an unloading auger under the perforated floor and a conveying system to move dry grain to storage that will convey a minimum of 2,000 bushels per hour.

The conveying system must be arranged so that moving the dry grain can be done with maximum convenience. Vertical legs can be used, but a combination of portable conveyors and permanently installed overhead augers will be less expensive and nearly as convenient. Figure 1001-2A and B is an example arrangement.

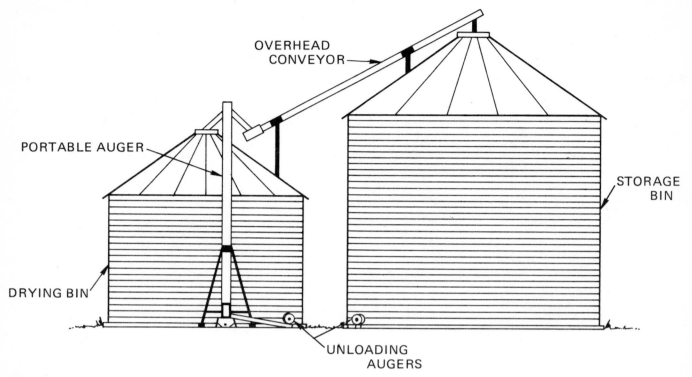

Figure 1001-2B   Front View

1001-5 *Drying with Circulating or Continuous-Flow Equipment* This drying method is most satisfactory when used as a continuous drying system with the corn moved to another storage unit. A minor disadvantage is that the grain must be cooled in storage. Storage bins must be equipped with aeration equipment.

As with stir drying, circulating equipment increases daily drying capacity of conventional bin-batch dryers. Since the drying rate is up to 200 to 250 bushels per hour, dry corn conveying equipment need not have high capacity. This is a major advantage for this method.

This method is appropriate for farmers who dry as little as 12,000 to 50,000 or more bushels of corn per year.

1001-6 *Bin-Batch, Stir Batch and Continuous-Flow Bin Drying* Encourage the operator to consider drying bins used for any of these three systems primarily as dryers and secondly as storage bins. It is easier to manage the drying

operation if these drying bins have a maximum grain depth of 10 to 12 feet.

With all three, if farmers have problems, it normally is not when they are drying the corn and moving it to other storage. Problems are much more common when the corn is dried and stored in the drying bin. The storage capacity of short bins is less, so there is less corn to have problems with.

As an example, assume one of your clients is considering buying one drying bin and one storage bin for 15,000 bushels of corn. Rather than buy two equal size bins (perhaps 27-foot diameter × 16-foot grain depth), suggest to him to consider a 5,000-bushel drying bin (probably a 27-foot diameter × 12-foot grain depth) and a 10,000-bushel storage bin (possibly a 27-foot diameter × 20-foot grain depth).

1001-7 *Roof Drying* With this method, corn is dried in a fixed batch in a cone-shaped perforated

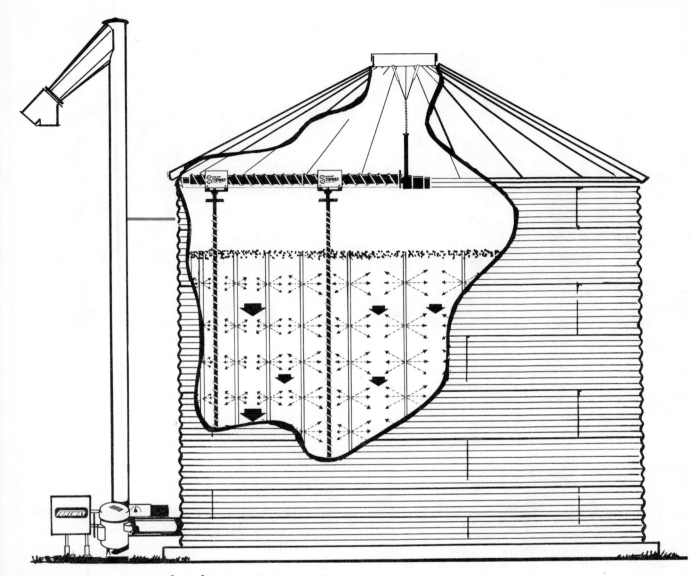

Figure 1001-4 Drying bin showing stirring equipment, perforated wall tubes, and grain unloading equipment. (Courtesy of Sukup Mfg. Co.)

floor installed under the bin roof. Maximum drying depth is 32 inches.

Four batch sizes are available, depending upon bin diameter: 21-foot diameter bin, 750 bushels; 24-foot bin, 1,000 bushels; 27-foot bin, 1,300 bushels; 30-foot bin, 1,600 bushels.

One to three batches per day can be dried. The corn may be cooled in the roof dryer; or to increase drying capacity, an aeration system can be installed in the lower storage area to cool the corn.

An advantage of this method is that the dry batch is dumped in 1 or 2 minutes to the storage area. There is no bottleneck of handling dry corn. Dry corn that accumulates in the storage area can also be slowly conveyed to additional storage bins.

A limitation of the system is that there is no wet corn holding. If more than one batch per day is dried in the bin, trucks and wagons must be available to accumulate the corn that is harvested while the previous batch dries.

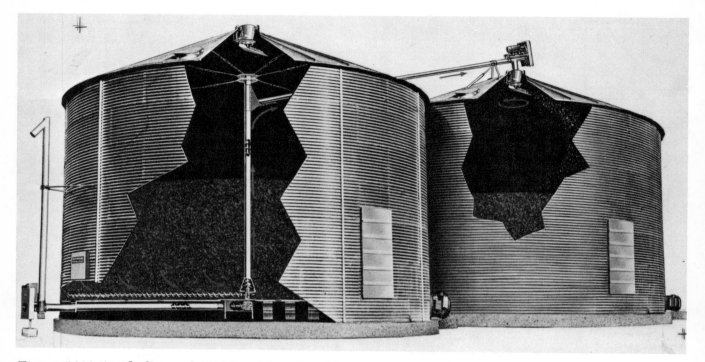

Figure 1001-5   *The bin on the left is equipped with circulating equipment for continuous-flow drying. The grain is stored and cooled in the bin on the right. (Photo courtesy Shivvers Enterprises, Inc.)*

Figure 1001-7   *Roof top dryer showing (1) filling cap; (2) grain retard rings to maintain a 32-inch drying depth; (3) perforated floor; (4) drying fan and heater; (5) trap doors to dump the grain to the storage area; and (6) the winch to lower the trap doors. (Photo courtesy of Stormor, Inc.)*

This system is suitable for farmers who dry 10,000 to 50,000 or more bushels per year.

1001-8   *All Bin Drying Systems* The fan is the key to drying capacity. Air and heat are required for drying corn. A common problem among farmers with bin drying systems is too small a fan. Extra investment for a high capacity fan when he first buys a bin may eliminate the necessity of later trading it for a bigger fan.

1001-9   *Portable Batch Drying* A limitation to portable batch dryers is that someone must be available to load and unload the dryer.

An advantage for portable batch dryers is they are self-contained drying and grain handling systems. The dryer is equipped with grain handling and unloading conveyors.

A portable dryer is most useful when storage is scattered on farms several miles apart or for custom operators.

A portable dryer can be moved from farm to farm. Only the dryer, LP gas tank and one conveyor to convey the corn from the dryer into dry storage needs to be moved.

At least 20,000 bushels of corn per year need

to be dried to economically justify a new portable batch dryer.

1001-10 *Automatic Batch and Continuous-Flow Dryers* These two drying methods require wet corn holding bins and conveying equipment to have a satisfactory drying system.

The total system cost normally requires at least 30,000 bushels of corn to be dried per year to economically justify either of these methods. If annual production of corn to be dried exceeds 50,000 bushels, one of these methods usually is the best choice.

1001-11 *Automatic Batch Dryers* These dryers are usually the best system if a single vertical leg is used to handle both wet corn from the field and dry corn coming from the dryer. These dryers are designed to be filled and emptied fast. High capacity (usually 3,000 bushels per hour) legs and wet corn holding bins mounted over the dryer to permit fast gravity filling of the dryer are the most common grain handling systems.

1001-12 *Continuous-Flow Dryers* These dryers commonly have drying capacities of from 150 to 300 bushels per hour. Since the dryer is almost continously filled with wet corn and the dry corn is almost continuously removed, high capacity conveyors are not needed. Wet corn can be stored in hopper-bottom bins mounted on the ground and augered to the dryer. It does require ample power to drive an auger to convey the wet corn. A double-V belt drive is practically a must.

The only great need for high capacity grain conveying in a continuous-flow drying system is to unload the grain wagons or trucks and move the corn into the wet corn holding bins. A minimum capacity of 2,000 bushels per hour is suggested.

1002 **High-Moisture Corn** The easiest way to store corn is as high-moisture corn. It is rare to find a farmer who is not satisfied with high-moisture corn storage systems.

High-moisture corn can be stored in trench silos, conventional upright silos and gastight silos. Either high-moisture shelled corn or ground ear corn can be fed to beef or dairy cattle. It is normally the least cost and most appropriate method of corn storage for the beef cattle feeder.

High-moisture shelled corn, usually stored in a gastight silo, can be a satisfactory storage method for swine producers. The corn does need to be fed once or twice a day during warm weather.

1002-1 *Storage of Chemically Treated Corn* Use of a fungicide such as propionic acid, acetic acid or a combination is the newest method for storing corn. Treated corn must be fed. It would be Sample Grade if sold because of foreign odor. Cost for fungicide-treated corn may be comparable to commercial drying.

At present it appears most logical that fungicide-treated corn will be most appropriate for swine production enterprises and smaller dairy and beef feeding enterprises.

Metal grain storage facilities may need to be sprayed with some type of paint to protect them from corroding if mild acid fungicides are used.

1003 **Locating Grain Storage Facilities**
A new grain storage facility is a permanent fixture on a farmstead. It is essential for a farmer to wisely select the correct site. You can provide a valuable service to your client if you can help him choose a site that he will be happy with for years to come. There are several important principles for locating and arranging grain storage centers. Keep them in mind when you consult with your client.

1003-1 *Expansion* This is probably the most important. Help him select a site to which he can not only add more storage structures but also one on which the center itself can be modified. For example, in the future the operator may find he needs to add new or a different type of drying facility. He may want to add grain cleaning equipment—or feed processing. A well-thought-out plan will allow for these changes. Often an area about 150 feet × 100 feet is ample for a fairly large center.

1003-2 *Proximity to Other Buildings* Select a site at least 150 to 200 feet away from residences to minimize noise and dust pollution. Locate grain bins or other buildings between drying fans and residences to serve as a noise shield. Consider locating the grain center so processed feed can be conveyed directly to livestock facilities. High-moisture grain storage structures are usually best located next to the beef or dairy cattle lots, such as suggested in the chapter on silage storage. It is best to locate grain centers 50 feet (100 feet, if possible) from other buildings for fire protection.

1003-3   *Drainage* This is always an important consideration for all new buildings. If possible, select a well drained hilltop or sidehill. If the best site is on a slope, build a terrace above the center to divert surface water around it. Raise the floor level of all buildings 12 to 18 inches above the existing grade to prevent any water from entering them.

1003-4   *Access* Locate the center close to an all-weather road. Do keep in mind farmsteads which have the farm home closest to the public road generally have the most pleasant appearance. The roads to and around the center should be graveled or rocked. Try to select a site so the roads to and around the center will not encounter a problem with drifting snow. Be sure there is ample room for large grain trucks to easily maneuver.

1003-5   *Sun* If the farmer is going to unload or load grain in the open, the south side is warmer than the north side.

1003-6   *Utilities* Be sure ample electric power is available. Advise your client to check early with his local power use advisor about his plans. He can provide valuable tips.

1003-7   *Complete Circuit Grain Conveying* Help the farmer develop a convenient grain conveying system. Strive for a system so he can mechanically convey grain from any one bin to any other bin or grain conditioning facility in the system. Permanent vertical legs are most convenient and expensive. If feeding processing equipment will be a part of the system, a vertical leg is most

easily justified. Portable inclined conveyors, particularly when used with permanently installed overhead augers, can be organized into a convenient, low-cost grain handling system. Figure 1001-2a is one example. Help the farmer develop a system so he does not need to frequently move portable conveyors during the harvesting season.

1003-8   *Select a New Site* The best choice for a new grain storage center may be a considerable distance from the existing farmstead. Be brave! If this appears to you to be a good choice, suggest it to the farmer. He may never have considered it. Six important reasons may justify moving as much as a mile or more away from the farmstead to a more favorable site. (1) Better drainage, (2) better road access, (3) a more central location, (4) availability to 3-phase electric power, (5) availability to natural gas, and (6) better expansion potential for livestock operations. There are disadvantages for a remote site. It is less convenient to manage grain drying equipment, to frequently check stored grain, and to prevent pilfering and vandalism.

1003-9   *Using an Existing Corncrib* Many farmers remodel structurally sound corncribs to shelled corn storage. If the crib is located so there is ample room around it for a convenient flow of traffic and space for expansion, a remodeled crib can be a wise choice as the best site to start a grain center. If the crib is poorly located, but structurally sound, perhaps it can be remodeled to be used for a grain resealing storage unit when the corn will be left in storage for a couple years or more. Figure 1003-9a(1) shows an example of how to organize a drying bin by a crib without an inside elevator. Figure 1003-9a is an example way to locate a drying bin and future storage bins around a crib with an inside elevator. Figure 1003-9a(2) is one more example layout with an inside elevator. It also shows how additional storage might be added. Any new system development should have space for additional storage.

1003-9A   *Remodeling the Crib* A crib remodeled for shelled corn will have a capacity of approximately twice as much shelled corn as ear corn. For example, a crib that will store 5,000 bushels of ear corn will store approximately 10,000 bushels of shelled corn. A crib will normally cost 10 to 20¢ per bushel for the total shelled corn capacity to convert. Ten thousand bushels of shelled corn in the example should cost between $1,000 and $2,000 to remodel.

The crib must be made graintight for shelled corn storage. It should also be weathertight for long-term, safe grain storage. Although the old cribbing is usually left on the crib, it's best to install some type of lining inside the crib so grain is not in contact with the old siding. If the grain is stored against the old siding, when the crib is emptied, a few kernels will remain on the edge of the old siding. This is an ideal place for stored grain insects to remain in the crib, which makes it difficult for the farmer to thoroughly clean the crib each year.

Most crib walls need to be structurally reinforced at three places.

1. The connection between the stud and sill.
2. About half way up the wall (either cables or rods and wales are commonly used).
3. And at the top of the wall.

Midwest Plan Service publication, "Remodeling Corn Cribs for Small Grain Storage," available from midwest extension agricultural engineers' offices, gives numerous alternatives for making a crib graintight and structurally reinforcing it.

1004 Construction Considerations

One of the first decisions to make in planning for grain storage is the space requirement. Table B11 (Appendix B) provides bulk density figures for most grain products. With these data, size and number of storage structures can be calculated when the management decision has been made on how much total grain storage is necessary as dictated by the cropping and/or feeding programs.

1004-1 *Foundations.* Foundation requirements for grain storage structures are calculated similarly to other farm buildings. The grain load must, however, be included as bin load. Table B11 can be used for calculating the total grain load. If the grain is stored in bulk, which is common, and the floor of the bin rests on the ground or

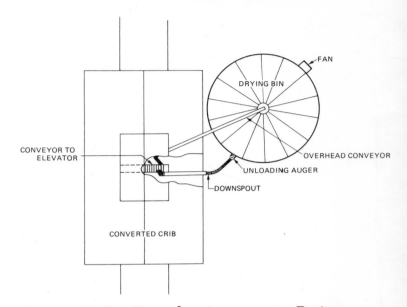

Figure 1003-9A   Example   Arrangement—Drying bin located adjacent to a crib with an inside elevator.

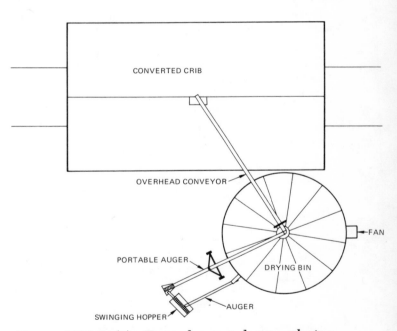

Figure 1003-9A(1)   Example way to locate a drying bin adjacent to a crib without an inside elevator.

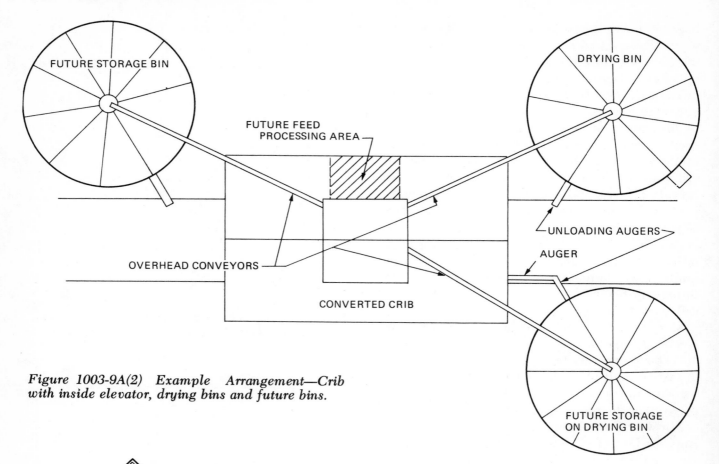

Figure 1003-9A(2) Example Arrangement—Crib with inside elevator, drying bins and future bins.

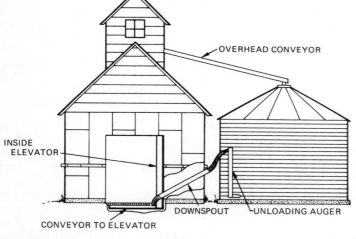

Figure 1003-9B End View

at least is separate from the perimeter foundation; then some proportion of the grain weight is transferred to the walls and the rest to the floor. These loads should be calculated by an engineer and the structure designed by him.

1004-2 *Anchoring.* The empty bin is most vulnerable to being shifted or lifted by the impact of wind, grain-handling equipment or livestock. The anchoring systems should not interfere with or be exposed to damage by farm equipment or livestock. For portable bins, the anchors should be easily installed and disconnected. Similar anchorage may also be required for temporary emergency bins if they cannot be filled immediately after erection.

1004-3 *Floors.* The floor should be designed to prevent any water penetration into the grain. It should also be tight enough to prevent excessive leakage of fumigant vapors. If a floor of perforated metal or similar material is used, the design should permit convenient and effective sealing of the space beneath the floor, to prevent entry of old grain and foreign material that may harbor stored grain insects or attract rodents. Structural details of fabricated materials that introduce obstructions, cracks, or pockets at the floor surface should be avoided if practical. This is particularly important if the bin will have a mechanical sweep-type unloader.

The design of hopper-bottom bins is critical. The floor slope must be 10° greater than the emptying angle of repose of the grain. See Table B15 for these angles. This will assure ready removal, except if wet grain is to be handled through the hopper bottom, it should have a slope 25° greater than the angle of repose for clean, dry grain as given in Table B15. The floor supporting system and the flooring material must be designed to withstand the vertical loads.

The flooring near doors and corners may be subjected to impact, abrasion, and tearing by shovels and grain-conveying equipment. Protection from or resistance to such damage should be provided. Similarly the floor should be resistant to or protected from gnawing by rodents or damage by termites. Structural features and material treatments that will prevent the loss of necessary strength and tightness due to wood rot, metal rust, or disintegration of masonry should be used, especially in permanent storages. Flooring materials that contact the grain should not, however, be treated with creosote as this will induce commercially objectionable foreign odors.

Figures 1004-3*a* and *b* show details for water proofing the floor and floor-wall junction, foundation and floor construction and a method of anchoring wall to foundation. Polyethylene film may be used for the vapor barrier in the floor in lieu of the indicated composition roofing.

1004-5 *Walls.* Exterior wall materials and joints should exclude draining water and rain or snow blown from any direction. Any exterior stay timbers or door frames, where snow or water may accumulate, should be flashed. Exterior walls should be protected from solar heat to retard or

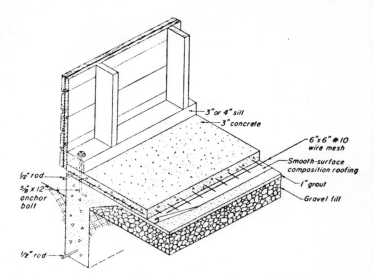

Figure 1004-3A Concrete Floor and Foundation for Wood Grain Bin, Showing Composition Roofing Used as Moisture Barrier. Note Anchor Bolts, Reinforcing Rods, and Wire Mesh.

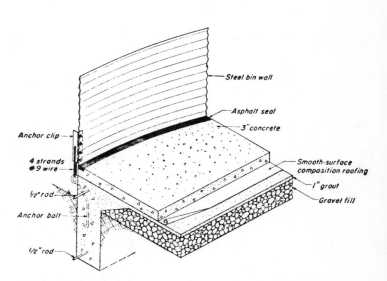

Figure 1004-3b Concrete Floor and Foundation for Steel Grain Bin. Floor is 1 Inch or More Above Lower Edge of Bin Wall. Note Moisture Barrier, Asphalt Seal at Wall, and Means of Anchoring Bin to Foundation.

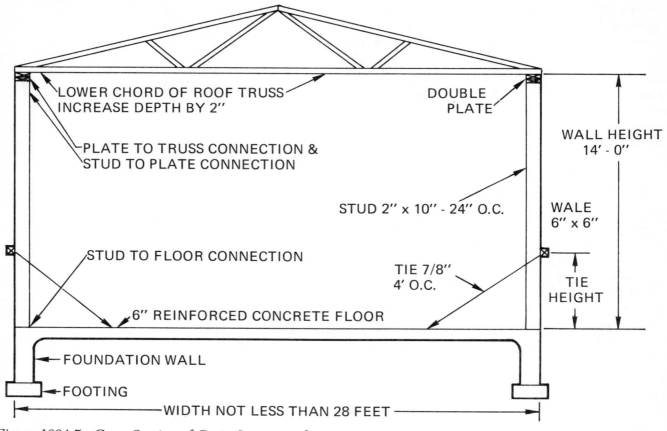

Figure 1004-5 Cross Section of Grain Storage with 14′ Wall Height.

prevent damage to bulk grain and possibly damage to the wall from overloading. White paint or other reflective surface and/or shading are most practical. If further insulation is used to eliminate daily fluctuations in grain temperature, it should have a thermal conductance equivalent to that of 12 in. of wheat, which is approximately 0.08 Btu/Ft^2 − Hr − °F. Storage bins that are equipped with a satisfactory aeration system have less need for insulated side walls except in the hot tropical and subtropical climates.

All walls should be tight enough to prevent excessive leakage of fumigant vapors. Any of the common wall materials, except perforated metal, will meet this requirement if kept in good repair. All parts of the interior wall should be self-cleaning to assure complete removal of old grain that might harbor insects.

Strength requirements for walls must be determined by an engineer. Design loads should allow for ordinary changes in pressure that may occur during filling and emptying or because of thermal expansion. Wall failures have been observed in corrugated metal bins for corn storage. The failure generally occurs where lighter gage sheets gradually fold down onto the heavier gage supporting sheets. This deformation always occurs on the wall receiving the most solar radiation.

While the round metal bins are mostly prefabricated, thus properly designed, tested and tried under practical conditions, the larger frame-type grain storage structures must each be designed. Fig. 1004-5 illustrates a cross section of a frame structure. Note that in general, these structures are at least twice as wide as they are high. A similar type of structure may be designed for pole construction. For frame and pole buildings, the size and spacing of vertical members, size and spacing of wall ties and wale size are all critical. These specifications are given in Table 1004-5.

Table 1004-5 Stud & Tie Recommendations for Large Grain Storages

Height of wall (feet)	Stud spacing (inches)	Stud size	Tie diameter** (inches) unthreaded	threaded	Wale Size	Tie Height
12	24	2″×8″	1/2-4′oc.	3/4-4′oc	6×6	3′0″
12	16	2″×6″	1/2-4′oc.	3/4-4′oc	4×6	3′0″
14	24	2″×10″	3/4-4′oc.		6×6	4′2″
14	16	2″×8″	3/4-4′oc.	7/8-32″oc	4×6	4′2″
16	16	2″×10″	3/4-4′oc.	7/8-32″oc	6×6	4′10″
16	12	2″×8″	3/4-4′oc.	3/4″×2′oc	6×6	4′10″
18	16	2″×10″	1″-4′oc.	1″-16″oc	°	5′5″
18	12	2″×10″	1″-4′oc	5/8″-1′oc	°	5′5″
20	12	2″×12″	3/4-2′oc	3/4-1′oc	°	6′0″

°No wale needed. Use metal plates to transfer load from tie to siding and studs.

°°1/2-4′ oc. means 1/2 inch diameter tie every 4 feet along the wall.

†Based on Group C Lumber.

The horizontal distance from the wall for the base tie connections is the same as the wall height. The tie forces are large, thus they must be properly anchored to deformed reinforcing bars in the concrete or specially designed commercial fasteners.

Table 1004-5A provides further information on siding materials and a nailing schedule. The

Table 1004-5A Siding Recommendations for Large Grain Storages

Height of wall (feet)	Stud spacing (inches)	Siding material	thickness	Nailing Schedule** size	number per foot
8	16	Plywood†	3/8″	8d	3
	24	Plywood†	5/8″	8d	4
	36	Lumber	1′°	10d	4
	24	Corrugated steel	2 1/2″-28 ga.	Should be applied to inside of studs.	
12	16	Plywood†	3/8″	8d	3
	24	Plywood†	5/8″	10d	3
	30	Lumber	1″°	12d	4
	18	Corrugated steel	2 1/2″-28 ga.	Should be applied to inside of studs.	
16	12	Plywood†	3/8″	8d	3
	16	Plywood†	1/2″	10d	3
	24	Plywood†	3/4″	12d	4
	24	Lumber	1″°	12d	4
20	12	Plywood†	1/2″	8d	4
	16	Plywood†	5/8″	10d	4
	16	Corrugated steel	2 1/2″-28 ga.	Should be applied to inside of studs.	

°Nominal dimension

°°*All nails are deformed shank nails,* ie., screw-nails or ring-shanked nails, except where lining is applied to inside of studs.

†Face grain of plywood should be perpendicular to the studs. All plywood wood to be exterior type.

stub-to-floor and stud-to-plate connections are particularly critical. They must withstand lateral pressures of from 400 to 600 lb depending on bin depth. Table B3 gives the allowable lateral load which can be resisted by different sized nails. Some special types of metal plate connectors should preferably be used. Where roof trusses are spaced four feet on center, its connection to the plate must resist the loads from two or three studs.

1004-6 *Roofs.* All roof joints should exclude draining or standing water and blowing rain or snow. Condensation on the underside of metal roofs should not normally be a problem when bins are filled with well conditioned grain that is safe for storage.

Roofs, as the side walls, that are protected from solar heat by white paint or with other reflective surfaces or shading, or both, provide a more comfortable space for workmen and retard insect activity by minimizing the temperature of the surface layers of grain. The eaves and other roof joints should not only be tight enough to turn away birds but also insects. Such construction will also help prevent the dissipation of fumigant vapors during windy weather.

The headroom should not be more than 2-1/2 ft. at a distance, not more than 3 ft. from any wall. This will permit reasonably convenient space for grain inspection. Bin capacity ratings should be based on this minimum headroom requirement; however, design loads should allow for the possible filling of the bin to the eaves.

1004-7 *Openings, Ducts and Closures.* The openings and closures of the structure often fail to exclude draining or standing water and blowing rain or snow. Inadequate flashing, defective joints, and deformation at the edges of openings and closures are common faults. Doors or hatch covers that do not fit properly may have to be pried open or hammered shut. Materials are often used without necessary protection or reinforcing to prevent warping and swelling or bending and buckling.

All ducts or spouts and the framework for openings should be easy to clean or self-cleaning. A 24- to 32-mesh screen should be used over all

openings to limit the entrance of insects. A small leakage of grain from defective joints may not be noticed until a large quantity has escaped and been consumed by rodents, birds or livestock.

1004-8 *General Requirements.* Portable bins for semi-permanent locations should meet all of the requirements for permanent storages. Materials and construction of the lightest weight that will meet these requirements should be used. If this is not possible, the bin dimensions should be reduced and additional units built to meet the required storage capacity.

1005 Silage Storage

When the farm builder advises livestock producers about the most appropriate type of silage storage to build, he should emphasize the best features of each.

Upright silos are most compatible when combined with conveyor feeding systems. They have lower storage losses (see Table 1005). Adverse weather, particularly heavy snow, does not affect the unloading operation. These systems do require better planning to develop a satisfactory system because the storage and feeding facilities are connected. Upright silos and conveyor feeding systems are most common for dairy farms and up to 1000-head beef feedlots.

Horizontal silos are better suited for wagon feeding systems. The investment per ton of silage is lower than for uprights. It is easier to expand size of the livestock operation with a combination of horizontal silos and bunks filled with self-unloading wagons. These systems are most com-

Table 1005. Estimated Average Silage Storage Losses Under Good Management, with Moisture Content Between 45 and 60 Percent

Type of Silo	Percent of Loss Average	Range
Gastight°	5	1–11
Concrete stave°	6	2–12
Bunker or trench	15	10–25
Stack	20	12–25

°Based on experiments by USDA at Beltsville, Md. and experiment stations at South Dakota, Illinois, Wisconsin and Pennsylvania.

mon for beef feeding operations of about 1000 head and greater.

1005-1 *Silo Size*
Use the tables on pages 234–246 of Appendix B to help the livestock producer determine the silage storage capacity he needs. First determine the total amount of silage needed. Then list the various silo sizes that will store that amount. Finally, select the size of silo so a minimum of 2 inches of silage is removed per day from a conventional upright silo and a 4-inch slice per day from a horizontal silo.

1005-2 *Upright Silos*
The tighter a silo is, the less the expected dry matter loss will be if all other good management practices are followed. Regardless of the type of silo, top management practices will minimize storage losses.

A silo should be filled as fast as possible. The silo should be equipped with a silage distributor so the silage will be loaded uniformly into the silo.

Conventional silos with tight walls and well sealed doors are fairly airtight except at the surface. Cover the top surface of stored silage with a sheet of plastic to minimize spoilage. Conventional concrete upright silos must have a good inner lining and tight doors.

Gastight silos do allow more flexibility. Feeding rate is not as critical as with conventional concrete silos. Feeding can be stopped for a time with less concern about spoilage.

If a farmer is considering storing large tonnages of silage in upright silos, have him consider more than one structure. In the future he might want to store two kinds of feedstuffs rather than one—perhaps silage and high-moisture corn. Two silos permit this. For example, if he needs 1000 tons of storage, one 30′ diameter × 60′ high silo would be sufficient; but two 20′ diameter × 70′ high silos will provide a similar capacity. Although the two silos will provide more flexibility, they will likely cost more.

Encourage farmers to use upright silos the year around in their feeding operation. A silo built for corn silage might be refilled with haylage in the spring for summer feeding.

1005-3 *Upright Silo Unloaders*
The unloading rate varies considerably with the type of material, length of cut and moisture content. Frozen material unloads more slowly than unfrozen.

The average unloading rate is about 1 ton per hour for each horsepower of the unloader for corn silage. This can vary from about 1/2 ton per hour to 1-1/2 tons per hour. The rate for haylage is about two-thirds of that for corn silage.

1005-4 *Horizontal Silos*
The farmer must be encouraged to follow proper management during filling and do a good job of sealing the surface to keep the storage losses to a minimum.

Thorough packing is necessary with horizontal silos because they do not have the advantage of extra weight to help pack the silage as in a vertical silo. A good plastic cover weighted to keep it from flapping in the wind can reduce top spoilage. Old tires, chopped forage or weeds have been used successfully for weighting.

1005-5 *Horizontal Silo Unloaders*
The labor requirement to fill self-unloading wagons can be high if high-capacity loading is not available. Most feeders use an industrial or heavy-duty front-end hydraulic loader to load wagons. This type of loader does loosen the silage and could result in increased surface spoilage if only a few inches were removed from the surface each day.

A 4-wheel-drive industrial loader or a tractor or truck-mounted horizontal silo unloader can be justified for larger operations. The horizontal silo unloader cuts material from the exposed vertical silage without disturbing the packed silage and introducing air. These unloaders can load a 2-ton wagon in 3 to 5 minutes.

1005-6 *Locating the Silo*
After the type and size of a new silo have been selected, the time has come to make one of the most important decisions—*where to locate it*. You can perform a valuable service to the farmer by helping him select the site. You can be more objective.

Remind the farmer that this decision will affect

Figure 1005-6 Two upright silos located outside of lot. They are equipped to discharge into feeding wagons. A mechanized feeding system could be developed in the future. (Photo courtesy of Waterloo Farm Systems, Inc.)

the feeding operations for years to come—and to think seriously about the future when making this decision.

Each farmer will have different conditions to meet when deciding where to locate new storage structures. They may desire to locate them close to existing facilities. On the other hand, help him carefully evaluate whether this is the best choice. For example, it does not make sense to build a new large-diameter silo close to an old one if they will both be out of date because of insufficient capacity and poor location in a few years.

Numerous farmers are very happy with their choice to move new storage structures several hundred feet to perhaps a mile from an old established site.

The specific location principles or the relationship of the storage facilities to the rest of the lot will vary between different types of storage structures because the feed is moved from them differently.

There are four characteristics that are important when locating and arranging new silage storage structures.

1005-6a *Good Drainage.* Locate silage storage facilities so there is drainage away from the site in all directions. Always avoid locating in a pothole area. There will not only be a continuous water problem, but wet subsoils do not satisfactorily support the foundations of upright structures. Tilting silos are frequently seen when they are built in areas of poor drainage.

If the best location is on a hillside, a terrace built above the facilities will divert water away from the storage area.

To assure that no surface water will enter silage storage facilities, the floor level should be 12 to 18 inches above the existing grade. Figures 1005-6a(1) and (2) are examples of the type of drainage to strive for.

1005-6b *Effects of Sun and Wind.* In open-lot beef and dairy feeding areas that have cold winter weather, locate all tall structures, such as storage facilities, on the north side or on the northeast or northwest corner of the lot as shown in Fig. 1005-6b. Facilities so located will cast very little, if any, shadows into the lot. Therefore, the sun has a better chance to thaw manure that will freeze in the lots in cold weather.

If it's necessary to locate tall structures on the south side of the lot, erect them as far away from the lot fence as possible to minimize the shading.

There are other good reasons to locate the storage facilities as shown in Fig. 1005-6A (2). Properly arranged storage structures located on the north side of the lot will provide some wind-break protection from the cold northerly winds.

Don't locate a building closer than 100 feet south of an open shed if winter winds come from a northerly direction. The winds can "bounce" back toward the shed and cause drafts or even snowdrifting problems.

If summer breezes generally come from a southern direction, it is better not to have any facilities along the south side of the lot to block these breezes.

1005-6c *Convenience* Silage must be moved into and out of storage. Good all-weather access roads are a necessity. Locate the roads so snow-drifting will not be a problem.

Year-around access to silage storage facilities is more convenient if there are no gates to open and close. Do not locate inside the lot area.

1005-6d *Flexibility* Plan upright silo systems so they can be expanded in the future and also so the method of feeding from them can be changed. For example, a silo might be erected so that feed could be hauled away from it in a self-unloading wagon to feed in a fenceline system. In the future a mechanical bunk system might be added. Therefore, locate silos with the flexibility of using either system.

Always leave space in the plans for at least two and perhaps three or four more silos in the future.

1005-7 **Tips** Following are specific arrangement, location and construction tips for horizontal and upright silos.

1005-7a *Horizontal silos*
Do not locate horizontal silos too close to a residence. Odors may be a nuisance.

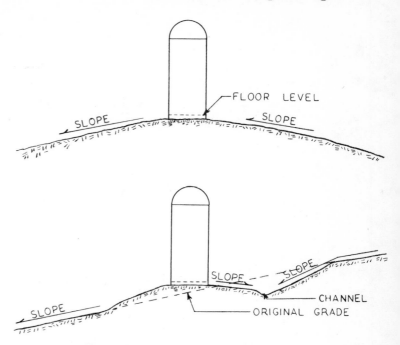

Figure 1005-6A(1) Drainage away from silos.

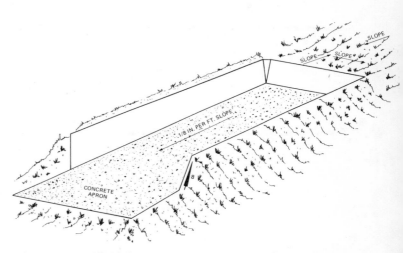

Figure 1005-6A(2) Drainage around horizontal silo.

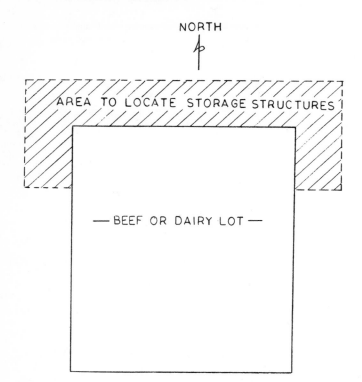

Figure 1005-6B   Suggested area to locate silos.

Dimensions, feet	
H	A
12	4
14	5
16	5
18	5

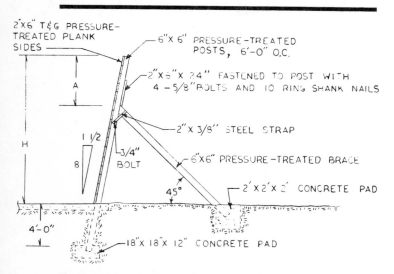

Figure 1005-7A(1)   Example post and plank horizontal silo wall cross section.

Be sure drainage from the end of a silo does not enter a well or stream where it could cause pollution.

Deeper silos minimize storage losses. Build them at least 6 feet deep and 10 to 12 feet or higher is better. Don't build them too deep to satisfactorily remove the silage with available equipment.

Slope the sidewalls out 1 foot for each 8 feet of height so the silage will not pull away from the walls as it settles.

The concrete floor should be a minimum of 5 inches thick to accommodate heavy vehicle traffic. Pour the concrete on a sheet of 4-mil plastic and keep the top surface wet for maximum strength. Thicken the edge where vehicles enter the silo to 8 inches. Extend the concrete floor 10 to 20 feet in front of the silo to minimize mud problems. The floor should slope a minimum of 1/8 inch per foot out of the silo for drainage.

In most soils, a permanent silo should have concrete or wood side walls to prevent annual wall maintenance.

The location of a horizontal silo in relation to the lot is not as critical as for upright silos since the feed is commonly hauled away from the silo in wagons. Do choose a well-drained site with good access for filling and unloading. If a hillside is available, this is usually the best choice. It is better to have the open end facing south for maximum sun exposure.

The type of construction you will recommend depends primarily on the type of material and building equipment you are best suited to provide. Figure 1005-7A (1) is an example post and plank, above-ground horizontal silo and Figures 1005-7A (2) and 1005-7A (3) show example construction details for below-ground tilt-up concrete silos. There are many sources of technical literature available to provide you with structural details. One excellent example is Midwest Plan Service 15, Tilt-Up Concrete Horizontal Silo Construction. It is available from many County Extension offices and all extension agricultural engineering offices in the Mid-Central States.

If you are going to build the silo, be sure you and the farmer are in complete agreement about all points. Get the agreement in writing. Such points as strength of concrete, type of concrete finish, thickness of concrete floors, etc. should be included. Too many disagreements, even lawsuits, result from the farm builder and farmer having a different concept in their minds about what the end product will be like.

1005-7b *Vertical Silos*

A good location for a vertical silo for a beef or dairy feeding operation is close to but not in the cattle yard. If it's located at least 16 feet from the lot fence as shown in Figure 1005-7b (1), there is adequate access room in front of most silos to fill a wagon. With this location, a mechanical bunk system can be adapted to the silo either as part of the original construction or at some time in the future. An example of this is shown in Figure 1005-7b (2). Figure 1005-7b (3) shows how the original single silo can be expanded into a four-silo system.

Remember—the best location for a feed storage and processing center is in the north side or northeast or northwest corner of the lot, as shown in Fig. 1005-6b.

At the present time most farmers do not have elaborate feed processing and metering equipment. Some are changing and more undoubtedly will in the future. A small control building in front of silos is common to house electrical controls and feed processing and metering equipment.

H, Feet	Tie Bar Size
12	4
14	4
16	6
18	6

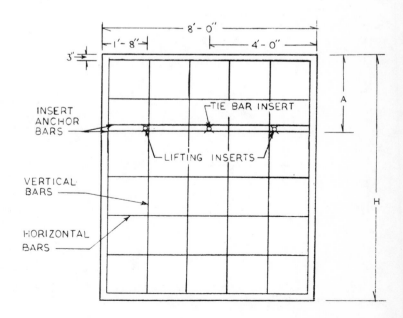

Figure 1005-7A(2) Example cross section of below-grade tilt-up horizontal silo.

Table 1005-7A 5-1/2″ Thick—8′ Wide Panel Dimension and Reinforcing Schedule

H Feet	Vertical Bars	Horizontal Bars	Insert Reinforcing Bars	A Feet
12	6 #4 @ 16″	8 #4 @ 18″	2 #5	3′—0″
14	8 #4 @ 12″	9 #4 @ 18″	2 #5	3′—6″
16	13 #4 @ 7-1/2″	11 #4 @ 18″	3 #5	4′—0″
18	19 #4 @ 5″	12 #4 @ 18″	3 #5	4′—6″

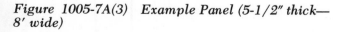

Figure 1005-7A(3) Example Panel (5-1/2″ thick— 8′ wide)

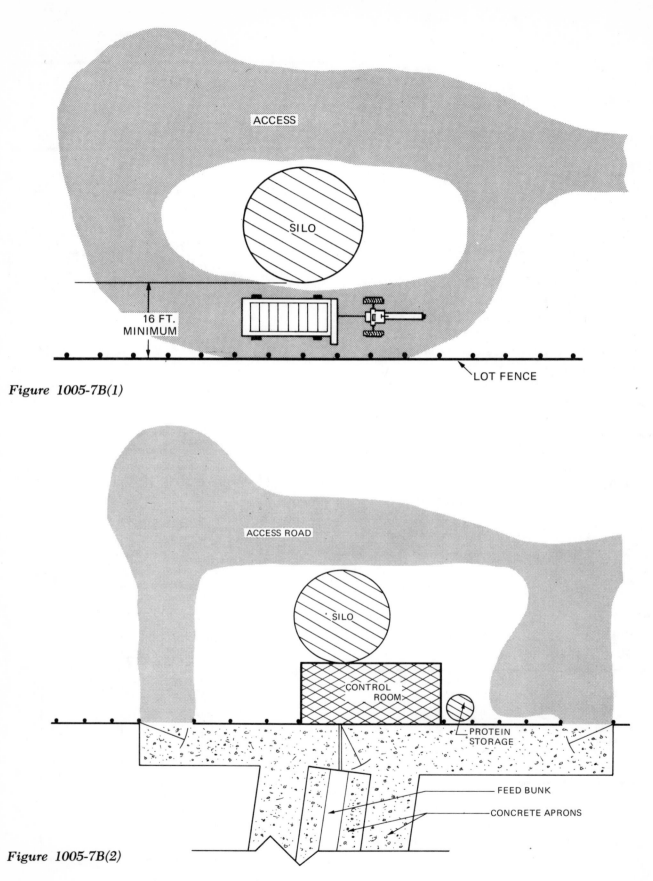

Figure 1005-7B(1)

ACCESS

SILO

16 FT. MINIMUM

LOT FENCE

ACCESS ROAD

SILO

CONTROL ROOM

PROTEIN STORAGE

FEED BUNK

CONCRETE APRONS

Figure 1005-7B(2)

166

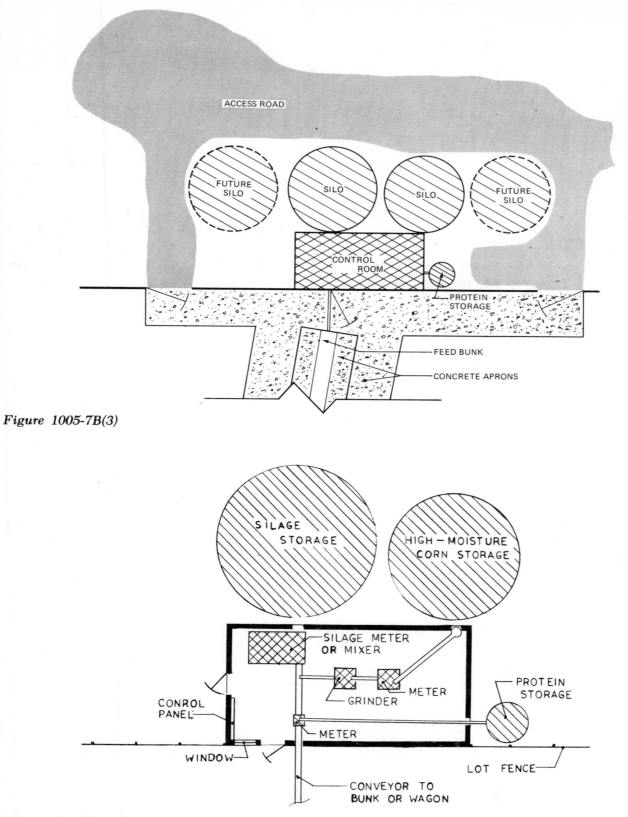

Figure 1005-7B(3)

Figure 1005-7B(4)   Optional Equipment in a Control Room.

Leave room to add other additional equipment in the future. A building 16 to 20 feet wide and 20 to 30 feet long should have sufficient room to include all of the equipment shown in Fig. 1005-7b (4) if the need arises in the future.

Note the control room is not built around a silo. It is only attached to the front. This is an easier way to connect it. Do not make any physical connection between the silo and control room until the silo has been filled the first time. A new silo will settle several inches because of the silage weight.

The National Silo Association, 1201 Waukegan Road, Glenview, Illinois, 60025, has Recommended Practices for Construction of Concrete Stave Silos. It includes such items as standard minimum construction tolerances for roundness, plumb, bulging, etc.

1005-7c *Convenience and Safety*

In conclusion, help the farmer develop silage storage and handling facilities for convenience and safety. The two go hand-in-hand. For example, a start-stop switch for a silo unloader in the silo provides both when checking the operation of the unloader. This switch should be wired so the unloader can't be accidentally started from the ground when anyone is working on the unloader.

Chapter 11

METAL BUILDINGS

by GEORGE E. BRUNNER, JR.
Editor and Publisher, Metal Building Review

1101 Unlike other chapters which relate to site built structures, this chapter attempts to review pre-fabricated metal buildings for which the engineering and the component design have been completely accomplished at the factory.

The responsibility of the farm builder is to erect the structure in accordance with the manufacturer's directions on foundations appropriate to the design of the structure, the soil conditions, and in conformity with applicable building codes.

1102 Types

Factory built metal buildings generally consist of four basic types as described by the Metal Building Manufacturers Association.

1102-1 Rigid Frame

This type of building is a continuous frame consisting of rafters (tapered or uniform depth) rigidly connected to vertical, fixed, or pin-based columns (tapered or uniform depth). The frame spans across the width of the building and is spaced on predetermined bay lengths and supports the secondary framing and the roof and wall covering.

1102-2 Beam and Column

This type of building utilizes a tapered or uniform depth beam or girder supported on columns and can be either a clear span or a multi-span structure. This primary framing is spaced on predetermined bay lengths and supports the secondary framing and the roof and wall covering.

1102-3 Truss Frame

This type of building can be either a single span or multi-span structure. The truss properly braced is supported by columns. This primary framing is spaced on pre-determined bay lengths and supports the secondary framing and the roof and wall covering.

1102-4 Self-Framing

This type of building can be a single span or multi-span structure utilizing the roof and wall covering as a load bearing diaphragm in addition to its function as an exterior skin of the building.

1103 Erection

Because metal buildings for farm use are manufactured in so many types and sizes, it is not possible to write a set of erection instructions which will pertain to all or even most of them. However, there are some features that are common to all.

When shipments are received in the field, two inspections are necessary:

1103-1 Boxes, crates, bundles, uncrated large structural members should be checked with the packing list as they are unloaded from the carrier.

1103-2 When bundles, crates, cartons or boxes are opened during the erection of the building, another check must be performed to determine quantity and condition of the contents. If during inspection No. 1 damages or shortages are found, a report should be filed with the carrier immediately at the site. When bundles, crates, cartons, boxes have been obviously damaged, they should be opened and inspected thoroughly at the time the shipment is received. Panel crates should be

Figure 1100A-1 *This horse and livestock show arena is a clearspan 200' × 20' rigid frame structure manufactured by Braden Steel Corp. of Tulsa. Accompanying pictures show how these frames were erected.*

Figure 1100A-2 *Two-piece center portion of the 200' roof beam is bolted together on the ground.*

opened and inspected for water damage. Galvanized panel crates should always be opened and inspected for white rust.

If during inspection No. 2, damages to or shortages of items are found upon opening the crates or cartons, then a written claim should be sent to the carrier within five working days of discovering the damage or shortage. If a shortage is discovered within a container, then a written notice should be mailed to the manufacturer at the same time the claim is sent to the carrier.

1104 Design Loads

Factory manufactured metal buildings are engineered to meet published design data. Included in this data are dead load, which is the weight of all permanent construction; roof live load, which includes all loads exerted on a roof except dead, wind and lateral loads; wind load, which is the load caused by the wind blowing from any horizontal direction; impact load, the assumed load resulting from the motion of machinery, elevators, craneways and hoists; seismic load, which is the assumed lateral load acting in any horizontal direction on the structural frame due to the action of earthquakes.

Buildings should not be compared on the basis of weight, which may not necessarily be indicative of ability to withstand the desired wind, live and other loads. It is standard practice to design each part of a building for maximum economy within the limits of good engineering practice. Parts are precision made, assuring the required strength as well as interchangeability.

Figure 1100A-3 *Crane lifts the bolted center of the roof beam into position while gin pole trucks secure the outer portions of the roof beam which have been bolted to the columns.*

Steels, likewise, are made under controlled conditions and have known properties. Since uniformity of size and material is obtained in all parts, and since these components have been integrated into an engineering system with highly predictable design values, the farm builder must erect each structure exactly in accordance with the manufacturer's drawings. Columns and roof beams, purlins and girts, end wall posts and other major structural components should not be shortened or lengthened in the field without the advice of the manufacturer.

Flange braces, wind bracing and other components of the package must not be deleted, nor substituted for, without the manufacturer's advice. Equipment and hoists must not be suspended from the building structure without the advice of the factory.

Anchor bolts must be set with precision in order to simplify erection and to obtain full design capacity.

1105 Foundations

The farm builder must not assume that because he has designed foundations for frame wall and masonry buildings, he can safely design foundations for metal buildings. The foundation that will support the building that is being erected will not necessarily withstand the tremendous outward thrust that a snow load will impose at the column base of a rigid frame structure.

Manufacturers furnish column reactions to the loading conditions for which each building is designed. The farm builder must be sure that the foundations are adequate to withstand these forces. Where there is any doubt about foundation design, a professional engineer should be retained.

1106 Insulation

More than 90% of all metal buildings are insulated with flexible fiberglass blankets from 3′ to 6′ wide in thicknesses of 1″, 1-1/2″ and 2″ faced with a vaporseal. Vaporseals are of unsupported vinyl film, aluminum foil, and combinations of vinyl film, foil and kraft paper with a reinforcing skrim. Choice of materials involves cost versus impermeability to passage of water vapor, ability to apply the material at low temperature, UL flame

171

Figure 1100A-4 Center portion is bolted in place to complete the primary frame which is composed of the roof beam and the two columns.

Figure 1100A-5 As frames are erected, purlins and girts are secured to hold each frame in alignment.

Figure 1100B Open web columns and beams are a distinctive feature of Cuckler rigid frame buildings on farms all over the country.

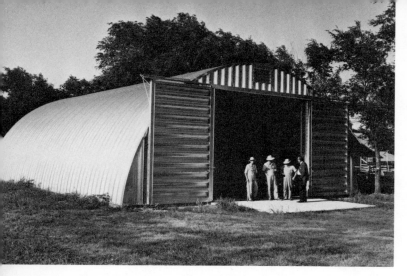

Figure 1100C This Behlen arched building is a familiar sight on midwestern farms.

Figure 1100D This self-framing building by Behlen shows that the deep ribbed panel used in the arch structure can also serve to erect farm buildings with straight sidewalls and gable roofs.

spread rating, wrinkle and sag-free appearance, abrasion resistance. Tabs, glued or folded and stapled, make seams vapor tight. Metal trim strips can be used to cover the seams for a neater appearance. Poultry netting is sometimes used to support insulation. Patching tape is available for repairing insulation facings.

Rigid insulation boards, foamed polyurethane and polystyrene have been used successfully to insulate metal buildings. They provide excellent appearance and greater resistance to damage, but higher cost has limited their use. A possible compromise has recently been offered by several suppliers—a rolled, semi-rigid fiberglass material with an unplasticized vinyl vapor barrier. This product presents a flat, wrinkle-free appearance without stretching. A lapping tab provides an almost invisible joint that seals out vapor without folding, gluing or stapling. Applied cost is said to be competitive with the flexible, faced blankets properly installed.

Sprayed-on urethane foams and cellulose materials have been used with success. UL ratings and integral colors can be obtained with the cellulose spray materials. Acoustical as well as thermal insulation properties are excellent with cellulose, and a carefully applied job can provide a decorative appearance.

1107 Fasteners

Structural to structural joining is generally accomplished with bolts, although field welded connections are not unknown in the industry. Bolted connections must be made using those furnished or specified by the manufacturer and tightened in accordance with the manufacturer's instructions.

Panel to structural and panel to panel fastening is accomplished with a variety of fasteners, among them: nuts and bolts, self-clinching rivets, self-

Figure 1100E This ten building complex accommodates 350,000 layers. Each of the 40' × 400' A&S Steel Buildings is connected by an egg conveyor system and integrated with a central packing system. The buildings have wall to wall flat deck cage systems with an overhead tram system.

172

tapping screws, self-drilling screws in which a pre-drilled hole is not required, and a number of specialized fasteners for installing rigid board insulation and field fabricated sandwich panels. For best results, drills, hole sizes, and manufacturer's suggested methods for stacking and drilling sheets should be followed exactly.

For a truly weathertight roof, tape sealants must be used on all panel to panel side-lap connections. Care must be taken to see that the sealant is placed on the weather side of the fasteners.

Fastener heads are available to match colored panels.

Clip attached panels are offered by some manufacturers as a means of avoiding or reducing the number of holes in the roof. These panel side-lap, or panel to panel connections, are generally made by self-propelled roll-forming machines that lock or hem panel edges after they have been placed on the roof structure.

Figure 1100F Rigid boards of polystyrene and polyurethane foams have found acceptance in the erection of metal buildings.

1108   Color Coatings

At the present there are no industry standards to guide the buyer in his selection of a color coating system for roof and wall panels. For several years it was the practice of a number of metal building manufacturers to offer a 20-year guarantee on their top of the line finishes. Most have recently withdrawn this guarantee. Responsibility for the finish begins with the galvanizer, then becomes dependent on the workmanship and materials applied by the coater of the galvanized coil, and finally the integrity of the coating film depends upon the fabricator who brakes or roll forms the sheet to various configurations. Because a great variety of panel finishes are available today, the farm builder ought to be aware of them and their salient features, if only to field questions from his prospects. An abridged list of those coatings most commonly used and their descrip-

Figure 1100G Insulated metal sandwich panels eliminate girts and provide a clean, decorative inner wall with a minimum of erection labor.

173

Figure 1100H This Sommer Steel Building marries wood posts to steel roof beams and purlins to combine the low cost pole building foundation with larger clear-span areas generally associated with steel construction.

Figure 1100I Self-propelled roll former crimps panel edges, which have a factory applied sealant, to produce a permanently weathertight roof.

tion as prepared by the National Coil Coaters Association is as follows:

1108-1 *Thermoset Acrylics* have excellent stain, abrasion and mar resistance coupled with excellent durability but their formability is rather limited. They have full-gloss appearance, making them suitable for decorative purposes, and are also available in low to medium gloss range. Typical uses include exterior building products (siding, rain carrying equipment and other components), appliance housings, cabinets, lighting fixtures and cabinetry, and over-finishes for polished metals and for printed coatings.

1108-2 *Silicone modified (alkyds, polyesters and acrylics)* are usually a chemical combination of an alkyd, polyester, or acrylic, and silicone intermediates, which are combined in the resin kettle prior to combination with other materials during the formulation of the coating. They have outstanding exterior durability; in fact, it is their superior non-chalking property and gloss retention that are almost solely responsible for their increasing use. They are somewhat limited in flexibility. Also, they often require a primer coat. In spite of these drawbacks, the constant search for better durability is leading to increased use of these materials. Typical uses—any exterior application, especially industrial building sheet and residential siding.

1108-3 *Vinyl-Alkyds* give a compromise between the economy of alkyds and the outstanding flexibility of the vinyls. With fair exterior durability, these systems are desirable where forming is involved and cost is a factor. Common uses: roof decking and any application where a straight alkyd would be used but where more than normal fabrication is involved.

1108-4 *Plastisols and Organosols* have excellent scuff and mar resistance, good formability, and many fine decorative properties. Both belong to the vinyl dispersion family. Plastisols may be applied in extremely heavy film thicknesses, permitting embossing and printing in different designs. They can be produced in colors across the full spectrum, and have excellent exterior durability and high chemical resistance. Most types require a primer to ensure good adhesion. Typical uses: TV cabinets and appliance housings, high-grade shelving and cabinets, interior wall paneling, protective linings for metal containers, metal furniture, gasketing, and exterior residential siding and commercial and industrial building panels.

1108-5 *Fluorocarbons* are premium coatings, unexcelled in their combination of outstanding properties, including formability, color retention, resistance to solvents, and chalking. A slow film erosion rate assures long-term durability under field service conditions. At present, these semi-gloss coatings are produced in a limited range of colors. Typical uses: curtain wall, residential siding, and industrial building components.

1108-6 *Fluorocarbon film laminates* provide long life and durability. Uses include exterior siding and other exterior building product applications.

1108-7 *Acrylic film laminates* are extremely weatherable, thick, mar-resistant, colored or patterned films produced using time-proven, extremely durable polymers. Used most commonly in the surfacing of exterior metal, film laminates virtually eliminate problems of chalking, fading, chipping, peeling or other forms of coating deterioration. Being a solid plastic, acrylic film laminates may be supplied in thick coatings, economically, to minimize marring, providing a balance of fabrication, mar-resistance, thickness and toughness not obtainable with liquid systems. Acrylic film laminates have wide use in building applications.

1109 *Sources* There are two sources of information with which all farm builders contemplating a metal building franchise should acquaint themselves: Metal Building Manufacturers Association, and Metal Building Dealers Association. These two organizations representing the major manufacturers and many of the top dealer-contractors are authoritative sources for information on design and erection of metal buildings, and on fire insurance, building codes, safety regula-

Figure 1100J Flexible fiberglass blanket with a vinyl vapor seal stretched from eave to eave provides a low-cost, efficient insulation for most metal buildings. When properly applied, material enhances the interior, as shown in this photograph of a Butler building used as a riding arena.

Figure 1100K Interior of this Stormor building shows how bulk grain and machinery storage are combined in one structure. This versatility is one of the advantages of metal buildings for farm use.

tions and union craft jurisdiction as they pertain to the metal building industry. The MBDA has about forty regional chapters that meet regularly, bringing suppliers and contractors together for a vital exchange of information. There is also a national Metal Building Industry Show held each year in February. The Show is sponsored by the MBDA.

The address of the Metal Building Manufacturers Association is:

2130 Keith Building
Cleveland, Ohio 44115

The address of the Metal Building Dealers Association is:

1406 Third National Building
Dayton, Ohio 45402

Appendix "D" contains the definitions of the terms commonly used in metal building construction.

STRUCTURAL DESIGN DATA

Tables of Maximums and Minimums

A-1   The purpose of this appendix is to provide tables for the various structural elements of farm buildings *(and pole type buildings used for industrial purposes)* together with the basic structural design data from which the tables were developed. This will permit the design of buildings differing from the norms suggested herein.

A-2   The structure, including the component parts, shall have sufficient strength and rigidity to support the design load and to resist deformation without exceeding the allowable design stress provided herein.

A-3   The strength and rigidity of individual members or assemblies shall be determined by a qualified engineer in accordance with recognized engineering analysis procedures. Where assemblies or details of construction do not permit of such analysis, the structural properties shall be determined by suitable tests.

A-4   Industrial Uses

Since many farm builders, particularly pole builders, frequently find themselves building structures for human occupancy, and under building codes, such as factories, warehouses, etc., the tables under **"Load Zone 50"** are provided. Buildings constructed with these tables will have a higher factor of safety and comply with most recognized building codes.

A-5   **Design Dead Loads** shall consist of actual weights of all materials making up the construction including walls, floors, roofs, ceilings, partitions, and fixed service equipment.

A-6   Design Live Loads

Design live loads shall consist of the weight of all moving and variable loads that may be placed in the building, including loads on floors, operational loads on roofs and ceilings and wind, snow and earthquake loads which may act upon the structure, either singly or in combination with other dead and live loads.

A-7   Roof Loads

Load Zone Map A7 is for a 25 year recurrence interval as recommended by ASAE R 288.1 *(Rev. 1967)*. The snow pack on the ground has been converted to the load occurring on a 4/12 slope roof. The load on the horizontally projected area in the several zones are developed as follows:

Load Zone	Live Load	Dead Roof Load	Dead Ceiling Load
20 psf	12.4 psf	5.4 psf	2.2 psf
25 psf	17.1 psf	5.7 psf	2.2 psf
30 psf	22.8 psf	5 psf	2.2 psf
50 psf	30 psf	10 psf	10 psf

Notes:
1.   Although many farm buildings have no ceiling, for the sake of simplicity, all tables have been developed including this small load. It is also recommended that truss designers include the ceiling load on future designs.
2.   Dead roof loads allow for the weight of the truss, roofing, and purlins *(for sheathing)*. Dead ceiling loads allow for a ceiling material, insulation and furring.

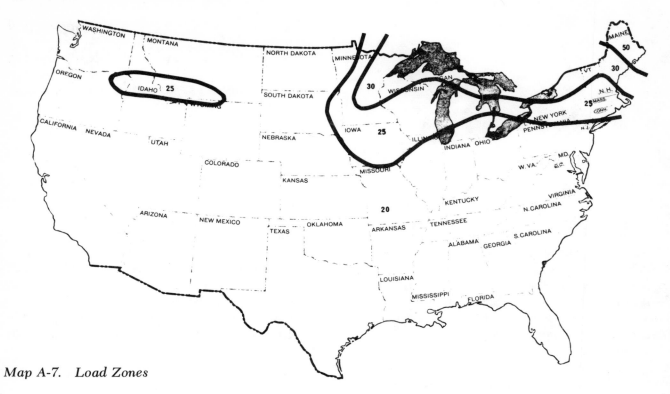

Map A-7.   Load Zones

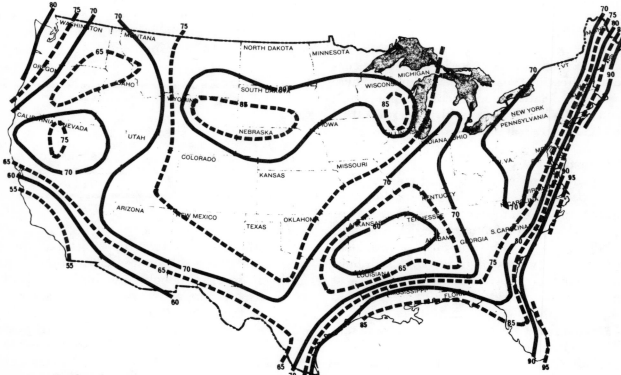

Map A-8   Wind Velocities

A-8 Wind Loads

Wind Map A-8 is for a 25 year recurrence interval and shows that a design value based on 85 mph winds covers the entire country except for a narrow fringe up the east coast.

A-9 Stress Increases Allowed

All tables are calculated on an increase in allowable stresses as follows:

Increase	Load Zone
33 1/3%	20
33 1/3%	25
15%	30°
33 1/3%	50

°Approximately the same as "Load Zone 35" with a 1/3 increase.

The tables for load zone 50 *(industrial)* are also deemed adequate for farm buildings only in that portion of Northern New England lying beyond load zone 30. By farm buildings is meant buildings with only the light dead loads described for load zones 20, 25, 30.

A-10 Deflection of

1/180 of span was considered in making up the tables, except in those tables extracted from the National Forest Products Assn. (Rafters and Floor Joists)

A-11 Tables

in this appendix are grouped by load zone so that you will find tables for pads, purlins, rafters, overhangs and plates for each load zone all in one section.

A-12 Posts and Poles

Tables indicate the maximum span of truss to be supported by posts and poles of the various sizes, spacings and eave heights.

Posts and poles are further classified by the type of load, like this;

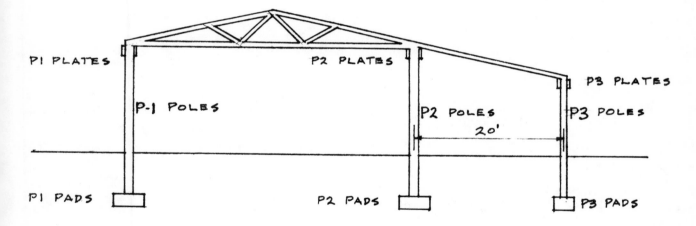

Further, poles and posts are divided into two groups according to strength characteristics.

Group A—Douglas Fir, West Coast
    Douglas Fir, Inland
    Western Larch
    Southern Pine

Group B—Western Red Cedar
    Ponderosa Pine
    Jack Pine
    Lodge Pole Pine
    Norway Pine *(Red Pine)*

Group A round poles are assigned a stress value of 3500 psi.

Group A square posts are assigned a stress value of 1750 psi.

Group B round poles are assigned a stress value of 2625 psi.

Group B square posts are assigned a stress value of 1313 psi.

All of the above figures include 33% allowable increase in stresses for wind. Embedment is assumed to be not less than specified in 405-1. The maximum 85 mph wind velocity is assumed.

A-13   Footings and Pads.
Required sizes are shown for the P-1, P-2 and P-3, Poles and Posts related to the span of the truss and the spacing of the poles. Drawings referred to are 404-1, a, b, c, & e. Bearing capacity of the soil is classified as follows:

Good—10,000 psf. Compact coarse sand, compact gravel or sand gravel mixture, hard-pan, shale, bedrock or hard clay.

Medium—6,000 psf. Compact fine sand, loose gravel or sand-gravel mixture, compact sandy loam or medium clay.

Poor—2,000 psf. Soft clay, fine and loose sand, clay loam, clay containing large amounts of silt.

A-14   Lumber is grouped by grade and species as follows.

Any lumber species or grade which meets the requirements of "E" and "F_b" specified below for groups C, D, E and F may be used in the group. Consult Tables for values assigned to grades and species. The F_b values below have been made consistent with those shown in the tables, so no further adjustment need be made.

	E	F_b
"C" Group	1,800,000	2050
"D" Group	1,400,000	1750
"E" Group	1,200,000	1350
"F" Group	800,000	800

Note: 2 × 3 ripped from wider widths is not acceptable without culling of large knots and other defects which would be permissible in 2 × 6 and wider.

A-15   Plates.
For the four load zones, tables are shown for each type loading situation on P-1, P-2, and P-3, Posts or Poles.

Rather than show 2 × 14's or 2 × 16's in the tables, since they are not generally available to the farm builder, we show vertically-built-up beams like those shown in Det. 408-2. Panel-Clip truss clips are shown as an example only. Other truss plate manufacturers can furnish similar de-

signs for openings wider than those shown in the tables, beams like those shown in Details 408-5A *(flitch plate)* 408-5B *(plywood box beam)* and 408-5C *(Truss Girder)* may be used.

Where plate braces are used similar to those shown in Det. 414, the maximum truss span in the tables for a given plate size may be increased by 10%.

A-16   Rafters
For each load zone, the maximum span of rafters is given for various spacings. Span is measured horizontally and pitch is assumed to be 4/12. For flat roof joists use floor joist tables.

Where a 4 × 8, 10, or 12 is shown, it is assumed that this is made by spiking two rafters tightly together or to spacing blocks when one rafter is on each side of the pole. The tables take into consideration 15% increase in stress for upgrading due to doubling members.

A-17   Purlins
Tables give the maximum span of the purlin for the various sizes, spacings and load zones.

A-18   Floor Joists
Tables are based on a 40 lb. live load plus a dead of 10 lbs. per sq. ft. This is the maximum residential load (living rooms, etc.) and deflection is limited to 1/360th of span. Floor framing for heavy loads, grain, feed storage, etc., should be specially engineered.

A-19   Roof Trusses—Design Criteria.
Roof trusses shall be designed for the loads specified in A-5, 6, 7, and 8. Allowable increase in short time loading as specified in A-9. Trusses shall be designed in accordance with the following recognized design procedures in addition to the above.

Metal Plate Trusses—TPI 70 Truss Plate Institute.

Glued Trusses—TR-1 Midwest Plan Service; also MWPS-9 "Designs for Glued Trusses."

Split Ring Trusses—MWPS-10 "Designs for Split Ring Trusses" Midwest Plan Service.

National Design Specifications for Stress Grade Lumber and Its Fastenings, National Forest Products Association.

Nailed Trusses—MWPS-11, "Designs for Nailed Trusses" Midwest Plan Service.

Design loads for 20, 25 and 30 load zones incorporate a minimum ceiling load. For simplicity, it is suggested that all farm building trusses incorporate this load.

Where ceiling-suspended cages are used in poultry operations, trusses shall be designed for this additional load. Par. 701-1f recommends 5 lbs. psf of ceiling for each deck of birds.

A-20 Safe Loads for Bolts

Bolted joints should be designed in accordance with the "Timber Construction Manual," American Institute of Timber Construction. For occasional and non-critical use the following may be used.

1. Douglas Fir, Larch or Southern Pine, Dry Lumber.
2. Assumes one 1-5/8" member bolted to a member of equal or greater thickness, such as 1-5/8" to 1-5/8"; 1-5/8" to 3-1/2" or 1-5/8" to 5-1/4".
3. When used for bracing, etc., not for long term loads such as stored materials, loads may be increased as follows:
   Load Zones 20, 25 and 50—33-1/3%
   Load Zone 30   15%
4. Bolt holes should be 1/16" larger than bolt. Washers or metal plates are assumed between the wood and the bolt head and nuts. Nuts should be tightened snugly, not to cause crushing under washer.
5. For more than one bolt per joint, multiply by the number of bolts, provided that bolts are staggered and with adequate end and edge distance.

Angle of Load to Grain	1/2"	5/8"	3/4"
0°	650 lbs.	1000 lbs.	1400 lbs.
15°	600 lbs.	900 lbs.	1300 lbs.
30°	600 lbs.	850 lbs.	1150 lbs.
45°	550 lbs.	750 lbs.	850 lbs.
60°	500 lbs.	625 lbs.	750 lbs.
90°	475 lbs.	575 lbs.	650 lbs.

Example I

A pole type building with 40 foot span trusses; trusses and poles 8 foot o.c.; 12 foot eave height and an 18 foot extension on one side. Location: Nebraska; loose gravel soil.

Step 1   From the Map A-7 we find that Nebraska is in Load Zone 20. Turn to tables for load zone 20.

Step 2   In the Pad Table, for medium soil, we find that the pads for the P-1 poles *(the side without the extension)* should be 12 inches diameter by 6 inches in thickness. For the P-2 Poles *(with the extension)* the same pad size is required. For the P-3 Poles *(carrying the extension only)* no pad is required; use anchor blocks only.

Step 3   In the Pole Tables, we find six options:
   4" Top Pole, "A" species
   4" Top Pole, "B" species
   6 × 6 Rough Posts, "A" species
   6 × 6 Dressed Post, "A" species
   6 × 6 Rough Post, "B" species
   6 × 6 Dressed Post, "B" species

Step 4   From the P-1 Plate Table, since trusses and posts are the same spacing, we may use 1-2 × 6 for the plate of either "C" or "D" species.

Step 5   Before selecting P-2 Plates, check the Rafter Tables. The 40 foot trusses have a 2 × 10 top chord and it will be desirable to have the rafters for the 18 foot extension match these. The Rafter Table shows that double 2 × 10 rafters in Group "C" species will span 18 feet, 4 inches, spaced 96 inches *(8 feet)* o.c. Therefore, we can use a single 2 × 6 plate on both P-2 and P-3 poles, because rafters and trusses occur only at the posts.

Step 6   Purlin Spacing. Assuming that the manufacturer's recommendation on the metal roofing will permit, 2 × 4 Group "C" species can be used on edge at 32 inches on center.

Step 7   Wall Girts. From the girt table we find that we can use a 2 × 3 spaced 36" o.c. on edge for 8 foot o.c. poles or a 2 × 4 on flat for 32 inches o.c., Group "C."

Step 8 The embedment of posts should also be checked. See paragraph 405-1. This shows a 6 × 6 in average soil should be 4 feet, 6 inches.

Example II:

A pole-type building with posts 12 feet on center; 50 foot span roof trusses, 4 feet on center; 14 feet eave height; maximum overhang both sides; plate braces; one 23 foot opening on one side; located in the vicinity of Duluth, Minnesota and soil is loose sand.

Step 1 From Map A-7, we find that load zone 30 applies.

Step 2 In load zone 30 Pad Table, we find under poor soil that with poles 12 feet o.c. and trusses of 50 foot span, the P-1 pads required are 28 inches in diameter and 16 inches deep. But wait!! We have neglected the overhang. From the Overhang Table, we find that the maximum overhang for a 2 × 8 (*top chord of a 50' truss*) spaced 48 inches o.c. is 6 feet, 2 inches. (*The overhang could be increased, if desired to 9 feet, 7 inches, by changing the top chords to 2 × 12.*)

This now means that the pads, poles, plates, etc. must be figured at a truss span of 62 feet.

The corrected pad would then be 34 inches by 18 inches thick (*next highest over 60 feet*).

Step 3 We can then select the posts from the load zone 30 table at 14 feet eave height. The 6 × 6 rough size is adequate, in "A" group species.

Step 4 The plate sizes are selected from the P-1 Plate Table. Since plate braces are used, the figure for 60 foot truss span is adequate (*because of the 10% factor in Par. 414-2.1*). The options are:
4–2 × 10 "C" or "D" group; or
2-Vertically Built up Beams 15 inch "C" group
or
3-Vertically Built up Beams 15 inch "D" group

Step 5 Roof purlins selected from the load zone 30 table can take advantage of the 12% factor in the footnote. 2 × 4's flat, "D" group can be spaced 36 inches o.c., provided 2 × 4 16's are used.

Step 6 Over the 23 foot opening we must use a specially designed header, or by calculating the load per lineal foot (*31 feet 1/2 span × 30 p.s.f. load = 930 lbs. per lineal foot*) we can see that five of the girders shown in 408-5C are adequate when well nailed together. Posts at opening should be cut off to provide bearing for these and pads should be increased approximately 50% in area to about 40 inches by 20 inches.

MAXIMUM SPAN OF GIRTS

LUMBER Size & Grade		16″	24″	GIRT SPACING 32″	36″	48″
Group C						
2 x 6	Flat	15-6	12-8	11-0	10-4	8-11
2 x 6	Edge	16-0	16-0	16-0	16-0	16-0
2 x 4	Flat	10-0	10-0	8-9	8-3	7-2
2 x 4	Edge	10-0	10-0	10-0	10-0	10-0
2 x 3	Flat	8-0	8-0	7-5	7-0	6-1
2 x 3	Edge	8-0	8-0	8-0	8-0	7-9
Group D						
2 x 6	Flat	14-4	11-9	10-2	9-7	8-3
2 x 6	Edge	16-0	16-0	16-0	16-0	15-11
2 x 4	Flat	10-0	9-4	8-1	7-8	6-7
2 x 4	Edge	10-0	10-0	10-0	10-0	10-0
2 x 3	Flat	8-0	7-11	6-10	6-5	5-7
2 x 3	Edge	8-0	8-0	8-0	8-0	7-3
Group E						
2 x 6	Flat	12-10	10-6	9-1	8-7	7-5
2 x 6	Edge	16-0	16-0	16-0	16-0	14-2
2 x 4	Flat	10-0	8-4	7-3	6-10	5-11
2 x 4	Edge	10-0	10-0	10-0	10-0	9-0
2 x 3	Flat	8-0	7-1	6-2	5-9	5-0
2 x 3	Edge	8-0	8-0	7-11	7-5	6-5
Group F						
2 x 6	Flat	9-10	8-0	6-11	6-6	5-8
2 x 6	Edge	16-0	15-4	13-3	12-6	10-10
2 x 4	Flat	7-10	6-5	5-6	5-3	4-6
2 x 4	Edge	10-0	9-9	8-5	8-0	6-11
2 x 3	Flat	6-8	5-4	4-8	4-5	3-10
2 x 3	Edge	8-0	6-11	6-0	5-8	4-11

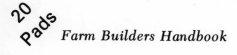

MINIMUM SIZES CONCRETE PADS OR FOOTINGS FOR POSTS OR POLES (DIAMETER & THICKNESS) LOAD ZONE - 20

P-1 POLES

SOIL	POLE SPACING	24'		28'		32'		36'		40'		50'		60'	
Good	8'	12"	6"	12"	6"	12"	6"	12"	6"	12"	6"	12"	6"	12"	6"
	12'	12"	6"	12"	6"	12"	6"	12"	6"	12"	6"	12"	6"	12"	6"
	16'	12"	6"	12"	6"	12"	6"	12"	6"	12"	6"	12"	6"	12"	6"
	20'	12"	6"	12"	6"	12"	6"	12"	6"	12"	6"	12"	6"	14"	7"
Medium	8'	12"	6"	12"	6"	12"	6"	12"	6"	12"	6"	12"	6"	12"	6"
	12'	12"	6"	12"	6"	12"	6"	12"	6"	12"	6"	12"	6"	14"	7"
	16'	12"	6"	12"	6"	12"	6"	12"	6"	14"	7"	14"	7"	16"	8"
	20'	12"	6"	12"	6"	14"	7"	14"	7"	14"	7"	16"	8"	18"	10"
Poor	8'	12"	6"	14"	7"	14"	7"	16"	8"	16"	8"	18"	10"	20"	12"
	12'	16"	8"	16"	8"	18"	10"	18"	10"	20"	12"	22"	12"	24"	14"
	16'	18"	10"	18"	10"	20"	12"	20"	12"	22"	12"	24"	14"	26"	15"
	20'	20"	12"	20"	12"	22"	12"	24"	14"	24"	14"	28"	16"	30"	18"

P-2 POLES

SOIL	POLE SPACING	24'		28'		32'		36'		40'		50'		60'	
Good	8'	12"	6"	12"	6"	12"	6"	12"	6"	12"	6"	12"	6"	12"	6"
	12'	12"	6"	12"	6"	12"	6"	12"	6"	12"	6"	12"	6"	12"	6"
	16'	12"	6"	12"	6"	12"	6"	12"	6"	12"	6"	12"	6"	14"	7"
	20'	12"	6"	12"	6"	12"	6"	14"	7"	14"	7"	14"	7"	16"	8"
Medium	8'	12"	6"	12"	6"	12"	6"	12"	6"	12"	6"	12"	6"	14"	7"
	12'	12"	6"	12"	6"	12"	6"	14"	7"	14"	7"	14"	7"	16"	8"
	16'	14"	7"	14"	7"	14"	7"	16"	8"	16"	8"	16"	8"	18"	10"
	20'	16"	8"	16"	8"	16"	8"	16"	8"	18"	10"	18"	10"	20"	12"
Poor	8'	16"	8"	18"	10"	18"	10"	18"	10"	18"	10"	20"	12"	22"	12"
	12'	20"	12"	20"	12"	22"	12"	22"	12"	24"	14"	24"	14"	26"	15"
	16'	22"	12"	24"	14"	24"	14"	26"	15"	26"	15"	28"	16"	30"	18"
	20'	26"	15"	26"	15"	28"	16"	28"	16"	30"	18"	32"	18"	34"	20"

P-3 POLES

SOIL	POLE SPACING		
Good	8'	none	
	12'	none	
	16'	8"	5"
	20'	8"	5"
Medium	8'		
	12'	8"	5"
	16'	10"	5"
	20'	10"	5"
Poor	8'	12"	6"
	12'	14"	7"
	16'	16"	8"
	20'	18"	10"

NOTE: Use P-3 Pads for end wall poles.

SOIL CLASSIFICATIONS:
GOOD: Compact coarse sand, compact gravel or sand-gravel mixture, hardpan, shale, bed rock, or hard clay.
MEDIUM: Compact fine sand, loose gravel or sand-gravel mixture, compact sandy loam, or medium clay.
POOR: Soft clay, fine and loose sand, clay loam, clay containing large amounts of silt.

POLE OR POST SPACING

EAVE HEIGHT	4' Top/Pole	4' Post	8' Top/Pole	8' Post	12' Top/Pole	12' Post	16' Top/Pole	16' Post	20' Top/Pole	20' Post
8'	A-4	A 4x4R 4x4D	A-4	A 4x4R 4x4D	A-4	A 4x6R 4x6D	A-4	A 4x6R 6x6D	A-4	A 6x6R 6x6D
8'	B-4	B 4x4R 4x4D	B-4	B 4x4R 4x6D	B-4	B 4x6R 6x6D	B-4	B 6x6R 6x6D	B-5	B 6x6R 6x6D
10'	A-4	A 4x4R 4x6D	A-4	A 4x6R 6x6D	A-4	A 6x6R 6x6D	A-5	A 6x6R 6x6D	A-5	A 6x6R 6x8D
10'	B-4	B 4x6R 4x6D	B-4	B 6x6R 6x6D	B-5	B 6x6R 6x6D	B-5	B 6x6R 6x8D	B-5	B 6x8R 8x8D
12'	A-4	A 4x4R 4x6D	A-4	A 6x6R 6x6D	A-5	A 6x6R 6x8D	A-5	A 6x8R 8x8D	A-6	A 6x8R 8x8D
12'	B-4	B 4x6R 6x6D	B-4	B 6x6R 6x6D	B-5	B 6x8R 8x8D	B-6	B 8x8R 8x8D	B-6	B 8x8R 8x8D
14'	A-4	A 6x6R 6x6D	A-5	A 6x6R 6x6D	A-5	A 6x8R 8x8D	A-6	A 8x8R 8x8D	A-6	A 8x8R 8x8D
14'	B-4	B 6x6R 6x6D	B-5	B 6x8R 6x6D	B-6	B 8x8R 8x8D	B-6	B 8x8R ---	B-7	--- ---
16'	A-4	A 6x6R 6x8D	A-5	A 6x8R 8x8D	A-5	A 8x8R 8x8D	A-6	A 8x8R ---	A-7	
16'	B-4	B 6x6R 6x8D	B-5	B 8x8R 8x8D	B-6	B 8x8R ---	B-7	--- ---	B-7	
18'	A-4	A 6x6R 6x8D	A-5	A 8x8R 8x8D	A-6	A 8x8R ---	A-7		A-7	
18'	B-4	B 6x6R 6x8D	B-6	B 8x8R 8x8D	B-7	--- ---	B-7		B-8	
20'	A-4	A 6x6R 6x8D	A-5	A 8x8R 8x8D	A-6	A 8x8R ---	A-7		A-8	
20'	B-4	B 6x8R 8x8D	B-6	B 8x8R ---	B-7		B-8		B-10	

MINIMUM POLE SIZE REQUIREMENTS   LOAD ZONE - 20

Note: For "A" & "B" Post or Pole Species see Par. 301-1 and A-12.

185

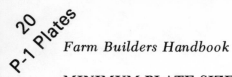

MINIMUM PLATE SIZES (ALTERNATES) LOAD ZONE - 20
P-1 POLES

POLE SPACING	TRUSS SPACING	TRUSS SPAN						
		24'-0"	28'-0"	32'-0"	36'-0"	40'-0"	50'-0"	60'-0"
8'	4'	2-2x8 C 3-2x6 C 2-2x8 D 3-2x6 D	2-2x8 C 2-2x10 D 3-2x8 D	2-2x10 C 3-2x8 C 2-2x10 D 3-2x8 D	2-2x10 C 3-2x8 C 2-2x10 D 3-2x8 D	2-2x10 C 3-2x8 C 2-2x10 D 3-2x8 D	2-2x10 C 2-2x12 D 3-2x10 D	2-2x12 C 2-2x12 D 3-2x10 D
	6'	2-2x10 C 3-2x8 C 2-2x10 D 3-2x8 D	2-2x10 C 3-2x8 C 2-2x10 D	2-2x10 C 2-2x12 D	2-2x12 C 3-2x10 C 2-2x12 D 3-2x10 D	2-2x12 C 3-2x10 C 2-2x12 D 3-2x10 D	2-2x12 C 3-2x10 C 3-2x12 D 2-VB 13 D	4-2x12 D 3-VB 13 D
	See Note 8'	1-2x6 C 1-2x6 D	1-2x6 C 1-2x6 D	1-2x6 C 1-2x6 D	1-2x6 C 1-2x6 D	1-2x6 C 1-2x6 D	1-2x6 C 1-2x6 D	1-2x6 C 1-2x6 D
12'	4'	2-2x8 C 2-2x10 D 3-2x8 D	2-2x10 C 3-2x8 C 2-2x10 D 3-2x8 D	2-2x10 C 3-2x8 C 2-2x10 D 3-2x8 D	2-2x10 C 3-2x8 C 2-2x12 D 3-2x10 D	2-2x10 C 2-2x12 D 3-2x10 D	2-2x12 C 3-2x10 C 2-2x12 D 3-2x10 D	2-2x12 C 3-2x10 C 3-2x12 D 4-2x10 D
	6'	2-2x8 C 3-2x6 C 2-2x8 D	2-2x8 C 2-2x10 D 3-2x8 D	2-2x10 C 3-2x8 C 2-2x10 D 3-2x8 D	2-2x10 C 3-2x8 C 2-2x10 D 3-2x8 D	2-2x10 C 3-2x8 C 2-2x12 D 3-2x10 D	2-2x12 C 3-2x10 C 2-2x12 D 3-2x10 D	2-2x12 C 3-2x10 C 3-2x12 D 4-2x10 D
	8'	2-2x10 C 3-2x8 C 2-2x10 D 3-2x8 D	2-2x10 C 3-2x8 C 2-2x10 D	2-2x10 C 2-2x12 D	2-2x12 C 3-2x10 C 2-2x12 D 3-2x10 D	2-2x12 C 3-2x10 C 2-2x12 D 3-2x10 D	2-2x12 C 3-2x10 C 3-2x12 D 4-2x10 D	3-2x12 C 4-2x10 C 3-2x12 D 2-VB 15 D
16'	4'	2-2x10 C 2-2x12 D 3-2x10 D	2-2x12 C 3-2x10 C 2-2x12 D 3-2x10 D	2-2x12 C 3-2x10 C 2-2x12 D 3-2x10 D	2-2x12 C 3-2x10 C 3-2x12 D 4-2x10 D	3-2x12 C 4-2x10 C 3-2x12 D 4-2x10 D	3-2x12 C 4-2x10 C 4-2x12 D 2-VB 15 D	4-2x12 C 2-VB 15 C 4-2x12 D 3-VB 13 D
	6'	2-2x10 C 3-2x8 C 2-2x12 D 3-2x10 D	2-2x12 C 3-2x10 C 2-2x12 D 3-2x10 D	2-2x12 C 3-2x10 C 2-2x12 D 3-2x10 D	2-2x12 C 3-2x10 C 3-2x12 D 4-2x10 D	2-2x12 C 3-2x10 C 3-2x12 D 4-2x10 D	3-2x12 C 4-2x10 C 3-2x12 D 2-VB 15 D	3-2x12 C 2-VB 15 C 4-2x12 D 2-VB 15 D
	8'	2-2x10 C 2-2x12 D	2-2x12 C 3-2x10 C 2-2x12 D	2-2x12 C 3-2x10 C 2-2x12 D	2-2x12 C 3-2x10 C 3-2x12 D 4-2x10 D	3-2x12 C 4-2x10 C 3-2x12 D 4-2x10 D	3-2x12 C 4-2x10 C 4-2x12 D 2-VB 15 D	4-2x12 C 2-VB 15 C 4-2x12 D 3-VB 13 D
20'	4'	3-2x12 C 4-2x10 C 3-2x12 D 4-2x10 D	3-2x12 C 4-2x10 C 3-2x12 D 2-VB 15 D	3-2x12 C 2-VB 15 C 4-2x12 D 2-VB 15 D	4-2x12 C 3-VB 13 C 4-2x12 D 3-VB 13 D	4-2x12 C 3-VB 15 C 4-2x12 D 3-VB 15 D	3-VB 15 C 4-VB 13 C 3-VB 15 D 4-VB 13 D	3-VB 15 C 4-VB 13 C 3-VB 17 D 4-VB 15 D
	6'	3-2x12 C 4-2x10 C 3-2x12 D 4-2x10 D	3-2x12 C 4-2x10 C 3-2x12 D 2-VB 15 D	3-2x12 C 2-VB 15 C 4-2x12 D 2-VB 15 D	4-2x12 C 2-VB 15 C 4-2x12 D 3-VB 15 D	4-2x12 C 3-VB 13 C 3-VB 15 D 4-VB 13 D	3-VB 15 C 4-VB 13 C 3-VB 15 D 4-VB 13 D	3-VB 17 C 4-VB 15 C 3-VB 17 D 4-VB 15 D
	8'	3-2x12 C 4-2x10 C 3-2x12 D 4-2x10 D	3-2x12 C 4-2x10 C 3-2x12 D 2-VB 13 D	3-2x12 C 2-VB 15 C 4-2x12 D 2-VB 15 D	4-2x12 C 3-VB 13 C 4-2x12 D 3-VB 13 D	4-2x12 C 3-VB 13 C 3-VB 15 D 4-VB 13 D	3-VB 15 C 4-VB 13 C 3-VB 17 D 4-VB 15 D	3-VB 17 C 4-VB 15 C 3-VB 17 D 4-VB 15 D

V-B Vertically Built-Up Beams as described in 408-2.
For C & D Groups of Lumber See Appendix A-14.

MINIMUM PLATE SIZES FOR P-2 and P-3 POLES (ALTERNATES) LOAD ZONE - 20
P-2 POLES

POLE SPACING	TRUSS SPACING	TRUSS SPAN 24'-0"	28'-0"	32'-0"	36'-0"	40'-0"	50'-0"	60'-0"	P-3 POLES 20' SPAN RAFTER
8'-0"	4'-0"	2-2x10 C 4-2x8 C 2-2x10 D 4-2x8 D	2-2x10 C 2-2x12 D 3-2x10 D	2-2x12 C 3-2x10 C 2-2x12 D 3-2x10 D	2-2x12 C 3-2x10 C 2-2x12 D 3-2x10 D	2-2x12 C 3-2x10 C 2-2x12 D 3-2x10 D	2-2x12 C 3-2x10 C 3-2x12 D 4-2x10 D	3-2x12 C 4-2x10 C 3-2x12 D 4-2x10 D	2-2x6 C 2-2x6 D
	6'-0"	2-2x12 C 3-2x10 C 3-2x10 D	2-2x12 C 3-2x10 C 3-2x12 D 4-2x10 D	3-2x12 C 4-2x10 C 3-2x12 D 4-2x10 D	3-2x12 C 4-2x10 C 3-2x12 D 4-2x10 D	3-2x12 C 4-2x10 C 3-2x12 D 4-2x10 D	3-2x12 C 2-VB 15 C 4-2x12 D 3-VB 15 D	4-2x12 C 2-VB 15 C 4-2x12 D 3-VB 13 D	
	See Note 8'-0"	2-2x6 C 2-2x6 D	2-2x6 C 2-2x6 D	2-2x6 C 2-2x6 D	2-2x6 C 2-2x6 D	2-2x6 C 2-2x6 D	2-2x6 C 2-2x6 D	2-2x6 C 2-2x6 D	
12'-0"	4'-0"	2-2x12 C 3-2x10 C 2-2x12 D 3-2x10 D	2-2x12 C 3-2x10 C 2-2x12 D 3-2x10 D	2-2x12 C 3-2x10 C 2-2x12 D 3-2x10 D	2-2x12 C 3-2x10 C 3-2x12 D 4-2x10 D	2-2x12 C 3-2x10 C 3-2x12 D 4-2x10 D	3-2x12 C 4-2x10 C 3-2x12 D 4-2x10 D	3-2x12 C 4-2x10 C 4-2x12 D 3-VB 13 D	2-2x8 C 3-2x6 C 2-2x8 D 3-2x6 D
	6'-0"	2-2x10 C 4-2x8 C 2-2x12 D 3-2x10 D	2-2x12 C 3-2x10 C 3-2x10 D 4-2x8 D	2-2x12 C 3-2x10 C 3-2x10 D	2-2x12 C 3-2x10 C 3-2x10 D	2-2x12 C 3-2x10 C 3-2x12 D 4-2x10 D	3-2x12 C 4-2x10 C 3-2x12 D 4-2x10 D	3-2x12 C 4-2x10 C 3-2x12 D 2-VB 15 D	
	8'-0"	2-2x12 C 3-2x10 C 3-2x10 D 2-VB 13 D	2-2x12 C 3-2x10 C 3-2x12 D 4-2x10 D	3-2x12 C 4-2x10 C 3-2x12 D 4-2x10 D	3-2x12 C 4-2x10 C 3-2x12 D 4-2x10 D	3-2x12 C 4-2x10 C 3-2x12 D 2-VB 15 D	3-2x12 C 4-2x12 D 2-VB 15 D	4-2x12 C 3-VB 13 C 4-2x12 D 3-VB 13 D	
16'-0"	4'-0"	3-2x12 C 4-2x10 C 3-2x12 D 4-2x10 D	3-2x12 C 4-2x10 C 3-2x12 D 2-VB 15 D	3-2x12 C 2-VB 15 C 4-2x12 D 2-VB 15 D	3-2x12 C 2-VB 15 C 4-2x12 D 2-VB 15 D	4-2x12 C 2-VB 15 C 4-2x12 D 3-VB 13 D	4-2x12 C 3-VB 13 C 3-VB 15 D	3-VB 15 C 3-VB 15 D	2-2x10 C 3-2x8 C 2-2x10 D 3-2x8 D
	6'-0"	3-2x12 C 4-2x10 C 3-2x12 D 4-2x10 D	3-2x12 C 4-2x10 C 3-2x12 D 2-VB 15 D	3-2x12 C 4-2x10 C 3-2x12 D 2-VB 15 D	3-2x12 C 2-VB 13 C 4-2x12 D 2-VB 15 D	3-2x12 C 2-VB 15 C 4-2x12 D 2-VB 15 D	4-2x12 C 2-VB 15 C 4-2x12 D 3-VB 15 D	4-2x12 C 3-VB 15 C 3-VB 15 D	
	8'-0"	3-2x12 C 2-VB 13 C 3-2x12 D 2-VB 15 D	3-2x12 C 2-VB 13 C 3-2x12 D 2-VB 15 D	3-2x12 C 2-VB 15 C 4-2x12 D 2-VB 15 D	3-2x12 C 2-VB 15 C 4-2x12 D 2-VB 15 D	4-2x12 C 2-VB 15 C 4-2x12 D 3-VB 13 D	4-2x12 C 3-VB 13 C 3-VB 15 D	3-VB 15 C 4-VB 13 C 3-VB 15 D 4-VB 13 D	
20'-0"	4'-0"	4-2x12 C 3-VB 13 C 3-VB 15 D	3-VB 15 C 3-VB 15 D	3-VB 15 C 3-VB 15 D	3-VB 15 C 3-VB 17 D	3-VB 15 C 3-VB 17 D	4-VB 17 C 4-VB 17 D	4-VB 15 C 4-VB 17 D	2-2x12 C 3-2x10 C 2-2x12 D 3-2x10 D
	6'-0"	4-2x12 C 3-VB 15 C 3-VB 15 D	3-VB 15 C 3-VB 15 D	3-VB 15 C 3-VB 17 D	3-VB 15 C 3-VB 17 D	3-VB 17 C 3-VB 17 D	3-VB 17 C 4-VB 17 D	4-VB 17 C 4-VB 17 D	
	8'-0"	3-VB 15 C 3-VB 15 D	3-VB 15 C 3-VB 15 D	3-VB 15 C 3-VB 17 D	3-VB 15 C 3-VB 17 D	3-VB 17 C 3-VB 17 D	3-VB 17 C 4-VB 17 D	4-VB 15 C 4-VB 17 D	

V-B Vertically Built-Up Beams as described in 408-2.
For C & D Groups of Lumber See Appendix A-14.
Note: If Rafters from P-2 to P-3 plates are spaced same as poles, a single member plate may be used.

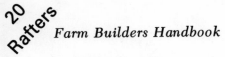

MAXIMUM SPAN OF RAFTERS HORIZONTAL SPAN LOAD ZONE - 20

LUMBER Size & Grade	RAFTER SPACING 12"	16"	24"	32"	36"	48"	72"	96"
Group C								
2 x 4	11-0	10-0	8-9	7-11	7-7	6-11		
2 x 6	17-3	15-9	13-9	12-5	12-0	10-9		
2 x 8		20-9	18-1	16-5	15-10	14-4	12-7	11-5
2 x 10					20-2	18-4	16-0	14-6
2 x 12						22-3	19-5	17-8
2-2 x 8						18-2	15-10	14-4
2-2 x 10							20-2	18-4
2-2 x 12								22-3
Group D								
2 x 4	10-1	9-3	8-0	7-3	7-0	6-4		
2 x 6	15-11	14-5	12-7	11-5	11-0	10-0		
2 x 8		19-1	16-8	15-1	14-7	13-2	11-7	10-6
2 x 10				19-3	18-7	16-10	14-8	13-4
2 x 12						20-6	17-11	16-3
2-2 x 8					18-4	16-8	14-7	13-3
2-2 x 10						21-3	18-7	16-10
2-2 x 12								20-6
Group E								
2 x 4	9-7	8-9	7-7	6-11	6-8	6-0		
2 x 6	15-1	13-9	12-0	10-10	10-5	9-6		
2 x 8		18-1	15-10	14-4	13-10	12-7	11-0	9-0
2 x 10			20-2	18-4	17-7	16-0	14-0	12-8
2 x 12					21-5	19-5	17-0	15-5
2-2 x 8					17-5	15-10	13-10	12-7
2-2 x 10						20-2	17-7	16-0
2-2 x 12							21-5	19-5

MAXIMUM LENGTH OF OVERHANGS LOAD ZONE - 20

LUMBER Size & Grade	TRUSS OR RAFTER SPACING							
	12"	16"	2'-0"	3'-0"	4'-0"	6'-0"	8'-0"	12'-0"
Group C								
2 x 12	11-0	11-0	11-0	11-0	11-0	9-9	8-10	7-7
2 x 10	10-0	10-0	10-0	10-0	9-2	8-0	7-3	6-3
2 x 8	10-0	10-0	9-0	7-11	7-2	6-3	5-8	4-11
2 x 6	8-8	7-10	6-10	6-0	5-5	4-9	4-4	3-9
2 x 4	5-6	5-0	4-4	3-9	3-5	3-0	2-9	2-4
Group D								
2 x 12	11-0	11-0	11-0	11-0	10-3	8-11	8-1	7-0
2 x 10	10-7	10-7	10-7	9-3	8-5	7-4	6-8	5-9
2 x 8	9-6	9-6	8-4	7-3	6-7	5-9	5-3	4-6
2 x 6	7-11	7-2	6-3	5-6	5-0	4-4	3-11	3-5
2 x 4	5-0	4-6	4-0	3-6	3-2	2-9	2-6	2-2
Group E								
2 x 12	10-8	10-8	10-8	10-8	9-8	8-6	7-8	6-3
2 x 10	10-0	10-0	10-0	8-9	8-0	6-11	6-4	5-2
2 x 8	9-0	9-0	7-11	6-11	6-3	5-5	4-11	4-1
2 x 6	7-6	6-10	6-0	5-2	4-9	4-2	3-9	3-1
2 x 4	4-9	4-4	3-9	3-4	3-0	2-5	2-4	1-11
Group F								
2 x 4	4-2	3-9	3-4	2-10	2-7	2-1	1-10	1-6

MAXIMUM SPANS OF ROOF PURLINS LOAD ZONE - 20

LUMBER Size & Grade		PURLIN SPACING				
		16"	24"	32"	36"	42"
Group C						
2 x 6	Edge	15-9	13-9	12-6	12-6	11-4
2 x 4	Flat	5-8	5-0	4-6	4-4	4-1
2 x 4	Edge	10-0	8-9	7-11	7-8	7-3
2 x 3	Flat	5-0	4-5	4-0	3-10	3-8
2 x 3	Edge	7-2	6-3	5-8	5-5	5-2
Group D						
2 x 6	Edge	14-5	12-8	11-6	11-0	10-2
2 x 4	Flat	5-3	4-6	4-2	4-0	3-9
2 x 4	Edge	9-3	8-0	7-4	7-0	6-8
2 x 3	Flat	4-8	4-0	3-9	3-6	3-4
2 x 3	Edge	6-6	5-9	5-3	5-0	4-9
Group E						
2 x 4	Flat	5-0	4-4	4-0	3-9	3-6
2 x 4	Edge	8-9	7-7	6-11	6-8	6-4
2 x 3	Flat	4-5	3-10	3-6	3-4	3-2
2 x 3	Edge	6-3	5-5	4-11	4-9	4-6
Group F						
2 x 4	Flat	4-4	3-9	3-5	3-2	3-1
2 x 4	Edge	7-7	6-8	6-0	5-10	5-6
2 x 3	Flat	3-10	3-4	3-0	2-11	2-9
2 x 3	Edge	5-5	4-9	4-4	4-2	3-11

Note: Where purlins span 3 or more spans, the allowable span may be increased 12%.

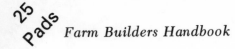
MINIMUM SIZES CONCRETE PADS OR FOOTINGS FOR POSTS OR POLES (DIAMETER & THICKNESS) LOAD ZONE - 25

P-1 POLES

SOIL	POLE SPACING	TRUSS SPAN FEET													
		24'		28'		32'		36'		40'		50'		60'	
Good	8'	12"	6"	12"	6"	12"	6"	12"	6"	12"	6"	12"	6"	12"	6"
	12'	12"	6"	12"	6"	12"	6"	12"	6"	12"	6"	12"	6"	14"	7"
	16'	12"	6"	12"	6"	12"	6"	12"	6"	12"	6"	12"	6"	14"	7"
	20'	12"	6"	12"	6"	12"	6"	12"	6"	12"	6"	14"	7"	16"	8"
Medium	8'	12"	6"	12"	6"	12"	6"	12"	6"	12"	6"	12"	6"	12"	6"
	12'	12"	6"	12"	6"	12"	6"	12"	6"	12"	6"	14"	7"	16"	8"
	16'	12"	6"	12"	6"	14"	7"	14"	7"	14"	7"	16"	8"	18"	10"
	20'	12"	6"	14"	7"	14"	7"	16"	8"	16"	8"	18"	10"	20"	12"
Poor	8'	14"	7"	14"	7"	16"	8"	16"	8"	18"	10"	20"	12"	22"	12"
	12'	16"	8"	18"	10"	20"	12"	20"	12"	22"	12"	24"	14"	26"	15"
	16'	20"	12"	20"	12"	22"	12"	24"	14"	24"	14"	28"	16"	30"	18"
	20'	22"	12"	22"	12"	24"	14"	26"	15"	28"	16"	30"	18"	34"	20"

P-2 POLES

SOIL	POLE SPACING	24'		28'		32'		36'		40'		50'		60'	
Good	8'	12"	6"	12"	6"	12"	6"	12"	6"	12"	6"	12"	6"	12"	6"
	12'	12"	6"	12"	6"	12"	6"	12"	6"	12"	6"	12"	6"	14"	7"
	16'	12"	6"	12"	6"	12"	6"	14"	7"	14"	7"	14"	7"	16"	8"
	20'	14"	7"	14"	7"	14"	7"	14"	7"	16"	8"	16"	8"	18"	10"
Medium	8'	12"	6"	12"	6"	12"	6"	12"	6"	12"	6"	14"	7"	14"	7"
	12'	14"	7"	14"	7"	14"	7"	14"	7"	16"	8"	16"	8"	18"	10"
	16'	16"	8"	16"	8"	16"	8"	16"	8"	18"	10"	18"	10"	20"	12"
	20'	18"	10"	18"	10"	18"	10"	18"	10"	20"	12"	20"	12"	22"	12"
Poor	8'	18"	10"	20"	12"	20"	12"	20"	12"	22"	12"	22"	12"	24"	14"
	12'	22"	12"	24"	14"	24"	14"	24"	14"	26"	15"	28"	16"	30"	18"
	16'	26"	15"	26"	15"	28"	16"	28"	16"	30"	18"	32"	18"	34"	20"
	20'	28"	16"	30"	18"	30"	18"	32"	18"	32"	18"	36"	21"	38"	24"

P-3 POLES

SOIL	POLE SPACING		
Good	8'	none	
	12'	8"	5"
	16'	8"	5"
	20'	10"	5"
Medium	8'	8"	5"
	12'	10"	5"
	16'	10"	5"
	20'	12"	6"
Poor	8'	12"	6"
	12'	16"	8"
	16'	18"	10"
	20'	20"	12"

NOTE: Use P-3 Pads for end wall poles.

SOIL CLASSIFICATIONS:
GOOD: Compact coarse sand, compact gravel or sand-gravel mixture, hardpan, shale, bed rock, or hard clay.
MEDIUM: Compact fine sand, loose gravel or sand-gravel mixture, compact sandy loam or medium clay.
POOR: Soft clay, fine and loose sand, clay loam, clay containing large amounts of silt.

POLE OR POST SPACING — LOAD ZONE - 30

EAVE HEIGHT		4' Top/Pole	4' Post	8' Top/Pole	8' Post	12' Top/Pole	12' Post	16' Top/Pole	16' Post	20' Top/Pole	20' Post
8'	A	A-4	A 4x4R 4x4D	A-4	A 4x4R 4x4D	A-4	A 4x6R 4x6D	A-4 & B-4 (spans to 47")	A 4x6R 6x6D	A-4 & B-5 (spans to 38")	A 6x6R 6x6D
	B	B-4	B 4x4R 4x4D	B-4	B 4x4R 4x6D	B-4	B 4x6R 6x6D	A-5 & B-5 (above 47")	B 6x6R 6x6D	A-5 & B-5 (above 38")	B 6x6R 6x6D
10'	A	A-4	A 4x4R 4x6D	A-4	A 4x6R 6x6D	A-5	A 6x6R 6x6D	A-5	A 6x6R 6x6D	A-5	A 6x6R 6x8D
	B	B-4	B 4x4R 4x6D	B-4	B 6x6R 6x6D	B-5	B 6x6R 6x6D	B-5	B 6x6R 6x8D	B-5	B 6x8R 8x8D
12'	A	A-4	A 4x4R 4x6D	A-4 & B-4 (spans to 47")	A 6x6R 6x6D	A-5	A 6x6R 6x6D	A-6	A 6x8R 8x8D	A-6	A 6x8R 8x8D
	B	B-4	B 4x6R 6x6D	A-5 & B-5 (above 47")	B 6x6R 6x6D	B-5	B 6x8R 8x8D	B-6	B 8x8R 8x8D	B-6	B 8x8R 8x8D
14'	A	A-4	A 6x6R 6x6D	A-4 & B-5 (spans to 37")	A 6x6R 6x6D	A-6	A 6x8R 8x8D	A-6	A 8x8R 8x8D	A-6	A 8x8R 8x8D
	B	B-4	B 6x6R 6x6D	A-5 & B-5 (above 37")	B 6x8R 6x6D	B-6	B 8x8R 8x8D	B-6	B 8x8R 8x8D	B-7	....
16'	A	A-4	A 6x6R 6x6D	A-5	A 6x8R 6x8D	A-6	A 8x8R 8x8D	A-6	A 8x8R 8x8D	A-7	....
	B	B-4	B 6x6R 6x6D	B-5	B 8x8R 8x8D	B-6	B 8x8R	B-7	B 8x8R	B-7	....
18'	A	A-4 & B-4 (spans to 50")	A 6x6R 6x6D	A-5 & B-6 (spans to 55")	A 8x8R 8x8D	A-6	A 8x8R	A-7		A-7	
	B	A-5 & B-5 (above 50")	B 6x6R 6x8D	A-6 & B-6 (above 55")	B 8x8R 8x8D	B-7	....	B-7		B-8	
20'	A	A-4 & B-4 (spans to 43")	A 6x6R 6x8D	A-5 & B-6 (spans to 47")	A 8x8R 8x8D	A-6		A-7		A-8	
	B	A-5 & B-5 (above 43")	B 6x8R 8x8D	A-6 & B-6 (above 47")	B 8x8R	B-7		B-8		B-10	

MINIMUM POLE SIZE REQUIREMENTS   LOAD ZONE - 30

Note: For "A" & "B" Post or Pole Species see Par. 301-1 and A-12.

MINIMUM PLATE SIZES (ALTERNATES) LOAD ZONE - 25
P-1 POLES

POLE SPACING	TRUSS SPACING	TRUSS SPAN						
		24'-0"	28'-0"	32'-0"	36'-0"	40'-0"	50'-0"	60'-0"
8'	4'	2-2x8 C 2-2x10 D 3-2x8 D	2-2x10 C 3-2x8 C 2-2x10 D 3-2x8 D	2-2x10 C 3-2x8 C 2-2x10 D 3-2x8 D	2-2x10 C 3-2x8 C 2-2x12 D 3-2x10 D	2-2x10 C 2-2x12 D 3-2x10 D	2-2x12 C 3-2x10 C 2-2x12 D 3-2x10 D	2-2x12 C 3-2x10 C 3-2x12 D 4-2x10 D
	6'	2-2x10 C 3-2x8 C 2-2x12 D 3-2x10 D	2-2x12 C 3-2x10 C 2-2x12 D 3-2x10 D	2-2x12 C 3-2x10 C 2-2x12 D 3-2x10 D	2-2x12 C 3-2x10 C 3-2x12 D 4-2x10 D	2-2x12 C 3-2x10 C 3-2x12 D 4-2x10 D	3-2x12 C 4-2x10 C 3-2x12 D 2-VB 15 D	3-2x12 C 2-VB 15 C 4-2x12 D 2-VB 15 D
	See Note 8'	1-2x6 C 1-2x6 D	1-2x6 C 1-2x6 D	1-2x6 C 1-2x6 D	1-2x6 C 1-2x6 D	1-2x6 C 1-2x6 D	1-2x6 C 1-2x6 D	1-2x6 C 1-2x6 D
12'	4'	2-2x10 C 3-2x8 C 2-2x10 D 3-2x8 D	2-2x10 C 3-2x8 C 2-2x10 D	2-2x10 C 2-2x12 D 3-2x10 D	2-2x12 C 3-2x10 C 2-2x12 D 3-2x10 D	2-2x12 C 3-2x10 C 2-2x12 D 3-2x10 D	3-2x12 C 4-2x10 C 3-2x12 D 4-2x10 D	3-2x12 C 4-2x10 C 3-2x12 D 2-VB 15 D
	6'	2-2x10 C 3-2x8 C 2-2x10 D 3-2x8 D	2-2x10 C 3-2x8 C 2-2x10 D 3-2x8 D	2-2x10 C 3-2x8 C 2-2x12 D 3-2x10 D	2-2x10 C 2-2x12 D 3-2x10 D	2-2x12 C 3-2x10 C 2-2x12 D 3-2x10 D	2-2x12 C 3-2x10 C 3-2x12 D 4-2x10 D	3-2x12 C 4-2x10 C 3-2x12 D 4-2x10 D
	8'	2-2x10 C 3-2x8 C 2-2x12 D 3-2x10 D	2-2x12 C 3-2x10 C 2-2x12 D 3-2x10 D	2-2x12 C 3-2x10 C 2-2x12 D 3-2x10 D	2-2x12 C 3-2x10 C 3-2x12 D 4-2x10 D	2-2x12 C 3-2x10 C 3-2x12 D 4-2x10 D	3-2x12 C 4-2x10 C 3-2x12 D 2-VB 15 D	3-2x12 C 2-VB 15 C 4-2x12 D 3-VB 13 D
16'	4'	2-2x12 C 3-2x10 C 2-2x12 D 3-2x10 D	2-2x12 C 3-2x10 C 3-2x12 D 4-2x10 D	3-2x12 C 4-2x10 C 3-2x12 D 4-2x10 D	3-2x12 C 4-2x10 C 3-2x12 D 2-VB 15 D	3-2x12 C 4-2x10 C 4-2x12 D 2-VB 15 D	4-2x12 C 3-VB 13 C 4-2x12 D 3-VB 13 D	4-2x12 C 3-VB 15 C 4-VB 13 D 3-VB 15 D
	6'	2-2x12 C 3-2x10 C 2-2x12 D 3-2x10 D	2-2x12 C 3-2x10 C 2-2x12 D 3-2x10 D	2-2x12 C 3-2x10 C 3-2x12 D 4-2x10 D	3-2x12 C 4-2x10 C 3-2x12 D 4-2x10 D	3-2x12 C 4-2x10 C 3-2x12 D 2-VB 15 D	4-2x12 C 2-VB 15 C 4-2x12 D 3-VB 13 D	4-2x12 C 3-VB 13 C 3-VB 15 D
	8'	2-2x12 C 3-2x10 C 2-2x12 D 3-2x10 D	2-2x12 C 3-2x10 C 3-2x12 D 4-2x10 D	3-2x12 C 4-2x10 C 3-2x12 D 4-2x10 D	3-2x12 C 4-2x10 C 3-2x12 D 4-2x12 D	3-2x12 C 4-2x10 C 4-2x12 D 2-VB 15 D	4-2x12 C 2-VB 15 C 4-2x12 D 3-VB 13 D	4-2x12 C 3-VB 15 C 3-VB 15 D
20'	4'	3-2x12 C 4-2x10 C 3-2x12 D 2-VB 15 D	3-2x12 C 2-VB 15 C 4-2x12 D 3-VB 13 D	4-2x12 C 2-VB 15 C 3-VB 15 D 4-VB 13 D	4-2x12 C 3-VB 13 C 3-VB 15 D 4-VB 13 D	3-VB 15 C 4-VB 13 C 3-VB 15 D 4-VB 13 D	3-VB 17 C 4-VB 15 C 3-VB 17 D 4-VB 15 D	3-VB 17 C 4-VB 15 C 4-VB 17 D
	6'	3-2x12 C 4-2x10 C 4-2x12 D 2-VB 15 D	4-2x12 C 2-VB 15 C 4-2x12 D 3-VB 13 D	4-2x12 C 3-VB 13 C 3-VB 15 D 4-VB 13 D	4-2x12 C 3-VB 15 C 3-VB 15 D 4-VB 13 D	3-VB 15 C 4-VB 13 C 3-VB 15 D 4-VB 13 D	3-VB 17 C 4-VB 15 C 3-VB 17 D 4-VB 15 D	3-VB 17 C 4-VB 15 C 4-VB 17 D
	8'	3-2x12 C 2-VB 15 C 4-2x12 D 2-VB 13 D	4-2x12 C 2-VB 15 C 4-2x12 D 2-VB 15 D	4-2x12 C 3-VB 13 C 3-VB 15 D 4-VB 13 D	3-VB 15 C 4-VB 13 C 3-VB 15 D 4-VB 13 D	3-VB 15 C 4-VB 13 D 3-VB 17 D 4-VB 15 D	3-VB 17 C 4-VB 15 D 3-VB 17 D 4-VB 15 D	4-VB 15 C 4-VB 17 D

V-B Vertically Built Up Beams as described in 408-2.
For C & D Groups of Lumber See Appendix A-14.

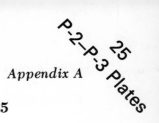

Appendix A

MINIMUM PLATE SIZES FOR P-2 and P-3 POLES (ALTERNATES) LOAD ZONE - 25
P-2 POLES

POLE SPACING	TRUSS SPACING	TRUSS SPAN 24'-0"	28'-0"	32'-0"	36'-0"	40'-0"	50'-0"	60'-0"	P-3 POLES 20' SPAN RAFTER
8'-0"	4'-0"	2-2x12 C 3-2x10 C 2-2x12 D 3-2x10 D	2-2x12 C 3-2x10 C 2-2x12 D 3-2x10 D	2-2x12 C 3-2x10 C 2-2x12 D 3-2x10 D	2-2x12 C 3-2x10 C 3-2x12 D 4-2x10 D	2-2x12 C 3-2x10 C 3-2x12 D 4-2x10 D	3-2x12 C 4-2x10 C 3-2x12 D 4-2x10 D	3-2x12 C 4-2x10 C 4-2x12 D 2-VB 15 D	
	6'-0"	3-2x12 C 4-2x10 C 3-2x12 D 4-2x10 D	3-2x12 C 4-2x10 C 3-2x12 D 2-VB 15 D	3-2x12 C 4-2x10 C 3-2x12 D 2-VB 15 D	3-2x12 C 2-VB 15 C 4-2x12 D 3-VB 13 D	3-2x12 C 2-VB 15 C 4-2x12 D 3-VB 13 D	4-2x12 C 2-VB 15 C 4-2x12 D 3-VB 15 D	4-2x12 C 3-VB 15 C 3-VB 15 D 4-VB 13 D	2-2x6 C 2-2x6 D
	See Note 8'-0"	2-2x6 C 2-2x6 D	2-2x6 C 2-2x6 D	2-2x6 C 2-2x6 D	2-2x6 C 2-2x6 D	2-2x6 C 2-2x6 D	2-2x6 C 2-2x6 D	2-2x6 C 2-2x6 D	
12'-0"	4'-0"	2-2x12 C 3-2x10 C 3-2x12 D 4-2x10 D	2-2x12 C 3-2x10 C 3-2x12 D 4-2x10 D	3-2x12 C 4-2x10 C 4-2x10 D 2-VB 13 D	3-2x12 C 4-2x10 C 4-2x10 D 2-VB 15 D	3-2x12 C 4-2x10 C 4-2x12 D 2-VB 15 D	3-2x12 C 2-VB 15 C 4-2x12 D 2-VB 15 D	4-2x12 C 2-VB 15 C 4-2x12 D 3-VB 13 D	
	6'-0"	2-2x12 C 3-2x10 C 3-2x10 D 2-VB 13 D	2-2x12 C 3-2x10 C 3-2x12 D 4-2x10 D	2-2x12 C 3-2x10 C 3-2x12 D 4-2x10 D	3-2x12 C 4-2x10 C 3-2x12 D 4-2x10 D	3-2x12 C 4-2x10 C 3-2x12 D 4-2x10 D	3-2x12 C 4-2x10 C 3-2x12 D 2-VB 15 D	3-2x12 C 2-VB 15 C 4-2x12 D 2-VB 15 D	2-2x8 C 2-2x10 D 3-2x8 D
	8'-0"	3-2x12 C 4-2x10 C 3-2x12 D 2-VB 13 D	3-2x12 C 4-2x10 C 3-2x12 D 2-VB 15 D	3-2x12 C 4-2x10 C 3-2x12 D 2-VB 15 D	3-2x12 C 2-VB 15 C 4-2x12 D 2-VB 15 D	3-2x12 C 2-VB 15 C 4-2x12 D 2-VB 15 D	4-2x12 C 2-VB 15 C 4-2x12 D 3-VB 15 D	4-2x12 C 3-VB 15 C 3-VB 15 D	
16'-0"	4'-0"	3-2x12 C 2-VB 15 C 4-2x12 D 2-VB 15 D	4-2x12 C 2-VB 15 C 4-2x12 D 3-VB 13 D	4-2x12 C 2-VB 15 C 4-2x12 D 3-VB 17 D	4-2x12 C 3-VB 13 C 3-VB 15 D 4-VB 13 D	4-2x12 C 3-VB 15 C 3-VB 15 D 4-VB 13 D	3-VB 15 C 4-VB 13 C 3-VB 17 D 4-VB 15 D	3-VB 17 C 4-VB 15 C 3-VB 17 D 4-VB 15 D	
	6'-0"	3-2x12 C 4-2x10 C 4-2x12 D 2-VB 15 D	3-2x12 C 2-VB 15 C 4-2x12 D 2-VB 15 D	4-2x12 C 2-VB 15 C 4-2x12 D 3-VB 13 D	4-2x12 C 2-VB 15 C 4-2x12 D 3-VB 15 D	4-2x12 C 3-VB 13 C 3-VB 15 D 4-VB 13 D	3-VB 15 C 4-VB 13 C 3-VB 15 D 4-VB 13 D	3-VB 15 C 4-VB 13 C 3-VB 17 D 4-VB 15 D	2-2x10 C 2-2x12 D 3-2x10 D
	8'-0"	3-2x12 C 2-VB 15 C 4-2x12 D 2-VB 15 D	4-2x12 C 2-VB 15 C 4-2x12 D 3-VB 13 D	4-2x12 C 2-VB 15 C 4-2x12 D 3-VB 15 D	4-2x12 C 3-VB 13 C 3-VB 15 D 4-VB 13 D	4-2x12 C 3-VB 15 C 3-VB 15 D 4-VB 13 D	3-VB 15 C 4-VB 13 C 3-VB 17 D 4-VB 15 D	3-VB 17 C 4-VB 15 C 3-VB 17 D 4-VB 15 D	
20'-0"	4'-0"	3-VB 15 C 4-VB 13 C 3-VB 17 D 4-VB 15 D	3-VB 15 C 4-VB 13 C 3-VB 17 D 4-VB 15 D	3-VB 17 C 4-VB 15 C 3-VB 17 D 4-VB 15 D	3-VB 17 C 4-VB 15 C 4-VB 15 D	3-VB 17 C 4-VB 15 C 4-VB 17 D	4-VB 17 C 4-VB 17 D	4-VB 17 C	
	6'-0"	3-VB 15 C 4-VB 13 C 4-VB 15 D	4-VB 15 C 3-VB 17 C 4-VB 15 D	4-VB 15 C 3-VB 17 C 4-VB 15 D	4-VB 15 C 3-VB 17 C 4-VB 17 D	4-VB 15 C 3-VB 17 C 4-VB 17 D	4-VB 17 C	4-VB 17 C	3-2x12 C 4-2x10 D 3-2x12 D
	8'-0"	3-VB 15 C 4-VB 13 C 4-VB 15 D	3-VB 17 C 4-VB 15 C 4-VB 15 D	3-VB 17 C 4-VB 15 C 4-VB 17 D	3-VB 17 C 4-VB 15 C 4-VB 17 D	4-VB 15 C 4-VB 17 D	4-VB 17 C		

V-B Vertically Built-Up Beams as described in 408-2.
For C & D Groups of Lumber See Appendix A-14.
Note: If Rafters from P-2 to P-3 plates are spaced same as poles, a single member plate may be used.

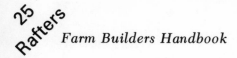
MAXIMUM SPAN OF RAFTERS HORIZONTAL SPAN LOAD ZONE - 25

LUMBER Size & Grade	RAFTER SPACING							
	12"	16"	24"	32"	36"	48"	72"	96"
Group C								
2 x 4	10-11	9-2	8-0	7-3	7-0	6-4		
2 x 6	15-11	14-6	12-7	11-5	11-0	10-0		
2 x 8		19-1	16-8	15-2	14-7	13-3	11-7	10-6
2 x 10			21-3	19-3	18-7	16-10	14-8	13-4
2 x 12					22-7	20-6	17-11	16-3
2-2 x 8					18-4	16-8	14-7	13-3
2-2 x 10						21-3	18-7	16-10
2-2 x 12							22-7	20-6
Group D								
2 x 4	9-3	8-5	7-3	6-8	6-5	5-10		
2 x 6	14-8	13-4	11-7	10-7	1C 2	9-2		
2 x 8		17-7	15-4	13-11	13-5	12-2	10-7	9-8
2 x 10			22-5	19-6	17-9	15-6	14-5	12-6
2 x 12					20-9	18-10	16-6	14-11
2-2 x 8					16-10	15-4	13-5	12-2
2-2 x 10						19-6	17-1	15-6
2-2 x 12							20-9	18-10
Group E								
2 x 4	8-9	8-0	7-0	6-4	6-1	5-6		
2 x 6	13-11	12-8	11-0	10-0	9-7	8-9		
2 x 8	18-4	16-8	14-7	13-3	12-9	11-7	10-1	8-9
2 x 10		21-3	18-7	16-10	16-2	14-8	12-10	11-2
2 x 12			22-7	20-6	19-9	17-10	15-8	13-7
2-2 x 8			18-4	16-8	16-0	14-7	12-9	11-7
2-2 x 10					20-5	18-7	16-2	14-8
2-2 x 12						22-7	19-9	17-11

MAXIMUM LENGTH OF OVERHANGS LOAD ZONE - 25

LUMBER Size & Grade	TRUSS OR RAFTER SPACING							
	12″	16″	2′-0″	3′-0″	4′-0″	6′-0″	8′-0″	12′-0″
Group C								
2 x 12	11-0	11-0	11-0	11-0	10-3	8-11	8-1	6-8
2 x 10	10-7	10-7	10-7	9-3	8-5	7-4	6-8	5-6
2 x 8	9-6	9-6	8-4	7-2	6-7	5-9	5-3	4-3
2 x 6	7-11	7-2	6-3	5-6	5-0	4-4	3-11	3-5
2 x 4	5-0	4-7	4-0	3-6	3-2	2-9	2-6	2-1
Group D								
2 x 12	10-0	10-0	10-0	10-0	9-5	8-3	7-5	6-2
2 x 10	9-9	9-9	9-9	8-6	7-9	6-9	6-1	5-1
2 x 8	9-8	8-8	7-8	6-8	6-0	5-3	4-10	4-0
2 x 6	7-4	6-8	5-9	5-0	4-7	4-0	3-8	3-0
2 x 4	4-8	4-2	3-8	3-2	2-10	2-6	2-4	1-11
Group E								
2 x 12	9-10	9-10	9-10	9-10	8-11	7-6	6-9	5-6
2 x 10	9-3	9-3	9-3	8-1	7-4	6-5	5-7	4-7
2 x 8	9-2	8-4	7-3	6-4	5-9	5-0	4-4	3-7
2 x 6	6-11	6-3	5-6	4-9	4-4	3-10	3-4	2-8
2 x 4	6-0	5-2	4-2	3-5	3-0	2-5	2-1	1-9
Group F								
2 x 4	3-10	3-6	3-1	2-8	2-3	1-10	1-7	1-4

MAXIMUM SPANS OF ROOF PURLINS LOAD ZONE - 25

LUMBER Size & Grade		PURLIN SPACING				
		16″	24″	32″	36″	42″
Group C						
2 x 6	Edge	14-6	12-8	11-6	11-0	10-6
2 x 4	Flat	5-2	4-6	4-1	3-11	3-9
2 x 4	Edge	9-2	8-0	7-3	7-0	6-8
2 x 3	Flat	4-8	4-0	3-8	3-6	3-4
2 x 3	Edge	6-6	5-9	5-2	5-0	4-9
Group D						
2 x 6	Edge	13-4	11-7	10-6	10-2	9-7
2 x 4	Flat	4-9	4-2	3-9	3-8	3-5
2 x 4	Edge	8-6	7-4	6-8	6-5	6-1
2 x 3	Flat	4-2	3-9	3-5	3-3	3-1
2 x 3	Edge	6-0	5-3	4-9	4-7	4-4
Group E						
2 x 4	Flat	4-6	4-0	3-7	3-5	3-3
2 x 4	Edge	8-0	7-0	6-4	6-1	5-10
2 x 3	Flat	4-0	3-6	3-3	3-1	2-11
2 x 3	Edge	5-9	5-0	4-6	4-4	4-2
Group F						
2 x 4	Flat	4-0	3-5	3-2	3-0	2-10
2 x 4	Edge	7-0	6-1	5-6	5-3	4-10
2 x 3	Flat	3-6	3-1	2-10	2-8	2-6
2 x 3	Edge	5-0	4-4	3-11	3-9	3-6

Note: Where purlins span 3 or more spans, the allowable span may be increased 12%.

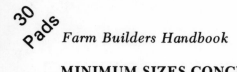

MINIMUM SIZES CONCRETE PADS OR FOOTINGS FOR POSTS OR POLES (DIAMETER & THICKNESS) LOAD ZONE - 30

P-1 POLES

SOIL	POLE SPACING	TRUSS SPAN FEET													
		24'		**28'**		**32'**		**36'**		**40'**		**50'**		**60'**	
Good	8'	12"	6"	12"	6"	12"	6"	12"	6"	12"	6"	12"	6"	12"	6"
	12'	12"	6"	12"	6"	12"	6"	12"	6"	12"	6"	12"	6"	14"	7"
	16'	12"	6"	12"	6"	12"	6"	12"	6"	14"	7"	14"	7"	16"	8"
	20'	12"	6"	12"	6"	14"	7"	14"	7"	14"	7"	16"	8"	18"	10"
Medium	8'	12"	6"	12"	6"	12"	6"	12"	6"	12"	6"	14"	7"	14"	7"
	12'	12"	6"	12"	6"	14"	7"	14"	7"	14"	7"	16"	8"	18"	10"
	16'	14"	7"	14"	7"	16"	8"	16"	8"	16"	8"	18"	10"	20"	12"
	20'	14"	7"	16"	8"	16"	8"	18"	10"	18"	10"	20"	12"	22"	12"
Poor	8'	16"	8"	18"	10"	18"	10"	20"	12"	20"	12"	22"	12"	24"	14"
	12'	20"	12"	22"	12"	22"	12"	24"	14"	24"	14"	28"	16"	30"	18"
	16'	22"	12"	24"	14"	26"	15"	28"	16"	28"	16"	32"	18"	34"	20"
	20'	24"	14"	26"	15"	28"	16"	30"	18"	32"	18"	36"	21"	38"	24"

P-2 POLES

SOIL	POLE SPACING	24'		28'		32'		36'		40'		50'		60'	
Good	8'	12"	6"	12"	6"	12"	6"	12"	6"	12"	6"	12"	6"	14"	7"
	12'	12"	6"	12"	6"	14"	7"	14"	7"	14"	7"	16"	8"	16"	8"
	16'	14"	7"	14"	7"	16"	8"	16"	8"	16"	8"	18"	10"	18"	10"
	20'	16"	8"	16"	8"	16"	8"	18"	10"	18"	10"	20"	12"	20"	12"
Medium	8'	12"	6"	14"	7"	14"	7"	14"	7"	14"	7"	16"	8"	16"	8"
	12'	16"	8"	16"	8"	16"	8"	18"	10"	18"	10"	20"	12"	20"	12"
	16'	18"	10"	18"	10"	20"	12"	20"	12"	20"	12"	22"	12"	24"	14"
	20'	20"	12"	20"	12"	22"	12"	22"	12"	22"	12"	24"	14"	26"	15"
Poor	8'	22"	12"	22"	12"	24"	14"	24"	14"	24"	14"	26"	15"	28"	16"
	12'	26"	15"	28"	16"	28"	16"	30"	18"	30"	18"	32"	18"	34"	20"
	16'	30"	18"	32"	18"	32"	18"	34"	20"	34"	20"	38"	24"	40"	24"
	20'	34"	20"	34"	20"	36"	21"	38"	24"	38"	24"	42"	24"	44"	26"

P-3 POLES

SOIL	POLE SPACING			
Good	8'	8"	5"	
	12'	8"	5"	**NOTE:** Use P-3 Pads for end wall poles.
	16'	10"	5"	
	20'	10"	5"	
Medium	8'	8"	5"	
	12'	10"	5"	
	16'	12"	6"	
	20'	14"	7"	
Poor	8'	14"	7"	
	12'	18"	10"	
	16'	20"	12"	
	20'	22"	12"	

SOIL CLASSIFICATIONS:
GOOD: Compact coarse sand, compact gravel or sand-gravel mixture, hardpan, shale, bed rock, or hard clay.
MEDIUM: Compact fine sand, loose gravel or sand-gravel mixture, compact sandy loam or medium clay.
POOR: Soft clay, fine and loose sand, clay loam, clay containing large amounts of silt.

POLE OR POST SPACING

EAVE HEIGHT	4' Top/Pole	4' Post	8' Top/Pole	8' Post	12' Top/Pole	12' Post	16' Top/Pole	16' Post	20' Top/Pole	20' Post
8'	A-4	A 4x4R 4x4D	A-4	A 4x4R 4x4D	A-4	A 4x6R 4x6D	A-4	A 4x6R 6x6D	A-4 (spans to 51')	A 6x6R 6x6D
	B-4	B 4x4R 4x4D	B-4	B 4x4R 4x4D	B-4	B 4x6R 6x6D	B-4	B 6x6R 6x6D	B-5	B 6x6R 6x6D
10'	A-4	A 4x4R 4x4D	A-4	A 4x6R 6x6D	A-4	A 6x6R 6x6D	A-5	A 6x6R 6x6D	A-5	A 6x6R 6x8D
	B-4	B 4x4R 4x6D	B-4	B 6x6R 6x6D	B-5	B 6x6R 6x6D	B-5	B 6x6R 6x8D	B-5	B 6x8R 8x8D
12'	A-4	A 4x4R 4x6D	A-4	A 6x6R 6x6D	A-5	A 6x6R 6x8D	A-5	A 6x6R 8x8D	A-6	A 6x8R 8x8D
	B-4	B 4x6R 6x6D	B-4	B 6x6R 6x6D	B-5	B 6x8R 8x8D	B-6	B 8x8R 8x8D	B-6	B 8x8R 8x8D
14'	A-4	A 4x6R 6x6D	A-4 (spans to 51')	A 6x6R 6x6D	A-5	A 6x8R 8x8D	A-6	A 8x8R 8x8D	A-6	A 8x8R 8x8D
	B-4	B 6x6R 6x6D	B-5	B 6x8R 6x8D	B-6	B 8x8R 8x8D	B-6	B 8x8R ----	B-7	--- ---
16'	A-4	A 6x6R 6x6D	A-5	A 6x8R 6x8D	A-5	A 8x8R 8x8D	A-6	A 8x8R ----	A-7	
	B-4	B 6x6R 6x8D	B-5	B 8x8R 8x8D	B-6	B 8x8R ----	B-7	--- ---	B-7	
18'	A-4	A 6x6R 6x8D	A-5	A 8x8R 8x8D	A-6	A 8x8R ----	A-7		A-7	
	B-4	B 6x6R 6x8D	B-6	B 8x8R 8x8D	B-7	--- ---	B-7		B-8	
20'	A-4	A 6x6R 6x8D	A-5	A 8c8R 8x8D	A-6	--- ---	A-7		A-8	
	B-4	B 6x8R 8x8D	B-6	B 8x8R ----	B-7		B-8		B-10	

MINIMUM POLE SIZE REQUIREMENTS   LOAD ZONE - 25

Note: For "A" & "B" Post or Pole Species see Par. 301-1 and A-12.

Farm Builders Handbook

MINIMUM PLATE SIZES (ALTERNATES) LOAD ZONE - 30
P-1 POLES

POLE SPACING	TRUSS SPACING	TRUSS SPAN						
		24'-0"	28'-0"	32'-0"	36'-0"	40'-0"	50'-0"	60'-0"
8'	4'	2-2x10 C 3-2x8 C 2-2x10 D	2-2x10 C 2-2x12 D 3-2x10 D	2-2x12 C 3-2x10 C 2-2x12 D 3-2x10 D	2-2x12 C 3-2x10 C 2-2x12 D 3-2x10 D	2-2x12 C 3-2x10 C 3-2x12 D 4-2x10 D	3-2x12 C 4-2x10 C 3-2x12 D 4-2x10 D	3-2x12 C 2-VB 15 C 4-2x12 D 2-VB 15 D
	6'	2-2x12 C 3-2x10 C 2-2x12 D 3-2x10 D	2-2x12 C 3-2x10 C 3-2x12 D 4-2x10 D	3-2x12 C 4-2x10 C 3-2x12 D 4-2x10 D	3-2x12 C 4-2x10 C 3-2x12 D 2-VB 15 D	3-2x12 C 2-VB 15 C 4-2x12 D 2-VB 15 D	4-2x12 C 2-VB 15 C 4-2x12 D 3-VB 15 D	3-VB 15 C 3-VB 15 D
	See Note 8'	1-2x6 C 1-2x6 D	1-2x6 C 1-2x6 D	1-2x6 C 1-2x6 D	1-2x6 C 1-2x6 D	1-2x6 C 1-2x6 D	1-2x6 C 1-2x6 D	1-2x6 C 1-2x6 D
12'	4'	2-2x12 C 3-2x10 C 2-2x12 D 3-2x10 D	2-2x12 C 3-2x10 C 2-2x12 D 3-2x10 D	2-2x12 C 3-2x10 C 3-2x12 D 4-2x10 D	3-2x12 C 4-2x10 C 3-2x12 D 4-2x10 D	3-2x12 C 4-2x10 C 3-2x12 D 4-2x10 D	3-2x12 C 2-VB 15 C 4-2x12 D 2-VB 15 D	4-2x12 C 2-VB 15 C 4-2x12 D 3-VB 15 D
	6'	2-2x10 C 3-2x8 C 2-2x12 D 3-2x10 D	2-2x12 C 3-2x10 C 2-2x12 D 3-2x10 D	2-2x12 C 3-2x10 C 2-2x12 D 3-2x10 D	2-2x10 C 3-2x10 C 3-2x12 D 4-2x10 D	3-2x12 C 4-2x10 C 3-2x12 D 4-2x10 D	3-2x12 C 4-2x10 C 3-2x12 D 2-VB 15 D	4-2x12 C 2-VB 15 C 4-2x12 D 3-VB 15 D
	8'	3-2x12 C 3-2x10 C 2-2x12 D	2-2x12 C 3-2x10 C 3-2x12 D	3-2x12 C 4-2x10 C 3-2x12 D	3-2x12 C 4-2x10 C 3-2x12 D	3-2x12 C 2-VB 15 C 4-2x12 D	4-2x12 C 3-VB 13 C 4-2x12 D	3-VB 15 C 3-VB 15 D
16'	4'	3-2x12 C 4-2x10 C 4-2x10 D 2-VB 13 D	3-2x12 C 4-2x10 C 4-2x12 D 2-VB 15 D	3-2x12 C 2-VB 15 C 4-2x12 D 2-VB 15 D	4-2x12 C 2-VB 15 C 4-2x12 D 3-VB 13 D	4-2x12 C 3-VB 13 C 3-VB 15 D	3-VB 15 C 3-VB 17 D	3-VB 17 C 3-VB 17 D
	6'	3-2x12 C 4-2x10 C 4-2x10 D 2-VB 13 D	3-2x12 C 4-2x10 C 4-2x12 D 2-VB 15 D	3-2x12 C 2-VB 15 C 4-2x12 D 2-VB 15 D	4-2x12 C 3-VB 13 C 4-2x12 D 3-VB 13 D	4-2x12 C 3-VB 13 C 4-2x12 D 3-VB 15 D	3-VB 15 C 3-VB 15 D	3-VB 15 C 3-VB 17 D
	8'	3-2x12 C 4-2x10 C 3-2x12 D	3-2x12 C 4-2x10 C 3-2x12 D	3-2x12 C 2-VB 15 C 4-2x12 D	4-2x12 C 2-VB 15 C 4-2x12 D	4-2x12 C 3-VB 13 C 3-VB 15 D	3-VB 15 C 3-VB 17 D	3-VB 17 C 3-VB 17 D
20'	4'	4-2x12 C 3-VB 13 C 3-VB 15 D 4-VB 13 D	3-VB 15 C 4-VB 13 C 3-VB 15 D 4-VB 13 D	3-VB 15 C 4-VB 13 C 4-VB 15 D	3-VB 17 C 4-VB 15 C 4-VB 15 D	3-VB 17 C 4-VB 15 C 4-VB 15 D	4-VB 17 C 4-VB 17 D	4-VB 17 C
	6'	3-VB 13 C 3-VB 15 D 4-VB 13 D	3-VB 15 C 4-VB 13 C 3-VB 15 D 4-VB 13 D	3-VB 15 C 4-VB 13 C 4-VB 15 D	3-VB 17 C 4-VB 15 D	3-VB 17 C 4-VB 17 D	4-VB 17 C	
	8'	3-VB 13 C 3-VB 15 D 4-VB 13 D	3-VB 15 C 4-VB 13 C 3-VB 17 D 4-VB 15 D	3-VB 15 C 4-VB 13 C 3-VB 17 D	3-VB 17 C 4-VB 15 C 3-VB 17 D	3-VB 17 C 4-VB 15 C 4-VB 17 D	4-VB 17 C	

V-B Vertically Built Up Beams as described in 408-2.
For C & D Groups of Lumber See Appendix A-14.

MINIMUM PLATE SIZES FOR P-2 and P-3 POLES (ALTERNATES) LOAD ZONE - 30
P-2 POLES

POLE SPACING	TRUSS SPACING	TRUSS SPAN 24'-0"	28'-0"	32'-0"	36'-0"	40'-0"	50'-0"	60'-0"	P-3 POLES 20' SPAN RAFTER
8'-0"	4'-0"	2-2x12 C 3-2x10 C 3-2x12 D 4-2x10 D	3-2x12 C 4-2x10 C 3-2x12 D 4-2x10 D	3-2x12 C 4-2x10 C 3-2x12 D 2-VB 15 D	3-2x12 C 4-2x10 C 3-2x12 D 2-VB 15 D	3-2x12 C 2-VB 15 C 4-2x12 D 2-VB 15 D	4-2x12 C 2-VB 15 C 4-2x12 D 3-VB 13 D	4-2x12 C 3-VB 15 C 3-VB 15 D 4-VB 13 D	2-2x6 C 2-2x8 D 3-2x6 D
	6'-0"	3-2x12 C 2-VB 15 C 4-2x12 D 3-VB 15 D	4-2x12 C 2-VB 15 C 4-2x12 D 3-VB 15 D	4-2x12 C 3-VB 13 C 3-VB 15 D 4-VB 13 D	4-2x12 C 3-VB 15 C 3-VB 15 D 4-VB 13 D	3-VB 15 C 4-VB 13 C 3-VB 15 D 4-VB 13 D	3-VB 15 C 4-VB 13 C 3-VB 17 D 4-VB 15 D	3-VB 17 C 4-VB 15 C 3-VB 17 D	
	See Note 8'-0"	2-2x6 C 2-2x8 D	2-2x6 C 2-2x8 D	2-2x6 C 2-2x8 D	2-2x6 C 2-2x8 D	2-2x6 C 2-2x8 D	2-2x6 C 2-2x8 D	2-2x6 C 2-2x8 D	
12'-0"	4'-0"	3-2x12 C 4-2x10 C 3-2x12 D 2-VB 15 D	3-2x12 C 2-VB 15 C 4-2x12 D 2-VB 15 D	3-2x12 C 2-VB 15 C 4-2x10 D 3-VB 13 D	4-2x12 C 2-VB 15 C 4-2x12 D 3-VB 13 D	4-2x12 C 2-VB 15 C 4-2x12 D 3-VB 15 D	4-2x12 C 3-VB 15 C 3-VB 15 D 4-VB 13 D	3-VB 15 C 4-VB 13 C 3-VB 17 D 4-VB 15 D	2-2x10 C 3-2x8 C 2-2x10 D 3-2x8 D
	6'-0"	3-2x12 C 4-2x10 C 3-2x12 D 4-2x10 D	3-2x12 C 4-2x10 C 3-2x12 D 2-VB 15 D	3-2x12 C 4-2x10 C 3-2x12 D 2-VB 15 D	3-2x12 C 2-VB 15 C 4-2x12 D 2-VB 15 D	4-2x12 C 2-VB 15 C 4-2x12 D 3-VB 13 D	4-2x12 C 3-VB 13 C 3-VB 15 D 4-VB 13 D	3-VB 15 C 4-VB 13 C 3-VB 15 D 4-VB 13 D	
	8'-0"	3-2x12 C 2-VB 15 C 4-2x12 D 3-VB 13 D	4-2x12 C 2-VB 15 C 4-2x12 D 3-VB 13 D	4-2x12 C 3-VB 13 C 3-VB 15 D 4-VB 13 D	4-2x12 C 3-VB 13 C 3-VB 15 D 4-VB 13 D	3-VB 15 C 4-VB 13 C 3-VB 17 D 4-VB 13 D	3-VB 15 C 4-VB 13 C 3-VB 17 D 4-VB 15 D	3-VB 17 C 4-VB 15 C 3-VB 17 D 4-VB 15 D	
16'-0"	4'-0"	4-2x12 C 3-VB 15 C 3-VB 15 D 4-VB 13 D	3-VB 15 C 4-VB 13 C 3-VB 15 D 4-VB 13 D	3-VB 15 C 4-VB 13 C 3-VB 17 D 4-VB 15 D	3-VB 17 C 4-VB 13 C 3-VB 17 D 4-VB 15 D	3-VB 17 C 4-VB 15 C 3-VB 17 D 4-VB 15 D	3-VB 17 C 4-VB 15 C 4-VB 17 D	4-VB 17 C 4-VB 17 D	2-2x12 C 3-2x10 C 3-2x12 D 4-2x10 D
	6'-0"	4-2x12 C 3-VB 13 C 3-VB 15 D 4-VB 13 D	3-VB 15 C 4-VB 13 C 3-VB 15 D 4-VB 13 D	3-VB 15 C 4-VB 13 C 3-VB 15 D	3-VB 15 C 4-VB 13 C 3-VB 17 D 4-VB 15 D	3-VB 15 C 4-VB 13 C 3-VB 17 D 4-VB 15 D	3-VB 17 C 4-VB 15 C 4-VB 15 D	4-VB 15 C 4-VB 17 D	
	8'-0"	4-2x12 C 3-VB 15 C 3-VB 15 D 4-VB 13 D	3-VB 15 C 4-VB 13 C 3-VB 15 D 4-VB 13 D	3-VB 15 C 4-VB 13 C 3-VB 17 D 4-VB 15 D	3-VB 15 C 4-VB 13 C 3-VB 17 D 4-VB 15 D	3-VB 17 C 4-VB 15 C 3-VB 17 D 4-VB 15 D	3-VB 17 C 4-VB 15 C 4-VB 17 D	4-VB 17 C 4-VB 17 D	
20'-0"	4'-0"	3-VB 17 C 4-VB 15 C 4-VB 17 D	4-VB 17 C 4-VB 17 D	4-VB 17 C	4-VB 17 C	4-VB 17 C			3-2x12 C 4-2x12 D
	6'-0"	4-VB 15 C 4-VB 17 D	4-VB 17 C 4-VB 17 D	4-VB 17 C	4-VB 17 C				
	8'-0"	4-VB 17 C 4-VB 17 D	4-VB 17 C 4-VB 17 D	4-VB 17 C	4-VB 17 C				

V-B Vertically Built-Up Beams as described in 408-2.
C & D Groups of Lumber See Appendix A-14.
Note: If Rafters from P-2 to P-3 plates are spaced same as poles, a single member plate may be used.

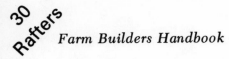

MAXIMUM SPAN OF RAFTERS HORIZONTAL SPAN LOAD ZONE - 30

LUMBER Size & Grade	RAFTER SPACING							
	12"	16"	24"	32"	36"	48"	72"	96"
Group C								
2 x 4	9-5	8-7	7-6	6-10	6-7	5-11		
2 x 6	14-11	13-6	11-10	10-9	10-4	9-4		
2 x 8	19-8	17-11	15-7	14-2	13-8	12-5	10-3	8-11
2 x 10		22-9	19-11	18-0	17-4	15-9	13-1	11-4
2 x 12			24-0	21-11	21-2	19-2	16-0	13-10
2-2 x 8			19-8	17-10	17-2	15-7	13-8	12-5
2-2 x 10					21-11	19-11	17-4	15-9
2-2 x 12						24-0	21-2	19-2
Group D								
2 x 4	8-8	7-10	6-10	6-3	6-0	5-5		
2 x 6	13-8	12-5	10-10	9-10	9-6	8-7		
2 x 8	18-1	16-5	14-4	13-0	12-6	11-5	9-6	8-3
2 x 10		20-11	18-3	16-7	15-11	14-6	12-2	10-6
2 x 12			22-3	20-2	19-5	17-8	14-9	12-10
2-2 x 8			18-1	16-5	15-10	14-4	12-6	11-5
2-2 x 10					20-1	18-3	15-11	14-6
2-2 x 12						22-3	19-5	17-8
Group E								
2 x 4	8-2	7-6	6-7	5-11	5-8	5-0		
2 x 6	13-0	11-10	10-4	9-4	9-0	7-11		
2 x 8	17-2	15-7	13-8	12-4	11-10	10-5	8-6	7-4
2 x 10		19-11	17-4	15-9	15-2	13-4	10-10	9-5
2 x 12			21-2	19-2	18-5	16-2	13-2	11-5
2-2 x 8			17-2	15-7	15-0	13-8	11-10	10-5
2-2 x 10					19-1	17-4	15-2	13-4
2-2 x 12						21-2	18-5	16-9

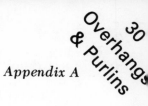

MAXIMUM LENGTH OF OVERHANGS LOAD ZONE - 30

LUMBER Size & Grade	TRUSS OR RAFTER SPACING							
	12″	16″	2′-0″	3′-0″	4′-0″	6′-0″	8′-0″	12′-0″
Group C								
2 x 12	10-6	10-6	10-6	10-6	9-7	8-0	6-11	5-8
2 x 10	9-11	9-11	9-11	8-8	7-10	6-7	5-8	4-8
2 x 8	8-11	8-11	7-9	6-10	6-2	5-2	4-5	3-8
2 x 6	7-5	6-9	5-11	5-2	4-8	3-11	3-4	2-9
2 x 4	4-8	4-3	3-9	3-3	3-0	2-6	2-2	1-9
Group D								
2 x 12	10-0	10-0	10-0	9-8	8-10	7-5	6-5	5-3
2 x 10	9-11	9-11	9-1	7-11	7-3	6-1	5-3	4-4
2 x 8	9-0	8-2	7-2	6-3	5-8	4-9	4-1	3-4
2 x 6	6-10	6-2	5-5	4-9	4-3	3-7	3-1	2-7
2 x 4	4-4	3-11	3-5	3-0	2-9	2-4	2-0	1-7
Group E								
2 x 12	10-0	10-0	10-0	9-3	8-1	6-7	5-9	4-8
2 x 10	9-11	9-11	8-8	7-6	6-8	5-5	4-8	3-10
2 x 8	8-7	7-9	6-9	5-11	5-2	4-3	3-8	3-0
2 x 6	6-6	5-11	5-2	4-6	3-11	3-3	2-10	2-3
2 x 4	4-1	3-9	3-3	2-10	2-6	2-1	1-9	1-5
Group F								
2 x 4	3-7	3-3	2-9	2-3	1-11	1-7	1-4	1-1

MAXIMUM SPANS OF ROOF PURLINS LOAD ZONE - 30

LUMBER Size & Grade		PURLIN SPACING				
		16″	24″	32″	36″	42″
Group C						
2 x 6	Edge	13-6	11-10	10-9	10-4	9-10
2 x 4	Flat	4-10	4-3	3-10	3-8	3-6
2 x 4	Edge	8-7	7-6	6-10	6-6	6-3
2 x 3	Flat	4-4	3-10	3-5	3-4	3-2
2 x 3	Edge	6-2	5-4	4-10	4-8	4-5
Group D						
2 x 6	Edge	12-5	10-10	9-10	9-6	9-0
2 x 4	Flat	4-6	3-11	3-6	3-5	3-3
2 x 4	Edge	7-11	6-11	6-3	6-0	5-9
2 x 3	Flat	4-0	3-6	3-2	3-0	2-11
2 x 3	Edge	5-8	4-11	4-5	4-3	4-0
Group E						
2 x 4	Flat	4-3	3-8	3-4	3-3	3-0
2 x 4	Edge	7-6	6-6	5-11	5-8	5-4
2 x 3	Flat	3-9	3-4	3-0	2-11	2-9
2 x 3	Edge	5-4	4-8	4-3	4-0	3-10
Group F						
2 x 4	Flat	3-8	3-3	2-11	2-10	2-8
2 x 4	Edge	6-6	5-5	4-8	4-5	4-1
2 x 3	Flat	3-4	2-11	2-7	2-5	2-3
2 x 3	Edge	4-8	3-11	3-4	3-1	2-11

Note: Where purlins span 3 or more spans, the allowable span may be increased 12%.

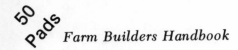

Farm Builders Handbook

MINIMUM SIZES CONCRETE PADS OR FOOTINGS FOR POSTS OR POLES (DIAMETER & THICKNESS) LOAD ZONE - 50

P-1 POLES

SOIL	POLE SPACING	24'		28'		32'		36'		40'		50'		60'	
Good	8'	12"	6"	12"	6"	12"	6"	12"	6"	12"	6"	12"	6"	14"	7"
	12'	12"	6"	12"	6"	12"	6"	14"	7"	14"	7"	16"	8"	16"	8"
	16'	12"	6"	14"	7"	14"	7"	16"	8"	16"	8"	18"	10"	20"	12"
	20'	14"	7"	14"	7"	16"	8"	16"	8"	18"	10"	20"	12"	22"	12"
Medium	8'	12"	6"	12"	6"	14"	7"	14"	7"	14"	7"	16"	8"	18"	10"
	12'	14"	7"	14"	7"	16"	8"	16"	8"	18"	10"	20"	12"	22"	12"
	16'	16"	8"	16"	8"	18"	10"	20"	12"	20"	12"	22"	12"	24"	14"
	20'	18"	10"	18"	10"	20"	12"	22"	12"	22"	12"	24"	14"	28"	16"
Poor	8'	20"	12"	20"	12"	22"	12"	24"	14"	24"	14"	28"	16"	30"	18"
	12'	24"	14"	24"	14"	26"	15"	28"	16"	30"	18"	34"	20"	36"	21"
	16'	26"	15"	28"	16"	30"	18"	32"	18"	34"	20"	38"	24"	42"	26"
	20'	30"	18"	32"	18"	34"	20"	36"	21"	38"	24"	42"	26"	46"	30"

P-2 POLES

SOIL	POLE SPACING	24'		28'		32'		36'		40'		50'		60'	
Good	8'	12"	6"	12"	6"	12"	6"	14"	7"	14"	7"	14"	7"	16"	8"
	12'	14"	7"	14"	7"	16"	8"	16"	8"	16"	8"	18"	10"	20"	12"
	16'	16"	8"	18"	10"	18"	10"	18"	10"	20"	12"	20"	12"	22"	12"
	20'	18"	10"	20"	12"	20"	12"	20"	12"	22"	12"	22"	12"	24"	14"
Medium	8'	16"	8"	16"	8"	16"	8"	16"	8"	18"	10"	18"	10"	20"	12"
	12'	18"	10"	20"	12"	20"	12"	20"	12"	22"	12"	22"	12"	24"	14"
	16'	20"	12"	22"	12"	22"	12"	24"	14"	24"	14"	26"	15"	28"	16"
	20'	24"	14"	24"	14"	26"	15"	26"	15"	28"	16"	30"	18"	32"	18"
Poor	8'	26"	15"	26"	15"	28"	16"	28"	16"	30"	18"	32"	18"	34"	20"
	12'	30"	18"	32"	18"	34"	20"	34"	20"	36"	21"	38"	24"	42"	24"
	16'	36"	21"	38"	24"	38"	24"	40"	24"	42"	24"	44"	26"		
	20'	40"	24"	42"	24"	42"	24"	44"	26"						

P-3 POLES

SOIL	POLE SPACING	Diameter	Thickness
Good	8'	8"	5"
	12'	10"	5"
	16'	12"	6"
	20'	14"	7"
Medium	8'	10"	5"
	12'	12"	6"
	16'	14"	7"
	20'	16"	8"
Poor	8'	18"	10"
	12'	22"	12"
	16'	24"	14"
	20'	28"	16"

NOTE: Use P-3 Pads for end wall poles.

SOIL CLASSIFICATIONS:
GOOD: Compact coarse sand, compact gravel or sand-gravel mixture, hardpan, shale, bed rock, or hard clay.
MEDIUM: Compact fine sand, loose gravel or sand-gravel mixture, compact sandy loam, or medium clay.
POOR: Soft clay, fine and loose sand, clay loam, clay containing large amounts of silt.

POLE OR POST SPACING

MINIMUM POLE SIZE REQUIREMENTS   LOAD ZONE - 50

Note: For "A" & "B" Post or Pole Species see Par. 301-1 and A-12.

EAVE HEIGHT		4' Top/Pole	4' Post	8' Top/Pole	8' Post	12' Top/Pole	12' Post	16' Top/Pole	16' Post	20' Top/Pole	20' Post
8'			A 4x4R 4x4D	A-4	A 4x4R 4x6D	A-4 & B-4 (spans to 43')	A 4x6R 6x6D	A-4 & B-4 (spans to 33')	A 6x6R 6x6D	A-4 & B-5 (spans to 26')	A 6x6R 6x6D
8'			B 4x4R 4x4D	B-4	B 4x4R 4x6D	A-5 & B-5 (above 43')	B 4x6R 6x6D	A-5 & B-5 (above 33')	B 6x6R 6x6D	A-5 & B-5 (above 26')	B 6x6R 6x6D
10'			A 4x4R 4x6D	A-4 & B-4 (spans to 44')	A 4x6R 6x6D	A-4 & B-5 (spans to 30')	A 6x6R 6x6D	A-5 & B-5 (spans to 51')	A 6x6R 6x6D	A-5 & B-5 (spans to 41')	A 6x6R 6x8D
10'			B 4x4R 4x6D	A-5 & B-5 (above 44')	B 6x6R 6x6D	A-5 & B-5 (above 30')	B 6x6R 6x6D	A-6 & B-6 (above 51')	B 6x6R 6x8D	A-6 & B-6 (above 41')	B 6x8R 8x8D
12'			A 4x4R 4x6D	A-4 & B-4 (spans to 33')	A 6x6R 6x6D	A-5 & B-5 (spans to 50')	A 6x6R 6x8D	A-6	A 6x8R 8x8D	A-6	A 6x8R 8x8D
12'			B 4x6R 6x6D	A-5 & B-5 (above 33')	B 6x6R 6x6D	A-6 & B-6 (above 50')	B 6x8R 8x8D	B-6	B 8x8R 8x8D	B-6	B 8x8R 8x8D
14'		A-4 & B-4 (spans to 51')	A 4x6R 6x6D	A-5 & B-5 (spans to 57')	A 6x6R 6x6D	A-6	A 6x8R 8x8D	A-6 & B-6 (spans to 56')	A 8x8R 8x8D	A-7	A 8x8R 8x8D
14'		A-5 & B-5 (above 51')	B 6x6R 6x6D	A-6 & B-6 (above 57')	B 8x8R 8x8D	B-6	B 8x8R 8x8D	A-7 & B-7 (above 56')	B 8x8R	B-7	....
16'		A-4 & B-4 (spans to 41')	A 6x6R 6x6D	A-5 & B-5 (spans to 46')	A 8x8R 8x8D	A-6	A 8x8R 8x8D	A-7	A 8x8R	A-7	
16'		A-5 & B-5 (above 41')	B 6x6R 6x8D	A-6 & B-6 (above 46')	B 8x8R 8x8D	B-6	B 8x8R	B-7		B-7	
18'		A-4 & B-4 (spans to 35')	A 6x6R 6x8D	A-5 & B-6 (spans to 38')	A 8x8R 8x8D	A-7	A 8x8R	A-7		A-8	
18'		A-5 & B-5 (above 35')	B 6x8R 8x8D	A-6 & B-6 (above 38')	B 8x8R	B-7	....	B-7		B-8	
20'		A-4 & B-4 (spans to 30')	A 6x8R 8x8D	A-6		A-7		A-8		A-8	
20'		A-5 & B-5 (above 30')	B 8x8R	B-6	B 8x8R	B-7		B-8		B-10	

Farm Builders Handbook

MINIMUM PLATE SIZES (ALTERNATES) LOAD ZONE - 50
P-1 POLES

POLE SPACING	TRUSS SPACING	TRUSS SPAN						
		24'-0"	28'-0"	32'-0"	36'-0"	40'-0"	50'-0"	60'-0"
8'	4'	2-2x12 C 3-2x10 C 2-2x12 D 3-2x10 D	2-2x12 C 3-2x10 C 3-2x12 D 2-VB 13 D	3-2x12 C 4-2x10 C 3-2x12 D 2-VB 13 D	3-2x12 C 4-2x10 C 3-2x12 D 2-VB 15 D	3-2x12 C 4-2x10 C 4-2x12 D 2-VB 15 D	4-2x12 C 3-VB 13 C 4-2x12 D 3-VB 13 D	4-2x12 C 3-VB 15 C 3-VB 15 D 4-VB 13 D
	6'	3-2x12 C 2-VB 15 C 3-2x12 D 2-VB 15 D	3-2x12 C 2-VB 15 C 4-2x12 D 3-VB 15 D	4-2x12 C 3-VB 13 C 4-2x12 D 3-VB 15 D	4-2x12 C 3-VB 15 C 3-VB 15 D 4-VB 13 D	4-2x12 C 3-VB 15 C 3-VB 15 D	3-VB 17 C 4-VB 15 C 3-VB 17 D 4-VB 15 D	4-VB 15 C 4-VB 15 D
	See Note 8'	1-2x8 C 1-2x8 D	1-2x8 C 1-2x8 D	1-2x8 C 1-2x8 D	1-2x8 C 1-2x8 D	1-2x8 C 1-2x8 D	1-2x8 C 1-2x8 D	1-2x8 C 1-2x8 D
12'	4'	2-2x12 C 3-2x10 C 3-2x12 D 4-2x10 D	3-2x12 C 4-2x10 C 3-2x12 D 4-2x10 D	3-2x12 C 4-2x10 C 4-2x12 D 2-VB 15 D	3-2x12 C 2-VB 15 C 4-2x12 D 2-VB 15 D	4-2x12 C 2-VB 15 C 4-2x12 D 3-VB 13 D	3-VB 15 C 4-VB 13 C 3-VB 15 D 4-VB 13 D	3-VB 15 C 4-VB 13 C 3-VB 17 D 4-VB 15 D
	6'	2-2x12 C 3-2x10 C 3-2x12 D 4-2x10 D	3-2x12 C 4-2x10 C 3-2x12 D 4-2x10 D	3-2x12 C 4-2x10 C 3-2x12 D 2-VB 15 D	3-2x12 C 4-2x10 C 4-2x12 D 2-VB 15 D	3-2x12 C 2-VB 15 C 4-2x12 D 2-VB 15 D	4-2x12 C 3-VB 13 C 3-VB 15 D 4-VB 13 D	3-VB 15 C 4-VB 13 C 3-VB 15 D 4-VB 13 D
	8'	3-2x12 C 4-2x10 C 3-2x12 D 2-VB 15 D	3-2x12 C 2-VB 15 C 4-2x12 D 2-VB 15 D	4-2x12 C 2-VB 15 C 4-2x12 D 3-VB 13 D	4-2x12 C 3-VB 13 C 3-VB 15 D 4-VB 13 D	4-2x12 C 3-VB 15 C 3-VB 15 D 4-VB 13 D	3-VB 15 C 4-VB 13 C 3-VB 17 D 4-VB 15 D	3-VB 17 C 4-VB 15 C 4-VB 15 D
16'	4'	4-2x12 C 2-VB 15 C 4-2x12 D 3-VB 13 D	4-2x12 C 3-VB 13 C 3-VB 15 D 4-VB 13 D	3-VB 15 C 4-VB 13 C 3-VB 15 D 4-VB 13 D	3-VB 15 C 4-VB 13 C 3-VB 17 D 4-VB 15 D	3-VB 17 C 4-VB 15 C 3-VB 17 D 4-VB 15 D	3-VB 17 C 4-VB 15 C 4-VB 17 D	4-VB 17 C
	6'	3-2x12 C 2-VB 15 C 4-2x12 D 2-VB 15 D	4-2x12 C 2-VB 15 C 4-2x12 D 3-VB 15 D	4-2x12 C 3-VB 13 C 3-VB 15 D 4-VB 13 D	3-VB 15 C 4-VB 13 C 3-VB 15 D 4-VB 13 D	3-VB 15 C 4-VB 13 C 3-VB 17 D 4-VB 15 D	3-VB 17 C 4-VB 15 C 4-VB 17 D	4-VB 17 C 4-VB 17 D
	8'	4-2x12 C 2-VB 15 C 4-2x12 D 3-VB 13 D	4-2x12 C 3-VB 13 C 3-VB 15 D 4-VB 13 D	3-VB 15 C 4-VB 13 C 3-VB 15 D 4-VB 13 D	3-VB 15 C 4-VB 13 C 3-VB 17 D 4-VB 15 D	3-VB 17 C 4-VB 15 C 3-VB 17 D 4-VB 15 D	3-VB 17 C 4-VB 17 D	4-VB 17 C
20'	4'	3-VB 15 C 4-VB 13 C 3-VB 17 D	3-VB 17 C 4-VB 15 C 4-VB 17 D	4-VB 15 C 4-VB 17 D	4-VB 17 C	4-VB 17 C		
	6'	3-VB 17 C 4-VB 15 C 3-VB 17 D 4-VB 15 D	3-VB 17 C 4-VB 15 C 4-VB 17 D	4-VB 17 C 4-VB 17 D	4-VB 17 C	4-VB 17 C		
	8'	3-VB 17 C 4-VB 15 D 3-VB 17 D 4-VB 15 D	3-VB 17 C 4-VB 15 C 4-VB 17 D	4-VB 17 C 4-VB 17 D	4-VB 17 C			

V-B Vertically Built Up Beams as described in 408-2.
For C & D Groups of Lumber See Appendix A-14.

MINIMUM PLATE SIZES FOR P-2 and P-3 POLES (ALTERNATES) LOAD ZONE - 50
P-2 POLES

POLE SPACING	TRUSS SPACING	TRUSS SPAN 24'-0"	28'-0"	32'-0"	36'-0"	40'-0"	50'-0"	60'-0"	P-3 POLES 20' SPAN RAFTER
8'-0"	4'-0"	3-2x12 C 2-VB 15 C 4-2x12 D 2-VB 15 D	4-2x12 C 2-VB 15 C 4-2x12 D 3-VB 13 D	4-2x12 C 2-VB 15 C 4-2x12 D 3-VB 15 D	4-2x12 C 3-VB 13 C 3-VB 15 D 4-VB 13 D	4-2x12 C 3-VB 15 C 3-VB 15 D 4-VB 13 D	3-VB 15 C 4-VB 13 C 3-VB 17 D 4-VB 15 D	3-VB 17 C 4-VB 15 C 3-VB 17 D 4-VB 15 D	2-2x8 C 3-2x6 C 2-2x8 D 3-2x6 D
	6'-0"	3-VB 15 C 4-VB 13 C 3-VB 15 D 4-VB 13 D	3-VB 15 C 4-VB 13 C 3-VB 17 D 4-VB 15 D	3-VB 15 C 4-VB 13 C 3-VB 17 D 4-VB 15 D	3-VB 17 C 4-VB 15 C 3-VB 17 D 4-VB 15 D	3-VB 17 C 4-VB 15 C 4-VB 15 D	4-VB 15 C 4-VB 17 D	4-VB 17 C	
	See Note 8'-0"	2-2x8 C 2-2x8 D	2-2x8 C 2-2x8 D	2-2x8 C 2-2x8 D	2-2x8 C 2-2x8 D	2-2x8 C 2-2x8 D	2-2x8 C 2-2x8 D	2-2x8 C 2-2x8 D	
12'-0"	4'-0"	4-2x12 C 3-VB 13 C 3-VB 15 D 4-VB 13 D	4-2x12 C 3-VB 15 C 3-VB 15 D 4-VB 13 D	3-VB 15 C 4-VB 13 C 3-VB 15 D 4-VB 13 D	3-VB 15 C 4-VB 13 C 3-VB 17 D 4-VB 15 D	3-VB 15 C 4-VB 13 C 3-VB 17 D 4-VB 15 D	3-VB 17 C 4-VB 15 C 3-VB 17 D 4-VB 15 D	3-VB 17 C 4-VB 15 C 4-VB 17 D	2-2x12 C 3-2x8 C 2-2x12 D 3-2x10 D
	6'-0"	4-2x12 C 2-VB 15 C 4-2x12 D 3-VB 13 D	4-2x12C 3-VB 13 C 3-VB 15 D 4-VB 13 D	4-2x12 C 3-VB 13 C 3-VB 15 D 4-VB 13 D	3-VB 15 C 4-VB 13 C 3-VB 15 D 4-VB 13 D	3-VB 15 C 4-VB 13 C 3-VB 15 D 4-VB 13 D	3-VB 15 C 4-VB 13 C 3-VB 17 D 4-VB 15 D	3-VB 17 C 4-VB 15 C 4-VB 15 D	
	8'-0"	3-VB 15 C 4-VB 13 C 3-VB 15 D 4-VB 13 D	3-VB 15 C 4-VB 13 C 3-VB 17 D 4-VB 15 D	3-VB 15 C 4-VB 15 C 3-VB 17 D 4-VB 15 D	3-VB 17 C 4-VB 15 C 3-VB 17 D 4-VB 15 D	3-VB 17 C 4-VB 15 C 4-VB 15 D	4-VB 15 C 4-VB 17 D	4-VB 17 C	
16'-0"	4'-0"	3-VB 17 C 4-VB 15 C 4-VB 15 D	3-VB 17 C 4-VB 15 C 4-VB 17 D	4-VB 15 C 4-VB 17 D	4-VB 17 C 4-VB 17 D	4-VB 17 C			3-2x12 C 2-VB 15 C 4-2x12 D 3-VB 13 D
	6'-0"	3-VB 17 C 4-VB 15 C 3-VB 17 D 4-VB 15 D	3-VB 17 C 4-VB 15 C 4-VB 15 D	3-VB 17 C 4-VB 15 C 4-VB 17 D	4-VB 15 C 4-VB 17 D	4-VB 17 C 4-VB 17 D	4-VB 17 C		
	8'-0"	3-VB 17 C 4-VB 15 C 4-VB 15 D	3-VB 17 C 4-VB 15 C 4-VB 17 D	4-VB 15 C 4-VB 17 D	4-VB 17 C 4-VB 17 D	4-VB 17 C			
20'-0"	4'-0"								3-VB 15 C 4-VB 13 C 3-VB 15 D 4-VB 13 D
	6'-0"								
	8'-0"								

V-B Vertically Built-Up Beams as described in 408-2.
C & D Groups of Lumber See Appendix A-14.
Note: If Rafters from P-2 to P-3 plates are spaced same as poles, a single member plate may be used.

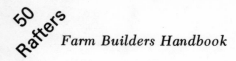

MAXIMUM SPAN OF RAFTERS HORIZONTAL SPAN LOAD ZONE - 50

LUMBER Size & Grade	RAFTER SPACING							
	12"	16"	24"	32"	36"	48"	72"	96"
Group C								
2 x 4	8-3	7-7	6-8	6-0	5-9	5-3		
2 x 6	13-2	12-0	10-5	9-6	9-2	8-4		
2 x 8	17-5	15-10	13-10	12-7	12-1	10-11	9-3	8-0
2 x 10		20-2	17-7	16-0	15-4	13-11	11-9	10-2
2 x 12			21-5	19-6	18-8	17-0	14-4	12-5
2-2 x 8			17-5	15-10	15-2	13-10	12-1	10-11
2-2 x 10				20-2	19-5	17-7	15-4	13-11
2-2 x 12						21-5	18-8	17-0
Group D								
2 x 4	7-8	7-0	6-1	5-6	5-4	4-10		
2 x 6	12-1	11-0	9-7	8-9	8-5	7-7		
2 x 8	16-0	14-7	12-8	11-7	11-1	10-1	8-6	7-5
2 x 10	20-5	18-7	16-2	14-8	14-2	12-10	10-11	9-5
2 x 12		22-7	19-8	17-10	17-2	15-8	13-3	11-6
2-2 x 8			16-0	14-7	14-0	12-8	11-1	10-5
2-2 x 10					17-10	16-2	14-2	12-10
2-2 x 12					21-8	19-8	17-2	15-8
Group E								
2 x 4	7-4	6-8	5-9	5-3	5-0	4-6		
2 x 6	11-6	10-6	9-2	8-4	8-0	7-1		
2 x 8	15-3	13-10	12-1	11-0	10-6	9-4	7-8	6-7
2 x 10	19-5	17-7	15-4	14-0	13-5	11-11	9-9	8-5
2 x 12		21-5	18-8	17-0	16-4	14-6	11-10	10-3
2-2 x 8			15-3	13-10	13-3	12-1	10-6	9-3
2-2 x 10			19-5	17-7	16-10	15-4	13-5	12-2
2-2 x 12					20-7	18-8	16-4	14-10

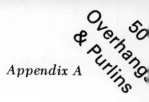

MAXIMUM LENGTH OF OVERHANGS LOAD ZONE - 50

LUMBER Size & Grade	TRUSS OR RAFTER SPACING							
	12"	16"	2'-0"	3'-0"	4'-0"	6'-0"	8'-0"	12'-0"
Group C								
2 x 12	10-0	10-0	10-0	9-4	8-6	7-2	6-2	5-1
2 x 10	9-11	9-11	8-9	7-8	7-0	5-11	5-1	4-2
2 x 8	8-8	7-10	6-10	6-0	5-6	4-7	4-0	3-3
2 x 6	6-7	6-0	5-2	4-7	4-2	3-6	3-0	2-6
2 x 4	4-2	3-9	3-4	2-10	2-7	2-3	1-11	1-7
Group D								
2 x 12	10-0	10-0	9-10	8-7	7-9	6-8	5-9	4-8
2 x 10	10-0	9-3	8-1	7-1	6-5	5-5	4-9	3-10
2 x 8	8-0	7-3	6-4	5-6	5-0	4-3	3-8	3-0
2 x 6	6-0	5-6	4-9	4-2	3-9	3-3	2-10	2-3
2 x 4	3-10	3-6	3-0	2-8	2-5	2-1	1-9	1-6
Group E								
2 x 12	10-0	10-0	9-4	8-2	7-3	5-11	5-2	4-2
2 x 10	9-8	8-9	7-8	6-8	6-0	4-11	4-3	3-5
2 x 8	7-7	6-11	6-0	5-3	4-8	3-10	3-4	2-8
2 x 6	5-9	5-2	4-6	4-0	3-7	2-11	2-6	2-1
2 x 4	3-8	3-4	2-10	2-6	2-3	1-10	1-7	1-4
Group F								
2 x 4	3-2	2-10	2-5	2-0	1-9	1-5	1-3	1-0

MAXIMUM SPANS OF ROOF PURLINS LOAD ZONE - 50

LUMBER Size & Grade		PURLIN SPACING				
		16"	24"	32"	36"	42"
Group C						
2 x 6	Edge	12-0	10-5	9-6	9-2	8-8
2 x 4	Flat	4-4	3-9	3-5	3-3	3-1
2 x 4	Edge	7-7	6-8	6-0	5-9	5-6
2 x 3	Flat	3-10	3-4	3-0	2-11	2-9
2 x 3	Edge	5-5	4-9	4-3	4-2	3-11
Group D						
2 x 6	Edge	11-0	9-7	8-9	8-5	8-0
2 x 4	Flat	3-11	3-5	3-2	3-0	2-10
2 x 4	Edge	7-0	6-1	5-6	5-4	5-1
2 x 3	Flat	3-6	3-1	2-10	2-8	2-6
2 x 3	Edge	5-0	4-4	3-11	3-10	3-7
Group E						
2 x 4	Flat	3-9	3-3	3-0	2-10	2-9
2 x 4	Edge	6-8	5-9	5-3	5-1	4-10
2 x 3	Flat	3-4	2-11	2-8	2-6	2-5
2 x 3	Edge	4-9	4-2	3-9	3-7	3-5
Group F						
2 x 4	Flat	3-3	2-10	2-7	2-6	2-4
2 x 4	Edge	5-10	4-10	4-2	3-11	3-8
2 x 3	Flat	2-11	2-7	2-4	2-2	2-0
2 x 3	Edge	4-2	3-5	3-0	2-10	2-7

Note: Where purlins span 3 or more spans, the allowable span may be increased 12%.

RAFTER SPAN, CONVERSION DIAGRAM

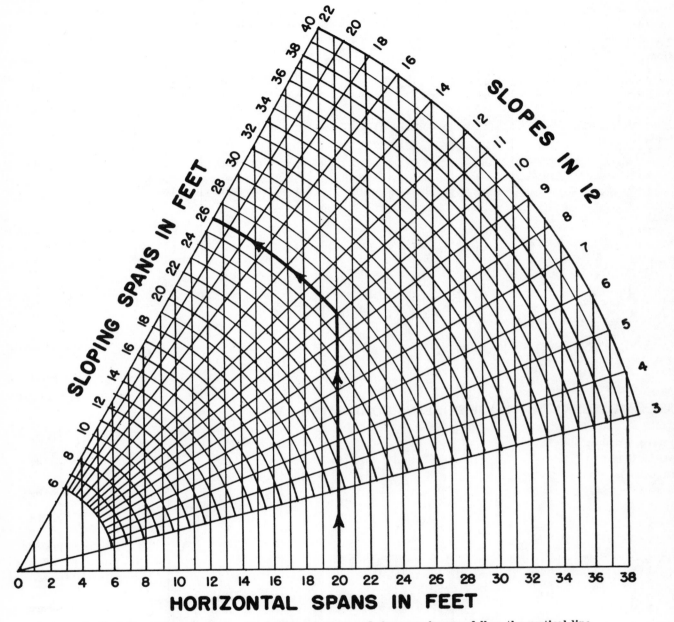

HORIZONTAL SPANS IN FEET

To find the rafter span when its horizontal span and slope are known, follow the vertical line from the horizontal span to its intersection with the radial line of the slope. From the intersection follow the curve line to the sloping span. The diagram also may be used to determine the horizontal span when the sloping span and slope are known, or to determine the slope when the sloping and horizontal spans are known.

Example: For a horizontal span of 20 feet and a slope of 10 in 12, the sloping span of the rafter is read directly from the diagram as 26 feet.

Span Tables, Joists and Rafters
(Recommended by National Forest Products Assn.)

Explanation
These span tables for joists and rafters are calculated on the basis of a series of modules of elasticity (E) and fiber bending stress (F_b) values. The range of values in the tables provides allowable spans for species and grades of nominal 2-inch framing lumber customarily used in farm building.

Table A-21 lists spans for floor joists used over a single span with calculations based on E and the required F_b values shown.

Tables A-22 and A-23 list spans for rafters used over a single span with calculations based on F_b and the required E values shown. For normal farm building construction, we can use these rafter tables through Load Zone 50. For spacings wider than 24" o.c. use the rafter tables provided for each load zone.

Table A-24 shows the E and F_b values for various grades, species and sizes.

Moisture Content
The listed dry and green sizes are related at 19 percent maximum moisture content. Tabulated spans are calculated on the basis of the dry sizes and are also applicable to the corresponding green sizes. The spans in these tables are intended for use in covered structures or where moisture content in use does not exceed 19 percent.

Allowable Span
The allowable span is the clear distance between supports. For sloping rafters the span is measured along the horizontal projection. Page 208 provides a chart by which horizontal distance can be converted to sloping distance, or vice versa. Where rafters are spaced over 24" o.c. the rafter tables in the individual load zone classification should be used.

How to Use the Span Tables
Example 1. Floor Joists. Assume a required span of 12'9" and a live load of 40 pounds per square foot (psf) and joists spaced 16" o.c. Reading the line 2 × 8—16" o.c. across in Table A-21 we find that the first time we exceed 12'9" is at $\frac{12'10''}{1250}$.

Therefore any grade of 2 × 8 with an F_b equal or over 1250 and an E value of 1,600,000 (1.6 at the top of the table) will do the job.

Now suppose that you have KD Southern Pine and Douglas Fir-Larch available in your area. From Table A-24 we find under "Normal duration" for 2 × 6 and wider that No. 2 has an F_b of 1450 and an E of 1,700,00. Since both exceed the 1250 and 1,600,000 determined above we muse use No. 2 Douglas Fir-Larch 2 × 8 spaced 16" o.c. (or any better grade) for this span, spacing and loading.

Likewise under Southern Pine KD in Table A-24 we find that grade No. 2 MG meets these requirements.

Example 2. Assume a rafter length of 20 feet, a slope of 4/12, a live load of 20 lbs. psf and a spacing of 16" o.c. Douglas fir is available.

First, we change the rafter length of 20' to a horizontal span of 19' by using the conversion diagram on Page 000.

Second, by inspection we determine that 2 × 6 rafters must be spaced 12" o.c. to qualify so we go to 2 × 8. We find that a 2 × 8 requires an E of 1,370,000 and an F_b of 2000 to handle a 19'5" span at 16" o.c. From Table A-24 on Douglas Fir we find that Dense #1 grade meets these requirements.

Table A-21
FLOOR JOISTS
40 Lbs. Per Sq. Ft. Live Load
(All rooms except those used for sleeping areas and attic floors.)

Recommended by National Forest Products Assn.

DESIGN CRITERIA:
Deflection - For 40 lbs. per sq. ft. live load.
Limited to span in inches divided by 360.
Strength - Live Load of 40 lbs. per sq. ft. plus
dead load of 10 lbs. per sq. ft. determines the
required fiber stress value.

Each cell shows the allowable span (feet-inches) and, below it, the required extreme fiber stress in bending, "F_b", in pounds per square inch.

Joist Size (IN)	Spacing (IN)	0.4	0.5	0.6	0.7	0.8	0.9	1.0	1.1	1.2	1.3	1.4	1.5	1.6	1.7	1.8	1.9	2.0	2.2	2.4
2x6	12.0	6-9 / 450	7-3 / 520	7-9 / 590	8-2 / 660	8-6 / 720	8-10 / 780	9-2 / 830	9-6 / 890	9-9 / 940	10-0 / 990	10-3 / 1040	10-6 / 1090	10-9 / 1140	10-11 / 1190	11-2 / 1230	11-4 / 1280	11-7 / 1320	11-11 / 1410	12-3 / 1490
	13.7	6-6 / 470	7-0 / 550	7-5 / 620	7-9 / 690	8-2 / 750	8-6 / 810	8-9 / 870	9-1 / 930	9-4 / 980	9-7 / 1040	9-10 / 1090	10-0 / 1140	10-3 / 1190	10-6 / 1240	10-8 / 1290	10-10 / 1340	11-1 / 1380	11-5 / 1470	11-9 / 1560
	16.0	6-2 / 500	6-7 / 580	7-0 / 650	7-5 / 720	7-9 / 790	8-0 / 860	8-4 / 920	8-7 / 980	8-10 / 1040	9-1 / 1090	9-4 / 1150	9-6 / 1200	9-9 / 1250	9-11 / 1310	10-2 / 1360	10-4 / 1410	10-6 / 1460	10-10 / 1550	11-2 / 1640
	19.2	5-9 / 530	6-3 / 610	6-7 / 690	7-0 / 770	7-3 / 840	7-7 / 910	7-10 / 970	8-1 / 1040	8-4 / 1100	8-7 / 1160	8-9 / 1220	9-0 / 1280	9-2 / 1330	9-4 / 1390	9-6 / 1440	9-8 / 1500	9-10 / 1550	10-2 / 1650	10-6 / 1750
	24.0	5-4 / 570	5-9 / 660	6-2 / 750	6-6 / 830	6-9 / 900	7-0 / 980	7-3 / 1050	7-6 / 1120	7-9 / 1190	7-11 / 1250	8-2 / 1310	8-4 / 1380	8-6 / 1440	8-8 / 1500	8-10 / 1550	9-0 / 1610	9-2 / 1670	9-6 / 1780	9-9 / 1880
	32.0					6-2 / 1010	6-5 / 1090	6-7 / 1150	6-10 / 1230	7-0 / 1300	7-3 / 1390	7-5 / 1450	7-7 / 1520	7-9 / 1590	7-11 / 1660	8-0 / 1690	8-2 / 1760	8-4 / 1840	8-7 / 1950	8-10 / 2060
2x8	12.0	8-11 / 450	9-7 / 520	10-2 / 590	10-9 / 660	11-3 / 720	11-8 / 780	12-1 / 830	12-6 / 890	12-10 / 940	13-2 / 990	13-6 / 1040	13-10 / 1090	14-2 / 1140	14-5 / 1190	14-8 / 1230	15-0 / 1280	15-3 / 1320	15-9 / 1410	16-2 / 1490
	13.7	8-6 / 470	9-2 / 550	9-9 / 620	10-3 / 690	10-9 / 750	11-2 / 810	11-7 / 870	11-11 / 930	12-3 / 980	12-7 / 1040	12-11 / 1090	13-3 / 1140	13-6 / 1190	13-10 / 1240	14-1 / 1290	14-4 / 1340	14-7 / 1380	15-0 / 1470	15-6 / 1560
	16.0	8-1 / 500	8-9 / 580	9-3 / 650	9-9 / 720	10-2 / 790	10-7 / 850	11-0 / 920	11-4 / 980	11-8 / 1040	12-0 / 1090	12-3 / 1150	12-7 / 1200	12-10 / 1250	13-1 / 1310	13-4 / 1360	13-7 / 1410	13-10 / 1460	14-3 / 1550	14-8 / 1640
	19.2	7-7 / 530	8-2 / 610	8-9 / 690	9-2 / 770	9-7 / 840	10-0 / 910	10-4 / 970	10-8 / 1040	11-0 / 1100	11-3 / 1160	11-7 / 1220	11-10 / 1280	12-1 / 1330	12-4 / 1390	12-7 / 1440	12-10 / 1500	13-0 / 1550	13-5 / 1650	13-10 / 1750
	24.0	7-1 / 570	7-7 / 660	8-1 / 750	8-6 / 830	8-11 / 900	9-3 / 980	9-7 / 1050	9-11 / 1120	10-2 / 1190	10-6 / 1250	10-9 / 1310	11-0 / 1380	11-3 / 1440	11-5 / 1500	11-8 / 1550	11-11 / 1610	12-1 / 1670	12-6 / 1780	12-10 / 1880
	32.0					8-1 / 990	8-5 / 1080	8-9 / 1170	9-0 / 1230	9-3 / 1300	9-6 / 1370	9-9 / 1450	10-0 / 1520	10-2 / 1570	10-5 / 1650	10-7 / 1700	10-10 / 1790	11-0 / 1840	11-4 / 1950	11-8 / 2070
2x10	12.0	11-4 / 450	12-3 / 520	13-0 / 590	13-8 / 660	14-4 / 720	14-11 / 780	15-5 / 830	15-11 / 890	16-5 / 940	16-10 / 990	17-3 / 1040	17-8 / 1090	18-0 / 1140	18-5 / 1190	18-9 / 1230	19-1 / 1280	19-5 / 1320	20-1 / 1410	20-8 / 1490
	13.7	10-10 / 470	11-8 / 550	12-5 / 620	13-1 / 690	13-8 / 750	14-3 / 810	14-9 / 870	15-3 / 930	15-8 / 980	16-1 / 1040	16-6 / 1090	16-11 / 1140	17-3 / 1190	17-7 / 1240	17-11 / 1290	18-3 / 1340	18-7 / 1380	19-2 / 1470	19-9 / 1560
	16.0	10-4 / 500	11-1 / 580	11-10 / 650	12-5 / 720	13-0 / 790	13-6 / 850	14-0 / 920	14-6 / 980	14-11 / 1040	15-3 / 1090	15-8 / 1150	16-0 / 1200	16-5 / 1250	16-9 / 1310	17-0 / 1360	17-4 / 1410	17-8 / 1460	18-3 / 1550	18-9 / 1640
	19.2	9-9 / 530	10-6 / 610	11-1 / 690	11-8 / 770	12-3 / 840	12-9 / 910	13-2 / 970	13-7 / 1040	14-0 / 1100	14-5 / 1160	14-9 / 1220	15-1 / 1280	15-5 / 1330	15-9 / 1390	16-0 / 1440	16-4 / 1500	16-7 / 1550	17-2 / 1650	17-8 / 1750
	24.0	9-0 / 570	9-9 / 660	10-4 / 750	10-10 / 830	11-4 / 900	11-10 / 980	12-3 / 1050	12-8 / 1120	13-0 / 1190	13-4 / 1250	13-8 / 1310	14-0 / 1380	14-4 / 1440	14-7 / 1500	14-11 / 1550	15-2 / 1610	15-5 / 1670	15-11 / 1780	16-5 / 1880
	32.0					10-4 / 1000	10-9 / 1080	11-1 / 1150	11-6 / 1240	11-10 / 1310	12-2 / 1380	12-5 / 1440	12-9 / 1520	13-0 / 1580	13-3 / 1640	13-6 / 1700	13-9 / 1770	14-0 / 1830	14-6 / 1970	14-11 / 2080
2x12	12.0	13-10 / 450	14-11 / 520	15-10 / 590	16-8 / 660	17-5 / 720	18-1 / 780	18-9 / 830	19-4 / 890	19-11 / 940	20-6 / 990	21-0 / 1040	21-6 / 1090	21-11 / 1140	22-5 / 1190	22-10 / 1230	23-3 / 1280	23-7 / 1320	24-5 / 1410	25-1 / 1490
	13.7	13-3 / 470	14-3 / 550	15-2 / 620	15-11 / 690	16-8 / 750	17-4 / 810	17-11 / 870	18-6 / 930	19-1 / 980	19-7 / 1040	20-1 / 1090	20-6 / 1140	21-0 / 1190	21-5 / 1240	21-10 / 1290	22-3 / 1340	22-7 / 1380	23-4 / 1470	24-0 / 1560
	16.0	12-7 / 500	13-6 / 580	14-4 / 650	15-2 / 720	15-10 / 790	16-5 / 860	17-0 / 920	17-7 / 980	18-1 / 1040	18-7 / 1090	19-1 / 1150	19-6 / 1200	19-11 / 1250	20-4 / 1310	20-9 / 1360	21-1 / 1410	21-6 / 1460	22-2 / 1550	22-10 / 1640
	19.2	11-10 / 530	12-9 / 610	13-6 / 690	14-3 / 770	14-11 / 840	15-6 / 910	16-0 / 970	16-7 / 1040	17-0 / 1100	17-6 / 1160	17-11 / 1220	18-4 / 1280	18-9 / 1330	19-2 / 1390	19-6 / 1440	19-10 / 1500	20-2 / 1550	20-10 / 1650	21-6 / 1750
	24.0	11-0 / 570	11-10 / 660	12-7 / 750	13-3 / 830	13-10 / 900	14-4 / 980	14-11 / 1050	15-4 / 1120	15-10 / 1190	16-3 / 1250	16-8 / 1310	17-0 / 1380	17-5 / 1440	17-9 / 1500	18-1 / 1550	18-5 / 1610	18-9 / 1670	19-4 / 1780	19-11 / 1880
	32.0					12-7 / 1000	13-1 / 1080	13-6 / 1150	13-11 / 1220	14-4 / 1300	14-9 / 1380	15-2 / 1450	15-6 / 1520	15-10 / 1580	16-2 / 1650	16-5 / 1700	16-9 / 1770	17-0 / 1830	17-7 / 1950	18-1 / 2070

Modulus of Elasticity, "E", in 1,000,000 psi

Note: The required extreme fiber stress in bending, "F_b", in pounds per square inch is shown below each span.

Table A-22
LOW OR HIGH SLOPE RAFTERS
20 Lbs. Per Sq. Ft. Live Load
(Supporting Drywall Ceiling)

DESIGN CRITERIA:
Strength - 15 lbs. per sq. ft. dead load plus 20 lbs. per sq. ft. live load determines required fiber stress.
Deflection - For 20 lbs. per sq. ft. live load. Limited to span in inches divided by 240.

RAFTER SIZE (IN)	SPACING (IN)	Allowable Extreme Fiber Stress in Bending, "F_b" (psi).										
		300	400	500	600	700	800	900	1000	1100	1200	1300
2x6	12.0	6-7 0.12	7-7 0.19	8-6 0.26	9-4 0.35	10-0 0.44	10-9 0.54	11-5 0.64	12-0 0.75	12-7 0.86	13-2 0.98	13-8 1.11
	13.7	6-2 0.12	7-1 0.18	7-11 0.25	8-8 0.33	9-5 0.41	10-0 0.50	10-8 0.60	11-3 0.70	11-9 0.81	12-4 0.92	12-10 1.04
	16.0	5-8 0.11	6-7 0.16	7-4 0.23	8-1 0.30	8-8 0.38	9-4 0.46	9-10 0.55	10-5 0.65	10-11 0.75	11-5 0.85	11-10 0.96
	19.2	5-2 0.10	6-0 0.15	6-9 0.21	7-4 0.27	7-11 0.35	8-6 0.42	9-0 0.51	9-6 0.59	9-11 0.68	10-5 0.78	10-10 0.88
	24.0	4-8 0.09	5-4 0.13	6-0 0.19	6-7 0.25	7-1 0.31	7-7 0.38	8-1 0.45	8-6 0.53	8-11 0.61	9-4 0.70	9-8 0.78
2x8	12.0	8-8 0.12	10-0 0.19	11-2 0.26	12-3 0.35	13-3 0.44	14-2 0.54	15-0 0.64	15-10 0.75	16-7 0.86	17-4 0.98	18-0 1.11
	13.7	8-1 0.12	9-4 0.18	10-6 0.25	11-6 0.33	12-5 0.41	13-3 0.50	14-0 0.60	14-10 0.70	15-6 0.81	16-3 0.92	16-10 1.04
	16.0	7-6 0.11	8-8 0.16	9-8 0.23	10-7 0.30	11-6 0.38	12-3 0.46	13-0 0.55	13-8 0.65	14-4 0.75	15-0 0.85	15-7 0.96
	19.2	6-10 0.10	7-11 0.15	8-10 0.21	9-8 0.27	10-6 0.35	11-2 0.42	11-10 0.51	12-6 0.59	13-1 0.68	13-8 0.78	14-3 0.88
	24.0	6-2 0.09	7-1 0.13	7-11 0.19	8-8 0.25	9-4 0.31	10-0 0.38	10-7 0.45	11-2 0.53	11-9 0.61	12-3 0.70	12-9 0.78
2x10	12.0	11-1 0.12	12-9 0.19	14-3 0.26	15-8 0.35	16-11 0.44	18-1 0.54	19-2 0.64	20-2 0.75	21-2 0.86	22-1 0.98	23-0 1.11
	13.7	10-4 0.12	11-11 0.18	13-4 0.25	14-8 0.33	15-10 0.41	16-11 0.50	17-11 0.60	18-11 0.70	19-10 0.81	20-8 0.92	21-6 1.04
	16.0	9-7 0.11	11-1 0.16	12-4 0.23	13-6 0.30	14-8 0.38	15-8 0.46	16-7 0.55	17-6 0.65	18-4 0.75	19-2 0.85	19-11 0.96
	19.2	8-9 0.10	10-1 0.15	11-3 0.21	12-4 0.27	13-4 0.35	14-3 0.42	15-2 0.51	15-11 0.59	16-9 0.68	17-6 0.78	18-2 0.88
	24.0	7-10 0.09	9-0 0.13	10-1 0.19	11-1 0.25	11-11 0.31	12-9 0.38	13-6 0.45	14-3 0.53	15-0 0.61	15-8 0.70	16-3 0.78
2x12	12.0	13-5 0.12	15-6 0.19	17-4 0.26	19-0 0.35	20-6 0.44	21-11 0.54	23-3 0.64	24-7 0.75	25-9 0.86	26-11 0.98	28-0 1.11
	13.7	12-7 0.12	14-6 0.18	16-3 0.25	17-9 0.33	19-3 0.41	20-6 0.50	21-9 0.60	23-0 0.70	24-1 0.81	25-2 0.92	26-2 1.04
	16.0	11-8 0.11	13-5 0.16	15-0 0.23	16-6 0.30	17-9 0.38	19-0 0.46	20-2 0.55	21-3 0.65	22-4 0.75	23-3 0.85	24-3 0.96
	19.2	10-8 0.10	12-3 0.15	13-9 0.21	15-0 0.27	16-3 0.35	17-4 0.42	18-5 0.51	19-5 0.59	20-4 0.68	21-3 0.78	22-2 0.88
	24.0	9-6 0.09	11-0 0.13	12-3 0.19	13-5 0.25	14-6 0.31	15-6 0.38	16-6 0.45	17-4 0.53	18-2 0.61	19-0 0.70	19-10 0.78

Note: The required modulus of elasticity, "E", in 1,000,000 pounds per square inch is shown below each span.

Table A-22 (cont.)

RAFTERS: Spans are measured along the horizontal projection and loads are considered as applied on the horizontal projection.

Recommended by National Forest Products Assn.

Allowable Extreme Fiber Stress in Bending, "F_b" (psi).											RAFTER SPACING (IN)	SIZE (IN)
1400	1500	1600	1700	1800	1900	2000	2100	2200	2400	2700		
14-2 1.24	14-8 1.37	15-2 1.51	15-8 1.66	16-1 1.81	16-7 1.96	17-0 2.12	17-5 2.28	17-10 2.44			12.0	
13-3 1.16	13-9 1.29	14-2 1.42	14-8 1.55	15-1 1.69	15-6 1.83	15-11 1.98	16-3 2.13	16-8 2.28	17-5 2.60		13.7	
12-4 1.07	12-9 1.19	13-2 1.31	13-7 1.44	13-11 1.56	14-4 1.70	14-8 1.83	15-1 1.97	15-5 2.11	16-1 2.41		16.0	2x6
11-3 0.98	11-7 1.09	12-0 1.20	12-4 1.31	12-9 1.43	13-1 1.55	13-5 1.67	13-9 1.80	14-1 1.93	14-8 2.20		19.2	
10-0 0.88	10-5 0.97	10-9 1.07	11-1 1.17	11-5 1.28	11-8 1.39	12-0 1.50	12-4 1.61	12-7 1.73	13-2 1.97	13-11 2.35	24.0	
18-9 1.24	19-5 1.37	20-0 1.51	20-8 1.66	21-3 1.81	21-10 1.96	22-4 2.12	22-11 2.28	23-6 2.44			12.0	
17-6 1.16	18-2 1.29	18-9 1.42	19-4 1.55	19-10 1.69	20-5 1.83	20-11 1.98	21-5 2.13	21-11 2.28	22-11 2.60		13.7	
16-3 1.07	16-9 1.19	17-4 1.31	17-10 1.44	18-5 1.56	18-11 1.70	19-5 1.83	19-10 1.97	20-4 2.11	21-3 2.41		16.0	2x8
14-10 0.98	15-4 1.09	15-10 1.20	16-4 1.31	16-9 1.43	17-3 1.55	17-8 1.67	18-2 1.80	18-7 1.93	19-5 2.20		19.2	
13-3 0.88	13-8 0.97	14-2 1.07	14-7 1.17	15-0 1.28	15-5 1.39	15-10 1.50	16-3 1.61	16-7 1.73	17-4 1.97	18-5 2.35	24.0	
23-11 1.24	24-9 1.37	25-6 1.51	26-4 1.66	27-1 1.81	27-10 1.96	28-7 2.12	29-3 2.28	29-11 2.44			12.0	
22-4 1.16	23-2 1.29	23-11 1.42	24-7 1.55	25-4 1.69	26-0 1.83	26-8 1.98	27-4 2.13	28-0 2.28	29-3 2.60		13.7	
20-8 1.07	21-5 1.19	22-1 1.31	22-10 1.44	23-5 1.56	24-1 1.70	24-9 1.83	25-4 1.97	25-11 2.11	27-1 2.41		16.0	2x10
18-11 0.98	19-7 1.09	20-2 1.20	20-10 1.31	21-5 1.43	22-0 1.55	22-7 1.67	23-2 1.80	23-8 1.93	24-9 2.20		19.2	
16-11 0.88	17-6 0.97	18-1 1.07	18-7 1.17	19-2 1.28	19-8 1.39	20-2 1.50	20-8 1.61	21-2 1.73	22-1 1.97	23-5 2.35	24.0	
29-1 1.24	30-1 1.37	31-1 1.51	32-0 1.66	32-11 1.81	33-10 1.96	34-9 2.12	35-7 2.28	36-5 2.44			12.0	
27-2 1.16	28-2 1.29	29-1 1.42	29-11 1.55	30-10 1.69	31-8 1.83	32-6 1.98	33-3 2.13	34-1 2.28	35-7 2.60		13.7	
25-2 1.07	26-0 1.19	26-11 1.31	27-9 1.44	28-6 1.56	29-4 1.70	30-1 1.83	30-10 1.97	31-6 2.11	32-11 2.41		16.0	2x12
23-0 0.98	23-9 1.09	24-7 1.20	25-4 1.31	26-0 1.43	26-9 1.55	27-5 1.67	28-2 1.80	28-9 1.93	30-1 2.20		19.2	
20-6 0.88	21-3 0.97	21-11 1.07	22-8 1.17	23-3 1.28	23-11 1.39	24-7 1.50	25-2 1.61	25-9 1.73	26-11 1.97	28-6 2.35	24.0	

Note: The required modulus of elasticity, "E", in 1,000,000 pounds per square inch is shown below each span.

Table A-23
LOW SLOPE RAFTERS
Slope 3 in 12 or less - 20 Lbs. Per Sq. Ft. Live Load
(No Finished Ceiling)

DESIGN CRITERIA:

Strength - 10 lbs. per sq. ft. dead load plus 20 lbs. per sq. ft. live load determines required fiber stress.

Deflection - For 20 lbs. per sq. ft. live load. Limited to span in inches divided by 240.

RAFTER SIZE (IN)	SPACING (IN)	Allowable Extreme Fiber Stress in Bending, "F$_b$" (psi).										
		300	400	500	600	700	800	900	1000	1100	1200	1300
2x6	12.0	7-1 0.15	8-2 0.24	9-2 0.33	10-0 0.44	10-10 0.55	11-7 0.67	12-4 0.80	13-0 0.94	13-7 1.09	14-2 1.24	14-9 1.40
	13.7	6-8 0.14	7-8 0.22	8-7 0.31	9-5 0.41	10-2 0.52	10-10 0.63	11-6 0.75	12-2 0.88	12-9 1.02	13-3 1.16	13-10 1.31
	16.0	6-2 0.13	7-1 0.21	7-11 0.29	8-8 0.38	9-5 0.48	10-0 0.58	10-8 0.70	11-3 0.82	11-9 0.94	12-4 1.07	12-10 1.21
	19.2	5-7 0.12	6-6 0.19	7-3 0.26	7-11 0.35	8-7 0.44	9-2 0.53	9-9 0.64	10-3 0.75	10-9 0.86	11-3 0.98	11-8 1.10
	24.0	5-0 0.11	5-10 0.17	6-6 0.24	7-1 0.31	7-8 0.39	8-2 0.48	8-8 0.57	9-2 0.67	9-7 0.77	10-0 0.88	10-5 0.99
2x8	12.0	9-4 0.15	10-10 0.24	12-1 0.33	13-3 0.44	14-4 0.55	15-3 0.67	16-3 0.80	17-1 0.94	17-11 1.09	18-9 1.24	19-6 1.40
	13.7	8-9 0.14	10-1 0.22	11-4 0.31	12-5 0.41	13-4 0.52	14-4 0.63	15-2 0.75	16-0 0.88	16-9 1.02	17-6 1.16	18-3 1.31
	16.0	8-1 0.13	9-4 0.21	10-6 0.29	11-6 0.38	12-5 0.48	13-3 0.58	14-0 0.70	14-10 0.82	15-6 0.94	16-3 1.07	16-10 1.21
	19.2	7-5 0.12	8-7 0.19	9-7 0.26	10-6 0.35	11-4 0.44	12-1 0.53	12-10 0.64	13-6 0.75	14-2 0.86	14-10 0.98	15-5 1.10
	24.0	6-7 0.11	7-8 0.17	8-7 0.24	9-4 0.31	10-1 0.39	10-10 0.48	11-6 0.57	12-1 0.67	12-8 0.77	13-3 0.88	13-9 0.99
2x10	12.0	11-11 0.15	13-9 0.24	15-5 0.33	16-11 0.44	18-3 0.55	19-6 0.67	20-8 0.80	21-10 0.94	22-10 1.09	23-11 1.24	24-10 1.40
	13.7	11-2 0.14	12-11 0.22	14-5 0.31	15-10 0.41	17-1 0.52	18-3 0.63	19-4 0.75	20-5 0.88	21-5 1.02	22-4 1.16	23-3 1.31
	16.0	10-4 0.13	11-11 0.21	13-4 0.29	14-8 0.38	15-10 0.48	16-11 0.58	17-11 0.70	18-11 0.82	19-10 0.94	20-8 1.07	21-6 1.21
	19.2	9-5 0.12	10-11 0.19	12-2 0.26	13-4 0.35	14-5 0.44	15-5 0.53	16-4 0.64	17-3 0.75	18-1 0.86	18-11 0.98	19-8 1.10
	24.0	8-5 0.11	9-9 0.17	10-11 0.24	11-11 0.31	12-11 0.39	13-9 0.48	14-8 0.57	15-5 0.67	16-2 0.77	16-11 0.88	17-7 0.99
2x12	12.0	14-6 0.15	16-9 0.24	18-9 0.33	20-6 0.44	22-2 0.55	23-9 0.67	25-2 0.80	26-6 0.94	27-10 1.09	29-1 1.24	30-3 1.40
	13.7	13-7 0.14	15-8 0.22	17-6 0.31	19-3 0.41	20-9 0.52	22-2 0.63	23-6 0.75	24-10 0.88	26-0 1.02	27-2 1.16	28-3 1.31
	16.0	12-7 0.13	14-6 0.21	16-3 0.29	17-9 0.38	19-3 0.48	20-6 0.58	21-9 0.70	23-0 0.82	24-1 0.94	25-2 1.07	26-2 1.21
	19.2	11-6 0.12	13-3 0.19	14-10 0.26	16-3 0.35	17-6 0.44	18-9 0.53	19-11 0.64	21-0 0.75	22-0 0.86	23-0 0.98	23-11 1.10
	24.0	10-3 0.11	11-10 0.17	13-3 0.24	14-6 0.31	15-8 0.39	16-9 0.48	17-9 0.57	18-9 0.67	19-8 0.77	20-6 0.88	21-5 0.99

Note: The required modulus of elasticity, "E", in 1,000,000 pounds per square inch is shown below each span.

Table A-23 (cont.)

RAFTERS: Spans are measured along the
horizontal projection and loads are
considered as applied on the horizontal
projection.

Recommended by National Forest Products Assn.

| Allowable Extreme Fiber Stress in Bending, "F_b" (psi). | | | | | | | | | | RAFTER SPACING (IN) | SIZE (IN) |
1400	1500	1600	1700	1800	1900	2000	2100	2200	2400		
15-4 1.56	15-11 1.73	16-5 1.91	16-11 2.09	17-5 2.28	17-10 2.47					12.0	
14-4 1.46	14-10 1.62	15-4 1.78	15-10 1.95	16-3 2.13	16-9 2.31	17-2 2.49				13.7	
13-3 1.35	13-9 1.50	14-2 1.65	14-8 1.81	15-1 1.97	15-6 2.14	15-11 2.31	16-3 2.48			16.0	2x6
12-2 1.23	12-7 1.37	13-0 1.51	13-4 1.65	13-9 1.80	14-2 1.95	14-6 2.11	14-10 2.27	15-2 2.43		19.2	
10-10 1.10	11-3 1.22	11-7 1.35	11-11 1.48	12-4 1.61	12-8 1.75	13-0 1.89	13-3 2.03	13-7 2.18	14-2 2.48	24.0	
20-3 1.56	20-11 1.73	21-7 1.91	22-3 2.09	22-11 2.28	23-7 2.47					12.0	
18-11 1.46	19-7 1.62	20-3 1.78	20-10 1.95	21-5 2.13	22-0 2.31	22-7 2.49				13.7	
17-6 1.35	18-2 1.50	18-9 1.65	19-4 1.81	19-10 1.97	20-5 2.14	20-11 2.31	21-5 2.48			16.0	2x8
16-0 1.23	16-7 1.37	17-1 1.51	17-7 1.65	18-2 1.80	18-7 1.95	19-1 2.11	19-7 2.27	20-0 2.43		19.2	
14-4 1.10	14-10 1.22	15-3 1.35	15-9 1.48	16-3 1.61	16-8 1.75	17-1 1.89	17-6 2.03	17-11 2.18	18-9 2.48	24.0	
25-10 1.56	26-8 1.73	27-7 1.91	28-5 2.09	29-3 2.28	30-1 2.47					12.0	
24-2 1.46	25-0 1.62	25-10 1.78	26-7 1.95	27-4 2.13	28-1 2.31	28-10 2.49				13.7	
22-4 1.35	23-2 1.50	23-11 1.65	24-7 1.81	25-4 1.97	26-0 2.14	26-8 2.31	27-4 2.48			16.0	2x10
20-5 1.23	21-1 1.37	21-10 1.51	22-6 1.65	23-2 1.80	23-9 1.95	24-5 2.11	25-0 2.27	25-7 2.43		19.2	
18-3 1.10	18-11 1.22	19-6 1.35	20-1 1.48	20-8 1.61	21-3 1.75	21-10 1.89	22-4 2.03	22-10 2.18	23-11 2.48	24.0	
31-4 1.56	32-6 1.73	33-6 1.91	34-7 2.09	35-7 2.28	36-7 2.47					12.0	
29-4 1.46	30-5 1.62	31-4 1.78	32-4 1.95	33-3 2.13	34-2 2.31	35-1 2.49				13.7	
27-2 1.35	28-2 1.50	29-1 1.65	29-11 1.81	30-10 1.97	31-8 2.14	32-6 2.31	33-3 2.48			16.0	2x12
24-10 1.23	25-8 1.37	26-6 1.51	27-4 1.65	28-2 1.80	28-11 1.95	29-8 2.11	30-5 2.27	31-1 2.43		19.2	
22-2 1.10	23-0 1.22	23-9 1.35	24-5 1.48	25-2 1.61	25-10 1.75	26-6 1.89	27-2 2.03	27-10 2.18	29-1 2.48	24.0	

Note: The required modulus of elasticity, "E", in 1,000,000 pounds per inch is shown below each span.

Table A-24 Working Stresses for Joists and Rafters—Visual Grading

These "F_b" values are for use where repetitive members are spaced not more than 24 inches. For wider spacing, the "F_b" values should be reduced 13 percent.

Values for surfaced dry or surfaced green lumber apply at 19 percent maximum moisture content in use.

Species and Grade	Size	Allowable Unit Stress in Bending "F_b"			Modulus of Elasticity "E"	Grading Rules Agency
		Normal Duration	Snow Loading	7-Day Loading		
DOUGLAS FIR—LARCH (Surfaced dry or surfaced green)						
Dense Select Structural		2800	3220	3500	1,900,000	
Select Structural		2400	2760	3000	1,800,000	
Dense No. 1		2400	2760	3000	1,900,000	
No. 1 & Appearance		2050	2360	2560	1,800,000	West Coast
Dense No. 2	2x4	1950	2240	2440	1,700,000	Lumber
No. 2		1650	1900	2060	1,700,000	Inspection
No. 3		925	1060	1160	1,500,000	Bureau
Construction		1200	1380	1500	1,500,000	
Standard		675	780	840	1,500,000	Western Wood
Utility		325	370	410	1,500,000	Products
Studs		925	1060	1160	1,500,000	Association
Dense Select Structural		2400	2760	3000	1,900,000	
Select Structural		2050	2360	2560	1,800,000	
Dense No. 1	2x6	2050	2360	2560	1,900,000	
No. 1 & Appearance	and	1750	2010	2190	1,800,000	
Dense No. 2	wider	1700	1960	2120	1,700,000	
No. 2		1450	1670	1810	1,700,000	
No. 3		850	980	1060	1,500,000	
DOUGLAS FIR SOUTH (Surfaced dry or surfaced green)						
Select Structural		2300	2640	2880	1,400,000	
No. 1 & Appearance		1950	2240	2440	1,400,000	
No. 2		1600	1840	2000	1,300,000	Western Wood
No. 3	2x4	875	1010	1090	1,100,000	Products
Construction		1150	1320	1440	1,100,000	Association
Standard		650	750	810	1,100,000	
Utility		300	340	380	1,100,000	
Studs		875	1010	1090	1,100,000	
Select Structural		1950	2240	2440	1,400,000	
No. 1 & Appearance	2x6	1650	1900	2060	1,400,000	
No. 2	and	1350	1550	1690	1,300,000	
No. 3	wider	800	920	1000	1,100,000	
EASTERN SPRUCE (Surfaced dry or surfaced green)						
Select Structural		1750	2010	2190	1,400,000	Northeastern
No. 1		1500	1720	1880	1,400,000	Lumber
No. 2	2x4	1200	1380	1500	1,200,000	Manufacturers
No. 3		675	780	840	1,100,000	Association
Appearance		1250	1440	1560	1,400,000	
Construction		875	1010	1090	1,100,000	Northern
Standard		500	580	620	1,100,000	Hardwood
Utility		225	260	280	1,100,000	& Pine
Studs		675	780	840	1,100,000	Manufacturers
Select Structural		1500	1720	1880	1,400,000	Association
No. 1 & Appearance	2x6	1250	1440	1560	1,400,000	
No. 2	and	1000	1150	1250	1,200,000	
No. 3	wider	600	690	750	1,100,000	

Recommended by National Forest Products Assn.

Table A-24   Working Stresses for Joists and Rafters—Visual Grading

These "F_b" values are for use where repetitive members are spaced not more than **24** inches. For wider spacing, the "F_b" values should be reduced **13** percent.

Values for surfaced dry or surfaced green lumber apply at 19 percent maximum moisture content in use.

Species and Grade	Size	Allowable Unit Stress in Bending "F_b"			Modulus of Elasticity "E"	Grading Rules Agency
		Normal Duration	Snow Loading	7-Day Loading		
ENGELMANN SPRUCE (ENGELMANN SPRUCE—LODGEPOLE PINE) (Surfaced dry or surfaced green)						
Select Structural		1550	1780	1940	1,200,000	
No. 1 & Appearance		1300	1500	1620	1,200,000	
No. 2	2x4	1100	1260	1380	1,100,000	Western Wood
No. 3		600	690	750	1,000,000	Products
Construction		775	890	970	1,000,000	Association
Standard		425	490	530	1,000,000	
Utility		200	230	250	1,000,000	
Studs		600	690	750	1,000,000	
Select Structural		1350	1550	1690	1,200,000	
No. 1 & Appearance	2x6	1150	1320	1440	1,200,000	
No. 2	and	925	1060	1160	1,100,000	
No. 3	wider	550	630	690	1,000,000	
HEM—FIR (Surfaced dry or surfaced green)						
Select Structural		1900	2180	2380	1,500,000	
No. 1 & Appearance		1600	1840	2000	1,500,000	West Coast
No. 2		1300	1500	1620	1,400,000	Lumber
No. 3	2x4	725	830	910	1,200,000	Inspection
Construction		975	1120	1220	1,200,000	Bureau
Standard		525	600	660	1,200,000	
Utility		250	290	310	1,200,000	Western Wood
Studs		725	830	910	1,200,000	Products
Select Structural		1650	1900	2060	1,500,000	Association
No. 1 & Appearance	2x6	1400	1610	1750	1,500,000	
No. 2	and	1150	1320	1440	1,400,000	
No. 3	wider	675	780	840	1,200,000	
NORTHERN PINE (Surfaced dry or surfaced green)						
Select Structural		1850	2130	2310	1,400,000	Northeastern
No. 1		1600	1840	2000	1,400,000	Lumber
No. 2	2x4	1300	1500	1620	1,300,000	Manufacturers
No. 3		725	830	910	1,100,000	Association
Appearance		1400	1610	1750	1,400,000	
Construction		950	1090	1190	1,100,000	Northern
Standard		525	600	660	1,100,000	Hardwood
Utility		250	290	310	1,100,000	& Pine
Studs		725	830	910	1,100,000	Manufacturers
Select Structural		1600	1840	2000	1,400,000	Association
No. 1 & Appearance	2x6	1400	1610	1750	1,400,000	
No. 2	and	1100	1260	1380	1,300,000	
No. 3	wider	650	750	810	1,100,000	

Recommended by National Forest Products Assn.

Table A-24 Working Stresses for Joists and Rafters—Visual Grading

These "F_b" values are for use where repetitive members are spaced not more than 24 inches. For wider spacing, the "F_b" values should be reduced 13 percent.

Values for surfaced dry or surfaced green lumber apply at 19 percent maximum moisture content in use.

Species and Grade	Size	Allowable Unit Stress in Bending "F_b"			Modulus of Elasticity "E"	Grading Rules Agency
		Normal Duration	Snow Loading	7-Day Loading		
PONDEROSA PINE—SUGAR PINE (PONDEROSA PINE—LODGEPOLE PINE) (Surfaced dry or surfaced green)						
Select Structural		1650	1900	2060	1,200,000	
No. 1 & Appearance		1400	1610	1750	1,200,000	
No. 2	2x4	1150	1320	1440	1,100,000	Western Wood
No. 3		625	720	780	1,000,000	Products
Construction		825	950	1030	1,000,000	Association
Standard		450	520	560	1,000,000	
Utility		225	260	280	1,000,000	
Studs		625	720	780	1,000,000	
Select Structural		1400	1610	1750	1,200,000	
No. 1 & Appearance	2x6	1200	1380	1500	1,200,000	
No. 2	and	975	1120	1220	1,100,000	
No. 3	wider	575	660	720	1,000,000	
SITKA SPRUCE (Surfaced dry or surfaced green)						
Select Structural		1800	2070	2250	1,500,000	
No. 1 & Appearance		1550	1780	1940	1,500,000	
No. 2	2x4	1250	1440	1560	1,300,000	West Coast
No. 3		700	800	880	1,200,000	Lumber
Construction		925	1060	1160	1,200,000	Inspection
Standard		500	580	620	1,200,000	Bureau
Utility		250	290	310	1,200,000	
Studs		700	800	880	1,200,000	
Select Structural		1550	1780	1940	1,500,000	
No. 1 & Appearance	2x6	1300	1500	1620	1,500,000	
No. 2	and	1050	1210	1310	1,300,000	
No. 3	wider	600	690	750	1,200,000	
SUBALPINE FIR (WHITE WOODS)(MIXED SPECIES) (Surfaced dry or surfaced green)						
Select Structural		1400	1610	1750	900,000	
No. 1 & Appearance		1200	1380	1500	900,000	
No. 2	2x4	1000	1150	1250	900,000	
No. 3		550	630	690	800,000	Western Wood
Construction		725	830	910	800,000	Products
Standard		400	460	500	800,000	Association
Utility		200	230	250	800,000	
Studs		550	630	690	800,000	
Select Structural		1200	1380	1500	900,000	
No. 1 & Appearance	2x6	1050	1210	1310	900,000	
No. 2	and	850	980	1060	900,000	
No. 3	wider	500	580	620	800,000	

Recommended by National Forest Products Assn.

Table A-24 Working Stresses for Joists and Rafters—Visual Grading

These "F_b" values are for use where repetitive members are spaced not more than 24 inches. For wider spacing, the "F_b" values should be reduced 13 percent.

Values for surfaced dry or surfaced green lumber apply at 19 percent maximum moisture content in use.

Species and Grade	Size	Allowable Unit Stress in Bending "F_b"			Modulus of Elasticity "E"	Grading Rules Agency
		Normal Duration	Snow Loading	7-Day Loading		
SOUTHERN PINE (Surfaced dry)						
Select Structural		2400	2760	3000	1,800,000	
Dense Select Structural		2800	3220	3500	1,900,000	
No. 1		2000	2310	2520	1,800,000	
No. 1 Dense		2350	2710	2950	1,900,000	
No. 2		1450	1650	1800	1,400,000	
No. 2 MG		1650	1920	2080	1,600,000	
No. 2 Dense	2x4	1950	2250	2440	1,700,000	
No. 3		950	1090	1190	1,400,000	Southern
No. 3 Dense		1100	1260	1380	1,500,000	Pine
Construction		1200	1380	1500	1,400,000	Inspection
Standard		700	800	880	1,400,000	Bureau
Utility		325	375	410	1,400,000	
Studs		950	1090	1190	1,400,000	
Select Structural		2050	2360	2560	1,800,000	
Dense Select Structural		2400	2760	3000	1,900,000	
No. 1		1750	2010	2190	1,800,000	
No. 1 Dense	2x6	2050	2380	2590	1,900,000	
No. 2	and	1200	1380	1500	1,400,000	
No. 2 MG	wider	1450	1670	1810	1,600,000	
No. 2 Dense		1650	1900	2060	1,700,000	
No. 3		825	950	1030	1,400,000	
No. 3 Dense		975	1120	1220	1,500,000	
SOUTHERN PINE (Surfaced at 15 percent moisture content—KD)						
Select Structural		2600	2990	3250	1,900,000	
Dense Select Structural		3050	3510	3810	2,000,000	
No. 1		2200	2510	2730	1,900,000	
No. 1 Dense		2600	2980	3230	2,000,000	
No. 2		1550	1790	1940	1,500,000	
No. 2 MG	2x4	1800	2050	2230	1,700,000	
No. 2 Dense		2150	2450	2660	1,800,000	
No. 3		1000	1150	1250	1,500,000	Southern
No. 3 Dense		1200	1380	1500	1,600,000	Pine
Construction		1300	1500	1620	1,500,000	Inspection
Standard		750	860	940	1,500,000	Bureau
Utility		350	400	440	1,500,000	
Studs		1000	1150	1250	1,500,000	
Select Structural		2250	2590	2810	1,900,000	
Dense Select Structural		2600	2990	3250	2,000,000	
No. 1		1900	2180	2380	1,900,000	
No. 1 Dense	2x6	2200	2530	2750	2,000,000	
No. 2	and	1300	1500	1620	1,500,000	
No. 2 MG	wider	1550	1780	1940	1,700,000	
No. 2 Dense		1800	2070	2250	1,800,000	
No. 3		925	1040	1120	1,500,000	
No. 3 Dense		1050	1210	1310	1,600,000	

Recommended by National Forest Products Assn.

Table A-24 Working Stresses for Joists and Rafters—Visual Grading

These "F_b" values are for use where repetitive members are spaced not more than 24 inches. For wider spacing, the "F_b" values should be reduced 13 percent.

Values for surfaced dry or surfaced green lumber apply at 19 percent maximum moisture content in use.

Species and Grade	Size	Allowable Unit Stress in Bending "F_b"			Modulus of Elasticity "E"	Grading Rules Agency
		Normal Duration	Snow Loading	7-Day Loading		
SPRUCE—PINE—FIR (Surfaced dry or surfaced green)						
Select Structural		1650	1900	2060	1,500,000	
No. 1		1400	1610	1750	1,500,000	
No. 2	2x4	1150	1320	1440	1,300,000	
No. 3		650	750	810	1,200,000	
Appearance		1400	1610	1750	1,500,000	Nat'l. Lumber Grades Auth. (A Canadian Agency—See notes 1 and 2)
Construction		850	980	1060	1,200,000	
Standard		475	550	590	1,200,000	
Utility		225	260	280	1,200,000	
Stud		650	750	810	1,200,000	
Select Structural		1450	1670	1810	1,500,000	
No. 1	2x6	1200	1380	1500	1,500,000	
No. 2	and	1000	1150	1250	1,300,000	
No. 3	wider	575	660	720	1,200,000	
Appearance		1200	1380	1500	1,500,000	
RED PINE (Surfaced dry or surfaced green)						
Select Structural		1600	1840	2000	1,300,000	
No. 1		1350	1550	1690	1,300,000	
No. 2	2x4	1100	1270	1380	1,200,000	
No. 3		625	720	780	1,000,000	
Appearance		1350	1550	1690	1,300,000	Nat'l. Lumber Grades Auth. (A Canadian Agency—See notes 1 and 2)
Construction		800	920	1000	1,000,000	
Standard		450	520	560	1,000,000	
Utility		225	260	280	1,000,000	
Stud		625	720	780	1,000,000	
Select Structural		1350	1550	1690	1,300,000	
No. 1	2x6	1150	1320	1440	1,300,000	
No. 2	and	950	1090	1190	1,200,000	
No. 3	wider	550	630	690	1,000,000	
Appearance		1150	1320	1440	1,300,000	
WESTERN WHITE PINE (Surfaced dry or surfaced green)						
Select Structural		1550	1780	1940	1,400,000	
No. 1		1300	1500	1630	1,400,000	
No. 2	2x4	1050	1210	1310	1,300,000	
No. 3		600	690	750	1,200,000	
Appearance		1300	1500	1630	1,400,000	Nat'l. Lumber Grades Auth. (A Canadian Agency—See notes 1 and 2)
Construction		775	890	970	1,200,000	
Standard		425	490	530	1,200,000	
Utility		200	230	250	1,200,000	
Stud		600	690	750	1,200,000	
Select Structural		1300	1500	1630	1,400,000	
No. 1	2x6	1150	1320	1440	1,400,000	
No. 2	and	925	1060	1160	1,300,000	
No. 3	wider	550	630	690	1,200,000	
Appearance		1150	1320	1440	1,400,000	

Table A-24 Footnotes Applicable to Visually Graded Joists and Rafters

1. National Lumber Grades Authority is the Canadian rules writing agency responsible for preparation, maintenance and dissemination of a uniform softwood lumber grading rule for all Canadian species.

2. When 2" lumber is manufactured at a maximum moisture content of 15 percent (grade-marked MC-15) and used in a condition where the moisture content does not exceed 15 percent the design values shown in Table W-1 for "surfaced dry or surfaced green" lumber may be increased eight percent (8%) for allowable unit stress in bending "F_b", and five percent (5%) for Modulus of Elasticity "E".

USEFUL TABLES
AND OTHER DATA

Table B-1

BOARD MEASURE

NOMINAL SIZE OF PIECE	BOARD FEET CONTENT WHEN LENGTH IN FEET OR NUMBER OF LINEAR FEET EQUALS												
	1	2	3	4	5	6	7	8	9	10	11	12	14
1 x 1	1/12	1/6	1/4	1/3	5/12	1/2	7/12	2/3	3/4	5/6	11/12	1	1-1/6
1 x 2	1/6	1/3	1/2	2/3	5/6	1	1-1/6	1-1/3	1-1/2	1-2/3	1-5/6	2-	2-1/3
1 x 3	1/4	1/2	3/4	1	1-1/4	1-1/2	1-3/4	2	2-1/4	2-1/2	2-3/4	3	3-1/2
1 x 4	1/3	2/3	1	1-1/3	1-2/3	2	2-1/3	2-2/3	3	3-1/3	3-2/3	4	4-2/3
1 x 5	5/12	5/6	1-1/4	1-2/3	2-1/12	2-1/2	2-11/12	3-1/3	3-3/4	4-1/6	4-7/12	5	5-5/6
1 x 6	1/2	1	1-1/2	2	2-1/2	3	3-1/2	4	4-1/2	5	5-1/2	6	7
1 x 8	2/3	1-1/3	2	2-2/3	3-1/3	4	4-2/3	5-1/3	6	6-2/3	7-1/3	8	9-1/3
1 x 10	5/6	1-2/3	2-1/2	3-1/3	4-1/6	5	5-5/6	6-2/3	7-1/2	8-1/3	9-1/6	10	11-2/3
1 x 12	1	2	3	4	5	6	7	8	9	10	11	12	14
1 x 14	1-1/6	2-1/3	3-1/2	4-2/3	5-5/6	7	8-1/6	9-1/3	10-1/2	11-2/3	12-5/6	14	16-1/3
1 x 16	1-1/3	2-2/3	4	5-1/3	6-2/3	8	9-1/3	10-2/3	12	13-1/3	14-2/3	16	18-2/3
1-1/4 x 1	5/48	5/24	5/16	5/12	25/48	5/8	35/48	5/6	15/16	1-1/24	1-7/48	1-1/4	1-11/24
1-1/4 x 2	5/24	5/12	5/8	5/6	1-1/24	1-1/4	1-11/24	1-2/3	1-7/8	2-1/12	2-7/24	2-1/2	2-11/24
1-1/4 x 3	5/16	5/8	15/16	1-1/4	1-9/16	1-7/8	2-3/16	2-1/2	2-13/16	3-1/8	3-7/16	3-3/4	4-3/8
1-1/4 x 4	5/12	5/6	1-1/4	1-2/3	2-1/12	2-1/2	2-11/12	3-1/3	3-3/4	4-1/6	4-7/12	5	5-5/6
1-1/4 x 5	25/48	1-1/24	1-9/16	2-1/12	2-19/48	3-1/8	3-31/48	4-1/6	4-11/16	5-5/24	5-35/48	6-1/4	7-7/24
1-1/4 x 6	5/8	1-1/4	1-7/8	2-1/2	3-1/8	3-3/4	4-3/8	5	5-5/8	6-1/4	6-7/8	7-1/2	8-3/4
1-1/4 x 8	5/6	1-2/3	2-1/2	3-1/3	4-1/6	5	5-5/6	6-2/3	7-1/2	8-1/3	9-1/6	10	11-2/3
1-1/4 x 10	1-1/24	2-1/12	3-1/8	4-1/6	5-5/24	6-1/4	7-7/24	8-1/3	9-3/8	10-5/12	11-11/24	12-1/2	14-7/12
1-1/4 x 12	1-1/4	2-1/2	3-3/4	5	6-1/4	7-1/2	8-3/4	10	11-1/4	12-1/2	13-3/4	15	17-1/2
1-1/4 x 14	1-11/24	2-11/12	4-3/8	5-5/6	7-7/24	8-3/4	10-5/24	11-2/3	13-1/8	14-7/12	16-1/24	17-1/2	20-5/12
1-1/4 x 16	1-2/3	3-1/3	5	6-2/3	8-1/3	10	11-2/3	13-1/3	15	16-2/3	18-1/3	20	23-1/3
1-1/2 x 1	1/8	1/4	3/8	1/2	5/8	3/4	7/8	1	1-1/8	1-1/4	1-3/8	1-1/2	1-3/4
1-1/2 x 2	1/4	1/2	3/4	1	1-1/4	1-1/2	1-3/4	2	2-1/4	2-1/2	2-3/4	3	3-1/2
1-1/2 x 3	3/8	3/4	1-1/8	1-1/2	1-7/8	2-1/4	2-5/8	3	3-3/8	3-3/4	4-1/8	4-1/2	5-1/4
1-1/2 x 4	1/2	1	1-1/2	2	2-1/2	3	3-1/2	4	4-1/2	5	5-1/2	6	7
1-1/2 x 5	5/8	1-1/4	1-7/8	2-1/2	3-1/8	3-3/4	4-3/8	5	5-5/8	6-1/4	6-7/8	7-1/2	8-3/4
1-1/2 x 6	3/4	1-1/2	2-1/4	3	3-3/4	4-1/2	5-1/4	6	6-3/4	7-1/2	8-1/4	9	10-1/2
1-1/2 x 8	1	2	3	4	5	6	7	8	9	10	11	12	14
1-1/2 x 10	1-1/4	2-1/2	3-3/4	5	6-1/4	7-1/2	8-3/4	10	11-1/4	12-1/2	13-3/4	15	17-1/2
1-1/2 x 12	1-1/2	3	4-1/2	6	7-1/2	9	10-1/2	12	13-1/2	15	16-1/2	18	21
1-1/2 x 14	1-3/4	3-1/2	5-1/4	7	8-3/4	10-1/2	12-1/4	14	15-3/4	17-1/2	19-1/4	21	24-1/2
1-1/2 x 16	2	4	6	8	10	12	14	16	18	20	22	24	28
2 x 2	1/3	2/3	1	1-1/3	1-2/3	2	2-1/3	2-2/3	3	3-1/3	3-2/3	4	4-2/3
2 x 3	1/2	1	1-1/2	2	2-1/2	3	3-1/2	4	4-1/2	5	5-1/2	6	7
2 x 4	2/3	1-1/3	2	2-2/3	3-1/3	4	4-2/3	5-1/3	6	6-2/3	7-1/3	8	9-1/3
2 x 5	5/6	1-2/3	2-1/2	3-1/3	4-1/6	5	5-5/6	6-2/3	7-1/2	8-1/3	9-1/6	10	11-2/3
2 x 6	1	2	3	4	5	6	7	8	9	10	11	12	14
2 x 7	1-1/6	2-1/3	3-1/2	4-2/3	5-5/6	7	8-1/4	9-1/3	10-1/2	11-2/3	12-5/6	14	16-1/3
2 x 8	1-1/3	2-2/3	4	5-1/3	6-2/3	8	9-1/3	10-2/3	12	13-1/3	14-2/3	16	18-2/3
2 x 9	1-1/2	3	4-1/2	6	7-1/2	9	10-1/2	12	13-1/2	15	16-1/2	18	21
2 x 10	1-2/3	3-1/3	5	6-2/3	8-1/3	10	11-2/3	13-1/3	15	16-2/3	18-1/3	20	23-1/3
2 x 12	2	4	6	8	10	12	14	16	18	20	22	24	28
2 x 14	2-1/3	4-2/3	7	9-1/3	11-2/3	14	16-1/3	18-2/3	21	23-1/3	25-2/3	28	31-2/3
2 x 16	2-2/3	5-1/3	8	10-2/3	13-1/3	16	18-2/3	21-1/3	24	26-2/3	29-1/3	32	37-1/3
2 x 18	3	6	9	12	15	18	21	24	27	30	33	36	42
2 x 20	3-1/3	6-2/3	10	13-1/3	16-2/3	20	23-1/3	26-2/3	30	33-1/3	36-2/3	40	46-2/3
3 x 3	3/4	1-1/2	2-1/4	3	3-3/4	4-1/2	5-1/4	6	6-3/4	7-1/2	8-1/4	9	10-1/2
3 x 4	1	2	3	4	5	6	7	8	9	10	11	12	14
3 x 5	1-1/4	2-1/2	3-3/4	5	6-1/4	7-1/2	8-3/4	10	11-1/4	12-1/2	13-3/4	15	17-1/2
3 x 6	1-1/2	3	4-1/2	6	7-1/2	9	10-1/2	12	13-1/2	15	16-1/2	18	21
3 x 7	1-3/4	3-1/2	5-1/4	7	8-3/4	10-1/2	12-1/4	14	15-3/4	17-1/2	19-1/4	21	24-1/2
3 x 8	2	4	6	8	10	12	14	16	18	20	22	24	28
3 x 9	2-1/4	4-1/2	6-3/4	9	11-1/4	13-1/2	15-3/4	18	20-1/4	22-1/2	24-3/4	27	31-1/2
3 x 10	2-1/2	5	7-1/2	10	12-1/2	15	17-1/2	20	22-1/2	25	27-1/2	30	35
3 x 12	3	6	9	12	15	18	21	24	27	30	33	36	42
3 x 14	3-1/2	7	10-1/2	14	17-1/2	21	24-1/2	28	31-1/2	35	38-1/2	42	49
3 x 16	4	8	12	16	20	24	28	32	36	40	44	48	56
3 x 18	4-1/2	9	13-1/2	18	22-1/2	27	31-1/2	36	40-1/2	45	49-1/2	54	63
3 x 20	5	10	15	20	25	30	35	40	45	50	55	60	70
4 x 4	1-1/3	2-2/3	4	5-1/3	6-2/3	8	9-1/3	10-2/3	12	13-1/3	14-2/3	16	18-2/3
4 x 5	1-2/3	3-1/3	5	6-2/3	8-1/3	10	11-2/3	13-1/3	15	16-2/3	18-1/3	20	23-1/3
4 x 6	2	4	6	8	10	12	14	16	18	20	22	24	28
4 x 7	2-1/3	4-2/3	7	9-1/3	11-2/3	14	16-1/3	18-2/3	21	23-1/3	25-2/3	28	32-2/3
4 x 8	2-2/3	5-1/3	8	10-2/3	13-1/3	16	18-2/3	21-1/3	24	26-2/3	29-1/3	32	37-1/3
4 x 9	3	6	9	12	15	18	21	24	27	30	33	36	42
4 x 10	3-1/3	6-2/3	10	13-1/3	16-2/3	20	23-1/3	26-2/3	30	33-1/3	36-2/3	40	46-2/3
4 x 12	4	8	12	16	20	24	28	32	36	40	44	48	56
4 x 14	4-2/3	9-1/3	14	18-2/3	23-1/3	28	32-2/3	37-1/3	42	46-2/3	51-1/3	56	65-1/3
4 x 16	5-1/3	10-2/3	16	21-1/3	26-2/3	32	37-1/3	42-2/3	48	53-1/3	58-2/3	64	74-2/3
4 x 18	6	12	18	24	30	36	42	48	54	60	66	72	84
4 x 20	6-2/3	13-1/3	20	26-2/3	33-1/3	40	46-2/3	53-1/3	60	66-2/3	73-1/3	80	93-1/3
5 x 5	2-1/12	4-1/6	6-1/4	8-1/3	10-5/12	12-1/2	14-7/12	16-2/3	18-3/4	20-5/6	22-11/12	25	29-1/6
5 x 6	2-1/2	5	7-1/2	10	12-1/2	15	17-1/2	20	22-1/2	25	27-1/2	30	35
5 x 7	2-11/12	5-5/6	8-3/4	11-2/3	14-7/12	17-1/2	20-5/12	23-1/3	26-1/4	29-1/6	32-1/12	35	40-5/6
5 x 8	3-1/3	6-2/3	10	13-1/3	16-2/3	20	23-1/3	26-2/3	30	33-1/3	36-2/3	40	46-2/3
5 x 9	3-3/4	7-1/2	11-1/4	15	18-3/4	22-1/2	26-1/4	30	33-3/4	37-1/2	41-1/4	45	52-1/2
5 x 10	4-1/6	8-1/3	12-1/2	16-2/3	20-5/6	25	29-1/6	33-1/3	37-1/2	41-2/3	45-5/6	50	58-1/3
5 x 12	5	10	15	20	25	30	35	40	45	50	55	60	70
5 x 14	5-5/6	11-2/3	17-1/2	23-1/3	29-1/6	35	40-5/6	46-2/3	52-1/2	58-1/3	64-1/6	70	81-2/3
5 x 16	6-2/3	13-1/3	20	26-2/3	33-1/3	40	46-2/3	53-1/3	60	66-2/3	73-1/3	80	93-1/3
5 x 18	7-1/2	15	22-1/2	30	37-1/2	45	52-1/2	60	67-1/2	75	82-1/2	90	105
5 x 20	8-1/3	16-2/3	25	33-1/3	41-2/3	50	58-1/3	66-2/3	75	83-1/3	91-2/3	100	116-2/3
6 x 6	3	6	9	12	15	18	21	24	27	30	33	36	42
6 x 8	4	8	12	16	20	24	28	32	36	40	44	48	56
8 x 8	5-1/3	10-2/3	16	21-1/3	26-2/3	32	37-1/3	42-2/3	48	53-1/3	58-2/3	64	74-2/3

Table B-1

BOARD MEASURE

NOMINAL SIZE OF PIECE	\-	\-	\-	\-	\-	\-	\-	\-	\-	\-	\-	\-	\-
	BOARD FEET CONTENT WHEN LENGTH IN FEET OR NUMBER OF LINEAR FEET EQUALS												
	16	**18**	**20**	**22**	**24**	**26**	**28**	**30**	**32**	**34**	**36**	**38**	**40**
1 x 1	1-1/3	1-1/2	1-2/3	1-5/6	2	2-1/6	2-1/3	2-1/2	2-2/3	2-5/6	3	3-1/6	3-1/3
1 x 2	2-2/3	3	3-1/3	3-2/3	4	4-1/3	4-2/3	5	5-1/3	5-2/3	6	6-1/3	6-2/3
1 x 3	4	4-1/2	5	5-1/2	6	6-1/2	7	7-1/2	8	8-1/2	9	9-1/2	10
1 x 4	5-1/3	6	6-2/3	7-1/3	8	8-2/3	9-1/3	10	10-2/3	11-1/3	12	12-2/3	13-1/3
1 x 5	6-2/3	7-1/2	8-1/3	9-1/6	10	10-5/6	11-2/3	12-1/2	13-1/3	14-1/6	15	15-5/6	16-2/3
1 x 6	8	9	10	11	12	13	14	15	16	17	18	19	20
1 x 8	10-2/3	12	13-1/3	14-2/3	16	17-1/3	18-2/3	20	21-1/3	22-2/3	24	25-1/3	26-2/3
1 x 10	13-1/3	15	16-2/3	18-1/3	20	21-2/3	23-1/3	25	26-2/3	28-1/3	30	31-2/3	33-1/3
1 x 12	16	18	20	22	24	26	28	30	32	34	36	38	40
1 x 14	18-2/3	21	23-1/3	25-2/3	28	30-1/3	32-2/3	35	37-1/3	39-2/3	42	44-1/3	46-2/3
1 x 16	21-1/3	24	26-2/3	29-1/3	32	34-2/3	37-1/3	40	42-2/3	45-1/3	48	50-2/3	53-1/3
1-1/4 x 1	1-2/3	1-7/8	2-1/12	2-7/24	2-1/2	2-17/24	2-11/12	3-1/8	3-1/3	3-13/24	3-3/4	3-23/24	4-1/6
1-1/4 x 2	3-1/3	3-3/4	4-1/6	4-11/24	5	5-5/12	5-7/12	6-1/4	6-2/3	7-1/12	7-1/2	7-11/12	8-1/3
1-1/4 x 3	5	5-5/8	6-1/4	6-7/8	7-1/2	8-1/8	8-3/4	9-3/8	10	10-5/8	11-1/4	11-7/8	12-1/2
1-1/4 x 4	6-2/3	7-1/2	8-1/3	9-1/6	10	10-5/6	11-2/3	12-1/2	13-1/3	14-1/6	15	15-5/6	16-2/3
1-1/4 x 5	8-1/3	9-3/8	10-5/12	11-11/24	12-1/2	13-13/24	14-7/12	15-5/8	16-2/3	17-17/24	18-3/4	19-19/24	20-5/6
1-1/4 x 6	10	11-1/4	12-1/2	13-3/4	15	16-1/4	17-1/2	18-3/4	20	21-1/4	22-1/2	23-3/4	25
1-1/4 x 8	13-1/3	15	16-2/3	18-1/3	20	21-2/3	23-1/3	25	26-2/3	28-1/3	30	31-2/3	33-1/3
1-1/4 x 10	16-2/3	18-3/4	20-5/6	22-11/12	25	27-1/12	29-1/6	31-1/4	33-1/3	35-5/12	37-1/2	39-7/12	41-2/3
1-1/4 x 12	20	22-1/2	25	27-1/2	30	32-1/2	35	37-1/2	40	42-1/2	45	47-1/2	50
1-1/4 x 14	23-1/3	26-1/4	29-1/6	32-1/12	35	37-11/12	40-5/6	43-3/4	46-2/3	49-7/12	52-1/2	55-5/12	58-1/3
1-1/4 x 16	26-2/3	30	33-1/3	36-2/3	40	43-1/3	46-2/3	50	53-1/3	56-2/3	60	63-1/3	66-2/3
1-1/2 x 1	2	2-1/4	2-1/2	2-3/4	3	3-1/4	3-1/2	3-3/4	4	4-1/4	4-1/2	4-3/4	5
1-1/2 x 2	4	4-1/2	5	5-1/2	6	6-1/2	7	7-1/2	8	8-1/2	9	9-1/2	10
1-1/2 x 3	6	6-3/4	7-1/2	8-1/4	9	9-3/4	10-1/2	11-1/4	12	12-3/4	13-1/2	14-1/4	15
1-1/2 x 4	8	9	10	11	12	13	14	15	16	17	18	19	20
1-1/2 x 5	10	11-1/4	12-1/2	13-3/4	15	16-1/4	17-1/2	18-3/4	20	21-1/4	22-1/2	23-3/4	25
1-1/2 x 6	12	13-1/2	15	16-1/2	18	19-1/2	21	22-1/2	24	25-1/2	27	28-1/2	30
1-1/2 x 8	16	18	20	22	24	26	28	30	32	34	36	38	40
1-1/2 x 10	20	22-1/2	25	27-1/2	30	32-1/2	35	37-1/2	40	42-1/2	45	47-1/2	50
1-1/2 x 12	24	27	30	33	36	39	42	45	48	51	54	57	60
1-1/2 x 14	28	31-1/2	35	38-1/2	42	45-1/2	49	52-1/2	56	59-1/2	63	66-1/2	70
1-1/2 x 16	32	36	40	44	48	52	56	60	64	68	72	76	80
2 x 2	5-1/3	6	6-2/3	7-1/3	8	8-2/3	9-1/3	10	10-2/3	11-1/3	12	12-2/3	13-1/3
2 x 3	8	9	10	11	12	13	14	15	16	17	18	19	20
2 x 4	10-2/3	12	13-1/3	14-2/3	16	17-1/3	18-2/3	20	21-1/3	22-2/3	24	25-1/3	26-2/3
2 x 5	13-1/3	15	16-2/3	18-1/3	20	21-2/3	23-1/3	25	26-2/3	28-1/3	30	31-2/3	33-1/3
2 x 6	16	18	20	22	24	26	28	30	32	34	36	38	40
2 x 7	18-2/3	21	23-1/3	25-2/3	28	30-1/3	32-2/3	35	37-1/3	39-2/3	42	44-1/3	46-2/3
2 x 8	21-1/3	24	26-2/3	29-1/3	32	34-2/3	37-1/3	40	42-2/3	45-1/3	48	50-2/3	53-1/3
2 x 9	24	27	30	33	36	39	42	45	48	51	54	57	60
2 x 10	26-2/3	30	33-1/3	36-2/3	40	43-1/3	46-2/3	50	53-1/3	56-2/3	60	63-1/3	66-2/3
2 x 12	32	36	40	44	48	52	56	60	64	68	72	76	80
2 x 14	37-1/3	42	46-2/3	51-1/3	56	60-2/3	65-1/3	70	74-2/3	79-1/3	84	88-2/3	93-1/3
2 x 16	42-2/3	48	55-1/3	58-2/3	64	69-1/3	74-2/3	80	85-1/3	90-2/3	96	101-1/3	106-2/3
2 x 18	48	54	60	66	72	78	84	90	96	102	108	114	120
2 x 20	53-1/3	60	66-2/3	73-1/3	80	86-2/3	93-1/3	100	106-2/3	113-1/3	120	126-2/3	133-1/3
3 x 3	12	13-1/2	15	16-1/2	18	19-1/2	21	22-1/2	24	25-1/2	27	28-1/2	30
3 x 4	16	18	20	22	24	26	28	30	32	34	36	38	40
3 x 5	20	22-1/2	25	27-1/2	30	32-1/2	35	37-1/2	40	42-1/2	45	47-1/2	50
3 x 6	24	27	30	33	36	39	42	45	48	51	54	57	60
3 x 7	28	31-1/2	35	38-1/2	42	45-1/2	49	52-1/2	56	59-1/2	63	66-1/2	70
3 x 8	32	36	40	44	48	52	56	60	64	68	72	76	80
3 x 9	36	40-1/2	45	49-1/2	54	58-1/2	63	67-1/2	72	76-1/2	81	85-1/2	90
3 x 10	40	45	50	55	60	65	70	75	80	85	90	95	100
3 x 12	48	54	60	66	72	78	84	90	96	102	108	114	120
3 x 14	54	63	70	77	84	91	98	105	112	119	126	133	140
3 x 16	64	72	80	88	96	104	112	120	128	136	144	152	160
3 x 18	72	81	90	99	108	117	126	135	144	153	162	171	180
3 x 20	80	90	100	110	120	130	140	150	160	170	180	190	200
4 x 4	21-1/3	24	26-2/3	29-1/3	32	34-2/3	37-1/3	40	42-2/3	45-1/3	48	50-2/3	53-1/3
4 x 5	26-2/3	30	33-1/3	36-2/3	40	43-1/3	46-2/3	50	53-1/3	56-2/3	60	63-1/3	66-2/3
4 x 6	32	36	40	44	48	52	56	60	64	68	72	76	80
4 x 7	37-1/3	42	46-2/3	51-1/3	56	60-2/3	65-1/3	70	74-2/3	79-1/3	84	88-2/3	93-1/3
4 x 8	42-2/3	48	53-1/3	58-2/3	64	69-1/3	74-2/3	80	85-1/3	90-2/3	96	101-1/3	106-2/3
4 x 9	48	54	60	66	72	78	84	90	96	102	108	114	120
4 x 10	53-1/3	60	66-2/3	73-1/3	80	86-2/3	93-1/3	100	106-2/3	113-1/3	120	126-2/3	133-1/3
4 x 12	64	72	80	88	96	104	112	120	128	136	144	152	160
4 x 14	74-2/3	84	93-1/3	102-2/3	112	121-1/3	130-2/3	140	149-1/3	158-2/3	168	177-1/3	186-2/3
4 x 16	85-1/3	96	106-2/3	117-1/3	128	138-2/3	149-1/3	160	170-2/3	181-1/3	192	202-2/3	213-1/3
4 x 18	96	108	120	132	144	156	168	180	192	204	216	228	240
4 x 20	106-2/3	120	133-1/3	146-2/3	160	173-1/3	186-2/3	200	213-1/3	226-2/3	240	253-1/3	266-2/3
5 x 5	33-1/3	37-1/2	41-2/3	45-5/6	50	54-1/6	58-1/3	62-1/2	66-2/3	70-5/6	75	79-1/6	83-1/3
5 x 6	40	45	50	55	60	65	70	75	80	85	90	95	100
5 x 7	46-2/3	52-1/2	58-1/3	64-1/6	70	75-5/6	81-2/3	87-1/2	93-1/3	99-1/6	105	110-5/6	116-2/3
5 x 8	53-1/3	60	66-2/3	73-1/3	80	86-2/3	93-1/3	100	106-2/3	113-1/3	120	126-2/3	133-1/3
5 x 9	60	67-1/2	75	82-1/2	90	97-1/2	105	112-1/2	120	127-1/2	135	142-1/2	150
5 x 10	66-2/3	75	83-1/3	91-2/3	100	108-1/3	116-2/3	125	133-1/3	141-2/3	150	158-1/3	166-2/3
5 x 12	80	90	100	110	120	130	140	150	160	170	180	190	200
5 x 14	93-1/3	105	116-2/3	128-1/3	140	151-2/3	163-1/3	175	186-2/3	198-1/3	210	221-2/3	233-1/3
5 x 16	106-2/3	120	133-1/3	146-2/3	160	173-1/3	186-2/3	200	213-1/3	226-2/3	240	253-1/3	266-2/3
5 x 18	120	135	150	165	180	195	210	225	240	255	270	285	300
5 x 20	133-1/3	150	166-2/3	183-1/3	200	216-2/3	233-1/3	250	266-2/3	283-1/3	300	316-2/3	333-1/3
6 x 6	48	54	60	66	72	78	84	90	96	102	108	114	120
6 x 8	64	72	80	88	96	104	112	120	128	136	144	152	160
8 x 8	85-1/3	96	106-2/3	117-1/3	128	138-2/3	149-1/3	160	170-2/3	181-1/3	192	202-2/3	213-1/3

Table B2

Actual Dimensions of dry lumber: (Dressed 4 sides—S4S)								
Nominal	1″	2″	3″	4″	6″	8″	10″	etc.
Actual	3/4	1 1/2	2 1/2	3 1/2	5 1/2	7 1/4	9 1/4	

1 × 6 measures 3/4″ × 5 1/2″
2 × 8 measures 1 1/2″ × 7 1/4″c

Table B-3

NAILS

SIZE	LENGTH INCHES	WIRE GAGE	APPROX. NO./LB.	APPROX. STRENGTH POUNDS	
				Pull (1)	Lateral (2)
COMMON NAILS					
2d	1	15	847	Douglas Fir, Larch or Southern Pine	
3d	1 1/4	14	543		
4d	1 1/2	12 1/2	294		
5d	1 3/4	12 1/2	254		
6d	2	11 1/2	167	29	63
7d	2 1/4	11 1/2	150		
8d	2 1/2	10 1/4	101	34	78
9d	2 3/4	10 1/4	92		
10d	3	9	69	38	94
12d	3 1/4	9	63	38	94
16d	3 1/2	8	49	42	107
20d	4	6	31	49	139
30d	4 1/2	5	24	53	154
40d	5	4	18	58	176
50d	5 1/2	3	14	63	202
60d	6	2	11	68	223
SPIKES					
10d	3	6	32	49	139
12d	3 1/4	6	31	49	139
16d	3 1/2	5	24	53	155
20d	4	4	19	58	176
30d	4 1/2	3	14	63	202
40d	5	2	12	68	223
50d	5 1/2	1	10	73	248
60d	6	1	9	73	248
5/16	7	5/16	6	80	289
3/8	8-12	3/8”	5-3	96	380
HARDENED THREADED NAILS					
6d	2	12	190	80	69
8d	2 1/2	11	117	90	82
10d	3	10	78	100	94
12d	3 1/4	10	73	100	94
16d	3 1/2	9	57	110	107
20d	4	7	36	135	139
30d	4 1/2	7	31	135	139
40d	5	7	27	135	139
50d	·5 1/2	7	23	135	139
60d	6	7	18	135	139

(1) Per inch penetration of point
(2) For penetration of 11 diameters

WIRE GAGES
ACTUAL SIZE

NO.	SIZE	NO.	SIZE
1	.2830	8	.1620
2	.2625	9	.1483
3	.2437	10	.1350
4	.2253	11	.1205
5	.2070	12	.1055
6	.1920	13	.0915
7	.1770	14	.0800
		15	.0720

Table B-3 *Continued*

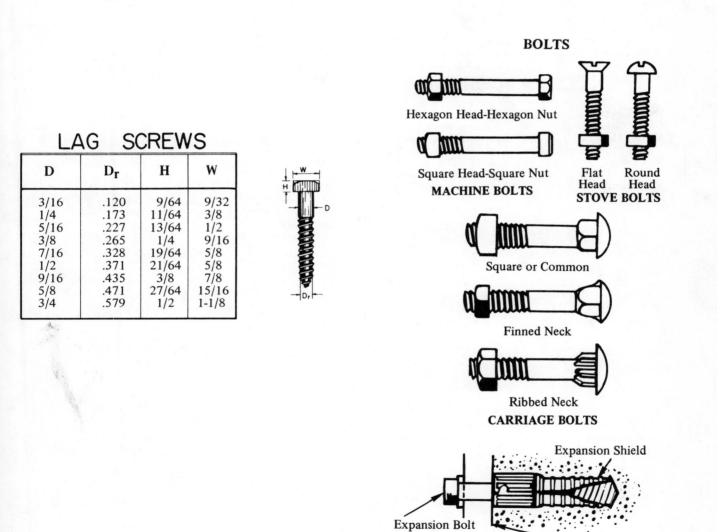

LAG SCREWS

D	D_r	H	W
3/16	.120	9/64	9/32
1/4	.173	11/64	3/8
5/16	.227	13/64	1/2
3/8	.265	1/4	9/16
7/16	.328	19/64	5/8
1/2	.371	21/64	5/8
9/16	.435	3/8	7/8
5/8	.471	27/64	15/16
3/4	.579	1/2	1-1/8

BOLTS

Hexagon Head-Hexagon Nut

Square Head-Square Nut
MACHINE BOLTS

Flat Head   Round Head
STOVE BOLTS

Square or Common

Finned Neck

Ribbed Neck
CARRIAGE BOLTS

Expansion Shield

Expansion Bolt

Wooden Cleat

Table B-4

ELECTRIC USES AND NEEDS
Estimated Kilowatt-Hour Use by Farm Electric Chore Equipment

General	Average KWH Use
Conveyor—Auger	4 per 1000 bushel
Elevator—Auger	10 per 1000 bushel
Bucket	3 per 1000 bushel
Feed Grinder *(general)*	5 per ton
Mixer *(general)*	1 per ton
Feeder *(automatic)*	2 per ton
Grain Drying Air only	1 per bushel
Heated	.2 per bushel
Hay Drying Air only	40 per ton
Heated	12 per ton
Silo Unloader Grass	4 per ton
Corn	2 - 5 per ton
Water Pump Shallow	1 per 1000 gallon
Deep	2 per 1000 gallon
Water Tank Heater	250 per year
De Icer	100 per year

Dairy Equipment	
Gutter Cleaner	0.5 per month per cow
Milking Machine	2 per month per cow
With pipeline	3 per month per cow
Milk Cooler can	1 per 10 gallon
Bulk	11 per month per cow
Ventilator	3 per month per cow
Water Heater	7 per month per cow
Water Fountain *(auto)*	1 per month per cow

Swine Equipment	Average KWH Use
Brooding *(infrared)*	40 per litter
Farrowing—Floor Cable	30 per sow farrowed
Ventilator	1 per month per pig
Water fountains *(auto)*	.5 per month per pig
Bunk feeder	1 per month per pig
Feed grinding	.3 per month per pig

Poultry Equipment	
Brooding—Hover	.5 per chicken
Infrared	.8 per chicken
Egg Cooler	1 per year per layer
Egg Washer	1 per 2000 eggs
Feed Grinder	5 per ton
Feeders *(auto)*	.3 per year per layer
Incubator	.2 per egg
Water Fountain	.1 per month per bird
Water Warmer	4 per month per 100 birds
Ventilator	.4 per month per bird

Farm Lighting	
General yard	20 per month per 100 watts
All night *(auto)*	35 per month per 100 watts

Farm Shop	
Arc Welding	5 per month
Battery Charging	2 per battery charged
Drill Press, Lathe, Grinder, and Saw	1.3 per hour used

Table B-5

COMPUTING ELECTRICAL DEMAND

Residence 1500 sq. ft.

General lighting and small appliance load		4575 w.
Range		12000 w.
Fixed equipment other than range		
Water heater	4500 w.	
Dishwasher	1200 w.	
Automatic washer	600 w.	
Water pump	600 w.	
Clothes dryer	7000 w.	
	13900 @ 75% =	10,400 w.
Total		26,975 w.

Dairy Barn

5 h.p. Hay dryer	35 amp. 230 v.
5 h.p. Silo unloader	28 amp. 230 v.
3 h.p. Milk cooler	17 amp. 230 v.
1-1/2 h.p. Milker	10 amp. 230 v.
4500 w. Water heater	20 amp. 230 v.
1.5 kw. Milk house heater	6.5 amp. 230 v.
1/3 h.p. Venti-	
lating Fan	7.2 amp. 115 v.
32 Lighting	
outlets	48 amp. 115 v.
12 Convenience	
outlets	18 amp. 115 v.
	73 amp. 115 v. = 36 amp. 230 v.
Total	156 amp. 230 v.

Use 200 amp. entrance to barn

Shop

Largest motor 1 h.p.		10 amp. 230 v.
Other motors 2—1/2 h.p.		9.5 amp. 230 v.
Welder		35 amp. 230 v.
10 Lighting		
outlets	15 amp. 115 v.	
6 Convenience		
outlets	9 amp. 115 v.	
	24 amp. 115 v. =	12 amp. 230 v.
Total		66.5 amp. 230 v.

Use 100 amp. entrance

2—5 h.p. grain dryer		60 amp. 230 v.
2—1/2 h.p. augers		10 amp. 230 v.
Total		70 amp. 230 v.

Use 100 amp. entrance

Total Entrance Requirements

Largest demand		
(dairy barn)	156 amp. @ 100% =	156 amp.
Second Largest demand		
(residence)	117 amp. @ 75% =	88 amp.
Third Largest demand		
(grain dryers)	70 amp. @ 65% =	45 amp.
Remaining		
demand	66.5 amp. @ 50% =	33 amp.
Total		322 amp.

This operation would require a 400 amp. entrance

w.=watts   v.=volts   amp.=amperes

Table B6. Tables of Length, Area, Volume, and Weight

Standard Measurements

Measure of length (linear measure)

4 inches	=	1 hand
9 inches	=	1 span
12 inches	=	1 foot
3 feet	=	1 yard
6 feet	=	1 fathom
5-1/2 yards—16-1/2 feet	=	1 rod or 11 poles
40 poles	=	1 furlong
8 furlongs	=	1 mile
5,280 feet—1,760 yards—320 rods	=	1 mile
3 miles	=	1 league

Measure of surface (area)

144 square inches	=	1 square foot
9 square feet	=	1 square yard
30-1/4 square yards	=	1 square rod
40 square rods	=	1 rood
4 square roods	=	1 square area
160 square rods	=	1 acre
43,560 square feet	=	1 acre
640 square acres	=	1 square mile
36 square miles	=	1 township

Liquid measure

2 cups	=	1 pint
4 gills	=	1 pint
16 fluid ounces	=	1 pint
2 pints	=	1 quart
4 quarts	=	1 gallon
31-1/2 gallons	=	1 barrel
2 barrels	=	1 hogshead
1 gallon	=	231 cubic inches
1 cubic foot	=	7.48 gallons
1 teaspoon	=	.17 fluid ounces (1/6 oz.)
3 teaspoons (level)	=	1 tablespoon (1/2 oz.)
2 tablespoons	=	1 fluid ounce
1 cup (liquid)	=	16 tablespoons (8 oz.)
1 teaspoon	=	5 to 6 cubic centimeters
1 tablespoon	=	15 to 16 cubic centimeters
1 fluid ounce	=	29.57 cubic centimeters

Apothecaries' weight

20 grains	=	1 scruple
3 scruples	=	1 dram
8 drams	=	1 ounce
12 ounces	=	1 pound
27-11/32 grains	=	1 dram
16 drams	=	1 ounce
16 ounces	=	1 pound
2,000 pounds	=	1 ton (short)
2,240 pounds	=	1 ton (long)

Table B6 (cont)

Metric Equivalents

Capacity

1 U.S. fluid ounce	=	29,573 milliliters
1 U.S. liquid quart	=	.946 liter
1 U.S. dry quart	=	1.101 liters
1 U.S. gallon	=	3,785 liters
1 U.S. bushel	=	.3524 hectoliters
1 cubic inch	=	16.4 cubic centimeters
1 liter	=	1,000 milliliters or 1,000 cubic centimeters
1 cubic foot water	=	7.43 gallons or 62-1/2 pounds
231 cubic inches	=	1 gallon
1 millimeter	=	.034 U.S. fluid ounce
1 liter	=	1.057 U.S. liquid quarts
1 liter	=	.908 U.S. dry quart
1 liter	=	.264 U.S. gallon
1 hectoliter	=	2.838 U.S. bushels
1 cubic centimeter	=	.061 cubic inch

Cubic measure (volume)

1,728 cubic inches	=	1 cubic foot
27 cubic feet	=	1 cubic yard
2,150.42 cubic inches	=	1 standard bushel
231 cubic inches	=	1 standard gallon (liquid)
1 cubic foot	=	4/5 of a bushel
128 cubic feet	=	1 cord (wood)
7.48 gallons	=	1 cubic foot
1 bushel	=	1.25 cubic feet

Table B7.

To Convert From	To	Multiply By
Acre feet	Gallons	325,851
Head (ft of water)	Pressure (lb/sq-in.)	0.434
Gallons	Cubic feet	0.133
Gallons	Pounds of water	8.33
Gallons per minute	Gallons per hour	60
Milligrams per liter	Parts per million	1
Pressure (lb/sq-in.)	Head (ft of water)	2.31
Cubic feet	Bushels ear corn	0.4
Sq ft 4″ floor	Cu yds concrete	0.0123
Sq ft 6″ floor	Cu yds concrete	0.0185

Board Foot = 1″ × 1′ × 1′ nominal dimensions.
Board Feet = thickness in inches × width in feet (4″ = 1/3′) × length in feet.
i.e.: 1 × 4 × 10′ = 1 × 1/3 × 10 = 3 1/3 fbm
2 × 6 × 12′ = 2 × 1/2 × 12 = 12 fbm

Table B-8

AREAS AND DIMENSIONS OF FARM VEHICLES AND EQUIPMENT

ITEM	Length* Ft.	Width Ft.	Height Ft.	Occupied Area** Sq. Ft.
Automobile	19	7	5	133
Truck—				
pickup, 8 foot box	17-1/2	6-1/2	6	104
livestock rack	26	8	10	208
grain bed	26	8	7	208
Tractor—				
Two Plow	10-1/2	7	6	53
Four Plow *(Case)*	11	8	8-1/2	60
Six Plow *(Case)*	14	8-1/2	10 w/cab	112
Eight Plow *(Case)*	16	9	10 w/cab	120
Crawler *(HD16 Allis-Chalmers)*	15-1/2	8	8	128
Plow, Tractor-drawn—				
two-furrow, mounted	5	3		12
three-furrow, mounted—no tail wheel	7	4-1/2		26
—with tail wheel	8	4-1/2		32
four-furrow, mounted	11-1/2	5		48
two-furrow, wheel type	12-1/2	5-1/2		50
three-furrow, wheel type	14-1/2	6-1/2		65
four-furrow, wheel type	16-1/2	7		92
five-furrow, mounted	13-1/2	9		
six-furrow, mounted	15	10		
seven-furrow, mounted	17	11		
eight-furrow, mounted	19	12-1/2		
Disc Harrow—				
8 ft. tractor-mounted	9-1/2	9	2-1/2	60
8 ft. transport-wheel type	10	9		65
10 ft. transport-wheel type	10-1/2	11		83
21 ft. Wing type	12	14	3	
Field Cultivator—				
8 ft. tractor-mounted	4	8		25
10 ft. tractor-mounted	6-1/2	10		48
Rotary Hoe	6	10	3	50

Table B-8

AREAS AND DIMENSIONS OF FARM VEHICLES AND EQUIPMENT

ITEM	Length* Ft.	Width Ft.	Height Ft.	Occupied Area** Sq. Ft.
Grain-Fertilizer Drill				
13 x 7, tractor-drawn	9	10	5-1/2	60
15 x 7, tractor-drawn	9	10	5-1/2	60
18 x 7, tractor-drawn	10	12-2/3	6	80
24 x 7, tractor-drawn	11	18	6	140
Forage Harvester				
tractor-drawn, 2-row corn head	15	9-1/2	10	136
windrow pickup attachment	6	6	4	27
Forage Blower, in transport position—				
Long hopper type	15-1/2	6	6	80
Short hopper type	8-1/2	5-1/2	6	47
Swather, self propelled—				
10 ft. cut	19	11-1/2	6-1/2	190
12 ft. cut	19	13-1/2	6-1/2	230
14 ft. cut	19	15-1/2	6-1/2	270
16 ft. cut	19	17-1/2	6-1/2	300
Combine, self propelled—				
10 ft. cut	23	11-1/2	13	250
12 ft. cut	23	13-1/2	13	270
14 ft. cut	23	15-1/2	13	290
16 ft. cut	23	18-1/2	13	310
18 ft. cut	26	20	16 w/cab***	
20 ft. cut	26	21	16 w/cab***	
24 ft. cut	26	25	16 w/cab***	
Combine, pull-type—				
6 ft. cut	22-1/2	11-1/2	10	220
10 ft. cut, tongue in transport position	22-1/2	11-1/2	10	220
Manure Spreader, tractor, 125 bu.	18-1/2	6-1/2	5-1/2	100
Feed Grinder-Mixer Unit				
tractor-drawn, p.t.o. driven	12-1/2	8-1/2	8-2/3	70
Bale Elevator, wheeled, 40 ft.	40	7-1/2		80

Table B-8

AREAS AND DIMENSIONS OF FARM VEHICLES AND EQUIPMENT

ITEM	Length* Ft.	Width Ft.	Height Ft.	Occupied Area** Sq. Ft.
Sugar Beet, Harvester,	14-1/2	19-1/2	13-1/2	
without elevator	14-1/2	14-1/2	4-1/2	210
Tomato Harvester, with canopy	23	10-1/2	11	230
(Less delivery and sorting platforms)				
Pickle Harvester, Transport	25-1/2	8	9	200
Peanut Combine	23-1/2	7-1/2	11	112
Cotton Stripper	23-1/2	9	13-1/2	168
Corn Planter				
2-row, tractor-mounted	6-1/2	5	6	30
4-row, tractor-mounted	6-1/2	12	9	78
4-row, tractor-mounted	10-1/2	12-14	9	90
Corn Planter—				
6-row, 42" rows	14	23		
8-row, 20" rows	14	21		
Potato Planter—				
2-row	10-1/2	6-1/2	5	60
4-row	11	13	5	132
Potato Harvester—				
Lockwood Markette	19	13	8 Boom Down	240
Lockwood Mark-aire	24-1/2	16-1/2	8 Boom Down	384
Allis Chalmers, 2-row	25	14-1/2	11-1/2	336
Lockwood M 600	25-1/2	16-1/2	10-1/2 Boom Down	420
Potato Sprayer—	13	8-1/2	7	110
Wheeleed Fertilizer Spreader—				
8-ft. spreading width	7	9-2/3		48
10-ft. spreading width	7	11-2/3		58

Table B-8

AREAS AND DIMENSIONS OF FARM VEHICLES AND EQUIPMENT

ITEM	Length* Ft.	Width Ft.	Height Ft.	Occupied Area** Sq. Ft.
Mower—				
tractor-drawn, 7 ft. bar up	7	7	7-1/2	28
tractor-rear-mounted, 7 ft. bar up	3	5	8	14
tractor-mid-mounted, 7 ft. bar down	5-1/2	10-1/2		26
rotary-Allis Chalmers	13	14	2-1/2	168
Hay Mower, Conditioner				
(New Holland)	7-1/2	8-1/2	3-1/2	56
(New Holland)	11-1/2	11-1/2	4	121
(Allis Chalmers)	12-1/2	12-1/2	6	120
Baler				
3 wire, New Holland	19-1/2	10-1/2	9	190
#303, Allis Chalmers	16	8-1/2	4-1/2	120
Haylner, New Holland	16-1/2	8-1/2	6-1/2	128
Bale Gatherer	22-1/2	12-1/2	14	264
Wagon				
Flat Platform	16	8	3	128
Self Unloading *(New Holland)*	23	8-1/2	12	176
V-Bottom Auger, 125 BU	10	6	12	54
Hopper, Dempster	14-1/2	7	7-1/2	98

*Length of machines includes the length of rigid draw tongues where used. The lengths of swinging tongues, such as on 4-wheeled farm wagons, are not included.

**Occupied area is not necessarily the product of length times width for all machines. Where the occupied area listed is less than the rectangular area, a deduction has been made for that part of the rectangular area, which could be used for other storage.

***A few current self-propelled combines are almost 16 ft. high. The majority of these machines are, however, 14 ft. high or less. Construction of implement storage to clear a combine 16 ft. high may not be necessary. Reference should be made to the specifications prepared by combine manufacturers.

Table B-9

```
AUGER    CONVEYORS  -  LIQUID    MANURE
          (11' length, tested with water)
```

4" Diameter

Speed rpm	Horse power	Angle degrees	Gallons per min.
1500	0.8	45	32
		60	17
		90	10
1700	1.6	45	48
		60	33
		90	19
1900	2.6	45	66
		60	51
		90	30

6" Diameter

Speed rpm	Horse power	Angle degrees	Gallons per min.
950	2.0	45	80
		60	40
		90	--
1150	2.8	45	180
		60	130
		90	85
1350	4.0	45	330
		60	255
		90	200

Liquid Manure with some solids: greater capacities than above, at same r.p.m. and horsepower. If length is doubled, required horsepower will double.

Consider a hydraulic motor off tractor hydraulic systems for auger drive. Power and speed can be adjusted on the tractor, and the light hydraulic motor is easy to handle.

Midwest Plan Service

Table B10. Weights of Commodities and Materials

Fruits and Vegetables

Commodity	Common measure	Weight, pounds	Pounds per cu. ft.
Apples	Northwest box (10 1/2 by 11 1/2 by 18)	44	38
	Eastern box (11 by 13 by 17)	54	
	Bushel	48	
Beets	Bushel	60	48
Carrots	Bushel	50	40
Onions	Bushel	57	45.6
Peaches	Bushel	48	36.4
Pears	Bushel	50	40
Peas	Bushel	60	48
Potatoes (Irish)	Bushel	60	48
Potatoes (sweet)	Bushel	50	40
Tomatoes	Bushel	60	48
Turnips	Bushel	55	44
Cherries	Box (3 3/4 by 11 1/2 by 14 1/8)	15	
	Bushel	64	51

Building and Other Materials

Commodity	Common measure	Weight, pounds	Pounds per cu. ft.
Brick	1,000	2.7 tons	
Cement	Barrel (4 bags)	376 lb.	99
Coal	Ton	2,000 lb	
Coal	Bushel	80 lb.	64
Cotton	Bale	500 lb.	
Cream	Gallon	8.4 lb.	62.9
Eggs	30-dozen crate	55–60 lb.	
Ice	Cubic foot		56
Kerosene	Barrel	385 lb.	
Lime	Barrel	320 lb.	
Lime	Bushel	75 lb.	60
Linseed Oil	Barrel	400 lb.	
Milk	Gallon	8.6 lb.	64.4
Milk	46.5 quarts	100 lb.	
Oil (fuel)	Barrel (42 gal.)	336 lb.	
Oil (fuel)	Gallon	8 lb.	
Salt	Barrel	280 lb.	
Sugar	Barrel	350 lb.	
Turpentine	Barrel	432 lb.	
Turpentine	Gallon	7.2 lb.	53.9
Vinegar	Barrel	400–500 lb.	
Water	Gallon	8.33 lb.	62.5

Table B11. Calculated Densities of Grain and Seeds Based on Weights and Measures Used in the Department of Agriculture

Grain or Seed	Unit	Approximate net weight, lb	Bulk density lb per cu ft
Alfalfa	bushel	60	48.0
Barley	bushel	48	38.4
Beans			
Lima, dry	bushel	56	44.8
Lima, unshelled	bushel	32	25.6
Snap	bushel	30	24.0
Other, dry	bushel	60	48.0
Other, dry	sack	100	48.0
Bluegrass	bushel	14–30	11.2–24.0
Broomcorn	bushel	44–50	35.2–40.0
Buckwheat	bushel	48–52	38.4–41.6
Castor beans	bushel	46	36.8
Clover	bushel	60	48.0
Corn:			
Ear, husked	bushel	70°	28.0
Shelled	bushel	56	44.8
Green sweet	bushel	35	28.0
Cottonseed	bushel	32	25.6
Cowpeas	bushel	60	48.0
Flaxseed	bushel	56	44.8
Grain sorghums	bushel	56 & 50	44.8 & 40.0
Hempseed	bushel	44	35.2
Hickory nuts	bushel	50	40.0
Hungarian millet	bushel	48 & 50	38.4 & 40.0
Katir	bushel	56 & 50	44.8 & 40.0
Kapok	bushel	35–40	28.0–32.0
Lentils	bushel	60	48.0
Millet	bushel	48–50	38.4–40.0
Mustard	bushel	58–60	46.4–48.00
Oats	bushel	32	25.6
Orchard grass	bushel	14	11.2
Peanuts, unshelled:			
Virginia type	bushel	17	13.6
Runners, Southeastern	bushel	21	16.8
Spanish			
Southeastern	bushel	25	19.7
Southwestern	bushel	25	19.8
Perilla	bushel	37–40	29.6–32.0
Popcorn:			
On ear	bushel	70°	28.0
Shelled	bushel	56	44.8
Poppy	bushel	46	36.8
Rapeseed	bushel	50 & 60	40.0 & 48.0
Redtop	bushel	50 & 60	40.0 & 48.0
Rice, rough	bushel	45	36.0
Rice, rough	bag	100	36.0
Rice, rough	barrel	162	36.0
Rye	bushel	56	44.8
Sesame	bushel	46	36.8
Sorgo	bushel	50	40.0
Soybeans	bushel	60	48.0
Spelt (p. wheat)	bushel	40	32.0
Sudan grass	bushel	40	32.0
Sunflower	bushel	24 & 32	19.2 & 25.6

Table B11 (cont)

Grain or Seed	Unit	Approximate net weight, lb	Bulk density lb per cu ft
Timothy	bushel	45	36.0
Velvet beans (hulled)	bushel	60	48.0
Vetch	bushel	60	48.0
Walnuts	bushel	50	40.0
Wheat	bushel	60	48.0

°The standard weight of 70 lb is usually recognized as being about two measured bushels of corn, husked, on the ear, because it requires 70 lb to yield 1 bu. or 56 lb of shelled corn.

SOURCE: ASAE Data: ASAE D241.1, 1967.

Table B12. Approximate Storage Requirements of Feed

Material	lb/cu ft	cu ft/ton
Alfalfa meal	15	134
Alfalfa, chopped	12	170
Barley meal	28	72
Barley, whole	38	53
Beet pulp, dried	15	134
Bran	16	125
Brewers grains, dry	15	134
Buckwheat bran	15	134
Buckwheat middlings	23	88
Coconut meal	38	53
Concentrates, typical	45	45
Corn meal	38	53
Corn & cob meal, dry	36	56
Cotton seed meal	38	53
Distillers' grains, dry	15	134
Gluten feed	33	61
Gluten meal	46	45
Hominy meal	28	72
Kaffir meal	27	74
Lime	60	33
Linseed meal	23	88
Malt sprouts	15	134
Mixed mill feed (bran & middlings)	15	134
Molasses	78	26
Molasses beet pulp	20	100
Meat scraps	34	59
Oats, ground	18–20	111–100
Rice bran	20	100
Rice polish	31	65
Salt, fine	50	40
Soybean meal	42	48
Tankage	32	63
Wheat bran	14	154
Wheat feed, mixed	15	134
Wheat, ground	45	46
Wheat middlings (Std)	20	100
Wheat screenings	27	77
Pellets, mixed feed	35–40	57–60
Pellets, ground hay	38–45	53–44

SOURCE: Based primarily on California Agricultural Circular 517.

Table B13. Approximate Storage Space Requirements for Silage and High Moisture Corn

Material Description	lb/cu ft	cu ft/ton
Corn shelled:		
25% moisture	43.1	46
30% moisture	39.7	51
Corn and cob meal:		
30% moisture	38.5	52
Silage:		
upright silo	40°	50
horizontal silo	35°	60
spread in bunk	25°	80

°Silage densities and weights are highly variable, depending on material, cut, moisture content and depth in the silo.

SOURCE: Purdue University AE Data: 2.4.

Table B14. Storage Space Requirements for Feed and Bedding

CROP	Lbs/ Bu	Lbs/ Cu Ft	Freshly Ground Lbs/ Bu	Freshly Ground Lbs/ Cu Ft	Hay-Straw	Cu Ft/ Ton	Lb/ Cu Ft
Corn 15 1/2%						LOOSE	
Shelled	56	44.8	48	38	Alfalfa	450-500	4.4-4
Ear	70	28.0	45	36	Non legume	450-600	4.4-3.3
Corn 30%	(Amounts to yield a bu or c ft						
	of 15 1/2% grain.)				Straw	670-1000	3-2
Shelled	67.5	54.0					
Ear, ground			89.6	35.8		BALED	
Barley 15%	48	38.4	37	28	Alfalfa	200-330	10-6
Flax 11%	56	44.8			Non legume	250-330	8-6
Grain							
Sorghum 15%	56	44.8			Straw	400-500	5-4
Oats 16%	32	25.6	23	18	CUT CHOPPED		
Rye 16%	56	44.8	48	38	Alfalfa 1 1/2"	285-360	7-5.5
Soybeans 14%	60	48.0			Non legume 3"	300-400	6.7-5
Wheat 14%	60	48.0	50	43	Straw	250-350	8-5.7

MWPS-15, Midwest Plan Service.

Table B15.   Angles of Repose and Some Coefficients of Friction for Clean and Dry Grains[1]

| Grain | Angles of repose | | Average coefficients of friction of grain on | | | | Wall board | |
	Emptying or funneling	Filling or piling	Smooth shiny tin	Smooth side Prestwood	Across grain of plywood	Rough side asbestos cement	Gypsum	Insulite
	Deg.	Deg.						
Rough rice (paddy)	36	20	0.479	0.554	0.530	0.368	0.637	0.662
Grain sorghum	33	20	.372	.306	.294	.331	.396	.321
Oats	32	18	.445	.398	.380	.362	.442	.429
Soybeans	29	16	.368	.295	.312	.301	.379	.306
Barley:								
Two row	28	16	.404	.264	.311	.308	.380	.360
Six row	28	16	.378	.266	.287	.298	.344	.354
Wheat:								
Hard red spring	28	17	.366	.335	.298	.333	.394	.325
Hard red winter	27	16	.340	.306	.294	.323	.392	.287
Soft red winter	27	16	.356	.306	.277	.292	.372	.300
Corn	27	16	.447	.306	.302	.264	.416	.257
Wheat, Durum	26	17	.414	.321	.321	.323	.418	.311
Rye	26	17	.406	.324	.330	.354	.398	.350
Flaxseed	25	14	.372	.300	.275	.323	.319	.350
Vetch	25	14	.327	.255	.249	.242	.340	.270

[1] Results of tests made in Grain Storage Laboratory, Ames, Iowa.

Table B16.   Approximate Capacity for Corn Silage in Trench or Bunker Silos with Sides Sloped Outward 1 1/2 Inches for Each Foot of Depth

| Bottom width | Approximate tons per foot of length Depth—feet | | | | |
(feet)	8	10	12	16	20
20	3.1	4.0			
30	4.6	5.9	7.1	9.6	
40	6.1	7.7	9.3	12.6	16.0
50	7.6	9.6	11.6	15.6	19.8
60		11.5	13.8	18.6	23.6
70			16.1	21.6	27.4
80			18.3	24.6	31.0
100				30.6	38.6

Materials Handled per Animal

Developing a farmstead by focusing on the handling of materials provides efficient labor organization and economy of investment—develop the handling system, then build the building to fit.

The following tables can be used as a guide to determine the amount of material that must be handled for different animals for average to above average performance. For the purpose of estimating storage needs and daily handling requirements, adjustments would be needed to fit specific feeding and operating practices.

Table B-17

DAIRY CATTLE
Estimated Hay and Silage Requirements for Holstein Cows*

Feeding Program		Fed Daily		Grain (Avg.)	Annual					
					240 days			365 days		
Hay	Sil.	Hay	Sil.		Hay	Sil.	Hay Eq.	Hay	Sil.	Hay Eq.
%	%	lb.	lb.		Tons			Tons		
25	75	10	80	12	1.2	9.0	4.4	2.0	14.6	6.7
50	50	20	60	12	2.4	7.2	4.8	3.7	10.9	7.2
75	25	30	36	12	3.6	4.3	5.1	5.5	6.6	7.7
100	—	43	—	12	5.2	—	5.2	7.9	—	7.9

*Approximately 1300 lb. body weight and 11000 lbs. milk production
  Grain ration - 3000 to 4000 lbs.
*Estimates do not include young stock
  Hay equivalent (hay eq.) can be estimated on the basis of 3 lb. of hay per hundred lbs. of body weight
  One ton of hay is equivalent to 3 tons of silage

Table B-18

ESTIMATED FEED REQUIREMENTS FOR YOUNG STOCK

Age	Milk or Equivalent	Hay	Grain
1-12 Mo.	5 cwt.	2 T	6 cwt.
12-24 Mo.		4.5 T or 2.5 T and 5 Mo. pasture	

Table B-19

BEEF STEER AND HEIFERS

	Annual				Daily			
	Hay	Sil.	Corn	Sup.	Hay	Sil.	Corn	Sup.
400 lb. steer calves fed to choice (10 Mo.)	600#	4 T	30 Bu	450#	2#	26#	5.6#	1.5#
400 lb. heifer calves fed to choice (8 Mo.)	500#	3 T	22 Bu	350#	3#	25#	5.1#	1.5#
400 lb. steer calves fed to good								
11 Mo.	2½T		25 Bu		14#		5#	
7 Mo. lot and 60 day pasture	½ T	4 T	8 Bu	400#	4.8#	38#		2.0#
650 lb. (yearling) (8 Mo.)	600#	4 T	30 Bu	350#	2.5#	33#	7#	1.4#

* Table refers to corn, silage, and 15% shelled corn and 44% supplement

* 1.2 Bu of 30% shelled or ear corn replace 1 Bu of 15% corn
   8 Bu of 15% ground ear corn replace 1 T of 70% corn silage
   9 Bu of 15% ground shelled corn replaces 1 T of 70% corn silage

Table B-20

BEEF COW AND CALF PROGRAM

	Hay		Oats	
	Annual	Daily	Total	Daily
Cow	2-1/4 T	20# - 9 Mo. Feed and 5 Mo. Pasture		
Replacement Heifer	1-1/2 T	15#	12 Bu.	3# - Jan 1 to pasture
Bull	2-3/4 T	25# (220 days)	10 Bu.	5# (April and May)

Table B-21

SWINE

	Annual		Daily	
	Corn	Supplement	Corn	Supplement
Sow and litter *(2)*	37	840	6-12 lbs.	1-2 lbs.
Pigs — 40 to 215 lbs.	10	110	3-7	1-2 lbs.
Boar *(365 days)*	32	175		

POULTRY

	Annual		Daily	
	Corn	Supplement	Corn	Supplement
Laying hen	65-70	25-20	2/10	1/10

SHEEP

	Annual			Daily	
	Hay	Grain	Pasture	Hay	Grain
Ewe	600 lbs.	1-2 Bu.	1/4 acre	4# Dec. 1 May 1	3/4# average 6 weeks before and 6 weeks after lambing
Feeder lambs *(30 lb. gain)*	120 lbs. *(Approx.)*	120 lbs. *(Approx.)*		Daily— 90 days	

BEDDING

Dairy cow	1-1/2 T	8-12 lbs.
Beef cow	1/3 T	3 lb. *(used for heifers and bull)*
Beef calf *(400-1000 lbs.)*	1/2 T	3 lb.
Sow litter		
Pig *(50-200 lbs.)*		
Ewe	50 lbs.	
Hen		

Vertical Silo Storage and Feeding Data for Beef-Type Animals

The following tables are presented to assist in planning for the necessary storage facilities for beef-type feeder operations. Table B22 relates the daily corn silage—high moisture corn ration requirements to beef-type feeder animals. Table B24 is designed as an aid for determining maximum silo diameters for varying sizes of herds and corn silage consumption. Table B25 is provided to aid in determining silo diameter to minimum daily removal for specific design situations not covered in Table B24. A silo capacity chart is presented in Table B23.

Table B-22

BEEF-TYPE CATTLE STORAGE REQUIREMENTS
BASED ON A CORN SILAGE – HIGH MOISTURE CORN PROGRAM

RATION	DAILY CONSUMPTION PER ANIMAL	STORAGE CAPACITY REQUIREMENTS FOR VARIOUS SIZED HERDS			
		100	200	500	1,000
CORN SILAGE	POUNDS	TONS	TONS	TONS	TONS
300-400 lb. Animal	12-16	3/4	1-1/2	3-3/4	7-1/2
500-600	20-24	1-1/4	2-1/2	6-1/4	12-1/2
700-800	28-32	1-3/4	3-1/2	8-3/4	17-3/4
900-1000	36-40	2-1/4	4-1/2	11-1/4	22-1/2
HIGH MOISTURE CORN	POUNDS [1]	POUNDS	POUNDS	POUNDS	POUNDS
300-400 lb. Animal	3-4	400	800	2000	4000
500-600	5-6	600	1200	3000	6000
700-800	7-8	800	1600	4000	8000
900-1000	9-10	1000	2000	5000	10000

[1] Figures in this table refer to 15% dry corn equivalent *(multiply by 1.22 for high moisture corn basis.)*

The following table and curves shows capacities of large silos based on data at the Minnesota Experiment Station. This data dealt with storages up to 20 feet in diameter and 40 feet high. No test work has been reported for larger silos. Capacities in these tables have been computed for silos up to 30' by 70'.

Capacities shown allow 1 foot of unused depth for settling on silos up to 30 feet high, and 1 added foot for each ten feet over 30. So a 60-foot silo would have 4 feet of unused depth.

Table below gives capacities for silos at height intervals of 10 feet. Figure 1—a graph of the same data—allows interpolation for silos of odd-numbered heights.

Table B-23

SILO CAPACITY IN TONS*

Silo Height in Feet	Inside Diameter of Silo										
	10'	12'	14'	16'	18'	20'	22'	24'	26'	28'	30'
20	33	48	66	86							
30	56	80	109	143	180	223	270	321	377		
40	77	110	150	196	248	307	371	442	520	600	690
50			193	252	320	394	477	570	668	773	886
60					392	483	585	697	818	947	1087
70						574	694	827	970	1125	1290

* Corn or grass silage of the same moisture content.

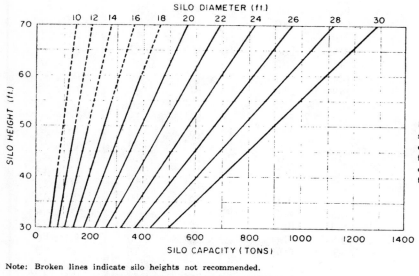

Example: Capacity of a 24' x 55' silo: Follow the curve from 24' diameter until it crosses the horizontal line from 55' height. Move down vertically and read tons capacity, 630 tons, on the horizontal axis.

Note: Broken lines indicate silo heights not recommended.

SILO CAPACITY IN TONS

Relating Silo Capacity to Herd Size

Silo capacities are usually based on a minimum removal of inches of silage per day. The following table is a guide for various herd sizes and feeding rates. It gives sizes for both 8-month and 12-month feeding programs.

Size is given for two silos rather than one in the 360-day feeding period. This size is recommended to remove silage fast enough to prevent spoilage.

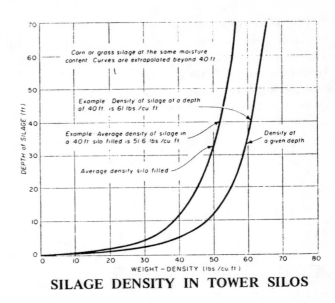

SILAGE DENSITY IN TOWER SILOS

Table B-24

PLANNING SILO CAPACITY TO HERD SIZE

Pounds per Animal per day					Total Pounds	FEEDING Period			
						240 Days		360 Days	
40	50	60	70	80	per	Total	Silo	Total	Silo[1]
		Number of Animals			day	Tons	Size	Tons	Size
20	—	—	—	—	800	96	12 x 36'	144	12 x 30'
—	—	15	—	—	900	108	12 x 40'	162	12 x 32'
25	20	—	15	—	1000	120	14 x 34'	180	12 x 34'
30	25	20	—	15	1200	144	16 x 32'	216	14 x 30'
35	—	—	20	—	1400	168	16 x 36'	252	14 x 34'
—	30	25	—	—	1500	180	16 x 38'	270	14 x 36'
40	—	—	—	20	1600	192	16 x 40'	288	16 x 32'
—	35	30	25	—	1800	216	16 x 44'	324	16 x 34'
50	40	—	—	25	2000	240	16 x 48'	360	16 x 38'
—	—	35	30	—	2100	252	18 x 40'	378	16 x 40'
60	—	40	35	30	2400	288	18 x 46'	432	18 x 36'
—	50	—	—	—	2500	300	18 x 48'	450	18 x 36'
—	—	—	40	35	2800	336	20 x 44'	504	18 x 42'
75	60	50	—	—	3000	360	20 x 46'	540	18 x 44'
—	—	—	—	40	3200	384	22 x 42'	576	20 x 38'
—	—	—	50	—	3500	420	22 x 44'	630	20 x 42'
—	—	60	—	—	3600	432	22 x 46'	648	20 x 44'
—	75	—	—	—	3800	456	22 x 48'	684	22 x 38'
100	—	—	—	50	4000	480	22 x 50'	720	22 x 40'
—	—	—	60	—	4200	504	24 x 44'	756	22 x 42'
—	—	75	—	—	4500	540	24 x 48'	810	22 x 44'
—	—	—	—	60	4800	576	24 x 50'	864	22 x 46'
—	100	—	—	—	5000	600	24 x 52'	900	22 x 48'
—	—	—	75	—	5200	624	24 x 54'	936	22 x 50'
—	—	100	—	75	6000	720	26 x 54'	1080	24 x 48'

1 Size given is for 2 silos of equal size

Table B-25

DATA ON VERTICAL SILO CAPACITY
FOR DETERMINING MINIMUM DAILY REMOVAL

SILO DIAMETER	VOLUME PER FOOT OF DEPTH (CU. FT.)	AMOUNT OF SILAGE IN 2" LAYER BASED ON 40# /CU. FT.
12	113.1	755
14	153.9	1,025
16	201.1	1,340
18	254.5	1,696
20	314.2	2,094
22	380.1	2,534
24	452.4	3,015
26	530.9	3,539
28	615.8	4,105
30	706.9	4,712
34	908.0	6,053
38	1134.1	7,560
42	1385.4	9,235
50	1963.5	13,089
60	2827.4	18,847

Table B-26

RELATING DAILY BEEF FEEDER SILAGE REQUIREMENTS
TO SILO SIZE

NUMBER OF ANIMALS CONSUMING CORN SILAGE POUNDS PER ANIMAL PER DAY								DAILY CONSUMPTION		Maximum Silo Diameter Based On Minimum Removal Of 2" Per Day
15	20	25	30	35	40	45	50	POUNDS	TONS	
—	100	80	—	—	50	—	40	2,000	1	20
200	150	120	100	—	75	—	60	3,000	1-1/2	24
—	200	160	—	—	100	—	80	4,000	2	28
—	250	200	—	—	125	—	100	5,000	2-1/2	30
400	300	—	200	—	150	—	120	6,000	3	34
—	350	280	—	200	175	—	140	7,000	3-1/2	34
—	—	320	—	—	200	—	160	8,000	4	38
—	—	360	300	—	225	200	180	9,000	4-1/2	38
—	500	400	—	—	250	—	200	10,000	5	42
—	625	500	—	—	—	—	250	12,000	6-1/4	42
1000	750	600	500	—	375	—	300	15,000	7-1/2	50
—	875	700	—	500	—	—	350	17,000	8-3/4	50
—	1000	800	—	—	500	—	400	20,000	10	60
1500	1125	900	—	—	—	500	450	22,500	11-1/4	—
—	1250	1000	—	—	625	—	500	25,000	12-1/2	—
2000	1500	1200	1000	—	750	—	600	30,000	15	—
—	1750	1400	—	1000	—	—	700	35,000	17-1/2	—
—	2000	—	—	—	1000	—	800	40,000	20	—
—	2250	—	—	—	—	1000	900	45,000	22-1/2	—
—	2500	2000	—	—	—	—	1000	50,000	25	—

High Moisture Corn Storage Space
Requirements for Beef-Type Feeder Programs

The recommended ration for finishing beef-type animals *(400 lb.)* to the grade of choice *(1000 lb.)* is as follows:

> 4-1/2 tons Corn Silage *(30% D.M.)*
>   28 lb. daily
> 32 bu. shelled corn *(15% moisture)*
>   6 lb. daily
> 300 lb. 64% protein supplement
>   1 lb. daily

In order to determine the high moisture corn storage space requirements, it is necessary to convert the 15% dry corn to a 30% high moisture corn basis. Equivalents are as follows:

> 32 bu. or 1792 lb. 15% shelled corn
> approximately equivalent are
> 39 bu. or 2193 lb. 30% H.M. corn

The following Tables B27 and B28 are presented to assist in planning for the necessary high moisture corn storage facilities for a beef-type feeder operation.

Table B27 relates the feed storage requirements for finishing 400 lb. beef-type animals to choice 1000 lb. animals. Table B28 relates the daily consumption of high moisture corn to various sized herds and silo diameters.

Table B-27

FEED STORAGE REQUIREMENTS FOR
BEEF-FEEDER TYPE ANIMALS FED TO CHOICE [1]

RATION	PER UNIT	HERD SIZE, NUMBER OF ANIMALS			
		100	200	500	1,000
Corn Silage	4½ t.	450 t.	900 t.	2,250 t.	4,500 t.
High Moisture Corn	50 cu. ft.	5,000 cu. ft.	10,000 cu. ft.	25,000 cu. ft.	50,000 cu. ft.
(30% Moisture)	2,193 lb.	110 t.	220 t.	550 t.	1,100 t.
64% Prot. Supplement	300 lb.	15 t.	30 t.	75 t.	150 t.

[1] 400 lb. Beef-Feeder Type to 1000 lb. Choice Animals.

Table B-28

RELATING DAILY BEEF-FEEDER HIGH MOISTURE CORN REQUIREMENTS TO SILO SIZE[2]

NUMBER OF ANIMALS CONSUMING 30% HIGH MOISTURE CORN POUNDS PER ANIMAL PER DAY				DAILY CONSUMPTION		MAXIMUM SILO DIAMETER BASED ON A MINIMUM REMOVAL OF 2" PER DAY
5	7½[3]	10	12½	POUNDS	TONS	
100	—	50	40	500	1/4	10'
150	100	75	60	750	3/8	12
200	—	100	80	1,000	1/2	14
250	—	125	100	1,250	5/8	14
300	200	150	120	1,500	3/4	16
400	—	200	160	2,000	1	18
500	—	250	200	2,500	1-1/4	22
600	400	300	240	3,000	1-1/2	24
750	500	375	300	3,750	1-7/8	26
1,000	—	500	400	5,000	2-1/2	30
1,250	—	650	500	6,250	3-1/8	—
1,500	1,000	750	600	7,500	3-3/4	—
2,000	—	1,000	800	10,000	5	—
2,500	—	1,250	1,000	12,500	6-1/4	

[2] Based on a high moisture corn density of 40 pounds per cubic foot.
The average density in a 30' depth is 46 pounds.

[3] The average daily consumption of H. M. Corn over the period from 400 to 1000 lb. beef-type animal.

The Occupational Safety and Health Act of 1970 which went into effect on April 17, 1971 applies to all non-governmental employees except those already covered by other safety laws such as railroaders and miners. This new law also covers farmers if they employ even one man for as little as one day, according to the Department of Labor. So, the structures you build for farmers must be within the provisions of this complex law or your customers will be in difficulty. Of course, your own operation must also comply.

The objective of the Act is "to assure safe and healthful working conditions for working men and women; by authorizing enforcement of the standards developed under the Act; by assisting and encouraging the States in their efforts . . .; by providing for research, information, education and training in the field of occupational safety and health; and for other purposes."

Recordkeeping Requirements
During the summer of 1971 every employer filing social security benefits for employees received a booklet, "Recordkeeping Requirements Under the Act." If you have misplaced this booklet or don't recall receiving it, get a replacement immediately. Many banks, county agent's offices and attorneys have extra copies. Or, you can contact your nearest area OSHA office. These same offices can supply copies of standards, reprints of the law and they welcome questions on compliance. They can not advise you as to whether your operation complies with the law except during an official inspection.

Here is what you *must* do under the recordkeeping portion of OSHA:

1. Display the centerpiece poster that comes in the recordkeeping booklet. This must be posted where employees normally gather or work.
2. OSHA Form No. 100, the next one in the booklet, is a log of occupational injuries and illnesses. Each recordable work injury or illness connected with the job must be entered on this log within 6 days of receiving information that the incident has occurred. The booklet defines "recordable" accidents.
3. OSHA Form No. 102 is a summary of occupational injuries and illnesses and must be prepared within one month following the end of each calendar year. This summary must then be posted for all employees to see. Alongside the centerpiece poster would be a good place. The summary must be left up for a minimum of 30 days. If you've had no "recordable" accidents or illnesses you'll still need to post the form or a notice to that effect.
4. OSHA Form No. 101 is a supplementary record of occupational injuries and illnesses and must be kept on file for each recordable injury or illness. Most Workman's Compensation Insurance reports will be accepted as a substitute for OSHA Form No. 101. Just make sure it contains the same information. Some builders may be requested to submit these supplemental reports to the Bureau of Labor Statistics for study of accident causes and rates.

Inspections
Any employer can be visited at any reasonable time by a Compliance Officer (inspector) to make sure that your operation meets the requirements of the law. He can levy a fine for not having

the poster displayed or not having your records up to date. However, his main interest will be in the safety of your employees on the job.

The inspectors will be concentrating on businesses that have experienced a fatal accident. Any such accident must be reported to your nearest OSHA office within 48 hours. This can be done orally. The same 48 hour notification also applies to any accident that hospitalizes 5 or more workers.

Next highest priority will be follow-up on complaints from employees. The visit will be without advance warning. In fact, a stiff fine can be inflicted on any individual who gives advance warning of a safety and health inspection.

If you should be inspected, be courteous and cooperative and show a desire to promote safety in your business. He'll probably notice, but it won't do any harm to point out the efforts you've made to make the operation safer.

If the inspector finds a violation of the Act he will issue a citation and set a fine. You will usually be given a certain amount of time to correct the situation. Failure to meet the deadline will result in even stiffer fines, usually per day until the violation is corrected. You can appeal the citation but this is a long and complicated process.

How to Comply
OSHA recommends following this outline for your compliance program. They recommend:

1. Familiarize certain people in your business both at the management and worker level with the Act in depth. Keep them informed of changes and additions in the standards and administration. Determine who shall go with the compliance officer should you be inspected.
2. Go over the safety and health conditions in your operation very critically. Consider the shop, warehouse, vehicles, as well as the field crew operations.
3. Where you see the need for strengthening the safety of your operation, make the change whether covered by an existing standard or not.
4. Get acquainted with the state program and what your state officials are doing in safety and health. Stay in touch with them.
5. If you have a large operation, designate one of your management team to maintain liaison

with OSHA in your region. Let OSHA know who this person is. Ask for any documents that relate to your operation.
6. Hold regular meetings of the entire management team to keep everybody up to date on OSHA requirements.
7. Study standards in effect, and future standards as they take effect. Think in terms of how they apply to your operation.
8. Develop and maintain an effective internal safety training program for all employees, especially the new hires.
9. Participate in your industry groups in their safety and health activities. Work with the committees that are involved in safety.
10. Cooperate when you are asked to help draft new or revised safety standards.
11. Set specific safety goals for your business. Cutting last year's accidents by one half would be a reasonable goal.

What to Look for in General
First of all, make sure that the poster is up in a place where it can be seen by all of the employees. Several employers report $50 fines for failing to have the poster displayed.

Sanitary conditions—will be high on the list of some of the inspectors. Hot as well as cold water in washrooms is one of the things for which they will be looking. Washroom containers must be covered. Food and lunches must be stored elsewhere. Drinking water and toilet facilities must be located within 200 feet of where employees normally work. If you have employees of both sexes, separate facilities must be provided.

Fire extinguishers—to be effective, must be easy to locate and reach. In shop, warehouse or office they should be mounted in front of a red background. The top of the extinguisher must be no more than 5 feet above the floor so that it can easily be reached. An inspector will check the tag for the last time the unit was inspected and/or tested. This must be done at least yearly.

Tools—Portable power tools must be grounded unless they are double insulated. Your wiring must be installed according to the National Electric Code. Three prong plug outlets will be required by the inspector. Make sure that hand tools like chisels and punches do not have "mushroomed" heads. If you use compressed air for cleaning around saws, drills or in the repair shop, the nozzle must have a device to limit the air pressure to 30 PSI or less.

Any belt driven tools or machines must have the belts guarded or be placed so that the employees can not accidentally get their hands in the belts while working. Guards must not only be available but must be in use at the time of inspection.

Power tools may no longer be equipped with an automatic "on" trigger. These can usually be easily deactivated.

Personal protective equipment—needs to be suited to the jobs being done. Hard hats will be required wherever there is danger of falling objects or blows to the head. All field construction crews will surely be required to wear head protection.

Anyone using grinders, mechanical breaking hammers or other tools that could trigger an eye damaging accident will have to be wearing safety glasses or goggles. Painters using spray equipment will be using masks. Field crews will be required to wear shoes with steel toe caps and perhaps even puncture resistant innersoles.

Sound levels may be measured and if employees are working in noise of over 90 decibels all day, they must have ear protection such as muffs or plugs.

Excavations—must now be shored or sloped back to less than the angle of repose of the soil. The minimum slope in soil is 6 inches back for each foot of depth. Soil must be stored at least 2 feet back from the bank. The regulations apply to any trench 5 feet or more deep.

Roll-Over Protective Structures (ROPS)—will be required on all tractors and mobile material handling equipment used in construction on a schedule depending on the age of the machine. All equipment manufactured on or after September 1, 1972 will be so equipped at the factory. If you buy an agricultural tractor to use in construction, it too will have to have the ROPS if it is new. The schedule for having the older equipment protected appears in Subpart W, Par. 1926.1000 c. Machines manufactured before 1969

are presently (1972) exempted from the ROPS requirement.

Shop-made ROPS will not qualify unless an identical frame has passed the tests described in the OSHA standards in Subpart W.

Miscellaneous items—are too numerous to list here. Knowledge of the actual standards is the only way to stay on top of the occupational safety situation. But, here are a few obvious conditions that should be corrected if they exist around shop, warehouse or job site.

* First aid kits must be well stocked. Don't try to get by with a box of adhesive bandages.
* Ladders must be in top shape. Destroy or repair any ladder that has any sign of weakness. All straight ladders must have safety feet.
* If you have a stairway, even one to a seldom used loft, it must be capable of carrying not less than 1,000 pounds or up to 5 times the maximum amount of load it might be called on to hold. Hand rails are required.
* Loading docks must have protective railings and toe boards plus guard rails on ramps and steps.
* Hallways, storerooms and all work areas must be clean, orderly and properly lighted. Exits must be marked with "lighted" signs.

Complaints, How They are Handled

If any employee feels he is working under unsafe conditions, he can make a complaint in writing to OSHA. The names of complainers do not have to be revealed and they are protected against any reprisal by the law. Also, a worker can complain orally during an actual inspection.

The Act requires that employees follow safety rules but there is no provision for enforcing such rules. Labor safety officials do suggest that compliance with all safety rules be enforced by making them a condition of employment. Failure of the employee to comply is sufficient cause for dismissal. Heavy construction has made this approach work over the last several years, especially in the area of hard hats.

Variances

If you feel that a standard under the act would force an undue hardship on your company or that you have solved the safety problem in a better way, you may ask for a "variance" from the rules. You can apply for this written permission to operate outside the rules by following the procedures in part 1905 of Title 29, USC 65 (Williams Stieger Occupational Safety and Health Act).

A Farm Builder's Safety Inspection Check List
The following outline is offered only as a guide for your own check list which you should develop for your own operation. Ask your insurance carrier for assistance in developing and carrying out the regular evaluations needed to keep your business a safe place to work.

1. Accident Prevention Program:
   a. Schedule for posting safety notices and reminders.
   b. Protective equipment requirements.
   c. Safety meetings scheduled and held.
2. Housekeeping and Sanitation:
   a. General neatness of working area.
   b. Regular disposal of waste and trash.
   c. Walkways clear.
   d. Adequate light.
   e. Tripping hazards and protruding nails removed.
   f. Waste containers provided and used.
   g. Sanitary facilities adequate and clean.
   h. Drinking water safe and in good supply.
   i. Drinking cups or sanitary bubblers for drinking.
3. First Aid:
   a. First aid station.
   b. First aid supplies.
   c. First aid instruction on the job.
   d. Telephone numbers and locations of nearby physicians.
   e. Telephone number and location of nearest hospital.
   f. Injuries reported promptly to proper persons.
4. Fire Prevention:
   a. Fire fighting instructions to workers.
   b. Fire extinguishers identified, checked and lighted.
   c. Fire department phone number posted.
   d. Access to hydrants open.
   e. Good housekeeping.

   f. No Smoking Signs Posted and Enforced.
5. Electrical Installations:
   a. Adequate wiring, properly installed.
   b. Fuses or circuit breakers provided.
   c. Electrical hazards posted.
   d. Type 'C' fire extinguishers provided.
6. Hand Tools:
   a. Right tools used for each job.
   b. Orderly storage.
   c. Tools inspected and maintained regularly.
   d. Damaged tools repaired or replaced promptly.
7. Power Tools:
   a. Good housekeeping where tools are used.
   b. Tools and cords in good condition.
   c. Proper grounding, three wire cords.
   d. Employees trained in tool use.
   e. All guards used.
   f. Right tools used for the job.
8. Power Actuated Tools:
   a. Make sure all operators are qualified.
   b. Tools and charges protected from unauthorized use.
   c. Tools checked and in good working order.
   d. Safety goggles or face shields used.
9. Ladders:
   a. Stock ladders inspected and in good condition.
   b. Siderails on fixed ladders extend above top landing.
   c. Rungs not over 12 inches on center.
   d. Stepladders fully open when in use.
   e. Metal ladders not used around electrical hazards.
   f. Proper maintenance and storage.
10. Motor vehicles:
    a. Regular inspection and maintenance.
    b. Qualified operators.
    c. Weight limits and load sizes controlled.
    d. Personnel carried in a safe manner.
11. Handling and Storage of Materials:
    a. Neat storage area, open lanes.
    b. Materials neatly stacked.
    c. Stacks on firm footings, not too high.
    d. Men picking up loads properly.
    e. Traffic routing and control.
12. Excavation and Shoring:
    a. Shoring of adjacent structures.

b. Shoring and sheathing as needed for soil and depth.

c. Materials not too close to excavation.

d. Water controlled.

e. Equipment at a safe distance from edge.

f. Frequent inspection.

13. Flammable Gases and Liquids:

a. All containers clearly identified.

b. Proper storage practices observed.

c. Proper number and type of fire extinguishers.

14. Welding and cutting:

a. Qualified operators.

b. Screens and shields to protect bystanders.

c. Goggles, gloves and heavy clothing used.

d. Equipment in good operating condition.

e. Electrical equipment grounded.

f. Power cables protected and in good repair.

g. Fire extinguishers of proper type nearby.

h. Inspection for fire hazards.

i. Flammable materials protected.

j. Gas cylinders chained upright.

15. Steel and Truss Erection:

a. Safety nets on high work.

b. Hard hats, safety shoes used.

c. Taglines for tools.

d. Ladders, stairs or other access provided.

e. Hoisting apparatus checked.

16. Concrete Construction:

a. Forms properly installed and braced.

b. Shoring in place until strength is attained.

c. Mixing and transport equipment traffic planned.

d. Adequate runways.

17. Masonry:

a. Proper scaffolding.

b. Masonry saws properly equipped, dust protection used.

c. Safe hoisting equipment.

TERM	DEFINITION
AISI	American Iron and Steel Institute.
AISC	American Institute of Steel Construction.
Base Angle	An angle secured to the perimeter of the foundation to support and close wall panels.
Base Plate	A plate attached to the base of a column which rests on a foundation or other support, usually secured by anchor bolts.
Bay	The space between frame center lines or primary supporting members in the longitudinal direction of the building.
Beam	A primary structural member, usually horizontal, that is subjected to bending loads. There are three types, simple, continuous and cantilever.
Beam and Column	A primary structural system consisting of a series of rafter beams supported by columns. Often used as the end frame of a metal building.
Bearing Plate	A steel plate that is set on the top of a masonry support on which a beam or purlin can rest.
Bent	The main frame of a structural system.
BOCA	Building Officials and Code Administration.
Brace Rods	Rods used in roof and walls to transfer loads, such as wind loads, and seismic and crane thrusts to the foundations. (Also often used to plumb buildings but not designed to replace erection cables.)
Built-Up Section	A structural member, usually an "I" section, made from individual flat plates by welding them together.
Butt Plate	The end plate of a structural member usually used to rest against a like plate of another member in forming a connection. Sometimes called a splice plate.
"C" Section	A member formed from steel sheet in the shape of a block "C," that may be used either singularly or back to back.
Camber	A predetermined curvature designed into a structural member to offset the anticipated deflection when loads are applied.
Cap Plate	A plate located at the top of a column or end of a beam for capping the exposed end of the member.
Channel— Hot Rolled	A member formed while in a semi-molten state at the steel mill to a shape having standard dimensions and properties specified by AISC or the steel producer.

TERM	DEFINITION	TERM	DEFINITION
Clip	A plate or angle used to fasten two or more members together.	Door Guide	An angle or channel guide used to stabilize or keep plumb a sliding or rolling door during its operation.
Closure Strip	A resilient strip, formed by the contour of ribbed panels used to close openings created by joining metal panels and flashing.	Drift Pin	A tapered pin used during erection to align holes in steel members to be connected by bolting or riveting.
Cold Form	The process of using press brakes or rolling mills to cold form steel into desired shapes at room temperature.	Eave	The line along the sidewall formed by the intersection of the faces of the roof and wall panels.
Collateral Loads	A load, in addition to normal live, wind, or dead loads, intended to account for loads such as sprinklers, lighting, etc.	Eave Height	The vertical dimension from finished floor to the eave.
Column	A main structural member used in a vertical position on a building to transfer loads from main roof beams, trusses, or rafters to the foundation.	Eave Strut	A structural member at the eave to support roof panels and wall panels. It may also transmit wind forces from roof brace rods to wall brace rods.
Continuity	The terminology given to a structural system denoting the transfer of loads and stresses from member to member as if there were no connections.	Elastic Design	A design concept utilizing the proportional behavior of materials when all stresses are limited to specified allowable values.
Covering	The exterior cover for a building.	End Frame	A frame at the endwall of a building to support the roof load from one half the end bay.
Curtain Wall	Perimeter wall panels which carry only their own weight and wind load.	Fascia	A decorative trim or panel projecting from the face of a wall.
Dead Load	The dead load of a building is the weight of all permanent construction, such as supported floors, roof, framing and covering members.	Finial	Gable closure at ridge.
		Fixed Base	A column base that is designed to resist rotation as well as horizontal or vertical movement.
Deflection	The displacement of a structural member or system under load.	Flange	The projecting edge of a structural member.
Design Loads	Those loads specified in building codes published by federal, state, or city agencies, or in owner's specifications to be used in the design of a building.	Flange Brace	A bracing member used to provide lateral support to the flange of a beam or girder.
Diaphragm Action	The resistance to racking generally offered by the covering system.	Force	The action of one body on another body which changes or tends to change its state of rest or motion. A force may be expressed in pounds, kips or other similar units and may act in any one of the following ways:

TERM	DEFINITION	TERM	DEFINITION
	a. Compression force: Is a force acting on a body tending to compress the body. (Pushing action).		commodate the high stress at such points. (Usually occurs at connection of column and rafter.)
	b. Shear force: Is a force acting on a body which tends to slide one portion of the body against the other side of the body. (Sliding action).	High Strength Bolts	Any bolt made from steel having a tensile strength in excess of 100,000 pounds per square inch. Some examples are: ASTM A-325, A-354, A-449, A-490.
	c. Tension force: Is a force acting on a body tending to elongate the body. (Pulling action).	Hinged Base	See "Pin Connection."
		High Strength Steel	Structural steel having a yield stress in excess of 36,000 pounds per square inch.
	d. Torsion force: Is a force acting on a body which tends to twist the body.	Hood (Door)	The metal flashing used over exterior slide door track along the full length of the door header to protect the tracks from weather and to conceal them for aesthetic purposes.
Framing	The primary and secondary members (columns, rafters, girts, purlins, brace rods, etc.) which go together to make up the skeleton of a structure to which the covering can be applied.	Hot-Rolled Shapes	Steel sections (angles, channels, I-beams, etc.) which are formed by rolling mills while the steel is in a semi-molten state.
Gable	A triangular portion of the end-wall of a building directly under the sloping roof and above the eave height line.	Impact Load	An assumed dynamic load resulting from the motion of machinery, elevators, craneways, vehicles, and other similar moving forces.
Gable Roof	A ridged roof that terminates in gables.	Jack Beam	A beam used to support another beam or truss and eliminate a column support.
Gage	The numerical designation for the thickness of sheet steel.	Jack Truss	A truss used to support another truss or beam and eliminate a column support.
Girder	A main horizontal or near horizontal structural member that supports vertical loads. It may consist of several pieces.	Kip	A unit of measure equal to 1,000 pounds.
Girt	A secondary horizontal structural member attached to sidewall or endwall columns to which wall covering is attached and supported horizontally.	Knee (or Haunch)	The connecting area of a column and rafter of a structural frame such as a rigid frame.
Gusset Plate	A steel plate used to distribute loads.	Knee Brace	A diagonal brace designed to resist horizontal loads usually from wind or moving equipment. This member normally has the lower end connected to a column and the upper end
"H" Section	A steel member with an H cross section.		
Haunch	The deepened portion of a column or rafter, designed to ac-		

TERM	DEFINITION	TERM	DEFINITION
	connected to a rafter or eave strut.		gable buildings with interior posts are examples.
Lean-To	A structure such as a shed, having only one slope or pitch and depending upon another structure for partial support.	Peak	The uppermost point of a gable.
		Peak Sign	A sign attached to the peak of the building at the endwall showing the building manufacturer.
Leveling Plate	A steel plate used on top of a foundation or other support on which a structural column can rest.	Piece Mark	A number given to each separate part of the building for erection identification. Also called mark number and part number.
Liner Panel	A panel applied as an interior finish.		
Live Load	Live load means all loads, including snow, exerted on a roof, except dead, wind and lateral loads.	Pier	A concrete structure designed to transfer vertical load from the base of a column to a footing.
Loads	Anything that causes a force to be exerted on a structural member. Examples of different types are: a. Dead Load b. Impact Load c. Roof Live Load d. Seismic Load e. Wind Load f. Crane Load g. Collateral Load	Pin Connection	In structural analysis; a member's connection to a foundation, another member or structure is designed in such a way that free rotation is assumed.
		Plastic Design	A design concept based on multiplying the actual loads by a suitable load factor and using the yield point as the maximum stress in any member.
Moment	The tendency of a force to cause rotation about a point or axis.	Portal Frame	A rigid frame structure so designed that it offers rigidity and stability in its plane. It is used to resist longitudinal loads where X-rods are not permitted. (Also wind bent).
Moment Connection	A connection between two members which transfers the moment from one side of the connection to the other side and maintains under application of load the same angle between the connected members that existed prior to the loading. Also, a connection that maintains continuity.		
		Post (End Post)	A secondary column at the end of a building to support the girts and in a beam-and-column endwall frame to additionally support the rafter.
Moment of Inertia	A physical property of a member, which helps define strength and deflection characteristics.	Pre-Painted Coil	Coil steel which receives a paint coating prior to the forming operation.
Multispan Building	Buildings consisting of more than one span across the width of the building. Multiple gable buildings and single	Primary Members	The main load carrying members of a structural system, generally the columns, rafters or other main support members.
		Primer Paint	This is the initial coat of paint applied in the shop to the

TERM	DEFINITION	TERM	DEFINITION
	structural framing of a building for protection against the elements during shipping and erection.		ments, joint sealants, or built-up roof.
Prismatic Beam	A beam having both flanges parallel about its longitudinal axis.	Roof Overhang	A roof extension beyond the endwall/sidewall of a building.
Purlin	A secondary horizontal structural member attached to the roof rafters which transfers the roof loads from the roofing to the roof beams or main frames.	Roof Slope	The angle that a roof surface makes with the horizontal. Usually expressed in units of vertical rise to 12 units of horizontal run.
Rafter	A primary beam supporting the roof system.	Sag Rod	A tension member used to limit the deflection of a girt or purlin in the direction of the weak axis.
Rake	The intersection of the plane of the roof and the plane of the gable. (As opposed to endwalls meeting hip roofs).	Sandwich Panel	A non-composite panel assembly used as covering; consists of an insulating core material with inner and outer skins.
Rake Angle	Angle fastened to purlins at rake for attachment of endwall panels.	Secondary Members	Members which carry loads to the main or primary members. In metal buildings this term includes base angles, purlins, girts, struts, knee braces, tie rods, headers, jambs, and flange braces.
Rake Trim	A flashing designed to close the opening between the roof and endwall panels.		
Reactions	The resisting forces at the column bases of a frame, holding the frame in equilibrium under a given loading condition.	Section Modulus	A physical property of a structural member. It is used in design and basically describes the bending strength of a member.
Ridge	Highest point on the roof of the building which describes a horizontal line running the length of the building.	Seismic Load	Seismic load is the assumed lateral load acting in any horizontal direction on the structural frame due to the action of earthquakes.
Ridge Cap	A transition of the roofing materials along the ridge of a roof. Sometimes called ridge roll or ridge flashing.	Self Drilling Screw	A fastener which combines the functions of drilling and tapping. It is used for attaching panels to purlins and girts.
Rigid Connection	See "Moment Connection."		
Rigid Frame	Any structure in a plane, made up of rigidly connected beams and columns, so designed that the frame depends on its own bending strength for transverse stability.	Self Tapping Screw	A fastener which taps its own threads in a predrilled hole. It is for attaching panels to purlins and girts and for connecting trim and flashing.
Roof Covering	The exposed exterior roof skin consisting of panels, attach-	Shear	The force tending to make two contacting parts slide upon each other in opposite direc-

TERM	DEFINITION	TERM	DEFINITION
	tions parallel to their plane of contact.		Metal Building Manufacturers Association.
Shear Diaphragms	Membrane-like members which are capable of resisting deformation when loaded by in-plane shear forces.	Stiffener	A member used to strengthen a plate against lateral or local buckling. Usually a bar welded perpendicular to the longitudinal axis of the member. Large concentrated loads, such as crane loads, usually require stiffeners at the point of connection.
Shim	A piece of steel used to level base plates or square beams.		
Shoulder Bolt	A fastener used to attach wall and roof paneling to the structural frame. It consists of a large diameter shank and a small diameter stud. The shank provides support for the panel rib.	Stiffener Lip	A short extension of material at an angle to the flange of cold formed structural members, which adds strength to the member.
Sill	The bottom horizontal framing member of an opening such as a window or door.	Stitch Screw	A fastener used to connect panels together at the side lap.
Sill Angle	See "Base Angle."	Strain	Is change in length per unit length. It is the deformation of a body that is acted upon by forces.
Simple Span	A term used in structural analysis to describe a support condition for a beam, girt, purlin, etc., which offers no resistance to rotation at the supports.		
Siphon Break	A small groove to arrest the capillary action of two adjacent surfaces.	Stress	A measure of the load on a structural member in terms of force per unit area (kips per sq. in.).
Soffit	The underside covering of any exterior portion of a metal building.	Structural Steel Members	Load carrying members. May be hot rolled sections, cold formed shapes, or built-up shapes.
Soil Pressure	The load per unit area a structure will exert through its foundation on the soil.	Strut	A brace fitted into a framework to resist force in the direction of its length.
Span	The distance between supports of beams, girders or trusses.	Suction	A partial vacuum resulting from wind loads on a building which cause a load in the outward direction.
Specifications	A statement of particulars of a given job, as to size of building, quality, and performance of men and materials to be used, and the terms of the contract. The most common specification found in the metal building industry is the "Recommended Guide Specifications For Metal Buildings Systems" published by the	Tapered Member	A built-up plate member consisting of flanges welded to a variable depth web which slopes from one end to the other.
		Tensile Strength	The longitudinal pulling stress a material can bear without tearing apart.
		Thrust	The horizontal component of a reaction.

TERM	DEFINITION	TERM	DEFINITION
Tie	A structural member that is always loaded in tension.		causes a load in the upward direction. (See "Suction").
Torque Wrench	A wrench containing an adjustable mechanism for measuring and controlling the amount of torque or turning force to be exerted—often used in tightening nuts of high strength bolts.	Wainscot	Sheeting or liner panel on the inside of a building that goes from floor to a girt that is below eave height. (Not full height).
Trim	The light gage metal used in the finish of a building, especially around openings and at intersections of surfaces. Often referred to as flashing.	Web	That portion of a structural member between the flanges.
		Web Member	A secondary structural member interposed between the top and bottom chords of a truss.
Truss	A structure made up of three or more members, with each member designed to carry a tension or compression force. The entire structure in turn acts as a beam.	Wind Column	A vertical member supporting a wall system designed to withstand horizontal wind loads.
		Wind Load	A load caused by the wind blowing from any horizontal direction.
Uplift	Wind load on a building which	"Z" Section	A member cold formed from steel sheet in the shape of a block "Z".

INDEX